MILTON STUDIES
XIX

MILTON STUDIES
James D. Simmonds, Editor

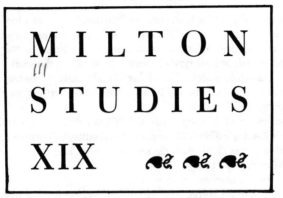

MILTON STUDIES XIX

Urbane Milton
The Latin Poetry

James A. Freeman
Anthony Low
Guest Editors

UNIVERSITY OF PITTSBURGH PRESS

MILTON STUDIES

is published annually by the University of Pittsburgh Press as a forum for Milton scholarship and criticism. Articles submitted for publication may be biographical; they may interpret some aspect of Milton's writings; or they may define literary, intellectual, or historical contexts — by studying the work of his contemporaries, the traditions which affected his thought and art, contemporary political and religious movements, his influence on other writers, or the history of critical response to his work.

Manuscripts should be upwards of 3,000 words in length and should conform to the *MLA Style Sheet*. Manuscripts and editorial correspondence should be addressed to James D. Simmonds, Department of English, University of Pittsburgh, Pittsburgh, Pa. 15260.

Milton Studies does not review books.

Within the United States, *Milton Studies* may be ordered from the University of Pittsburgh Press, Pittsburgh, Pa. 15260.

Overseas orders should be addressed to Feffer and Simons, Inc., 100 Park Avenue, New York, N.Y. 10017, U.S.A.

Library of Congress Catalog Card Number 69-12335

ISBN 0-8229-3492-2 (Volume XIX)

US ISSN 0076-8820

Published by the University of Pittsburgh Press, Pittsburgh, Pa. 15260

Feffer & Simons, Inc., London

Manufactured in the United States of America

CONTENTS

TEXTUAL NOTE

FOR CONSISTENCY the Latin text of Milton's poetry is quoted throughout from *The Works of John Milton*, ed. Frank A. Patterson et al. (New York: Columbia University Press, 1931–40), except that *&* is regularized as *et* and Latin titles are fully capitalized (with the exception of the bibliography). Permission of Columbia University Press to quote from this edition is gratefully acknowledged. Other texts and translations are as indicated in the individual essays.

COMMONLY USED ABBREVIATIONS

CM. *The Works of John Milton*, ed. Frank A. Patterson et al. (New York: Columbia University Press, 1931–40).

Variorum. A Variorum Commentary on the Poems of John Milton, ed. Merrit Y. Hughes et al. (New York: Columbia University Press, 1970–   ).

Bush, *Variorum*. Volume I of *A Variorum Commentary, The Latin and Greek Poems*, ed. Douglas Bush, J. E. Shaw, and A. Bartlett Giamatti (New York: Columbia University Press, 1970).

YP. *The Complete Prose Works of John Milton*, ed. Don M. Wolfe et al. (New Haven: Yale University Press, 1953–82).

PREFACE

THE PLEASURE that Milton experienced while writing his Latin poems awakened a corresponding pleasure in readers until very recently. His facility with meter, diction, and mythology appealed, by and large, to others who had undergone the same schooling. In England, the educational reforms that began in the early sixteenth century convinced both scholars and men of affairs that anyone who could manipulate the language of Homer and Virgil deserved special honor. On the Continent, writers in different countries gloried in sharing a common classical heritage. Thus all took pride in their spiritual citizenship, during that lingering summer when rising nationalism still seemed compatible with the universality of letters. Milton too was truly urbane, an Englishman but also a respected member of the city whose culture seemed everlasting.

Milton obviously valued his classical training. He preserved intact his early works and, in the English poems, often mined them for ideas. (One need only skim *In Quintum Novembris* to see how the idea of a demonic Great Consult stimulated him throughout his life.) Although he could read, write, and speak an awesome number of languages, Milton continually repaired to models like Ovid and Virgil, as well as to Statius and George Buchanan. All sang to him in their various keys — to an ear that, despite what has been said about the difficulty of writing poetry in a tongue other than that of one's birth, was extraordinarily sensitive to all the cadences and subtleties of Latin verse. Whatever the Latin compositions were that he chose to recite to his friends in the Florentine academies, they were judged (in the exuberant politeness of existing records) to be "extremely learned." Like other Neolatinists, Milton often lets himself go in the Latin poetry in a way that he does not permit himself in English. For him, and for his early readers, Latin was a living and a lively medium, in which he could share a joke with a close friend like Diodati, communicate across the fissures of time, distance, and religious difference with an Italian comrade, reveal his hopes and fears and his deepest feelings to a reader, and even achieve an intimacy with Ovid and Virgil closer than anything possible in English. To cite Milton's own words, spoken in a similar context: "hoc est, Auditores, omni aetati quasi vivus interesse, et velut ipsius temporis nasci contemporaneus" ("this means, my hearers, to reside in every age as if alive, to be born as though a contemporary of time itself").

Renaissance poets generally first learned to write by means of close reading and word-by-word imitation of choice Latin texts. As they grew older, they refined and adapted this elementary form of imitation and made it a basic constituent of their method of poetic composition. Imitation became a tool that could combine both respect and rivalry toward powerful classical predecessors. Milton, for example, had a lifelong, emulative, yet loving relationship with Virgil, which attained its fullest creative heights in *Paradise Lost*. It was while Milton was still working in the medium of Latin, however, that — as the Renaissance often put it — he mastered the art of transforming flowers culled from various sources into honey that was all his own. Thus Milton's subtle echoes, tributes, and revisions, which became so substantial and familiar an aspect of his English verse, immeasurably increasing the richness of its meaning and its stylistic texture, grew out of techniques that he learned from the writing of Latin verse. Doubtless other poets in the period served the same apprenticeship, both those whose Latin poetry has survived, like Herbert and Crashaw, and those whose youthful exercises have disappeared. But Milton was the master Neolatinist of his time and country, as he was also the master when he turned wholly to his native tongue. In such poems as *Ad Patrem, Mansus,* and *Epitaphium Damonis,* written in his maturity, a reader may still observe how a great poet borrows and transforms, in the language of his originals, the themes, phrases, and structures that he takes from such other great poets as Horace, Ovid, and Virgil.

As John B. Dillon's bibliography amply attests, a host of scholars have touched on the Latin poems. Many of their discussions, however, have been brief; many have focused on such technical concerns as chronology and prosody; and many have treated the Latin poems as no more than fodder for the biographer or the interpreter of the English poetry. Therefore relatively little has been done to help readers sense how self-sufficient the *Carmina* really are. After all, even if one chooses to look at one poem in order to illuminate another, or in order to understand better the life and mind of the poet who wrote it, the first requirement is to examine it with real attention. A subtler and more accurate reading of the poem in question is certain to result in an improved understanding of the whole life and works. Douglas Bush, to whom we all owe so much, has summed up much prior work in his volume of the *Variorum,* and has supplied future scholars with a vast network of echoes and allusions to Neolatin as well as classical poetry. Now what modern readers need, so they can begin to appreciate this whole neglected side of Milton's creative development and to see the Latin poetry for the major accomplishment it is — traditional yet innovative, impersonal yet heartfelt — what, in fact, we scholars need, is (to use Stephen Crane's word) "interpreters."

Therefore the guest editors commissioned these essays from readers who combined sensitivity with expertise. One of our first decisions was that all the essays should be entirely new and unpublished. Another was that foreign-language quotations should be translated to make them accessible to all readers. A third, more a hope than a rule, was that, while we would not impose an artificial unity on the contributors, we would hope that an organic unity might emerge, on the order of that house of which Milton speaks in *Areopagitica*. The end result, we now think, is better than we wished for. We are happy to be able to introduce a collection of first-rate, often definitive essays by various scholars that incorporate, as they should, a variety of approaches, touching, among other things, on rhetoric and audience, genre and style, biography and politics, and on both literary and historical contexts. Though one or two of the essays may jostle each other, they do so with a positive energy and a "goodly and graceful symmetry that commends the whole pile and structure."

Thus, for example, the point one essay raises, that the mature Milton of 1645 would surely have repudiated the politics that were implicit in his early elegies, balances instructively against other discussions of *Mansus*, *Ad Salsillum*, and *Ad Rousium*, to reveal that there were unexpected tensions between some of Milton's private friendships in that world represented by his Latin poetry and the public stance to which he committed himself in his English works as early as *Lycidas*. One wonders whether, with the publication of the *Poemata* in 1645, Milton knew that he was leaving behind forever the world of art and friendship that so many of the Latin poems commemorate, or whether, as he hints in the coda of *Ad Rousium*, he hoped that he was putting aside those civilized endeavors only for a time, while he strove by means of ideological polemics to restore or improve the world they had represented. In the event, Milton lost the urbane world of his youth forever, at least in terms that he could accept; that loss suggests one further reason why he kept silence in the tongue that had proved adequate to his mature poetic powers but now proved inadequate to confront the politics of a changing nation.

Other similar fruitful interactions among the essays might be cited. For example, the importance of audience to rhetorical stance and meaning, which one essay demonstrates in the case of *Ad Patrem*, is also evident in the discussions of *Ad Salsillum* and *Mansus*. For what all the essays have in common is a unifying subject matter, while the absence of much prior criticism has allowed most of the contributors to confront that subject matter frontally rather than peripherally (the fate of critics who arrive late on the scene, and one with which Miltonists are well accustomed to struggle). At the same time the freshness and urbanity of the poetry has, we think, inspired an answering degree of freshness in the essays. Like Job, we had heard of the vigor of Milton's verse; now we saw more clearly why it had been so much praised.

Without wishing to enter into disputes about dating, which modern editors have so far been unable to settle to their mutual satisfaction, we have arranged the essays in approximately the chronological order of the poems they treat. One result is the emergence of a substantial picture of Milton's artistic progress from youth to maturity. Like chapters in the biography of a mind, each essay reveals further details concerning how the poet responded to the Latin tradition in which he wrote, developing a power and a style that were characteristically his own. In the English poems, Milton explored (as Virgil had before him) the problem of how to create in his native language and culture works commensurate with the greatest achievements of poets who wrote in earlier languages. In the Latin poems, a modern reader can watch him wrestling with those poets in their own idiom, as his verse grows ever more resonant with allusions yet at the same time more powerful, self-assured, and original. Not surprisingly, the episodes these essays reveal from the life of John Milton, Neolatinist, correspond to the well-known story of John Milton, Englishman. Nevertheless, the shift in perspective afforded by close attention to the Latin poems is sufficient to throw a good deal of new light on Milton's growth as a poet and artificer.

The editors have not attempted complete coverage of the *Poemata*, although they have tried to seek out essays on all the important poems of Milton's maturity. For this reason they agreed that *Mansus*, clearly a major work, ought to be included, and when no volunteer could be found to perform that task, one of them undertook a second essay. Thus the presence of three essays by two editors is more the result of fate than of hubris. *Epitaphium Damonis*, to the contrary, inspired several essays, which approach it from different points of view: a coverage we judge appropriate to what may be the best and is certainly the best-known of the Latin poems. After all, *Epitaphium Damonis* is the only Latin poem of Milton's around which more than a sketchy critical tradition has previously developed, and it is a well-known principle that criticism begets criticism. If the present volume provokes its readers not only to reconsider the Latin poems, but to respond with further explorations, that would be one of its happiest fruits.

Because more than a decade had passed since publication of Bush's volume of the *Variorum* (which necessarily included in its bibliography many non-Miltonic items and did not attempt completeness), the editors commissioned an annotated bibliography from John Dillon. The result, surprising in its magnitude, has elicited praise for its sharp wit as well as its professional competence from two anonymous readers. The editors wish to thank those readers for various suggestions that have improved the volume. They also hope that the readers of *Urbane Milton* will find in it the same pleasure they experienced in bringing it together.

James A. Freeman
Anthony Low

MILTON STUDIES

XIX

GUNPOWDER AND THE PROBLEM OF THEATRICAL HEROIC FORM: *IN QUINTUM NOVEMBRIS*

John G. Demaray

WITH ITS unexpected revelations of learned audacity, fresh imaginative association, and adolescent melodrama, Milton's early Latin work *In Quintum Novembris* is a critically vexing poem. The range of its theatrical and literary resonances has yet to be sounded.[1]

In Quintum Novembris is strongly molded by classical conventions, labored with narrative contrivances, strident with youthful polemicism, filled with an impressive and at times overextended catalogue of classical and literary allusions, and weighted with an abrupt *deus-ex-machina* ending. The piece is clearly a Latin literary performance written to reflect partisan public sentiment on an English-Protestant national holiday and to demonstrate academic learning and linguistic skill. Yet the keen feeling of the author often charges the performance; and the finished composition represents an unusual attempt to blend literary artifice, engaged emotion, and Latin stylistic dexterity by a young author wavering in his posture between involvement and detachment. Milton at the age of seventeen is already composing something that, if not fully accomplished as a work of art, is surely special.

Normal literary categories and their subdivisions will not hold. *In Quintum Novembris* with its heroic but also its odd theatrical components is neither entirely a brief epic, a mock epic, nor an epic in miniature, although confining critical arguments might be advanced for the use of each of these labels. If a literary label is at all required, then the exercise is perhaps best described as a heroic-theatrical Latin occasional poem.

This early work probably would have very much pleased conscientious seventeenth-century schoolmasters such as Alexander Gill, Jr., of St. Paul's School or Joseph Meade of Cambridge; for Milton the fledgling scholar, with all the dutiful academic ardor of a student anxious to prove himself, embodied in his composition actual or possible references to, among others, Cicero, Pliny, Claudian, Augustine, Catullus, Juvenal, Lucretius, Propertius, Martial, Hesiod, and, above all, Ovid and Virgil.

3

But the heavy weight of classical imitation, a weight that "sank" many another Renaissance schoolboy, provided Milton with heroic character-types, actions, and thematic perspectives that in fact stimulated and liberated his imagination. Strong feelings and genuine poetic abilities were striving toward an as yet unrealized theatrical-literary form. The result was an episodic and uneven Latin poem, a work which lacks effective structural unity but displays heroic tonalities, occasional flashes of imaginative brilliance, and, in the opening and central passages, surprisingly direct emotional force.

Here Milton abandons the elegiac meter of Propertius and Tibullus and strikes out for the first time with heroic notes in the hexameter rhythms used in Ovid's *Metamorphoses* and Virgil's *Aeneid*. The young poet makes his opening statement with authority, establishing at once a firm narrative line and a metaphoric relationship linking King James I and his British subjects to Aeneas and the "Troy-born race." As Leicester Bradner has observed, Milton in employing hexameters introduces a "new seriousness" to his poems, a feeling that his verses "are poetry in their own right and not a youthful pastime, no matter how well done."[2]

For the first time in an exercise by Milton unintegrated patterns of theatrical and literary structure begin to emerge, patterns that the poet will develop and better control in his mature works. For the first time heroic archetypal figures are depicted on a cosmic canvas with references to the heavens, the underworld, the midregion of earth, the cyclical movement of the stars, and the regular passage of the hours of the day and night. The general theme, the destiny of the British king and nation, is conflated within the wider themes of religious strife and the war between good and evil. And even in youth the poet's imagination ranges beyond traditional literary divisions in drawing upon and seeking to join diverse genres, modes, and elements that will be elaborated throughout a lifetime. This experimental Latin exercise, showing the tensions that early accrue from these efforts, is of poetic interest in itself; but it is also of interest for the light that it casts upon the mature heroic poetry.

A fiery explosion designed by demonic plotters to hurl virtuous figures from this life to the next — this was the *topos* of evil that in 1626 stirred the adolescent imagination of John Milton. The young author had discovered, or perhaps a Cambridge tutor had assigned, what for this student writer was very possibly a "new" subject, one that provided scope for heroic development and yet was unknown to epic masters Homer and Virgil.

The published record of Milton's "disposition" of the *topos* shows evidence both of considerable work and of a continuing fascination with the noise, smoke, and sulphurous fumes of an imagined detonation. Five Latin epigrams on the general subject of a gunpowder explosion and of Guy Fawkes's plan to blow up British king and parliament appear in the 1645 and 1673 editions of the *Poems* just three pages before the 226-line poem *In Quintum Novembris*. The emotive strength of the epigrams, like that of the opening two-thirds of the longer Latin verse, lies in the economy with which they evoke an experience of awe, horror, and outrage at the machinations of evil.[3]

The *topos* expands in the epigrams almost of its own accord. Milton is invariably forced into imaginative projections of what happened "before" and "after" the discovery of the plot, and of what might have happened had the explosion taken place. The poet observes in the first epigram *In Proditionem Bombardicam* ("On the Gunpowder Plot") that Fawkes would like to seem merciful by sending James I to "high heaven, / in a sulphurous chariot with wheels of whirling fire" (5–6) ("atria caeli, / Sulphureo curru flammivolisque rotis"),[4] an ascent which the poet compares in simile to Elijah's journey to heaven from the banks of the Jordan River (2 Kings ii). But in the second epigram entitled *In Eandem* ("On the Same") the poet becomes aware that the blast never occurred, that the king has died in old age and has been removed to the stars. Milton then unleashes his pyrotechnic fantasies upon the alleged plotters:

> Sic potiùs foedos in caelum pelle cucullos,
>   Et quot habet brutos Roma profana Deos,
> Namque hac aut aliâ nisi quemque adjuveris arte,
>   Crede mihi caeli vix bene scandet iter.   (7–10)

> [Blow your detestable cowls, rather, up to the skies,
>   And all the idol gods that profane Rome professes;
> For unless you help them in this way or in some other,
>   Believe me, not one of them will climb very well
>   on the path to heaven.]

Attention in the third epigram *In Eandem* shifts to the theological reasons for the plot. James had written a tract against the existence of Purgatory, and Milton in his epigram begins with the statement: "Purgatorem animae derisit Iácobus ignem" (1) ("James derided the purgatorial fires that purge the soul"). Still, the poet returns with proper qualification to his explosive interests: "Nam prope Tartareo sublime rotatus ab igni / Ibat ad aethereas umbra perusta plagas" (11–12) ("For he did almost go, wheeled high by Tartarean fire, / a scorched shade to the celestial shore"). A whimsical paradox about what might have been appears in the fourth epigram *In Eandem*, for James is imagined both descending low and rising high. An "impia" (1) ("impious") Rome is said to have wished to consign the king to the Styx and the Taenarian gulf, but the poet adds that in fact Rome is prepared to lift the king to the stars and "cupit ad superos evehere usque Deos" (4) ("wishes to raise him aloft among celestial gods"). In the fifth epigram *In Inventorem Bombardae* ("On the Inventor of Gunpowder") Milton focuses only upon the gods and their fiery powers, comparing by oblique allusion Prometheus with his flame to a greater man with the "trifidum fulmen" (4) ("three-forked thunderbolt") of Jove.

In Quintum Novembris, apparently the final product of these epigrammatic musings, again discloses Milton's preoccupation with fire and detonation. But the argument of the exercise now initially "turns" upon announcements by evil figures of plans for a future explosion that never occurs. Following a procession in Rome of mendicant friars and others, Satan, deceitfully clothed to resemble the friar St. Francis, demands that the Pope take action to insure that the British king and his followers are blown limb from limb (119–21). The Pope in turn commands an antic consistory of figures to destroy the British enemies: "Illuc, sic jubeo, celeri contendite gressu, / Tartareoque leves difflentur pulvere in auras" (160–61) ("Go, such is my bidding, quickly with swift steps, / And let them be blown apart by Tartarean powder into the light air").

The impact of the epigrams and the exercise on the mature poetry can be strikingly illustrated, for Milton's intense adolescent association of the "Romans" with explosive force remained to be projected into *Paradise Lost* with a coarse, satiric harshness. Inventing an otherworldly "Paradise of Fools" to replace the Roman Purgatory that, as the poet noted in epigram three, King James had rejected, Milton pauses in his description of Satan pacing the windswept outermost sphere of the universe to interject fifty-three lines on the spirits who "hereafter" will inhabit the imagined realm. Among the spirits depicted marching in a future procession past the spheres toward the gate of St. Peter are the mendicant friars, the same figures who in the Latin exercise are presented in Rome moving in procession on the eve of St. Peter. And in the manner of Satan who in the exercise is depicted disguised in garments like those worn by St. Francis, some of the future otherworldly spirits have in "Dying put on the weeds of *Dominic*, / Or in *Franciscan* think to pass disguis'd" (III, 479–80).[5] With a jarring display of caustic physical humor and a rather self-conscious demonstration of poetic virtuosity, Milton now transmutes the imagined blast of gunpowder in epigram two into a blast from a tempestuous wind:

> when loe
> A violent cross wind from either Coast
> Blows them transverse ten thousand Leagues awry
> Into the devious Air; then might ye see
> Cowles, Hoods and Habits with thir wearers tost
> And flutterd into Raggs, then Reliques, Beads,
> Indulgences, Dispenses, Pardons, Bulls,
> The sport of Winds: all these upwhirld aloft
> Fly o're the backside of the World farr off
> Into a *Limbo* large and broad, since calld
> The Paradise of Fools.[6]   (III, 486–96)

Equally harsh as poetic elements deriving from adolescence, though elements certainly subject to critical defense and explanation, are Milton's metaphoric accounts of grossly physical gunpowder blasts from demonic cannon during the war between the immortal angels in heaven:

> those deep throated Engins belcht, whose roar
> Emboweld with outragious noise the Air,
> And all her entrails tore, disgorging foule
> Thir devilish glut.   (VI, 586–89)

The opposing virtuous angels, tossed helplessly about like the imagined victims of the gunpowder plot, "fell / By thousands, Angel on Arch-Angel rowl'd" (593–94), while in the demonic camp "Th' invention all admir'd" (498).

In the exploratory epigrams and in the exercise, Milton was forced by the evolution of his subject into seemingly discordant imaginative reflections about the raw materiality and physical force of gunpowder, about immortal beings in heaven among whom presumably was King James, and about the evil beings of the netherworld. The poet began to associate crass materiality with evil and its perpetrators and, by so doing, laid the foundations for the lavish and varied use of metaphors of corrupt matter in his epic depiction of the battling rebel angels. Milton's normal chain of association imaginatively lifted him in the fifth epigram to the heavens where two immortal gods, each carrying a different form of fire, became a source for the opposing champions in the angelic epic war in *Paradise Lost*. A Promethean Satan with his demonic "flame" (584) from cannon is no match for the greater man-god, the Son, who arrives from heaven in a chariot "with three-bolted Thunder stor'd" (764). The Son drives Satan "before him Thunder-struck" (858) until the Archfiend together with his legions falls through the gaping wall of heaven into hell. For Milton's early epigrams and exercise — with their combined stress

upon conspiracy, revolt, and physical power involving the opposed figures of Satan and the Almighty—thus served the poet as a general imaginative stimulus for the scenes of angelic rebellion and war in Books V
and VI of *Paradise Lost*.

The search for literary works directly influencing Milton's Latin exercise, a search extending beyond traditional classical and biblical materials, has had only marginal success in its concentration upon Renaissance
Latin verse and in particular upon Renaissance poetic narratives and occasional poems. The limited accessibility in England of early or foreign
printed texts in small editions makes it only possible that Milton was
familiar with the works cited: the over four-hundred-line, anonymously
written Latin poem *Pareus*, published in 1585, on a plot to overthrow
English political and religious authority; and Giambattista Marino's four-
book, over six-thousand-line Latin poem *La Strage degl' Innocenti*, published in Venice in 1610 and 1620, about the revolt of Lucifer and his
cohorts in hell against God. Phineas Fletcher's four-book, over eight-
hundred-line Latin poem *Locustae* and the English version *The Apol-
lyonists*, on the gunpowder plot, were not published until 1627, a year
after Milton composed his exercise, and in all likelihood would not have
been available in manuscript to a Cambridge student.[7]

Of these works *Pareus* and *Locustae* are, however, useful indexes
to the popular moods and literary designs of Milton's period. The two
poems mirror polemical Protestant sermons and public pronouncements
linking the "Romans" with Satan and hell. In the first poem about the
English traitor Dr. William Parry, Pluto is depicted dispatching the figure
Fraud to the Pope with a plan to undermine England; the Pope next sends
his own messenger to Dr. Parry who attempts but fails to subvert the island
nation. In Fletcher's *Locustae* the prince of the Jesuits, after attending
a council of Lucifer in hell, travels and speaks to the Pope in Rome and
there inspires others to join in the gunpowder plot. At the command of
the Almighty, a messenger descends from heaven to England, and the
plan is uncovered.

Milton "disposed" his exercise drawing upon or inventing popular
poetic arguments of this nature. The poet "framed" the antic actions concerning the gunpowder plot between two theatrical flights from heaven
to earth, one by Satan at the beginning to initiate evil, and one by Fame
at the end to reveal that evil and to introduce a final English triumph
in dance. The antic action encapsulated by the flights unfolds sequen-
tially on 28 and 29 June in Rome. There is a march by the Pope and his
train to a temple at dusk on the first day; the sinister appearance and
speech of Satan in the papal chambers later that night; and the Pope's

summoning and exhortation of allegorical Evils in an internal darkness which contrasts with the dawning outside of the second day. Then Satan, the Pope, and the Evils disappear from the exercise, and the sequence of antic action directly involving these figures is broken. The scene changes to an Olympian heaven where the Almighty laughs at the plotters and orders the figure Fame to fly from her tower to alert the English. Fame obeys, dressing and descending to earth. The exercise ends with a terse, matter-of-fact account of the suppression of the plot and the dancing of English youth. Reviewed as a whole, the work can be seen to divide in its structured action between opening and central episodes of evil followed by concluding episodes of virtue, the abstract "argument" providing the thematic link between the two sets of events.

A heroic mockery pervades Milton's description of the antic scenes in Rome and extends to include a few mildly ironic comments on the past actions of Lady Fame. But the work is not a true mock epic aimed at trivializing and thus satirizing heroic structures and devices. Epic elements are seriously introduced, and Milton's mockery is primarily directed against evil figures and their supposedly idolatrous rites. The viewpoint is best exemplified by the poet's representation of the Almighty ironically laughing at evil, a representation probably based upon lines about God's laughing (4) in Psalm II. Milton in the main avoids the trivial, even in his slighting depiction of Satan's disguise. For the poet informs the objects of poetic derision with an aura of blasphemy.

Although a driving energy animates the poetic presentation of Satan's soaring entry and flight over Europe to Rome, the resolution, involving Fame's descent to earth and announcement of the plot, lacks emotional force. There is a sudden turn from absorbed fascination with key evil figures — Satan, the Pope, and their followers — to a rather exterior description of the tower of Fame and of Fame's descent. Milton's obvious artistic problems with disposition and representation can be rather precisely delineated. On the one hand, the exercise discloses the young poet straining toward the character-types, form, and episodes of a brief epic like his *Paradise Regained* composed many years later. In that poem in four books, the action is dominantly and far more effectively centered upon two heroic biblical characters, the evil Satan and the virtuous Son, who participate throughout in a rising hierarchy of dramatic temptation scenes culminating in the Son's climactic and triumphant victory over Satan on the pinnacle of the temple. On the other hand, the work shows the strong theatrical influence of those Renaissance *intermezzi* and representations of a more external, iconographic kind that were "hinged" upon a contemporaneous political or social occasion, representations in which opening and central antic scenes and characters were often divided from and counterpoised against concluding virtuous scenes and characters. In Milton's early exercise the epic and theatrical elements do not satisfactorily merge.

An exclusively heroic structure drawn from Virgil has been found in the exercise by Macon Cheek who, by combining two antic scenes involving the Pope, posits just four "movements": the flight of Satan (1–53); the papal procession together with Satan's appearance before the Pope at night (53–132); the Pope's meeting with antic Evils (133–65); and the flight of Fame and her divulging of the plot (166–226).[8] This flat sequence of events joined by transitional comments is plainly there in the text, though it needs to be added that five "movements" can be distinguished because a transitional "time passage" (68–73) separates the papal procession from the papal confrontation with Satan. Cheek, moreover, usefully traces sources in the *Aeneid* for Milton's flight episodes; but he can understandably find only general parallels in Virgil for Milton's allusions to events in Rome that, like the "hinge" of a Renaissance spectacle, constitute a contemporaneous "occasion." For there is also in Milton's youthful work a startling though generally overlooked reflection of theatrical materials and of theatrical "representation" structure: the descent or entry of a heroic figure or figures; the antic activities of orgiastic evil figures; and the final "discovery" and defeat of evil in a spectacle involving the heavenly descent or entry of good figures, and the joyous, triumphant dancing of virtuous performers.

Milton's rhetorically inflated description of Satan's opening flight is unmistakably indebted to classical sources. Satan is identified as a wandering outcast of Olympus who has been banished to the realms of Pluto. Having left the underworld, the Archfiend now conducts an aerial survey of earth just as Jupiter in the *Aeneid* (IV, 219–37) surveys from above the Mediterranean nations. In a descent reminiscent of those of Mercury in the *Aeneid*, particularly Mercury's arrival in Libya (IV, 238–61), Satan initially flies over England where the Archfiend's hatred is aroused:

> Jamque fluentisonis albentia rupibus arva
> Apparent, et terra Deo dilecta marino,
> Cui nomen dederat quondam Neptunia proles.   (25–27)

> [Presently he sees the white lands and the wave-resounding
> Cliffs of the beloved country of the sea-god,
> The Land to which Neptune's son long ago gave his name.]

The Fiend oratorically curses this nation said to be dedicated to the true God, and then sails on to a landing in Rome.

Given Christian undertones beneath classical surfaces, there is a sense of enacted Renaissance spectacle in this theatrical description of winged journey and descent, of spacious vistas of a favored nation, of demonic wrath directed against the nation and its God. When in both the 1634 and 1637 drafts of Milton's masque *Comus* the Attendant Spirit is depicted descending or entering, this virtuous figure declaims from a different viewpoint but with similar thematic emphasis upon his movement from heaven, upon the beautiful appearance of "this Isle" England, "The greatest and the best of all the main" (27–29), and upon Neptune's deputation of governing authority over the island. Then too Giambattista Andreini opened his Italian sacred representation *L'Adamo* (Milan, 1613) with a cloud descent of heavenly figures; and Hugo Grotius began his Latin sacred representation *Adamus Exul* (The Hague, 1601) with an oration by an enraged Satan who, staring down from a mountain height above Eden, describes his reactions to the nations of earth. In Milton's final outline of the representation "Adam Unparadiz'd," probably written in the 1640s, it was a biblical figure, the angel Gabriel, who was depicted "descending or entering" past "the station of ye chorus" to Eden.[9]

At the end of the exercise, Milton's detached, iconographic presentation of Fame's tower, costume, and cloud descent is formal and artificial. The depiction undeniably owes much to the rendering of Fame in Virgil's *Aeneid* (IV, 178–80) and Ovid's *Metamorphoses* (XII, 39–65), but Milton's account also suggests staged masque and spectacle entries of the sort recorded by Ben Jonson and other seventeenth-century writers.[10] In Milton's Latin work Lady Fame is discovered on a lofty and brazen tower that is broad and "rutilis vicinior astris / Quàm superimpositum vel Athos vel Pelion Ossae" (173–74) ("closer to the ruddy stars / Than Athos or Pelion, piled upon Ossa"). Having been ordered by the Almighty to spread word of the gunpowder plot, Fame puts on wings and "Induit et variis exilia corpora plumis; / Dextra tubam gestat Temesaeo ex aere sonoram" (206–07) ("clothes her slender body with parti-colored feathers, / and in her right hand she takes a trumpet of Temesan bronze"). She outstrips the clouds, and "Nec mora jam pennis cedentes remigat auras" (208) ("Without delay on her wings she goes oaring through the yielding air").

The iconography and the general pattern of the cloud descent have a familiar theatrical quality. Ben Jonson arranged to have Lady Fame "attir'd in white, with white Wings. . . . In her hand . . . a trumpet"[11] descend from a scenic House of Fame in the main masque of *The Masque of Queenes*, published in 1609, the work having an antimasque showing a disorderly and ugly hell that may have later influenced infernal representations in *Paradise Lost*.[12] Fame reappeared in the main masque of Jonson's *Chloridia* (1631) when there "ariseth a Hill, and on top of it, a globe, on which *Fame* is seene standing, with her trumpet in hand" (175–77). And though Fame had a tower only in Ovid's *Metamorphoses*, being without one in Virgil's *Aeneid*, Giulio Parigi in *Il giudizio di Paride*, presented in Florence in 1608, unveiled a scenic palace and tower of Fame, with a winged Lady Fame holding a trumpet on the summit, that was copied by other illustrators and that influenced Inigo Jones in his designs for Fame or her house in four different masques including the two written by Jonson.[13]

The antic scenes that are placed in Milton's exercise between the flights of Satan and Fame, while denoting a supposedly historic occasion in Rome, are informed with a symbolism suggesting discord, idolatry, and blasphemous religious spectacle. In the darkness on the eve of St. Peter on 28 June, a procession of mendicant friars, kings, and the wearer of the triple crown, the last uplifted on a hand-borne chair, circles the city and then marches by candlelight to the evil, domed temple. "Panificosque Deos" (56) ("Gods made of bread") are said to be carried with the high priest. Employing a strained metaphor, Milton identifies the cries of the marching participants with those of wild revelers: "Qualiter exululat Bromius, Bromiique caterva, / Orgia cantantes in Echionio Aracyntho" (64–65) ("Such are the shrieks of Bacchus and the followers of Bacchus / When they chant their orgies on Theban Aracynthus").

The episode is brief and unelaborated, but its striking evocation of unholy religious rites is bound to the antic wildness of the satyr play. As commentators have pointed out, the description of the procession derives from passages about Bacchus and his votaries in the *Metamorphoses* (III, 702–19). Yet the theatrical quality of the allegedly demonic ritual in Rome is suggested by the fact that Milton later incorporated such bacchanal proceedings into the antimasque of *Comus*. There the evil enchanter Comus and his crew move from a dark wood, where by night they howl "doing abhorred rites" (535) in "barbarous dissonance" (550), to an evil palace in the navel of a wood.

It is in a following scene of *In Quintum Novembris*, set after the procession in the universal darkness of the papal chambers and the underworld, that Milton in rather crude fashion embraces the aesthetic and quite clearly captures the theatrical spirit of the Renaissance spectacle of strangeness. The Pope, urged on by a nocturnal visit from Satan, summons allegorical Evils from their lair in the terrible cavern of Murder and Treason, a place of noise, discord, and treachery. This den of horrors with its grisly inhabitants is somewhat haphazardly pieced together by the young poet from iconography in Ovid, Seneca, Lucian, Virgil, Statius, Petronius, and a host of other sources. Lines 152–53 describing the cave's outcropping rocks and darkness seem inserted almost as an afterthought. But even granting the exaggeration implicit in Renaissance iconographic representation, it must be admitted that Milton as a schoolboy, probably writing several days after All Hallows' Eve when evil spirits allegedly roamed the earth, takes an obvious, lurid delight in the grotesque and the sensational and so overdraws the episode. Amid rubble, shattered rock, unburied bones, and corpses lanced by steel, the figures Murder and Treason cower in their cave as ghosts shriek, deathly shadows hover inexplicably nearby, and pale Horror rushes around the enclosure. Milton provides gruesome iconographic labels for an entire family of Evils before recounting the departure of Treason and Murder, glancing fearfully backward, from their evil den. They go at once to the Pope who in darkness tells them of their mission.

Placing this patterned action in a dark cave of Evils "below" against the introduction in the next scene of antithetical patterned action involving Lady Fame and her tower "above," Milton begins to exhibit the scenic and theatrical "balances" employed by Jonson in his staged spectacles.[14] In the preface to the *Masque of Queenes* of 1609, for example, Jonson explains how he "devis'd that twelve Women . . . sustayning the persons of Ignorance, Suspicion, Credulity, &c. the opposites to good Fame" should represent "Evills" (16–19, 26) that come in discord from a hell that is generally believed to have been a scenic cavern like that in an Inigo Jones design for hell.[15] Dissonant sound, irregular movement, and grotesque appearance mark these "Evills" in the garb of Witches as antithetical to the harmonious movement and appearance of the figure Fame who moves down from her House to music in a main masque spectacle. Again in the antic spectacle of Jonson's *The Golden Age Restored,* published in 1615, there is a "calling forth" of allegorical "Evills"—Fraud, Slander, Treachery, Pride, and others—whose monstrous garb and erratic actions are the antithesis of those of "farre-fam'd spirits" (133) in the form of classical goddesses and poets who float directly to earth on cloud machines in the main masque.

The general theatrical background to Milton's short antic scene is wide, for a rich theatrical iconography interlaced with classical iconography to serve European and English writers. Grotesque scenic caves and grottoes abounded on Renaissance stages, and allegorical evils turned up regularly as characters in sacred representations such as Andreini's *L'Adamo* as well as in masques. It is accordingly significant that Milton at age seventeen, very possibly under the influence of Jonson, obtrudes into his work an overblown, schoolboy vision of a cave of Evils just before presenting the direct descent past clouds of a theatrically costumed Lady Fame. Whether or not by conscious design, a theatrical pattern of antithetical elements is developing.[16]

In the central antic episodes of the Latin exercise, the weak and outward representation of Satan in mendicant garb has a definite theatrical cast. Satan in a guise like that of St. Francis enters interior chambers and approaches the drowsing Pope.[17] Concealed by a false beard and tonsured wig, the Archfiend wears deceptive clothing as well:

>   cineracea longo
>   Syrmate verrit humum vestis, pendetque cucullus
>   Vertice de raso; et ne quicquam desit ad artes,
>   Cannabeo lumbos constrinxit fune salaces,
>   Tarda fenestratis figens vestigia calceis.   (81–85)
>
>   [with a long train
>   His ash-colored robe trailed on the ground; a hood
>   Hung from his shaven crown; and to complete his arts
>   His lustful loins are bound with hemp rope and
>   His slow-moving feet are fastened into latticed sandals.]

Milton's attendance at and participation in Latin plays at Cambridge, activities documented by the poet's satiric play *At a Vacation Exercise* (1628) and by his comments in *An Apology for Smectymnuus* (1642), may well have in part inspired the conception of this theatrical Satan in disguise. In the play author-actor Milton speaks of rummaging through theatrical "coffers" in search of antic or decorous costumes to clothe performers (31). And the poet in the exercise *In Quintum Novembris* exhibits the device of bifurcating evil nature into a seemingly virtuous outward disguise that is at variance with an inward evil reality.

Satan's call to the Pope for vengeance, while conventional, has in the exercise an underlying power. But the sharp, satiric edge of the scene is dulled by routine, polemical reference to the Pope's alleged concubines and by superficial concern for the details of Satan's external costume. This early Satan experiences no torment from the breach between appearance and inner nature. The heroic pain and inner conflict of evil character will be left for future years when Milton creates the Satan of *Paradise Lost*. The Satan of the Poet's youth is a posturing, "dressed up" oratorical performer, passionate but lacking in dimension, who requires little in the way of wily arts to induce his supposed old Roman ally to act.

The exercise's precipitate and mechanical ending is condensed into only seven lines (220–26). Fame warns the English of the gunpowder plot, and with help from the Almighty, the culprits are arrested. The poem concludes suddenly with the lines: "Turba choros juvenilis agit: Quintoque Novembris / Nulla Dies toto occurrit celebratior anno" (225–26) ("In throngs youth goes dancing. The fifth of November / No day throughout the whole year shall be more celebrated"). After beginning with the vigorous and theatrical epic journey of Satan, the young author pressed on to the theatrical but very formal, iconographic descent of Fame, and then, apparently losing interest in this formal treatment, hastily appended a reference to the dancing that, in court spectacles, regularly followed descents by virtuous character-types.

This weak resolution presages the future difficulties Milton will have with his endings, in his attempts to wed theatrical materials to recalcitrant literary themes and forms. "O what a Mask was there" (13), Milton writes in *The Passion* of the Son's death; but after struggling with lines that demonstrate an inability either to visualize or otherwise to render this spectacle of suffering, Milton abandons the poem. And in the last two books of *Paradise Lost,* containing a radically transformed reflection of "a mask of all the evills of this life & world" mentioned in the fourth outline of "Adam Unparadiz'd," there appears to be a lessening of poetic power in the representation of theatrical "speaking pictures" of evil.

In the Latin exercise structural deficiencies also partially explain Milton's inability to maintain poetic force throughout. Instead of beginning *in medias res* and alternating the normal sequence of action involving good and evil characters, the young poet chose to string out five scenes— two flights surrounding three antic representations— in normal sequence while reflecting Jonsonian structural practices by dividing the total action in half between first evil figures and then good figures. But while Milton separately depicts initiatory actions by immortal beings, first Satan and then the Almighty, the poet introduces no "core" episode that presents in immediate detail figures in England actually engaged in carrying out the gunpowder plot and in being thwarted. The youthful author, after indulging in explosive fantasies in the epigrams, is apparently inhibited in the more consciously constructed exercise by the knowledge that the planned explosion did not in fact take place. The focus of action is lost; and the overexpanded, episodic form of the exercise, lacking a central event, seems to cause even the young poet to grow weary. In his brief epic *Paradise Regained* Milton abandons the Jonsonian two-part division, interweaves the actions of good and evil figures, but again holds essentially to a sequential presentation of scenes depicting Satan's repeated encounters with the Son. It is in *Paradise Lost* that Milton, fusing structural devices of the classical epic with elements of theatrical form, demonstrates his greatest poetic power by beginning *in medias res*, "repositioning" heavenly flights, and employing epic "flashbacks" and prophetic visions of the future to focus upon a "core" event: the temptation and fall of Adam and Eve in Eden.

Even in early years Milton's limited but notable poetic achievement in the exercise *In Quintum Novembris* consists in an eclectic and unique bringing together, with manifest aesthetic effect, of disparate theatrical, classical, and literary materials appropriate to grand-scale, heroic themes of religious idolatry and political intrigue. Milton turns traditional conventions and elements to his own poetic ends by investing a contemporaneous occasion in Rome with heroic tonalities. Rich metaphor and an infused emotional vitality give strength to the narrative, particularly in the opening passages. But Milton's satire is crude and overdrawn. The diverse poetic materials are never successfully united, and the heroic mode is not sustained. Youthful poetic virtuosity is ultimately compromised by inflation, episodic treatment, superficial character-types, and structural flaws. *In Quintum Novembris*, then, is a youthful work of considerable originality that fails, but a work that remains a wellspring of the later heroic poetry.

What is incipient in the exercise becomes sharply defined in the later verse. The emerging theatrical structure of the Latin work, a structure existing in disjunctive tension with an unfolding epic form, is firmly grasped and developed by Milton in the antimasque/main masque structure of *Comus*. The figure Fame becomes a personified character mentioned in the staged entertainment *Arcades*. Theatrical descents of characters reappear regularly, not only at the beginning of *Comus* and in the fourth draft of "Adam Unparadiz'd," but also in the descents of Peace and other figures in *On the Morning of Christ's Nativity* and of a number of character-types in *Paradise Lost*.

In comparing the exercise to the epic, it becomes at once apparent that, in the early work, the march of a blasphemous group to a temple on St. Peter's Eve prefigures the movement of Satan and the devils to the palace Pandemonium, associated by commentators with St. Peter's basilica, in *Paradise Lost*. Antic noise and idolatry characterize both groups. The consistory of evil figures called by the Pope in the first work foreshadows the "secret conclave" of Satan and his council in the second. The groups meet to formulate evil plots opposed to the will of God. And in both poems, the Almighty gazes down and laughs at the powerlessness of those instigating evil. Then heavenly messengers are sent by the Almighty to earth to warn of impending danger. And in emotive passages of the Latin exercise, a vengeful but externalized Satan is a prefiguring type for the anguished rebel angel who soars and wanders, frequently in ingenious disguise, through the expansive poetic universe of *Paradise Lost*. The opening flight of that early Satan will someday be transformed into a grand, visionary celestial voyage when, in Book II of the epic, the Archfiend

> Weighs his spread wings, at leasure to behold
> Farr off th' Empyreal Heav'n, extended wide
> In circuit, undetermind square or round,
> With Opal Towrs and Battlements adorn'd
> Of living Saphire, once his native Seat;
> And fast by hanging in a golden Chain
> This pendant world, in bigness as a Starr
> Of smallest Magnitude close by the Moon.
> Thither full fraught with mischievous revenge,
> Accurst, and in a cursed hour he hies.   (1046–55)

Rutgers University

NOTES

1. A number of brief, conflicting judgments unsupported by extended analysis have been made on *In Quintum Novembris*. But in two relatively lengthy studies of Milton's poem, Douglas Bush provides twenty-nine pages of excellent footnotes, together with a five-page introductory background statement, in *Variorum*, pp. 167–200; and Macon Cheek in "Milton's 'In quintum Novembris': An Epic Foreshadowing," *Studies in Philology*, 54 (1957), 172–184, discusses Milton's debts primarily to Virgil, but also to other writers of classical epics, and presents a structural analysis of the exercise. Stella Purce Revard in *The War in Heaven and Paradise Lost* (Ithaca and London, 1980) has recently offered comments on Protestant sermons that, in her view, exerted "unquestionable" influence on the exercise (p. 88): William Barlow's *The Sermon Preached at Paules Crosse* (London, 1606), and James Ussher's *A Sermon Preached before the Commons House of Parliament* (printed 1620).

2. *Musae Anglicanae: A History of Anglo-Latin Poetry, 1500–1925* (New York, 1940), p. 116.

3. The internal details of the epigrams suggest that they were written as a body probably before *In Quintum Novembris* at a time when Milton was probing for suitable themes and materials for the Latin exercise. All are usually assumed by editors to have been penned after the death of James I on 27 March 1625, a dating based on a reference to that death in the second epigram. All were published in the same sequence following *Elegia Septima* and its postscript in both the 1645 and 1673 printings of the *Poems*. In these two printings *In Quintum Novembris* is located with the notation "Anno Aetatis 17" before *In Obitum Procancellarii Medici* ("On the Death of the Vice-Chancellor, a Physi-

cian"), a work assumed to have been written about October 1626. Though the epigrams are placed apart from the Latin exercise in the two published volumes, possibly by the printer for reasons of labeling or spacing, the slim historical evidence available also points to the view that the epigrams were composed after 27 March 1625 but before Milton's writing of the Latin exercise, probably in November 1626.

4. CM I, pt. 1, p. 224. All references to Milton's Latin poems and minor English poems are from this volume.

5. All references to *Paradise Lost* are from CM.

6. Merritt Y. Hughes in his edition of *John Milton: Complete Poems and Major Prose* (New York, 1957) cites for epigram two, without comment, the parallel "Paradise of Fools" passage in Milton's epic "*PL* II, 476–97" (p. 13n.), a comparison which this writer has independently observed and developed.

7. The short, printed poem *Pareus* (Oxford, 1585) is in the collection of the Huntington Library; a microfilm reproduction of the Huntington copy is available at the New York Public Library. See also *La Strage degl' Innocenti* in *Opere del Cavalier Giambattista Marino*, ed. Giuseppe Zirandini (Naples, 1861), pp. 451–87; and *Locustae* in *Giles and Phineas Fletcher, Poetical Works*, ed. F. S. Boas, 2 vols. (Cambridge, 1908–09).

8. Cheek, "Milton's 'In Quintum Novembris'," pp. 175–76.

9. A translation of Andreini's passages on opening descents and speeches appears in Watson Kirkconnell, *The Celestial Cycle* (Toronto, 1967), pp. 228–30. Satan's beginning oration in Grotius' *Adamus Exul* can also be found in *Cycle*, pp. 99–103; the Latin text from the first edition (1601) in the British Museum is printed opposite Kirkconnell's translation. The Trinity College manuscript of Milton's fourth draft of "Adam Unparadiz'd," with a line recording the angel Gabriel's entry or descent, is reproduced in *Johr Milton's Complete Poetical Works in Photographic Facsimile*, ed. Harris Francis Fletcher (Urbana, Ill., 1945), II, p. 26 (26). All references to the fourth draft of "Adam Unpara diz'd" are from this volume.

10. Although commentators have cited no theatrical sources for Milton's depictior of Fame and her descent, they note that Milton is somehow original in his borrowing from Virgil and Ovid. Edward Kennard Rand in "Milton in Rustication," *Studies in Phi lology*, 19 (1922), remarks that, while the poet's depiction of Fame "inevitably suggest: Ovid," there are differences in the presentation by Milton that make the "picture . . . fon all its borrowed details, his own" (p. 116). Concentrating on Milton's Latin usage, Bush in *A Variorum* observes that "In this ambitious poem . . . , he is, as usual, eclectic in style; and one thing of interest . . . is the way in which remote phrases from Ovid and others are embedded in or adapted to a very alien texture" (p. 171).

11. *Ben Jonson*, ed. C. H. Herford, Percy Simpson, and Evelyn Simpson (Oxford, 1941) VII, p. 305 (449–52). All line references to Jonson's masques are from this volume. A short account of the theatrical background and qualities of *In Quintum Novembris* appears in John G. Demaray, *Milton's Theatrical Epic* (Cambridge, Mass., 1980), pp. 9–10.

12. For comments on the setting for hell in the masque and on the hell scenes in *Paradise Lost*, see Demaray, *Theatrical Epic*, pp. 32, 69.

13. Jones's other settings of the palace and tower of Fame appeared in Thomas Carew's *Coelum Britannicum* (1634) and William Davenant's *Britannia Triumphans* (1638). Enid Welsford discusses the influence of this particular scenic design by Parigi on Jones in *The Court Masque* (Cambridge, 1927), pp. 186–87. See *Inigo Jones: The Theatre of the Stuart Court*, ed. Stephen Orgel and Roy Strong (Berkeley and Los Angeles, 1973), II, for reproductions of the following designs: the palace and tower of Fame by Remigio Cantagellina after Giulio Parigi (p. 679); three designs by Jones of the figure Fame for Jonson's masque

Chloridia (pp. 450–51); and the palace and tower of Fame by Jones for Davenant's *Britannia Triumphans*.

14. For remarks throughout on Jonson's development and use of anti-masque main masque form, see Stephen Orgel, *The Jonsonian Masque* (Cambridge, Mass., 1965); and Demaray, *Milton and the Masque Tradition* (Cambridge, Mass., 1968).

15. See design no. 260 in *Designs by Inigo Jones for Masques and Plays at Court*, intro. and notes by Percy Simpson and C. F. Ball (Oxford, 1924). A reproduction of this design may be found in *Inigo Jones: The Theatre*, ed. Orgel and Strong, II, pp. 792–93. The opinion that the flaming hell in *The Masque of Queenes* was presented within a cavern design is advanced by Allardyce Nicoll, *Stuart Masques and the Renaissance Stage* (New York, 1963), p. 68; and by Welsford, *The Court Masque*, p. 187.

16. Available to Milton in 1626 from the original printers in London were thirteen masques published by Jonson out of a total of twenty-four masques that the playwright had seen through performance. Available also in 1626 was a wide body of other recently published masques by authors of the stature of Samuel Daniel, Thomas Campion, George Chapman, Francis Beaumont, Thomas Middleton, and William Rawley. On Milton's possible knowledge of Jonson's works, see Demaray, *Milton and the Masque Tradition*, pp. 47–48.

17. Protestant Milton doubtless associated St. Francis with the mendicant friars and with the Roman Catholic practices of pilgrimage and veneration of relics. Acting upon the tradition that St. Francis made the pilgrimage from Egypt to the Holy Land, the Franciscans from the thirteenth century through Milton's period maintained hostels for pilgrims in the Middle East and in Europe.

ELEGIA SEPTIMA:
THE POET AND THE POEM

Anthony Low

F OR A great many years, critics who have commented on *Elegia Septima* have viewed it as the literal record of an incident in Milton's early life or, as the currents of criticism taught them to be warier of such assumptions, at least as representing his psychology as a young man. At the same time, the way each critic reads what he supposes to be Milton's real-life confessions about falling in love tends to change as the *Zeitgeist* changes. Thus in 1796, William Hayley read *Elegia Septima* essentially as the effusion of a young man of sentiment. He finds support in a couplet translation provided him by William Cowper. That he prints the Latin alongside Cowper's version suggests he was unaware of any damaging discrepancies. Hayley tells his late-eighteenth-century readers that Milton

felt, with the most exquisite sensibility, the magic of beauty, and all the force of female attraction. His seventh Elegy exhibits a lively picture of his first passion; he represents himself as captivated by an unknown fair, who, though he saw her but for a moment, made a deep impression on his heart. . . . [But she quickly vanishes.] The juvenile poet then addresses himself to love, with a request that beautifully expresses all the inquietude, and all the irresolution, of hopeless attachment. . . .

> Remove, no, grant me still this raging woe;
> Sweet is the wretchedness that lovers know.[1]

Marvell had anticipated the kind of large-scale social changes represented by this criticism more than a hundred years earlier: "I too transported by the Mode offend, / And while I meant to Praise thee must Commend."[2] To us, Hayley's remarks, with the support given them by Cowper's translation, may seem more than a little myopic; they reveal less about Milton's poem than about the critic and the translator. Warned by their example, we might consider whether we too are not separated from Milton by a gap of time and custom. For each age brings its own characteristic myopia to the reading of poetry, especially when that poetry touches on a subject so ambiguous but near the heart as love.

At the start of the nineteenth century, the Rev. H. J. Todd laid aside

21

his scholarly objectivity to join Hayley in admiration of Milton's sentiments. He too is moved to comment on the concluding lines: "There never
was a more beautiful description of the irresolution of love. He wishes
to have his woe removed, but recalls his wish; preferring the sweet misery
of those who love. Thus Eloisa wavers, in Pope's fine poem: 'Unequal
task! a passion to resign, / For hearts so touch'd, so pierc'd, so lost, as
mine'."[3] What appeals to these early critics is first the story, of a young
man's first love engagingly described, and then, arising from that story,
the sentiments. Of course, most of Todd's notes point to classical echoes
and allusions, but when he departs from such annotation it is to consider
the question (raised by Warton) of which park Milton was strolling in
when he encountered the young lady, or to commend him for expressing
his feelings so movingly. Another comment reads: "The fervour of his
love is inimitably expressed."[4] Later in the century, Masson continued
to read the seventh elegy as autobiography, but he dropped the now
unfashionable language of sentiment for a more matter-of-fact tone. By
his time, and ever since, the treatment of the elegy had been standardiz-
ed. Just as, when speaking about *Elegia Sexta*, one emphasized the beauty
of the water-drinking passage, so in speaking about *Elegia Septima* one
proceeded mainly by retelling the story and concluding with praise for
Milton's feelings — perhaps with a remark that Milton was not, after all,
always a sour Puritan. It became customary to emphasize the part about
the poet walking in the fields, since even the most naive biographer recognized that Milton did not really wake up to find Cupid standing by
his bed. Thus, Masson writes, "At line 51, the real story begins."[5] And
thus inevitably the first part of the poem became excess baggage.

　　In the twentieth century, critics no longer refer to Milton's "exquisite sensibility," yet otherwise their responses have been not altogether dis-
similar from those of their earliest predecessors. According to Tillyard,
for example, "there is little doubt that Milton is narrating an actual experience; and one is glad to think that at the age of nineteen he was not
in every way unlike other young men of that age. But later [in the retrac-
tion] he judged unkindly of his hasty passion."[6] John S. Diekhoff prints
the whole poem in his collection *Milton on Himself*, because, as he explains in the headnote: "The frequent assumption that this elegy and the
Italian sonnets are mere conventional poetic exercises robbed us for a long
time of the understanding of valuable biographical material."[7] James
Holly Hanford, in his influential and still important essay, "The Youth
of Milton," is more cautious about the relationship between poem and
life, yet still reads the elegy as a significant document in Milton's youthful development. "Whether or not these verses recount an actual inci-

dent they express real and acute sensations, and the poem as a whole gives evidence of an all but complete surrender to the Ovidian attitude and mood." Hanford also argues that beneath the whole body of Milton's youthful verse, including the elegies, "we may read the evidence of disturbing experiences and intimate reactions which belong characteristically to the period of adolescence."[8] *Plus ça change;* the terminology of sentiment has given way before the advance of modern psychology, but the critic still treats the poem as a self-revelation, not a literary work of art.

Recent years have brought new biographical speculations. In 1967, J. B. Broadbent wrote that "there seems to be a genuine experience here, and there may be discoveries of Milton's own about the nature of love." In 1977, Broadbent's coeditor, Robert Hodge, was first to see autobiographical implications in the Cupid episode. He puts forward a new possibility, partially withdraws it, then teasingly puts it forward again: "The image of Cupid appearing beside his bed is conventional in detail, but this Cupid is also an attractive boy, compared to two famous pretty boys from antiquity, Ganymede, beloved of Jove, and Hylas, boyfriend of Hercules. Is M suggesting early homosexual attraction (not of course any homosexual acts)? M's nickname at university was 'the lady of Christ's'. At university, boys slept two or three to a room, often with a tutor."[9] Although the *Zeitgeist* has changed indeed, still most of the critic's attention is on Milton's supposed self-revelations, now seen, as Hanford and Tillyard had begun to see them, as mainly unintended and unconscious. From praising Milton for painting his passions vividly, criticism progressed to the point where it celebrated Milton's artless and unwitting self-exposure. The poem still disappears behind the autobiographical document.

My point is not that we should return to New Criticism, and divorce Milton from his poems. Yet if the New Critics taught us anything, it was to look directly at the poem, and not to leap immediately to a one-for-one identification between author and protagonist. While the New Criticism was ascendant, it became customary for critics to remark that the incidents in the poem may not actually have occurred precisely as described; yet then they would propose readings essentially the same as those of Hayley and Todd. Thus the obligatory demurrals come to seem more like defenses of the critic's flank than significant changes in procedure.

What, then, is one to make of *Elegy VII*? Even if one hesitates to identify its protagonist simply with the poet, it still seems that the poem is a description of first love, largely in imitation of Ovid but, as critics generally agree, more youthful, romantic, and innocent in spirit. But such a reading, though it represents the consensus, leads to difficulties. Speaking of Milton's sweeping comparison of the bereft lover to Vulcan thrown from heaven, for example, Todd and Warton admit a certain inappropriateness: "The allusion . . . is perhaps less happy, although the compliment is greater."[10] While Hanford praises Milton's "eager delight," he regrets that the poem "smells of the oil of humanism." [11] In other words, the poem is only good insofar as it is autobiographical, and weak insofar as it is artful. Yet a parallel tradition of exegesis and footnotes, beginning with Warton and Todd and culminating in the *Variorum Commentary*, has shown that *Elegy VII* is a tissue of imitation, which can hardly be saved for "originality" by insisting that Milton sincerely meant what he said or that the action took place in the London suburbs.

The difficulty is posed most sharply by William Riley Parker, in remarks of typically Johnsonian pungency:

I do not doubt, though some have doubted, that Milton's seventh elegy records an actual experience. By his own statement he went for one of his customary walks, exchanging glances boldly with the pretty girls whom he passed. Then, out of his day-dreams into reality emerged a creature more beautiful than all the rest. The poet was on fire. . . . Milton's heart turned over like the page of a book. In another moment the adventure ended. The girl strolled on, blissfully unaware of her contribution to Anglo-Latin verse. . . .

The *Elegia Septima* . . . is conventionally extravagant. Its sentimental machinery creaks, rhythmically. . . . We are spectators at the immemorial ritual of Love-at-First-Sight, and we embarrass ourselves, not the performer, if we laugh at the fusty costumes and faded scenery. Stripped to cold and shivering prose, the young lover looks absurd. . . . But we shall understand Milton better, in his *Elegia Septima*, if we leave him in his ceremonial robes.[12]

In other words, the poem had better not be looked at too closely, for it is bookish, sentimental, creaking, fusty, faded, and potentially absurd. Therefore, let us use it as handy biographical evidence but forbear from putting critical hands on it, lest we destroy it. Surely, however, Milton is the last English poet whose work we should fear to damage by rough handling. As Humphrey Moseley announced in his preface to the 1645 poems: "Reader if thou art Eagle-eied to censure their worth, I am not fearful to expose them to thy exactest perusal" (CM I, p. 415).

Keeping in mind the cautionary lessons that our critical tour has suggested, let us accept Moseley's challenge. Yet what we have learned from that tour was not all negative, or I should not have extended it to such length. For one thing, what has been said about *Elegy VII* is only too typical of much of what has been said about the other Latin poems. For another, at least three things about the poem are revealed by the critical consensus: that its power resides first in its story, which is compulsively retold; that the feelings it expresses are moving; and that the poem can hardly be looked at before difficult issues crop up about the relationship between art and life. Yet those difficulties are not symptoms of problems in the poem. Far from being in trouble in some perilous balance between fusty humanism and awkward adolescence, Milton is deliberately exploring and exploiting the tensions between experience and artistic play. Perhaps all successful poetry must do something of the kind, in one degree or another, though the poet may hide his tracks like Wordsworth or, like the Milton of *Paradise Lost* and *Paradise Regained*, repudiate artifice even as he is making use of it.

At the beginning of *Elegy VII*, the narrator introduces himself by an address to Venus, which explains that he used to scorn the power of love as personified in Cupid (1–4). As he quotes his past insults to Cupid, the god overhears him and vows revenge (5–12). Time and setting are indefinite. This first part of the elegy is allusive, and therefore "literary," throughout; but its tone is more comic than pedantic. Milton uses an ancient situation not to prepare a cover for his nakedness, but to begin to laugh at human folly and the folly of such gods as Venus and Cupid. We may hear, lightly touched but unmistakable, that satirical note that Milton was to employ so effectively throughout his career, for the purpose of chastizing foolishness and pride, whether in politicians, prelates, fallen angels, or even in his own heroes:

> Tu puer imbelles dixi transfige columbas,
>   Conveniunt tenero mollia bella duci.
> Aut de passeribus tumidos age, parve, triumphos.[13]   (5–7)

["Boy," I said, "go shoot the unwarlike doves; gentle combats suit a tender champion; or else, little one, go keep your boasted triumphs over the sparrows."]

The reader immediately knows that Cupid is not the only butt of this satire; knowing the tradition, he confidently expects the speaker's downfall. That downfall, at least as seen from this point in the story, will be comically appropriate. Not even Chaucer's Troilus, after all, was spared the poet's barbs at an equivalent point in his story, when he is seen boasting his superiority to love in the Temple of Venus. And Chaucer raises that satirical note again when, in the well-known envoi, he lifts his tragedy to the level of divine comedy and reduces the lovers' romance to its appropriate level *sub specie aeternitatis*. So, even encountering Milton's poem for the first time, one knows from the start what to expect. A reader's interest has little to do with suspense or unexpected turns in the miniature story. Instead, he wants to see how the protagonist gets his comeuppance.

Milton first gives a specific time and place for his action in the second part. It is spring, morning, the first of May, and the sun's light pours down over the rooftops:

> Ver erat, et summae radians per culmina villae
> Attulerat primam lux tibi Maie diem.   (13–14)

The radiance of dawn blinds the poet, whose eyes still crave the retreating night (15–16) — not, surely, an early manifestation of Milton's failing sight, as some suggest, but both a natural response of someone waking up and a metaphorical indication that the speaker has been blind and is still attached to his darkness, but that he is about to confront some new experience and be forced, in some sense, to see. So far, the scene seems realistic. Into it, however, at a specific time and place — Mayday morning, beside the poet's bed — Amor suddenly reveals himself:

> Astat Amor lecto, pictis Amor impiger alis,
> Prodidit astantem mota pharetra Deum:
> Prodidit et facies, et dulce minantis ocelli,
> Et quicquid puero, dignum et Amore fuit.
> Talis in aeterno juvenis Sigeius Olympo
> Miscet amatori pocula plena Jovi;
> Aut qui formosas pellexit ad oscula nymphas
> Thiodamantaeus Naiade raptus Hylas.   (17–24)

[Then love stood beside my bed, Love the indefatigable with his painted wings. The swaying quiver betrayed the god as he stood; his features and his sweetly menacing eyes betrayed him and so did all else beseeming the boy who is Love. So the Phrygian youth appeared when he mixed the flowing cups for amorous Jove on everlasting Olympus; and so Hylas, the son of Theodamas, who lured the lovely nymphs to his kisses and was carried off by a Naiad.][14]

It is the sort of encounter that Chaucer might have claimed happened to him in a dream, but Milton claims, on the contrary, to have just woken up. While classical deities enter his early poetry by the dozens, this is the only time a pagan god enters the everyday, modern world of the poet and his readers, except briefly as a personification or an invisible presence, or metaphorically. Although Phoebus plays an important role in *Lycidas*, he is not really visualized, nor are the gods who appear at the feast in *Elegy VI*. Not only does Milton give us a detailed description of Cupid, however, insisting with a double "prodidit" how loudly his appearance proclaimed him, but he even introduces a double simile to magnify him further, in which he compares him to Ganymede and Hylas.

While the ostensible ground of the comparison is to Cupid's beauty, the double simile, in anticipation of one of Milton's mature techniques, has further indirect and proleptic implications, which are probably more important than the surface meaning. For what Ganymede and Hylas have in common, in addition to beauty, is that both are hapless victims of the gods and of love. Imperious Jove sent an eagle to carry off Ganymede, while Hylas, "going to fetch water from a pool, was drawn down into it by an enamored nymph."[15] When, in *Paradise Lost*, Milton introduces the rape of Proserpina in the process of saying that Paradise is lovelier than the fields of Enna where she gathered flowers, critics agree that the major effect of the image (though it is apparently subordinated to a comparison between gardens) is to look forward to Eve's seduction by Satan. When he brings in Ganymede and Hylas, Milton uses the same technique, though in their context they have far less power and resonance. Indeed, the discrepancy between their fates and the poet's, already signaled by the discrepancy between an elaborately feigned Cupid and his literal setting, is essentially comic. A reader who is familiar with the tradition and sympathetic to Milton's tone may fairly guess what to expect as an outcome; it will be surprising if it is tragic.

Now Cupid has his turn to boast (27–46) and proves much better at flyting than his opponent. As he recounts his many victories over great gods and heroes, from the Parthians who defeated Rome to Jove himself, his ostensible purpose is to magnify the power of his right arm. Once more, however, a secondary effect is to suggest parallels with the soon-to-be-hapless poet. If Cupid can conquer Apollo "in all his pride after he had slain the Python," or "Gigantic Orion," or "strong-handed Hercules," or "Jove himself" armed with thunderbolts, what hope is there for the poet? The discrepancy is not only between the boylike Cupid and his mighty opponents, but also between Hercules and the narrator. Although the style of the poem is mainly Ovidian, it partakes at times of a higher strain, what with its elevated similes and epithets: "strato Pythone superbum / . . . Phoebum," "ingens . . . Orion," "Herculeaeque manus" (31–32, 39, 40). This evident elevation in style is part of what has troubled critics about the poem; only, I think, because they have taken it seriously.

It may be helpful to ask what genre the poem belongs to. A classical love elegiac of a sort, its strong story line also makes it like an Aesopian tale, of the sort represented by Milton's early *Apologus de Rustico et Hero*. The moral, while not supplied, may be readily inferred: don't boast your superiority to love, or you will suffer the consequences. Yet the style and subject matter of the Cupid passages resemble epic delineation of single combat. Everything is there: the detailed presentation of the hero and his antagonist, their boasts of strength in combat and of past victories, their trading of insults. Consider Cupid's parting words:

> Caetera quae dubitas meliùs mea tela docebunt,
> Et tua non leviter corda petenda mihi.
> Nec te stulte tuae porterunt defendere Musae,
> Nec tibi Phoebaeus porriget anguis opem.   (43–46)

[Whatever other doubts you have shall be resolved by my shafts and by your own heart, at which I must aim no gentle stroke. Fool! Neither will your Muses be able to protect you nor will the serpent of Apollo afford you any help.]

This is nothing other than the conventional ending of a precombat flyting: blows, not words, will prove who is stronger. But, of course, these are *bella amoris*, the wars of love, and the style verges not on epic but mock-epic. Throughout, the poem is closer in spirit to "The Rape of the Lock" than to *Tristan and Iseult*.

Having uttered his last dire threats, Cupid shakes his golden arrow and departs. The narrator's reaction to the whole episode is simply to laugh:

> At mihi risuro tonuit ferus ore minaci,
> Et mihi de puero non metus ullus erat.   (49–50)

[But I was inclined to laugh at the threats that the angry fellow thundered at me and I had not the least fear of the boy.]

This laughter is not wholly misplaced, but it is misdirected; what he fails to understand, *stultus* that he is, is not that it isn't a joking matter but that he is about to become the chief butt.

In the third part, Milton sets the scene again:

> Et modò quà nostri spatiantur in urbe Quirites
> Et modò villarum proxima rura placent.   (51–52)

[Sometimes parts of the town where our citizens walk abroad and sometimes the suburban fields offer me their pleasures.]

This setting belongs to the same world as the one depicted in the second part. Indeed, Milton uses the word *villa* in both passages (plural in the second); the word might more accurately be translated as farm or country house, rather than village or suburb. The poet woke with the sun streaming over the roof-ridges of his country villa or its outbuildings, and when he isn't visiting the city he walks in the nearby fields. Whether the city recalls Rome or London, and whether the villa belongs to John Milton, Senior, or to Martial depends on where one puts the balance between life and art. In any event, if we are to connect the fields in which the

poet admires the passing girls with Hyde Park, Gray's Inn, or Covent
Garden, then by rights we ought logically to identify the place where
he saw Cupid as his bedroom at Hammersmith or Horton.

A connection between the passing girls and Cupid is suggested by
Milton's continued use of light imagery:

> Turba frequens, faciéque simillima turba dearum
>   Splendida per medias itque reditque vias.
> Auctaque luce dies gemino fulgore coruscat,
>   Fallor? an et radios hinc quoque Phoebus habet.   (53–56)

[Groups of radiant girls with divinely lovely faces come and go along the walks.
When they add their glory, the day shines with double splendor. Am I deceived,
or is it from them also that Phoebus has his rays?]

Two details call for comment. First is the wonderfully balanced line that
begins with the protagonist's romantic vision, "Splendida per medias,"
but ends with the poet's sly hint that the girls are showing themselves
off in immemorial fashion by promenading back and forth, "itque re-
ditque," as Milton's comical phrase captures the process. Second is the
question with which Milton ends: "Fallor?" Clearly the answer the protagonist expects is, No, you are not mistaken; just as clearly, I would argue,
the answer the poet expects is, Yes, you are sadly — but very humanly —
mistaken. The doubleness of Milton's meaning is often hard to capture
in translation; Hughes is as reliable and responsive a translator as any,
yet he cannot help but reduce the comic implications of Milton's "turba
frequens," a packed crowd of girls and of goddesses, to the more respectable "groups," probably because he did not expect comedy at this point.
My dictionary (Cassell's) gives "disorderly crowd, heap, swarm," as the
definition of *turba*; I am sure Milton could have found a more romantic
word had he wished.

The eyes of the night-blinded poet are about to suffer a further assault; filled with comic hubris, he walks about with the misplaced confidence of a young warrior, a mock Patroklos or Pallas, who is about to
learn what battles are really like:

> Haec ego non fugi spectacula grata severus,
>   Impetus et quò me fert juvenilis, agor.
> Lumina luminibus malè providus obvia misi,
>   Neve oculos potui continuisse meos.   (57–60)

[I did not turn (sternly) away from the pleasant sights, but was carried where
the impulse of youth led me. Heedlessly I sent my glances to encounter theirs
and lost all control of my eyes.]

Terribly careless; for it is through the eyes that one catches the disease of love. Compare Chaucer's Troilus, before events have turned his notes to tragic:

> Withinne the temple he wente hym forth pleyinge,
> This Troilus, of every wight aboute,
> On this lady, and now on that, lokynge,
> Wher so she were of town or of withoute;
> And upon cas bifel that thorugh a route
> His eye percede, and so depe it wente,
> Til on Criseyde it smot, and ther it stente.   (I, 267–73)

So much for Troilus, and in another line so much for the protagonist of *Elegy VII*:

> Unam forte aliis supereminuisse notabam,
>   Principium nostri lux erat illa mali.   (61–62)

[Then, by chance, I caught sight of one who was supreme above all the rest; her radiance was the beginning of my disaster.]

No translation could do justice, however, to the splendid phrase that Milton places at this turning point: "supereminuisse notabam." Can such sublime diction be taken at face value? Does it anticipate "With hideous ruin and combustion down / To bottomless perdition," or does it rather look forward to Milton's mockery of such language: "So Hills amid the Air encounter'd Hills / Hurl'd to and fro with jaculation dire"?[16]

Cupid dodges about this apparition, hurling his darts and striking the poet's breast "in a thousand places." As unfamiliar passions assail him, his heart is consumed by the fire of love (65–74). Having built up at great length to this crisis, however, Milton suddenly disappoints us:

> Interea misero quae jam mihi sola placebat,
>   Ablata est oculis non reditura meis.   (75–76)

[While I suffered, she who alone could give me happiness was borne away, never to return to my eyes again.]

Was she borne away by Jove's eagle or gloomy Dis? No, the stupified poet merely lacked the initiative to follow her and seek an introduction (77–80). It is this hesitation, incidentally, which is so much admired by the early critics as a fine exhibition of the gentle passion. To compare small things to great, the effect Milton achieves at this point is like what happens in *Paradise Lost* when he builds up the encounter between Satan and Death, and later between Satan and Ithuriel, only to pull the rug out from under the reader's expectations of a fine battle to come. In each case the effect is to subvert the genre. In *Paradise Lost* we are taught to admire not military valor but the higher heroism of suffering and martyrdom; in *Elegy VII* Milton overturns the conventions of the love elegiac more gently but just as thoroughly.

The point is driven home by what is surely the high point of mock-epic in the poem, at the same time that it is the high point of Milton's accomplished mastery of style:

> Sic dolet amissum proles Junonia coelum,
>   Inter Lemniacos praecipitata focos.
> Talis et abreptum solem respexit, ad Orcum
>   Vectus ab attonitis Amphiaraus equis.   (81–84)

[Such was the grief of Hephaestus for his lost heaven when he was hurled down among the hearths of Lemnos; such was the grief of Amphiaraus when he looked his last upon the sun as he was swept away to Hades by his thunder-driven horses.]

Critics have rightly admired this passage even as they have objected to it. Those objections may be answered if we posit that Milton was fully aware of the discrepancy between the poet's case and that of Vulcan or Amphiaraus — in fact, that the discrepancy is part of his point.

But Milton was not Dryden or Pope. Although he revealed a satirical strain all through his life, he seldom allowed it dominance. In such a passage as this, Milton has his cake and eats it. Just as in *Paradise Lost* he derides Satan constantly yet makes him, in spite of everything, the grandest Romantic figure of English poetry, so he can laugh at the largely self-inflicted wounds of young love yet show more than a little understanding for that condition. (After all, it does come more graciously to laugh at oneself.) True, the fall of Mulciber and the destruction of Amphiaraus are matters more serious than the simple disappearance of a girl the poet glimpsed in passing and never saw again; but the terrifying sublimity of their fates as evoked in Milton's magniloquent language is not so disproportionate to a young lover's feelings. They only become disturbingly disproportionate if we insist that the poet still is an unreflecting prisoner of his feelings and so has lost control of his poem. Clearly Milton does not despise young love, but although he can sympathize with it and probably has experienced it — and may even continue to feel its power — he is no longer wholly its victim as he writes.

The ending might seem to contradict that view. Although it shows a protagonist who no longer is callowly hubristic, it still shows him in a posture that, while opposite to the earlier one, is extreme and foolish:

Jam tuus O certè est mihi formidabilis arcus,
    Nate deâ, jaculis nec minus igne potens:
Et tua fumabunt nostris altaria donis,
    Solus et in superis tu mihi summus eris.
Deme meos tandem, verùm nec deme furores,
    Nescio cur, miser est suaviter omnis amans.   (95–100)

[Now, O child of the goddess, with your darts no less powerful than fire, your bow is beyond all doubt dreadful to me. Your altars shall smoke with my sacrifices, and, as far as I am concerned, you shall be sole and supreme among the gods. Take away madness, then! But rather, do not take it away. I cannot tell why, but every lover's misery is sweet.]

So, he prays to this new god of his, if ever he should love again, may he and his beloved be transfixed by a single dart (101–02).

We might accept as reasonable that the chastened poet should now fear Cupid's formidable bow; but, however little Milton may have been a Puritan at this early age, it is hard to imagine him taking seriously, even in metaphor, a duty to load Cupid's altars with smoking sacrifices, or to worship him as sole and supreme deity. The commandments are against it; yet the line is very emphatic; "Solus et in superis tu mihi summus eris." Far more probably, as the exaggerated language suggests, Milton still has his tongue in his cheek — as Horace often does in his odes, or Chaucer in the case of Troilus — and is no more at one with his protagonist's last state than he was with his first. Indeed, one error follows another, and his last state is surely much worse than his first. Milton's tone, of course, as it is throughout, is more sympathetically amused than censorious. If he hopes to teach his reader a further lesson (a real lesson, not the ostensible, pragmatic "moral" I spoke of earlier), he will do so not by scolding him but by making him laugh and, like the poet, laugh at himself, not at some detached figure in whom he has no sympathetic interest.

To read the poem in such a way depends on finding at least a partial distinction between Milton and his first-person protagonist. Moreover, that distinction, as an aspect of Milton's poetic strategy, must be conscious. If such a proposition — that Milton deliberately manipulated the relationship between poet and protagonist, and consequently the relationship between art and life — is not, as I have argued, sufficiently obvious in the tone, diction, and imagery of the elegy, then I think it is given away beyond dispute by a stylistic quirk not yet mentioned: the insistent use of the word *mihi*. Milton is, as much in Latin as in English, a careful stylist who does not repeat himself in vain; yet the word occurs twice in the passage last quoted, and twelve times in the poem as a whole. The personal pronoun, moreover, is more noticeable in an inflected language, which can indicate person in its verbs. Seven times the reflexive *mihi* appears at or near the emphatic beginning or end of a line. In every instance, it appears in such a context as to underline the speaker's egotistical and boastful foolishness. The word first crops up when the speaker says, "but as for me," my eyes "craved the retreating night" and could not bear the dawn (15).[17] Cupid in his turn says that Phoebus yielded "to me" (32); "to me" the Cydonian hunter yields (37); "my" shafts will teach your heart a lesson (44). "But as for me," the foolish narrator retorts, "I was inclined to laugh"; "and as for me," he repeats in the next line, "I had not the least fear of the boy" (49–50). Such close repetition, at the start of both lines in the distich, emphasizes his solipsistic blindness at this point.

Subsequently, having been vanquished by love in spite of his boasts, he can only cry out, "Hei mihi!", "alas for me — he struck my defenseless breast in a thousand places" (72). "She alone," he laments, "can solace me" (75). Would that it might be given "to me" to see her face to face (87). "Crede mihi," he then proceeds to tell his readers: "Believe me! No one ever suffered such misery in the fire of love" (91). That "Crede mihi" might almost sum up the poem. Do we believe, and in what respects should we believe, someone who talks like this? It is evident that he still has not learned his lesson when, in the conclusion, he tells Cupid, "to me your bow is beyond all doubt dreadful" (95); and "as for me you shall be sole and supreme among the gods" (98). Can we think, even here at the close, that this *mihi* who is speaking is John Milton?

There is a Milton behind the poem, of course, and, having attempted to read it as a literary whole rather than a fragment, we may properly return to where we began: to its biographical implications. What *Elegy VII* reveals, I think, is a more complicated young poet than most critics have admitted, and one far more in control of his art. He has either experienced, or can sympathetically imagine, both what it is like to be a callow young man who boasts about his superiority to love, and what it is like to be struck by a passing face or to fall in love for the first time. Then he can see that love both from the inside — as something supremely momentous — and from the outside — as something trivial, foolish, even blasphemous. While doing this, he can manipulate his classical sources and his language to such effect that multiple tones and viewpoints exist side by side without destroying one another. He is not a sentimentalist or a mooning romantic, nor is he a simple mocker or a spoilsport. If his vision, as revealed by *Elegia Septima*, can be summed up in a word, one that encompasses both his wryly detached balance and his human sympathy, that word might unexpectedly be *Chaucerian*.[18]

New York University

NOTES

1. William Hayley, *The Life of Milton* (London, 1796; facs. ed., Gainesville, 1970), pp. 20–21.

2. Andrew Marvell, "On *Paradise Lost*," 51–52.

3. *The Poetical Works of John Milton*, ed. H. J. Todd (London, 1826), VI, pp. 236–37.

4. Todd, VI, p. 235.

5. *The Poetical Works of John Milton*, ed. David Masson (London, 1882; rpt. 1903), I, p. 94.

6. E. M. W. Tillyard, *Milton*, rev. ed. (London, 1966), p. 22.

7. John S. Diekhoff, ed., *Milton on Himself* (London, 1939; rpt. 1966), p. 31.

8. James Holly Hanford, "The Youth of Milton: An Interpretation of His Early Literary Development" (1925), rpt. in *John Milton: Poet and Humanist* (Cleveland, 1966), pp. 27, 3; and see headnote in Hanford's edition of *The Poems*, 2d ed., p. 38.

9. J. B. Broadbent, *Some Graver Subject* (London, 1967), p. 31; John Milton, *Samson Agonistes, Sonnets, &c.*, ed. John Broadbent and Robert Hodge (Cambridge, 1977), p. 17.

10. Todd, VI, p. 236.

11. Hanford, "Youth of Milton," p. 27.

12. William Riley Parker, *Milton: A Biography* (Oxford, 1968), I, pp. 77–78.

13. Latin text from CM; translations by Merritt Hughes, ed., *John Milton, Complete Poems and Major Prose* (New York, 1957), except where otherwise indicated.

14. I correct a rare misprint in Hughes: "Theomadas."

15. Bush, *Variorum*, p. 133.

16. Bush, *Variorum* (p. 137) cites Virgil's "supereminet" (*Aeneid* I, 501), used to compare Dido, first glimpsed by Aeneas, to Diana outshining her followers; and Ovid's "supereminet" (*Met.* III, 182), also of Diana, as she is first spied by Actaeon among her maidens. Milton's form "supereminuisse" is even more splendid, and the precedent appearance of the word at those signal, even epic, meetings simply reinforces the comic effect. Should a reader remember the precedents, as readers trained like Milton in close study of the classics were likely to do, they would find still another instance of proleptic discrepancy as the sad fates of Dido and Actaeon are recalled.

17. Here and at times in these two paragraphs I give a translation more literal than Hughes's. My colleague Christopher Collins remarks that *mihi*, which may be variously scanned, is a "wonderful prosodic crutch" that even classical writers found convenient. But Milton uses the word three times as often per line in *Elegy VII* as in the other elegies, and in his other poems he usually employs it emphatically and in rhetorical clusters rather than as an unobtrusive filler (e.g., *El.* 5, 1–23, conclusions of *Ell.* 3, 4).

18. What consequence does reinterpretation of *El.* 7 have for our reading of Milton's retraction? First, without entering into disputed questions of dating, nothing he says

in *El*. 7 would have prevented him from writing it immediately afterward. I find it hard to believe that Milton meant readers to take its bombastic exaggerations wholly seriously. It too seems to have a double import. Readers who took offense at *El*. 7 (or amorous parts of others), because they took it at face value, might probably read the retraction literally and find the desired apology. Others, who entered into Milton's spirit of play, would find the retraction playful too, a continuation of the joke. The consequence of trying to save Milton from the stigma of prudishness by reading *El*. 7 as a youthful confession is to condemn him immediately afterward for a priggish and inhuman retraction (as more than one critic has done). Fairer to the text, fairer to what we are beginning to learn about Milton's sense of comedy, to regard the elegies as artistic creations from life, not naive self-revelations, and the retraction not as an effort to take back what was incautiously revealed, but as a small piece of artistry in its own right.

MILTON'S EARLY COSMOS
AND THE FALL OF MULCIBER

Christopher Collins

T HE M I L T O N I C model of the universe with which we are most fa-
    miliar, the model he elaborated in *Paradise Lost*, was not the cos-
mos of his early poetry. Though many of its features, both traditional
and idiographic, were to be fitted into his later cosmos, this earlier model
appears to be less spatially demarcated, less architectonic, more permeable to the risings and descendings of conscious beings. Judging from the
cosmological references in his early Latin and English poetry, we find
no adamantine barriers or "firm opacous" convexities. In their place we
find a number of operationally (therefore temporally) distinct *states of
being* through which souls, human and superhuman, pass after death
or in ecstatic trance-states or in moments of prophetic vision or after having lost their original status or simply on transcosmic missions.

The reasons why Milton's early cosmos should be divided into spiritual states rather than spatial realms readily suggest themselves. First,
the poet had no need as yet to formulate an extended and consistent visual
model of his universe. (We must not forget, by the way, that this cosmos
is the work of an experimenting poet between the ages of seventeen and
twenty-six and is inferred from textual references scattered through some
forty short poems and epigrams.) Secondly, he had not yet fully assimi-
lated or integrated the various models at his disposal, namely the Hebraic, Homeric, Ptolemaic, and Copernican *cosmoi*. Not having settled
on one nor yet fashioned his own amalgam, he could be free to adjust
his cosmology to the specific demands of each poem. Thirdly, being mer-
curially young and confident of his own powers, he no doubt preferred
to view the universe as open to exploration. What, after all, was to prevent a true poet from meditating with "thrice great *Hermes*" or from
unsphering the "spirit of *Plato* to unfold / What Worlds, or what vast
Regions hold / The immortal mind that hath forsook / Her mansion in
this fleshly nook"?[1] If virtue could teach one "how to climb / Higher then
the Spheary chime,"[2] to what plane might one not aspire on the wings
of virtue imped with prophetic inspiration and the art of song?

A wiser, if not wisest, Fate said "no" to such free transcosmic journeyings and the young Milton in his wiser moments dutifully accepted this pronouncement, but his earliest poetry was often too exuberant — indeed perhaps too hyperbolic — to be "wise." He had not sensed as yet the full inertial weight of original sin. Instead he saw himself as one of a line of prophetic poets (*vates*) whose work was the making of "divine song" ("vatis opus divinum . . . carmen"), a vocation "which more than anything else proclaims the celestial origins, the heavenly seed, of the human mind, retaining as it does the sacred traces of Promethean fire."[3]

> Quo nihil aethereos ortus, et semina caeli,
> Nil magis humanam commendat origine mentem,
> Sancta Prométhéae retinens vestigia flammae. (*Patrem*, 18–20)

The *vates* which the young poet aspired to be was clearly not a descendant of Adam but a son of the celestial voyager Prometheus. He was yet to learn the Augustinian lesson that, in order to ascend, one must first descend.

I. Cosmic Time Zones

The principal division of Milton's early cosmos are not those which we later find — empyreal heaven, the lower heavens, earth (as a center stage), then chaos and hell. As far as the young Milton is concerned, chaos is unthinkable and hell a cheerless prison, a classical Tartarus, but evidently not a very important place. Every really important place is above. It is as though terrestrial existence marked the lowest conceivable point on a scale which, like Jacob's ladder, was "set up on the earth, and the top of it reached to heaven: and behold the angels of God ascending and descending on it" (Gen. xxviii, 12). So much of his early poetry was, as we shall see, concerned with this "ascending and descending" through supernal cosmic planes of activity.

Instead of being spatially compartmentalized, these planes or zones are kept distinct by their dynamic operational differences. The transcosmic voyager passes through various states of being, a passage which is marked by changes in the way things appear to behave in time. In other words, the zones through which he passes are experienced as contiguous and permeable durational zones. The major division, of course, is between the eternity of heaven and the time of Creation. But the latter is further divided into the perfect cyclical realm of the superlunary spheres and the imperfect rhythms of sublunary nature. Of eternity little could be said in the time-bound idiom of man. The poem *In Obitum Praesulis Eliensis* makes this very point; Bishop Felton, after recounting his ascent into heaven, mentions the shining gates, the crystal palace, the court paved with emeralds, then stops abruptly:

> Sed hic tacebo, nam quis effari queat
> Oriundus humano patre
> Amoenitates illius loci, mihi
> Sat est in aeternum frui.   (65–68)

[But here I shall be silent, for who, sprung from a human father, could express the beauties of that place? It is enough for me that I enjoy it eternally.]

Yet the young Milton was not always ruled by such reticence. In *Ad Patrem*, his apologia in the form of an epistle addressed to his father, he speculates:

> Nos etiam patrium tunc cum repetemus Olympum,
> Aeternaeque morae stabunt immobilis aevi,
> Ibimus auratis per caeli templa coronis,
> Dulcia suaviloquo sociantes carmina plectro,
> Astra quibus, geminique poli convexa sonabunt.   (30–34)

[For we, when we regain our heavenly fatherland where the everlasting intervals of motionless eternity abide, then will we pass in gold crowns through the heavenly holy places, blending with the soft-voiced harp such sweet songs that the double-vaulted universe will resound.]

"Aeternae morae,"[4] then, is the durational state which stands in apposition to the spatial term "Olympus." Yet the poet could not resist investing this sublime concept with lower-worldly spatiotemporality—the father and son rambling through heaven making their music.

Perhaps one way to understand this treatment is to regard the real heaven as possessing in plenitude the durational characteristics of the lower realms, plus its own. In other words, heaven could have its "aeternae morae," plus the order and harmony of the lower heavens, plus the linear, irreversible time of the earthly realm of man, including the free will that properly characterizes and shapes human history. The lower heavens, on the other hand, could possess only cyclic order and harmony (as their chief characteristic) plus linear irreversibility (they were not eternal and their angelic engineers were possessed of free will). At the bottom of this scale, the sublunary realm of earthlings was ruled by linear, irreversible time; though granted heavenly grace (including vatic inspiration) and the edifying vision of the cycling spheres, humans were not granted the additional temporal prerogatives of the two higher realms. Theirs was the mutability of sublunar existence. This, I would submit, was the three-tiered cosmos of Milton's early poetry. Though it is set up schematically as a spatial hierarchy (and referred to as "three-tiered"), we should keep in mind that the spatiality of these realms, or more properly, states of being, was not stressed in this early poetry and was certainly not presented with the cosmographical explicitness found in *Paradise Lost*.

THE THREE REALMS AS COSMIC TIME ZONES

		TEMPORAL STATES		
		1 CHANGELESSNESS (Eternity)	2 ORDER (Cyclic Time)	3 MUTABILITY (Linear Time)
	1 EMPYREAL HEAVEN	distinctive temporal mode	additional attributes	
THE THREE REALMS	2 LOWER HEAVENS		distinctive temporal mode	additional attribute
	3 EARTHLY NATURE			*only* temporal mode

The empyreal heaven possesses as additional attributes the temporal modes of the two lower realms. Directly "beneath" this durational plenitude is the cyclic state of order (*cosmos*) represented by the wheeling of the firmament ("astra . . . geminique poli convexa," *Patrem*, 34) and the planetary spheres within it. Milton's academic exercise *Naturam Non Pati Senium* ("That Nature Does Not Suffer From Old Age") argues that the material universe, specifically the lower heavens, will not change or "run down" until the final world conflagration. According to the myth of Uranus, or Sky, and his son Chronos (traditionally confused with Kronos, the ogre-god who swallowed his own children one after another as they were born), he asks, "Shall insatiable Time devour the Sky and take into his entrails his own father?" Here "Time" ("Tempus") is the linear time, *tempus edax*, which gives birth to, then devours, the consecutive intervals of earthly existence. "Of course not" is the expected answer, for how could Jupiter, the Sky-Father, be so improvident as to build his citadels subject to such an outrage, to "that evil of Time" ("Temporis isto / . . . malo," 17–18)? If he had not foreseen this danger, his whole court would indeed have collapsed inevitably into that dread chaos of sublunary Time; he, too, he and his daughter Athena, would have reenacted the fall of "Juno's offspring," Vulcan, who long ago had been "hurled from the holy threshold of the sky and fell upon Aegean Lemnos":

> Qualis in Aegaeam proles Junonia Lemnon
> Deturbata sacro cecidit de limine caeli.   (23–24)

(We should note here that this classical myth was the only available *exemplum* of the casting down of a divine being from Olympus. In his early model of the universe, in which gravity and friction seem such negligible factors, this fall is a notable exception. As we shall see, when Milton needed a classical *exemplum* to typify the precipitous fall which goeth after pride and infatuation, he used the story of "Juno's offspring.")

These lower heavens are not subject to old age, or, as later cosmologists would term it, entropy or "heat-death." Their perpetual cycles are an imitation of the changelessness of the empyreal heaven. The time that they typify and embody Plato in the *Timaeus* had defined as the "moving image of eternity." This celestial machine was constructed like no machine we know on earth, for

> pater omnipotens fundatis fortius astris
> Consuluit rerum summae, certoque peregit
> Pondere fatorum lances, atque ordine summo
> Singula perpetuum jussit servare tenorem.
> Volvitur hinc lapsu mundi rota prima diurno;
> Raptat et ambitos sociâ vertigine caelos.   (33–38)

[The almighty father, considering the totality of things, founded the stars more firmly, established the scales of fate with definite weight, and commanded that in the sublime order each particular should maintain its perpetual course. Hence the primal wheel of the world turns in a daily motion and by its sympathetic rotation propels with it all the orbiting heavens.]

As we know, Milton made much of the long-held belief in the musical harmony of the lower heavens, a notion that was a continual source of imaginative inspiration to him throughout his career. As a poet, the son of a musician, his vocation was, as it were, a participation in that angel-thronged realm which lay like a bridge between the divine and the human.

The orbiting heavens, which after their fashion copied eternity, knew nothing of beginnings and endings. How could they? Their time, though it had its one beginning and would have its one end, was cyclic. To the angels who inhabited these spheres, the universe might well appear, as Goethe puts it, "herrlich wie am ersten Tag." Earthly time, however, was another matter. Beneath the moon, it was the realm of mutability and was ruled by the laws of beginnings and endings.

This is not to say that the lower time zone could not be *influenced* by the cyclic regularities of celestial motions. It therefore could have its festal, or liturgical, cycle. "This is the Month, and this the happy morn," the young poet could say to celebrate the recurrent feast of the Nativity. And the elegy on the coming of spring could begin:

> In se perpetuo Tempus revolubile gyro
> Jam revocat Zephyros vere tepente novos.
> Induiturque brevem Tellus reparata juventam,
> Jamque soluta gelu dulce virescit humus.   (*El.* 5, 1–4)

[Time, turning back upon himself in his perpetual cycle, now calls back the fresh Zephyrs, as the spring grows mild and the Earth, renewed, dons her brief youth and now the sweet ground, unloosened from frost, turns green.]

This "Tempus revolubile" is not the linear time of earthly history. It is not the path "our lingring Parents" took, on which each human lifetime is an irreversible step. It is the renewable time of the spheres and lifts the poet with it into its own zone:

> Jam mihi mens liquidi raptatur in ardua coeli,
>   Perque vagas nubes corpore liber eo.
> Perque umbras, perque antra feror penetralia vatum,
>   Et mihi fana patent interiora Deûm.   (*El.* 5, 15–18)

[Now mine is a mind that is rapt to the heights of the pellucid sky and through the wandering clouds I pass, freed of my body; through shades I am borne and through caverns, the secret dwelling places of the bards, and to me are disclosed the inner sanctuaries of the gods.]

Such is the enthusiasm, the ecstasy, of the young poet rapt like Ganymede into another state of being. The "tempus revolubile" of the lower heavens permits the annual recurrence of the liturgical year. Cyclic time as the *magnus annus* also permits the return of the paradisiacal golden age. Curiously, he prays that this age will restore Jupiter to the earth:

> Te referant miseris te Jupiter aurea terris
>   Saecla, quid ad nimbos aspera tela redis? (*El.* 5, 135–36)

[May the golden age return you, Jupiter, return you to the wretched earth! Why do you withdraw into the storm clouds, that cruel armory of yours?]

"Jupiter," of course, may be taken as a classical name for the Christian supreme deity. Yet Milton must have known that Jupiter was the god who brought the Saturnian golden age to a close and, as Virgil says in *Georgic* I, imposed on mankind a regime of unremitting toil. We see here what might well be an early indication of a conflict in the poet's mind between the images of God as the author of goodness and as the great taskmaster, a conflict which in the Nativity ode (written according to Bush about a half year later) took the form of a wish that time would "run back, and fetch the age of gold" together with the realization that redemptive history must after all run its painful course.

II. MULCIBER AND THE MOTIF OF THE SUDDEN COSMIC DESCENT

That word the Romantics were to make so much of, "forlorn," well characterizes the condition of humanity locked into linear time. The thematic complexity of vulnerability, loss, abandonment, and exile — so central to so much of Romanticism — appears throughout Milton's poetry. Its first tentative expression we find in his early Latin verse. Here his master was Ovid, not only the author of the *Metamorphoses*, the *Heroides*, and the *Fasti*, those handbooks of mythology, but Ovid the exile, the poet whose *Ars Amatoria* and *Remedia Amoris* (so the story went) prompted Augustus to banish him from Rome to Tomi, the imperial outpost on the Black Sea — Ovid the psalmist of the *Tristia*, those laments for the lost world of his past.

The first clear instance of this theme appears in *Elegy I* (*Ad Carolum Diodatum*). During his first year at Cambridge, he was suspended, apparently because of a difference with his tutor, William Chappell. His poem makes light of this suspension: he would much rather have his freedom in London than serve in Cambridge. He would not object should he be stigmatized as a "fugitive" ("profugus"), he so happily accepts the conditions of his banishment. If only Ovid had been similarly exiled! In somewhat forced-sounding tones of youthful bravado the poet extols the girls of London.[5] They are allurements to him, but he has not yet been snared by their Circean wiles.

In *Elegy VII*, however, he speaks of his vulnerability and subsequent sense of abandonment. The scene is set in a sort of Ovidian London on May Day. He had spurned Cupid and the irate god had chosen to make a convert of him. The *peripeteia* begins with his catching sight of a certain girl:

Sic Venus optaret mortalibus ipsa videri,
　Sic regina Deûm conspicienda fuit.
Hanc memor objecit nobis malus ille Cupido,
　Solus et hos nobis textuit antè dolos.　　　　　　(63–66)

[That was how Venus might have wanted to seem to the eyes of mortals. That was how the queen of the gods must have looked. Cupid—he was the one who deliberately and maliciously set her before me; he and he alone wove this snare for me.]

What happens next in the poem was perhaps as much a surprise for Milton the poet as the event had been for Milton the impressionable gallant. He loses her in the crowd and, in the poem, is brought through this sorrowful loss to a nobility of expression that presages the poet of *Paradise Lost* and *Samson Agonistes*.

Protinus insoliti subierunt corda furores,
　Uror amans intùs, flammaque totus eram.
Interea misero quae jam mihi sola placebat,
　Ablata est oculis non reditura meis.
Ast ego progredior tacitè querebundus, et excors,
　Et dubius volui saepe referre pedem.
Findor, et haec remanet, sequitur pars altera votum,
　Raptaque tàm subitò gaudia flere juvat.
Sic dolet amissum proles Junonia coelum,
　Inter Lemniacos praecipitata focos.
Talis et abreptum solem respexit, ad Orcum
　Vectus ab attonitis Amphiaraus equis.　　　　(*El.* 7, 73–84)

[All at once strange passions took shape in my heart. Burning inwardly with love, I was totally aflame. In the meantime she, she the only one who could delight me in my wretched state, was taken away, never again to appear before my eyes. As for me now, I go my way silently sorrowing. Foolish and hesitant, I have often wished to go back there. I am split in two: one part of me holds back, the other part follows its desire. It does some good to cry over joys like these which are suddenly snatched away. That was how Juno's child mourned[6] for his lost heaven, having been cast headlong down among the hearth-fires of Lemnos, and that was the way Amphiaraus looked his last upon the sun as he was carried into hell by his thunderstruck horses.]

The last two couplets are remarkable for several reasons. Douglas Bush noted that these "two examples of epic feeling and tone occur together, perhaps not without conscious hyperbole, in the most unlikely of contexts."[7] It is not unlikely that the eighteen- or nineteen-year-old poet would have erotic reactions intense enough to lead to extreme utterances. What is remarkable is the seriousness of these similes within a poem which began quite conventionally and was to end in a proper Valentine's Day effusion — that, if any girl is ever to be his, may one single arrow transfix them both and make them one. There is a passion in these compressed similes which could only have come from a deep sense of loss — a forlornness — which this incident reactivated. What is also remarkable is the candor with which he admits this scene of desolation, a candor which, as was suggested earlier, the Ovidian conventions made easier. As we know from his later poetry, he was more likely to use mythic personae to convey such feelings than to do so directly in the lyric mode. This shyness perhaps lay behind his early choice of epic over the intoxication of elegy (see *Elegy VI, Ad Carolum Diodatum Ruri Commorantem*).

Before we consider their function as personae, we will need to review briefly the myths associated with "Juno's offspring" and Amphiaraus. Juno's child ("proles Junonia") is Vulcan or Mulciber, in Greek Hephaistos. Juno had been annoyed by her consort's giving birth by himself to a daughter, Athena, and decided to counter that with a strictly matrilinear offspring. When, as a full-grown celestial, Mulciber intervened on her behalf in a family dispute, Jupiter threw him down from heaven. He landed finally upon the island of Lemnos where, according to one story, he learned the trade of blacksmith from the inhabitants.[8] Amphiaraus was a seer, a *vates*, one of the fabled Seven against Thebes, those Argive confederates who supported Polynices' attempt to regain the throne relinquished by his father, Oedipus. Fully aware that the campaign had been doomed by the Fates, he turned from the walls and tried to escape, but the earth broke open and he plunged headlong into the underworld, coincidentally a fall also engineered by Jupiter.[9]

Thus Milton associates two falls in this double simile, one from heaven to earth, the other from earth to Orcus, and in both *exempla* the doomed being is said to think of or look back plaintively to his lost upper world. One character is a divine queen's son, the other a doomed prophet: both the poet likens to himself in his sudden fit of forlornness. Of these two falls, Mulciber's apparently held a greater, indeed a special, fascination for Milton. He alluded to it in *Naturam Non Pati Senium*, evidently composed at or about the time of *Elegy VII* (circa 1628), and was to rework it some thirty years later in a celebrated set-piece in *Paradise Lost* which we will examine shortly.

III. THE LOVER'S "LOST HEAVEN"

Not every reader, however, has found this Mulciber simile striking or meaningful. On the contrary, more often it has been regarded as misconceived. Thomas Warton (1785) felt that the reference to Amphiaraus was beautiful from a young mind teeming with classical history and imagery. [But] the allusion, in the last couplet, to Vulcan, is perhaps less happy, although the compliment is greater. In the example of Amphiaraus, the sudden and striking transition from light and the sun to a subterranean gloom, perhaps is more to the poet's purpose.[10]

A century later David Masson (1874) concurred with Warton's judgment and added:

In the preceding lines he had compared his desolation of heart, as the unknown London beauty vanished from his gaze, and he knew he should never see her again, to the feelings with which Vulcan in Lemnos may have thought of the heaven from which he had been suddenly flung; now he mends the image by saying he is like Amphiaraus, who, as he sank in his chariot through the dark chasm that was to close over him, took one last look upward at the sky and the sun.[11]

More recently Douglas Bush found both of these similes "not without conscious hyperbole" and "in the most unlikely of contexts."[12]

There is no question but that they are hyperbolic indeed and introduce into a poem ostensibly aspiring to Ovidian urbanity a jarring note of desperation that seems to violate the decorum of the composition. Our task, however, is not to evaluate these lines or the poem in which they are placed but to understand them within the context of the poet's maturer work. If, as the critics have felt, these lines mark a temporary loss of artistic control, what might this loss of control signify?

Let us return to the first simile with its "proles Junonia" pathetically centered within his loss:

> Sic dolet amissum proles Junonia coelum,
>   Inter Lemniacos praecipitata focos.   (*El.* 7, 81–82)

Mulciber had lost heaven on account of his "sin" of *lèse majesté*. To put this in more mundane terms, he had been thrown out of his home for having tried to stop his violent (step)father from physically abusing his mother. His metronymic epithet clearly testifies to his allegiance. In short, he had lost heaven out of love for his mother.

What, one must ask, must these mythic connotations have to do with Milton's professed sense of loss at the disappearance of his anonymous *virgo*? Nothing, we might conclude, except for one intriguing bit of contextual evidence: in this elegy there are only three formal simile-passages, each a double *exemplum* — the poet, as we know, is likened to Mulciber and Amphiaraus; Cupid is likened to Ganymede and Hylas (21–24); but the *virgo* is somewhat oddly compared to Venus and the "regina Deûm"

(63–64). Here certainly is another apparent infelicity, for neither goddess would seem to be an appropriate image of *virginitas* (and Milton usually defined *virgo* quite strictly). Juno, the matronly "regina Deûm," is a model of older womanhood; just to cite one example, four years later he compared the septuagenarian Countess Dowager of Derby to Latona, Cybele, and Juno (*Arcades*, 20–25). If likening this *virgo* to Juno seems odd, likening her to Venus seems downright wrong.

Concerning this latter comparison, Walter MacKellar (1930) remarks: "Possibly an allusion to the meeting of Venus and Aeneas (*Aeneid* I, 314–417)."[13] Although the allusive connection is, on the surface, somewhat tenuous, MacKellar's observation is germane if one grants the possibility of an allusive substratum in this text. Virgil's hero is the special concern of two goddesses, Juno, who tries to destroy him, and Venus, who is his remote but ever-protective mother. Shipwrecked by Juno's connivance on the coast of Libya, he is met by his mother disguised as a *virgo* (*Aeneid* I, 316–20). After informing him about Carthage and its queen, she departs, betraying tokens of her divine identity, at which point Aeneas berates her for not appearing as herself to her son (405–09).

There is yet further evidence to link the Miltonic simile with Aeneas' encounter with his disguised mother. Bush, commenting on line 69 of this elegy, notes that the expression "virginis ori" ("to the maiden's face") is a stock phrase appearing three times in Ovid's *Metamorphoses* and once in the *Aeneid* (I, 315) where it is specifically used to describe the virginal disguise of the hero's mother, Venus.[14] Then, if we recall that Cupid makes his one appearance in the Virgilian corpus later on in Book I (657ff.) and behaves very much as he does in this elegy, we may fairly conclude that MacKellar's instincts were correct.

Is this *virgo* a masked image of the young man's mother, as was the *virgo* whom Aeneas encountered? The evidence for such a conclusion is scant and inferential. One explanation, in greater harmony with the context of the elegy, might be that this Juno- and Venus-likened maiden is a virginal composite of the two principal women in the Mulciber myth: the mother, for whose sake he was cast out of Heaven, and the wife, who with Mars cuckolded him. By themselves they are powerful *numina*, but when combined and contextually associated with Mulciber, they suggest the power of the feminine to hold sway over the masculine intellect and will, a situation which was to become a central theme in Milton's later work. Here in *Elegy VII* we already find that susceptibility and, by implication, submission to the power of a woman is followed by pain, banishment, and the distant vision of a lost heaven, an "amissum coelum."[15]

Who or what is this "lost heaven"? Is it the girl he has no sooner seen than lost? If so, she is "the heaven that leads man to this hell," for all she has (innocently no doubt) occasioned in the speaker is an "expense of spirit." If, as I have earlier suggested, the divisions in Milton's early cosmos represent spiritual states of being and if heaven connotes the untrammeled freedom of the soul, then the vengeful work of Cupid in this elegy effects in the speaker a fall from this state of inner freedom. His heaven is lost as soon as he sees and desires the girl. As Michael explains to Adam in the final book of *Paradise Lost* (XII, 79ff.), when reason is obscured, inner liberty is lost and when this inner liberty is lost, one is ready to be tyrannized by others.

Let us now for a moment look at some of the classical versions of the Haiphestos-Vulcan-Mulciber myth. The most famous *locus classicus* for the divine smith's fall occurs toward the end of *Iliad* 1. There is once again unrest in Olympus. Again Hera (Juno) is on a collision course with her husband. This time Hephaistos (Vulcan) reminds her of what happened long ago, adding that he is not likely to intervene again. He then describes how the "Olympian" took him by the foot and hurled him from the celestial threshold and how he fell helplessly all day until sundown when he landed upon Lemnos. After recounting this story, he returns to his unlikely role as cupbearer *pro tem*, a performance which the assembled celestials find hilarious.

Vulcan had indeed become something of a comic personage. Perhaps even in Homer's time he was a stock character in satyr plays and in Punch-and-Judy-style marital farces. Perhaps of comedic sources of this type we can trace such *fracassi* as his cuckolding by Aphrodite, his entrapment of her and her harlequin Ares, and even his expulsion from the brawling household of Olympus.

Another, somewhat more serious version is found in the *Argonautica* of Valerius Flaccus. As Valerius tells the story, early in his new regime Jupiter became aware of unrest among the gods. To demonstrate his power he began by suspending the queen of the gods from the edge of "swift-winged Olympus and pointing out to her the horrible chaos below her and the punishment of the abyss" ("Iunonem volucri primam suspendit Olympo / horrendum chaos ostendens poenasque barathri," *Argonautica* II, 85–86).

> mox etiam pavidae temptantem vincula matris
> solvere praerupti Volcanum vertice caeli
> devolvit; ruit ille polo noctemque diemque
> turbinis in morem. Lemni dum litore tandem
> insonuit. (87–91)

Englished in a somewhat Miltonic manner, Valerius might sound like this:

> Soon after, catching Vulcan in th' attempt
> To loose his trembling mother from her bonds,
> Him the god thrust sheer from the precipice
> Of heav'n: down from the pole through night he fell
> And day, twisting in air, until at length
> On Lemnos' shore resoundingly he struck.[16]

Afterward "the Father permitted him to reenter the heavenly citadel," Valerius tells us, but because of his fall he henceforth was unable to walk without a limp. His stepfather, or father as he was sometimes called, had need of Vulcan's metallurgical skill and, as everyone knows, Vulcan became the indispensable smith and armorer of the gods.

Despite the comic, not to mention slapstick associations of the myth, Milton seems to have emulated Valerius' tone and attempted to raise the smith momentarily to the stature of a tragic hero in this passage from *Elegy VII*. This elevation would have deserved no more than an appreciative footnote — we would not have wished to overload this delicate couplet with so much mythological analysis — had not Milton chosen to return to the legend of Juno's son and rework it in that remarkable passage near the close of *Paradise Lost*, Book I. People had heard of the story of Mammon in Greece, the epic poet declares, but they called him by a false name; in Italy they called him Mulciber.

> and how he fell
> From Heav'n, they fabl'd, thrown by angry *Jove*
> Sheer o're the Chrystal Battlements; from Morn
> To Noon he fell, from Noon to dewy Eve,
> A Summers day; and with the setting Sun
> Dropt from the Zenith like a falling Star,
> On *Lemnos* th' *Aegaean* Ile.   (740–46)

In *Mythology and the Renaissance Tradition* Bush is again struck by the extraordinary and unexpected intensity with which Milton treats this myth:

This allusion is a sort of postscript to the catalogue of false gods and is prefaced and concluded with expressions of hostile disbelief, while the myth itself is told with quite unnecessary richness of detail and is notable even in Milton for beauty of phrase and sound; there seems to be a momentary divorce between the Christian and the imaginative artist in this transmutation of Homeric comedy into romantic vision.[17]

That this is in actuality Mammon, "the least erected Spirit that fell / From heav'n" (I, 678–79), and that, as Alastair Fowler notes, the poet deflates the grandeur of the passage in the "casual but commanding dismissal" of "thus they relate, / Erring,"[18] only serve to accentuate its strange solemnity. Error or not, Mulciber's fall is presented not with derision but with rapt fascination.

Part of the special magic comes from the manner in which Milton presents this fall as a descent through zones which are both spatially and temporally differentiated: first, empyreal heaven with its fixity of crystal battlements; next, the lower heavens with their cyclic revolutions, diurnal and annual; finally, the sublunary world as the ultimate destination and the lowest plane possible for an exiled god. But why all this extraordinary, this "quite unnecessary richness of detail"?

In the mind of the mature Milton, I would venture to suggest, the figure of Mulciber was linked with those other men who had fallen victim to women. An unquestioningly loyal son, a too-trusting husband, Mulciber had suffered the pains of physical deformity and social derision, all because of his gallant allegiance to the women he loved. As such, he was a poignant caricature of Adam and Samson — and of the poet as well — a self-portrait not unlike that which Michelangelo painted into his *Last Judgment*.

By identifying him with Mammon, however, Milton adds a baser trait to this earnest fool of love. Mulciber-Mammon is "downward bent" (*PL* I, 681), not because of his fall from heaven, but because while in heaven he had stared continually at the gold pavements. He is introduced evidently in order to be exposed as a lover of appearance and self-gain only. This figure, whom the Greeks and Romans regarded as a hardworking artist, a loyal mother's son, and an all-too-trusting husband, was actually the patron demon of those who later "Rifl'd the bowels of thir mother Earth / For Treasures better hid" (*PL* I, 687–88). One cannot avoid the impression that, despite the sumptuous language he lavished on the Mulciberian fall, he intended to distance himself and his readers from this mythic figure. When read in relation to *Elegy VII*, his treatment of Mulciber in the epic appears to serve the function of a palinode.

The poet had already determined that aspects of his early poetry called for a palinode. When in 1645 his *Poems* were published and he placed *Elegy VII* at the end of his elegies, he appended to it an epilogue, a ten-line moral disclaimer of high Horatian wit. What wantonness a reader might detect in these poems was due to wayward youth: he had now safely passed beyond that stage. The flames are all extinguished; his breast so bristles with ice that Cupid and Venus would be terrified if they met him in battle.

Urbane as this palinode is (one senses here the tone he used in his elegies to Diodati), he was true to his resolve in that he never again played the courtly heart-sick lover in his poetry.[19] He must have come to recognize the self-deception of this Catullan "odi et amo" role and no doubt experienced the despair to which erotic vulnerability, when not a mere convention, often leads.

As we have seen, Milton's early cosmos was a set of spiritual planes ranging upward from the earthly to the divine, from the self-limited to the fully liberated. It was, on the whole, a hopeful model of reality: the only direction one could go was up and upward flights were what his early poetry so often celebrated. In *Elegy VII*, however, we see the poet contemplating a downward trajectory. The Adam-like fall of Mulciber and the Satan-like fall of Amphiaraus are both tinged with tragedy: like the speaker, they are victims of divine powers whose strength and vindictive fury they had not fully assessed.

The universe of his maturer poetry was ruled by divine justice. It was vast and awesome. Never again was it to possess the easy permeability of his youthful cosmos. Instead of zones differentiated mainly by modes of temporality, these planes were spatially demarcated realms. Instead of a god-filled cosmic voyager, the poet became a man like other men, a *vates* indeed, but earthbound and subject to the curse of Adam. Turning from the role of the courtly lover and elegist, the devotee of the eternal feminine, he came to view his life's work as the justification of a Father Omnipotent. This shift in orientation I believe we can trace in his unusual adaptations of the myth of Mulciber.

New York University

NOTES

1. *Il Penseroso*, 89–92. All quotations from Milton's English poetry are from CM.
2. *Comus*, 1020–21.
3. All translations are mine.
4. Concerning this line (31) Tillyard wrote: it is "quite clear and untranslatable . . . mature and perfect Milton; tense, serene, and, as benefits the subject, trancelike; unequalled till the description of heavenly beatitude in *Lycidas*." *Milton* (London,

1930), p. 78. I might also suggest that the phrase in the preceding line, "patrium Olympum," is also difficult to translate into English: "native Olympus," as it is often translated, does not preserve the specifically patriarchal character of the phrase.

5. "A funny, pathetic, normal effort of an adolescent boy to impress another boy with his indifference to something that has hurt him deeply." William R. Parker, *Milton; A Biography* (New York, 1968), I, p. 30. See also James Holly Hanford, *Studies in Shakespeare, Milton, and Donne*, ed. O. J. Campbell (New York, 1925), p. 109.

6. I have translated "dolet" in past tense, assuming that Milton chose the historical present for metrical reasons.

7. Bush, *Variorum*, p. 13.

8. There is a completely different tradition according to which Hera, dismayed at having brought to birth a crippled child, cast him out herself. Milton nowhere alludes to this version.

9. Statius was probably his primary source (*Thebais*, VII, 820–24).

10. Thomas Warton, ed., *Poems Upon Several Occasions, English, Latin, and Translations by John Milton* (London, 1785), p. 485.

11. David Masson, ed., *The Poetical Works of John Milton* (London, 1874), III, p. 508.

12. Bush, *Variorum*, p. 13.

13. Walter MacKellar, ed., *The Latin Poems of John Milton* (Ithaca, N.Y., 1930), p. 238.

14. Bush, *Variorum*, p. 138.

15. *Amissum coelum*, we should also note, also appears at the beginning of Milton's *Prolusion V*: Jupiter is said to have conceded Italy to Saturn as an "amissi coeli solatium." In *PL* the expelled angels are understandably obsessed with the notion of their "lost heaven" (see esp. I, 134–36 and II, 14–16). Only after having completed this paper was I able to consult Louis Martz' *Poet of Exile: A Study of Milton's Poetry* (New Haven, 1980). Though chapters 4, 5, and 11 bear somewhat on my theme, as a whole this fine book sets itself and achieves other objectives.

16. Even a casual comparison with *PL* I, 738–46 will reveal the superior care Milton lavished on his account of this fall.

17. Douglas Bush, *Mythology and the Renaissance Tradition* (New York, 1957), p. 287. (Italics added.) We might also recall that Milton's fall of Mulciber apparently made such an impression on William Blake that he made him the central figure of his visionary epics. As Urthona (and in the fallen state: Los), this titanic smith became the poet's own persona.

18. Alastair Fowler, ed., *Paradise Lost* (London, 1968), p. 87.

19. As early as *Elegy VI*, composed a year or so after *Elegy VII*, he declared as much to his friend Diodati.

MILTON'S *NATURAM*

William A. Sessions

W HATEVER THE occasion and dating of *Naturam Non Pati Senium* ("Nature does not undergo old age"),[1] the poem as we have it is a remarkable performance. In sixty-nine lines of dactylic hexameters, exhibiting a sophistication of meter and caesura, of figure and verbal structure, and of allusion surely remarkable for any Latin poet but especially for a boy not even twenty, Milton reflects the achievements, on every level, of the Renaissance *paideia*. If we date the poem and the occasion as early as 1628, as most commentators do, Milton was ending that ritualistic training of language and thought that modeled itself on another world, an ideal landscape that, as the humanists from the beginning were quick to point out, was to be the prototype for transforming the real time and place of each reader and student. Thus, whatever the private initiations through language, it was the *polis*, it was *civitas*, that demanded the definitions. Even an exercise, some "leviculas . . . nugas," as Milton wrote Gill,[2] could be for a very young poet on a July day at Cambridge no small means for ordering his own world, especially if these lines were the first of his ever to be published.

If Hakewill did indeed provide the theme for the Cambridge commencement that year, the poem or spoken *oratio* moves quickly beyond its obvious polemic, that nature does not decay, into the realm of performance. Here seasoned rhetorical strategy marks truth as much as overt reasoning. Although it is probable that Milton did not speak his Latin lines,[3] his sense of an undergraduate audience and of a dramatic event controlled by language had been tested by the *Prolusions* delivered earlier, if in fact we can date the *Prolusions* at all (Fletcher assumes that Milton's success in the Lenten term with the highly technical *Prolusion Four* had led to the sudden request by a senior fellow that Milton produce these verses for the July commencement).[4] The third year of undergraduate study at Cambridge, with its special attention to logic and the public *disputatio*, certainly required such public performances and, in fact, Milton's first major performance on his own took place within a few weeks after this reading of his *Naturam*. He would participate in the midsummer disputations and mock-exercises, a record of which can be found in his *Prolusion Six* and his English poem *At a Vacation Exer-*

cise in the Colledge dated "Anno Aetatis 19." According to Fletcher, by
this time in Milton's study, the composition of themes, developed since
St. Paul's, was brought to a height; particularly at this stage of training
all themes had to be logical, on an announced subject, polished in style
and conforming to the best classical Latin, memorized, and effectively
delivered to a public audience. Thus, "by the third year, though the usual
form of exercise in which these themes were delivered was the *disputatio,* usually in the college chapel, the theme itself was the form of an
oration, made as effective as the ability of the student could prepare and
deliver it."[5]

If Milton did follow this form of the oration, which he clearly did
in other works and speeches in his epics and dramas, then the lines of
his rhetorical strategy become immediately apparent and give the reader
and auditor a means to organize their apprehensions of his poem. Thus
the theme of his work, that nature does not undergo old age, is organized
into four sections of proof: an *exordium* (1–7); a *reprehensio* (8–32); a
confirmatio (33–middle of 65) with a *propositio* in the first four lines;
and a *peroratio* (middle of 65–69). The larger structural division of the
poem follows the kind of dialectic Milton was to find so congenial to his
purposes in the first and second parts of the Nativity ode and the companion poems *L'Allegro* and *Il Penseroso.* This division into a negative
response to the question at hand and then a full proposition and positive
response was little more than the subdividing so beloved in Ramist logic,
which as Ong has shown,[6] developed from Agricola and the whole tradition of place-logic but with the special organizational twist of Ramus.
Yet, if we follow the order of an oration suggested by the contemporary
John Clarke in 1624, that is, *exordium, propositio-confirmatio, exemplum,*
and *peroratio,*[7] Milton has his own variation. Like Sidney in his *Defense,*
Milton includes a *reprehensio* in his literary adaptation of the oration;
furthermore, like Francis Bacon who brought a similar order into his
scientific method,[8] Milton provides the negative instance before he confirms his proof of theme. He does not need to include a special place for
what Clarke calls the *exemplum* because, as we shall see, the whole of
the poem displays a texture of examples. From the first bold classical
allusion to the final conflagration from Biblical and classical texts, *Naturam* builds its case on allusions as "places" for proof. These *topoi* bulk
largely from the *Metamorphoses,* that book of myths whose author was,
from the first years of his *paideia,* a "strong personal presence," as Martz
notes.[9] Such allusions in Milton's spoken poem define the structure
throughout the various parts of the poem and do not need any specific
position for proof. In fact, the most fundamental proof for his whole

thema would exist, for Milton, in this very oratorical structure and its placement. Such a principle of demonstration was not merely one of rhetoric but, as Ong illustrates copiously, one of logic. The basis of the structure of *Naturam* in the oration was itself, at least for Milton, as much a product of logic as of rhetoric.

Whatever its intellectual origins, however, the poem begins with a magnificent sweep that at once distances it from the school curriculum. Although its dramatic flourish may have been possible only because of those linguistic structures discovered by his *paideia*, the total effect of the lines is Milton's.

> Alas, how the wandering mind of man cracks,
> exhausted and driven by perpetual error,
> and immersed in darkness, profound and of itself,
> it ponders only Oedipean night.[10]

The reader's attitude is immediately set by the allusion to Oedipus. Despite its probable linguistic origins in Statius' epic *Thebaid* and in a pivotal passage of the fifteenth book of the *Metamorphoses*,[11] Milton's figure evokes Sophocles: cracking up, exhausted and driven, a great human being like Oedipus did not recognize that there is, in the liturgical language Milton had recited at St. Paul's throughout his childhood, "no health in us."[12] Recognition by the reader of this initial state, his essential humanity, thus begins the therapeutic process ahead in which a true definition may arise. In a single myth Milton prepares his auditor and reader for a major part of his thesis: human comprehension is limited, and absurd analogies merely reveal the fragmented human mind. The next lines of the *exordium* continue this opening motif:

> Raging, it dares to measure god-deeds
> as its own, and to pretend that laws engraved
> in eternal adamant are its own, and lines
> of fate, never to be loosened in any age,
> it fetters within its passing hours.

The Oedipus motif dramatized a persistent belief of Milton's about the nature of man's understanding of the universe. It was to be the base note of a dialectic expounded at the other end in the achievements that he described, for example, in the humanist sage of *Prolusion Seven*. But such a note clearly resounds in Adam's "All human thoughts come short, Supream of things" (*PL* VIII, 414); in Jesus' "But these are false, or little else but dreams" (*PR* IV, 291); and in the chorus of *Samson Agonistes:* "As if they would confine th' interminable, / And tie him to his own prescript, / Who made our Laws to bind us, not himself" (307–09). It also appears in the *Commonplace Book,* under the heading *De Curiositate* (CM XVIII, p. 138), where, using St. Basil's comparison of Sophists to night-owls, Milton denounces false theologians, whom he will later see as having "found no end, in wandring mazes lost" (*PL* II, 561) and inhabiting the Paradise of Fools. Similarly the Lady will rail against Comus, who has dared to impute his ideas to Nature and who simply cannot "apprehend / The sublime notion, and high mystery" (784–85) of either nature or chastity. Finally, in *De Doctrina Christiana,* condemning theologians who have recourse to what "they call anthropopathy," Milton states categorically: "for to know God as he really is, far transcends the powers of man's thoughts, much more of his perception" (CM XIV, pp. 33, 31).

Although the religious and particularly the Reformed Christian texts provide the major background for his motif of the *exordium,* there are classical sources as well: the choruses from Aeschylus' *Agamemnon* and two linguistic parallels from Ovid. In *Metamorphoses,* V, 320, for denigrating the "facta deorum" and challenging the Muses, the daughters of Pierus are turned into birds with human voices; in XV, 814ff., Jupiter tells Venus that the tablets of the fates, engraved in everlasting adamant, relate the history of her Roman posterity (Ovid's parallel for Anchises' prophecy). The central religious text is Isaiah lv, 8, "For my thoughts are not your thoughts, neither are your ways my ways, saith the Lord." Echoed in Isaiah xl, Psalm xix, and in Job xxxviii, it found its Christian focus in two Pauline texts, Roman xi, 33–36 ("For who hath known the mind of the Lord? or who hath been his counsellor?") and 1 Corinthians ii, 16. What this intricate network of allusion suggests is that Milton had already developed a method out of the *paideia* that worked as powerfully as the modern symbolist tradition in poetry, so that, by no accident, the most spectacular use, for example, of the figure of catachresis (often with a basis in allusion) can be found in Milton, Mallarmé, and Hart Crane. As such poets knew, no amount of calculated logical or dyslogical effect, allusive or otherwise, is possible without a passionate contemporary focus, in attitudes if not subject matter; and this Milton found in the Hakewill controversy. Here too the Oedipus motif was prominent: "How long this age shall last," says Hakewill, is a mystery "lockt up in the cabinet of his own counsell, a secret which is neither possible neither profitable for us to know, as being not by God revealed unto us in his Word, much lesse then in the booke of Nature."[13]

There was another contemporary source for this motif which probably bulked in 1628 as large in audience appeal as any one of the others.

Francis Bacon, whose theory of two books Hakewill alludes to above, had stressed such a recognition as the essential part of his *pars destruens*, and *pars preparativa*, the first stage of his Instauration or renewal in which the mind would be cleansed of its "distempers" and "peccant humours" and "idols" before it approached the important work of his method in the New Organon. This fundamental stance occurs in the earliest description of his method, *Valerius Terminus* (1603). Milton's Cambridge audience would have recalled Bacon's therapeutic attack on the human mind as "an enchanted glass" and his desire for healing its sick nature as evidenced, for example, in the first book of the very popular *Advancement of Learning* (1605), when Bacon divides knowledge into the Book of God's Word and the Book of God's Works. But his essential call for humility before the study of nature is given in pristine form in the *Valerius:* "For as in the inquiry of divine truth, the pride of man hath ever inclined to leave the oracles of God's word and to vanish in the mixture of their own inventions; so in the self-same manner, in inquisition of nature they have ever left the oracles of God's works, and adored the deceiving and deformed imagery which the unequal mirrors of their own minds have represented unto them."[14] Bacon's implicit reference here is to the Catholic scholastic emphasis on theology and philosophy rather than the Bible (a favorite Protestant dichotomy whose propagandistic base Bacon overtly turns to advantage, as he does throughout all his work, for the winning of his audience). Bacon will transform this theme in the 1620 *Novum Organon* into the spider emblem of his insect imagery, one of the most popular images for English intellectuals for the next century.

In the next section of his oration, Milton continues the Oedipus motif by giving his speaker of the Latin poem more cause for a mocking and ironic tone. He builds a subtle logical connection in his thematic development between the point of his *exordium* and that of the *reprehensio*. Both this display of logic and the railing burlesque tone would have not only delighted his public audience but also followed the other two of Cicero's directives, to teach and persuade. Milton had spelled these out in *Prolusion Three*, itself another attack on scholastic philosophy that leads to direct praise of a humanist, if not Baconian, program. In fact, Milton had already presented to Cambridge audiences (or soon would) the force of Baconian error in its grappling with truth; the attacks in *Prolusion Three* on scholastic philosophers, echoing the Baconian criticism and the imagery itself, the description of Error at the opening of *Prolusion Four,* and the battles of Truth with Error in *Prolusion Five* provide proof of where Milton had found popular terms that would dramatize his own concerns and dialectic (CM XII, pp. 159–67; 173–77; 195–97).[15]

The logical nexus of the two parts thus lies in the premise that, if the Oedipus-mind is so foolish as to identify its laws as those engraved by the fates, then what might one expect? The series of rhetorical questions that now begin enunciates the absurd possibilities. An operative Latin word here is "ergo"; it opens the *reprehensio* and then, at a critical juncture of this section, it repeats and then begins the last part of the *reprehensio*. In both cases it introduces a catalogue of sorts, one a series of mythic allusions set as questions and the other a series of myths set as declarations, both climaxing in hyperbole taken to the level of cosmic and divine absurdity — the kind of joke that can make God laugh. Thus, "ergo," with its root senses of "paying out" as well as "bending and inclining,"[16] carries this transition from the logic of the *exordium*, where Man is Oedipus, to its absurd conclusions. A subtle mocking irony of tone is in order. And again, another invention begins to suffuse the lines as did the expanded Oedipus allusion. In this case a prosopopeia develops as a result of this tight logical and linguistic connection, one that will form an image that will become, quite literally, a matrix for the whole poem.

> Well, then, will the face of Nature really
> begin to wither, covered with wrinkles
> like plow-furrows? Will the common mother
> of all things become sterile through age,
> her womb opening for all now drawn tight?
> And having confessed herself old, will she go
> with tottering steps, shaking her head of stars?

With the figure of a decrepit Mother Nature (modeled on Ovid's description of a disguised Juno in the *Metamorphoses* (III, 175), Milton turns to his negative image, so to speak, of what would happen if indeed nature did undergo old age and decay. The contrasts establish absurdity: the sublime image of the face of Nature and her role as "publica mater" make the details of wrinkles, contracted womb, sterility, and tottering seem incongruous, an effect turned ludicrous in the final detail of the shaking of the heavens. The linguistic echoes in this latter image in Ovid and Seneca would certainly provide, if not for Milton's auditors, then for his sophisticated readers, a profound parody. The stars were immutable and could never shake, but such would be the result if this absurd proposition about nature's decay were true. Furthermore, behind Milton's prosopopeia lay the implicit contrast of the Great Mother herself. This literary archetype was, of course, no mere abstraction for Milton. Isis appears early in his work;[17] and like his audience, he would recall how Lucretius transforms the crown of Cybele, her "head of stars," into the turrets of her holy city (II, 606–07) and how Virgil, following his master, transforms the crown into a climax in Anchises' prophecy for Rome (*Aeneid* VI, 784–87). Most of all, this Cambridge audience of 1628 would recall Spenser's metamorphosis in *The Faerie Queene* of this same simile to glorify the crown of the bridegroom Thames in order to reveal the newest of the great cities, London (IV, 11, 28). In the very same book of the epic the young men would remember the fertile androgynous figure of Venus who would merge at the end of the epic into the bisexual Dame Nature. For an audience to whom Spenser was the English Virgil, and for a poet for whom Spenser represented a "sage and serious" master, Dame Nature represented the sublime figure before whom Mutability had to bow and learn the lesson from Venus' garden: "eterne in mutabilitie" (III, 6, 47). Thus the concept of wrinkles and sterility was absurd for "This great Grandmother of all creatures bred / Great *Nature*, euer young yet full of eld, / Still moouing, yet vnmoued from her sted" (VII, 7, 13).

In the next lines, the burlesque of the *reprehensio* develops the motif of nature's age as ridiculous by introducing a strange personification of Time that will lead logically to the questioning of Jupiter himself. This allusion, by name, to the father of the gods completes the section that had begun with first "ergo."

> And will loathsome old age or the everlasting
> hunger of years or squalor or dust
> and dirt actually shake the stars? Will
> insatiable Time really be hungry enough
> for heaven itself and ravish his father
> in his very depths? Alas, could not even
> Jupiter, thoughtless as ever, fortify his castles
> against this outrage and free them from that
> evil of time, conferring instead
> unceasing circles, year after year?

An immediate effect of Milton's reversal of the traditional myth about time is a curious physicality, a sustaining of a biting realism already suggested in the incestuous figure of Oedipus and the bodily deterioration of Mother Nature. Milton may have inherited mythology that Dr. Johnson suggested any undergraduate could find, but his dramatization of myths for this performance gives evidence that he found classical myth more than mere academic appendage to his thought. Another aspect of his dramatization is a counterpoint to the dominant realism and absurdity; that is, the speaker hints at a larger order (to be developed in the *confirmatio*) in the repeated image of the stars, the heaven of the defiled father, and the perennial circling of the spheres. This assurance is important for the reader here because the developing identifications of age/ hunger, Time/ravisher demonstrate the conclusion in the text that Jupiter seems to have lost control. Is it possible that the god of gods (rather imprudent as he is) cannot even stop this execration against heaven itself? Furthermore, the confusion over whether Jupiter, the son whom Father Saturn or Cronos wants to devour in Hesiod's version, is to be identified in any way with Milton's reversed figure adds to the general effect of ludicrous, if not terrifying, disorder.

This passage has disturbed readers, and Reiss's suggestion that Milton mocks "the folly of thinking that time could destroy matter in which resided the spirit of God,"[18] a theological point developed later in the *De Doctrina*, emphasizes the parody that Milton is attempting. Although time may have been created, as Reiss notes, before the universe and may not destroy matter *per se*, its effects are devastating. The figure is as hungry as Death in *Paradise Lost* and just as incestuous: as Milton remarks in *On Time*, written in the same early period, "And glut thy self with what thy womb devours. . . . And last of all thy greedy self consum'd" (II.4, 10). The Latin phrasing "insatiabile Tempus" (14) echoes a famous linguistic *topos* in Virgil where, on three crucial occasions, Virgil accentuates the devouring of human structures and activities by time.[19] Although Milton is certainly inheriting the traditional confusing of *Chronos* and *Cronos*, or Saturn and Time, the Latin *Tempus* and its epic associations indicate Milton's attempt at a personification independent of traditional myth or at least a rhetorical strategy that will use old associations for new effects of burlesque. The result is a sophisticated verbal and literary joke for the Cambridge audiences of 1628, punctuated by the mockheroic "heu" that introduces the impotent Jupiter. In such a universe, Milton is saying, where nature decays, Time would have to reverse its character and instead of being limited by the Father, would actually devour the Father, as though Hesiod's myth could be reversed! Milton's reversal thus serves as a polemical device to attack his opponent (implied or real): in the *disputatio* it is an undercutting by sarcasm and implicit absurdity based on an audience's (like the poet's) full response to the classical world. This response has the same simple basis as the Elder Brother's total faith in *Comus* that virtue "Shall in the happy trial prove most glory. / But evil on it self shall back recoyl" (592–93). Having established this sense of prevading irony, burlesque, and even mock-heroic, Milton now repeats these effects in the last section of his *reprehensio* but on a grander scale. Beginning once more with "ergo," he unleashes a catalogue of Ovidian myth.

Well, if not, then it will be, one day
or another, that the floor of heaven's vault
will fall down with a terrible sound, and the poles
exposed will scream with the blow, and the Olympian
will sink from his upper palace, as well as Pallas,
terrifying with her uncovered Gorgon's head.
Juno's child once sank like that, to Aegean Lemnos,
ejected from the sacred threshold of heaven.
Even you, Phoebus, copy the fall of your son,
in sinking chariot, and you rush downward
with a crash so sudden that Nereus will steam
as the torch of day is quite put out.
From the sea, thunderstruck, he hisses with death.
At that time even the peak of lofty Haemus,
foundations torn apart, will burst, and the Ceraunian
mountains used by Dis against the immortals,
in wars with his brothers, now dashed to the abyss
and sunken, will terrify the Stygian king.

Milton skillfully introduces here the Lucretian and Biblical motif of the final catastrophe in an ironical mode, to be changed at the end of *Naturam* into a serious and majestic event whose expression will be primarily Christian. Now, with grim absurdity, the speaker moves rapidly to the lively world of myth. Jupiter, who earlier could not prevent a rape of heaven, actually collapses and with him falls Athena, exposing Medusa's head on her shield. This collocation of Jupiter-Athena-head represents a source that will be transformed in *Paradise Lost* as will the following myths of Hephaestus and Phaethon, all three united by imagery of falling. Milton is using a primary principle of composition in his *reprehensio* that he will employ powerfully in his next section, the *confirmatio*. Mythology, for the early Milton, reflected the animistic universe that the Nativity ode most clearly defined. It was a specialized language, to be sure, easily apprehended (and even demanded) by the summer audience of 1628, and it was best understood when it was presented, as Angus Fletcher has noted,[20] in the cluster technique of the *Metamorphoses* (and not in the form of larger single myths developed slowly but profoundly, as in the *Aeneid* and the Homeric epics). Especially for a thesis in which the myths themselves are proof, the cluster method dramatizes the argument more cogently. Furthermore, with this method, it is also clusters of reality that Milton is dramatizing, pointillist configurations like Seurat's which in Milton start from allusion but end in specifically dramatized human reality. Obversely, as in *L'Allegro* and *Il Penseroso*, specific landscapes can become ideal ones and even allusions themselves. This is the process of mythologizing inherent in language that Milton had discovered as early as the *Naturam*. Because such clusters cannot be so easily abstracted or codified, they are a valuable device for turning the spoken performance of an oration into a moving exploration of reality far beyond a mere *disputatio*.

For this reason these myths that end the *reprehensio* present a compelling reality in which the negative appears before the positive in the same way that Milton, for one example among many, will present in *Paradise Lost* a parody of the Trinity before the divine figures themselves. These negative instances reinforce the *reductio ad absurdum* already begun: not just Jupiter but the Olympian falls; the maiden warrior Athena loses control of her shield; even Phoebus Apollo cannot direct the sun; and Nereus, the solid old man of the sea (often confused with the powerful Proteus) turns to steam. It is, as Irene Samuel has remarked on Milton's use of comedy, "as though to laugh were only another way of denouncing error."[21] Finally the conclusion, with its confusion of the collapsing mountains and its use of zeugma to connect Dis and the war of the Titans, emphasizes the same ludicrous and in this case raucous absurdity. Milton dramatizes the scene so vividly that, if the reader forgets the sophisticated burlesque that is here to denounce error, he may be frightened and remember what the Elder Brother also said: "if this fail, / The pillar'd firmament is rott'nness, / and earths base built on stubble" (597–99). The Oedipus-mind always threatens.

With the third part of *Naturam*, Milton's great affirmation begins. It is a moment for which Milton has carefully prepared his reader and auditor, and when the familiar Latin "At pater omnipotens" with its echoes in Lucretius, Virgil, and Ovid rolled across the Cambridge audience, Milton's performance was reaching its climax. Section three of *Naturam* is essentially another catalogue, or cluster, of myths that in many cases directly answer the myths of the second part. Syntactically, it is organized around a series of comparatives and a series of conjunctives or adverbs showing comparison beginning with "fortius" in Milton's magnificent first line: "At pater omnipotens fundatis fortius astris."[22] The result is that this part of *Naturam* has a tightly woven argument and progression that leaves the auditor satisfied and convinced. The majestic "Pater" that controls the thematic development, like a hypothesis governing data, reveals a familiar Miltonic strategy: the classical atmosphere around Jupiter and his surrogates has turned into that "higher mood" of *Lycidas* reflecting the Hebraic and Christian. The Father has become the universal underlying all the particulars which the myths have displayed; they will display this Ovidian vitality until the *peroratio* where, again, the Father is in control of events, destroying his "machina mundi" for its greater bliss. "Pater" is thus a key juncture in *Naturam* summing up from the past and looking ahead. It provides the unity any performance, especially a spoken one, demands. Like Sabrina in *Comus*, the figure of the Father is a climax in terms of both content and form.

The Father is also one of Milton's subtlest inventions. In a series of specific metamorphoses, this carefully constructed prosopopeia has developed through their living texture, through clusters of identity, to this full announcement of his being. Thus, in the *exordium*, the confused father-son Oedipus marks the essential human condition. Next, the female parent Mother Nature cannot sustain herself in a world where Time prevails, and Time the son actually rapes and eats the loins of his father in heaven, an execration even Father Jupiter is too weak and imprudent to prevent. Time, mutability, has won this mock-heroic war, like the parodic victories of Satan; it is a victory in which, furthermore, the Father Olympian with his daughter born of himself will sink, as Juno's son once fell, in which Father Apollo imitating his son will burn up turning the old father of the sea Nereus into hissing steam, and in which Dis, the father of the truly terrible, collapses beneath the weight of mountains, one of which Spenser thought (VII, 7, 12) was the scene for the wedding that precipitated the great original sin of the classical world, the Trojan War, and the other, a battlefield where the fathers fought the fathers. Into this disorder, cosmic and yet mocking because it is logically absurd, the true Father reveals himself.

At the opening of the *confirmatio*, Milton's figure is the center of an inverted Ovidian typology in which the myths, with their open merging identities as flexible as Mother Nature herself, turn to the Father who directs and guides the auditor to salvation from his Oedipus-madness. In the first four lines of the *confirmatio*, Milton's *propositio* for his oration, the Father gives the reader this full assurance for total faith. He will reveal the truth that nature does not suffer old age and decay but is a self-renewing source of processes and functions which the same classical mythology, negative before, can now demonstrate as unchanging.

> But the Father, with firmer control of the stars,
> all-powerful, has watched over the very sum
> of things, and with certainty he has set
> in balance the scales of the fates, especially
> decreeing that each single thing keep
> its own perpetual, uninterrupted course
> and all within his highest order.

As the decorum of his argument demanded, however, statement was not enough, and so Milton continues his method, derived from Thomistic logic, of proof by analogy. The myths that he will now use build on an order that Milton had already adumbrated (or soon would) in *Prolusion Two:* Pythagorean and Platonic. The argument from the stars (and for Milton this included Copernican outer space) was an ancient one that would be translated into Milton's supreme dramatizations and statements of it in *Paradise Lost;* it had already been implicit in the dialectic of the *reprehensio* of *Naturam* where it stood for eternal order. Thus, in Milton's first line of the *confirmatio*, the Father controls the stars and more firmly than to allow all the previous images of falling. Because the Father is dramatized as astral order, it is logical that the next section of the *confirmatio* develop in a progression through outer space to earth: the "Prime Wheel" hurrying along the spheres and "no later than usual" Saturn at the end of space near the Primum Mobile and then "flashing red" Mars "as fierce as ever." With Phoebus, "eternally fresh," who does not imitate the reckless Phaeton but "runs along the same tracks of his wheel," Milton's auditor would draw closer to earth, the center of his universe. The star of Venus that collects the other stars like orderly sheep in a heavenly pasture, dividing "the kingdoms of time into twin colors," and the rhythmic brightening and fading of Delia are proof from space that nature continues the same. Even on earth, the four elements do not "change their faith and, as usual," thunderbolts of fire strike the rocks and cliffs of the earth; the winds Corus and Aquilo rage "no lighter" and the latter wind (a brilliant image in *Fair Infant*)[23] "huddles the armed Russians with the same shivering." Neptune, "as he usually does," crashes against Sicilian Pelorus; Triton sounds "his raucous shell" across the sea-surfaces; and across them, "with no less huge bulk," the giant Aegaeon is supported on the backs of Balearic whales. In this orderly progression of the four elements, like the processions in Spenser's *Mutabilitie Cantos,* earth, the last to be reviewed, has "that primitive vigor of her ancient time" and so Narcissus keeps his fragrance and the beautiful boys whom Phoebus and Venus love have their same grace. Milton ends his progression and catalogue with the negative side of his dialectic (the obverse of his second section): evil continues with the same lack of decay as the good, "for just as rich as before, the conscious earth hides gold given to crime in her mountains and gems under the waves." Not even steadfastness of Nature can rule out evil or the resources for evil; Nature and the Father are not the same. Thus the last of Milton's progressing catalogue (a theme of earthly riches to be developed as a major motif in Comus' arguments, in Milton's descriptions of hell, and Satan's arguments in *Paradise Regained*) is a subtle but sober reminder that neither human beauty nor natural order nor astral harmony is finally enough. Significantly, this last statement in the third part of *Naturam* is without any mythic allusion.

It is a preparation and muting before the *peroratio* not only of the poem but of nature itself.

The rhetorical principle that organizes this third section of *Naturam* is a progressive order within the multiplication of a classical landscape. Whatever the actual relationship of Milton's Latin poem to Hakewill, there are verbal parallels, and by no accident they best show in the *confirmatio* of the poem. Of course, like most writers of the day, Hakewill was a repository of classical and Biblical traditions. The result is that, for example, when Milton's progression of astral and natural harmonies reflects passages that derive from Hooker and possibly Arnobius and with full echoes of Boethius, the reader must be satisfied with Milton's rhetorical handling of them, not the originality of any ideas. Thus, in his use of the scales image in his *propositio*, Milton is not only drawing on the Homeric image later to be put to dramatic purpose in *Paradise Lost* but also is evoking for his Protestant audience the Biblical references in Daniel, Job, Isaiah, I Samuel, and Proverbs. From both traditions Milton is summing up allusions that suit his rhetorical purpose at this juncture of his poem: to invent an elaborate prosopopeia necessary for the decorum of his poem and to elicit from his audience associations, conscious or unconscious, that would enhance the dramatization of the Father as total power. When Milton translates himself, as, for example, when line 34 in the *propositio* becomes in *Paradise Lost:* "Had not th' Almightie Father where he sits / Shrin'd in his Sanctuarie of Heav'n secure, / Consulting on the sum of things, foreseen / This tumult, and permitted all, advis'd" (VI, 671–74), the complexity redoubles. Networks begin to arise such as the metamorphosis of the image in lines 58–59 of Aegaeon supported by whales. This image, originating in Hesiod, repeated in the *Iliad* and the *Aeneid*, takes its specific physical details (arms thrown over a pair of huge whales) from *Metamorphoses* (II, 9–10). Its final transformation in *Paradise Lost* (I, 199) reveals, once more, how the classical landscape works by incremental analogy. As part of a simile for Satan, the image reverts to the Hesiodic Briareos and, reinforced by an allusion from Aeschylus, its whale association carries beyond the name to the Leviathan figure that climaxes this first epic simile in the text, an illustration of Satan's mysterious physical and spiritual power.

Landscape here is, of course, inscape, and as such, classical landscape functions as a means not merely of bringing psychic order to the real world of Hobson's Cambridge, Laud's Canterbury, and Caroline England but also of evoking ideal landscapes themselves, such as the soon-to-be-produced *L'Allegro* and *Il Penseroso*, and these within the same social, political, and physical landscapes as those of the poet himself. These

idealized landscapes are built on a network of allusion that strengthens
the force of the argument or thesis of the work and, significantly, does
not delay it, that is, if we grant Milton his mode of arguing by analogy
and through place-logic. The method of allusion would be deepened later
on as Milton's mind, assaulted by external realities, strengthened its own
network of reality that had been nourished first in a classical landscape.
Allusion then would be a point in the text where Milton's reader could
cut beneath the thrusting argument and find a network of support (now
Milton's own transformed landscape and allusion) for the passionate line
of argument. The simplicity of the method — argument and allusion —
allowed the text to conserve and enrich its own sensuous rhetoric and
music. In this sense it is not only that T. S. Eliot missed Milton's elaborate network of allusion and emblem, conserved from traditions as rich
as any an individual talent might arise from, but that he also missed the
fact that such a network was focused into life in the only place where
the reader could begin and end.[24] In such a passionate metamorphosis
as Milton's of past traditions and landscapes, his reader was left, correctly,
with only one central document: the poetic text itself, a true Alpha and
Omega.

II

In his *peroratio* Milton turns to a Christian commonplace. All landscapes, even the classical, the vital myths of Ovid, must burn in order
to reach another metamorphosis, the transfiguration figured by Christ
himself and called in Greek Christianity the Feast of Metamorphosis.
Patrides has fully defined the place of the final conflagration in Milton's
Christian heritage,[25] and to it Milton's Cambridge auditor would have
added the original classical *locus* in Lucretius (V, 96), Ovid's parody of
it in *Amores* (I, 15, 234) and Jupiter's prophecy in the *Metamorphoses*
(I, 256-58). Thus, all theories of progression, even Bacon's "plus ultra,"
imply an end; and theories of progressive linear history, Marxist or Christian, as opposed to the cyclical, always demand, as a matter of logic, a
culmination and gathering up of meaning. A teleology for history need
not deny, however, vitality within that history. On the contrary, as Lewalski has shown, such a view of history in which types are not only "re-
capitulated in antitypes, but also surpassed; prophecies are fulfilled, but
according to a higher spiritual meaning which transcends the literal
terms,"[26] is one of enormous novelty and re-creation precisely because
there is direction. Metamorphosis is heightened by teleology, and this is
certainly implicit in Milton's own view: "There can be no doubt that every
thing in the world, by the beauty of its order, and the evidence of a de-

terminate and beneficial purpose which pervades it, testifies that some supreme efficient Power must have pre-existed, by which the whole was ordained for a specific end" (CM XIV, p. 27).

The specific end of *Naturam* is appropriately somber and inevitable, therefore, because it indicates the moment of death and transfiguration. The lines are simpler here and without allusion although they fully echo the Petrine letter, the *locus classicus* for Christians of the idea: "the heavens shall pass away with a great noise, and the elements shall melt with fervent heat, the earth also and the works that are therein shall be burned up. . . . Nevertheless we, according to his promise, look for new heavens and a new earth, wherein dwelleth righteousness" (2 Pet. iii, 10, 13). Nature therefore will never decay or grow old, but it will die in order to give its functioning body greater vitality and greater transformation: a *felix culpa* out of its own principle of life.

In the poem, its very last words, the world that will be burned is called "machina mundi," and Milton's Latin phrase is itself the ending of the Lucretian description of the collapse of the world. Those beautiful processes and strategies (suiting Lucretius' military etymology for the word) that Lucretius describes so fully will vanish. But, as Michael promises in *Paradise Lost* (XII, 459), "this worlds dissolution shall be ripe," and the justice of the burning of the world Milton reinforces with his verbal echo of Virgil's "series longissima rerum" (*Aeneid* I, 641), where succession and "a long lineage of glory" are celebrated, in the line (66) "series justissima rerum." Milton calls on the highest form of classical teleology here to support his adaptation of the Petrine text; for the end alone tells the true meaning of Virgil's succession, or "the righteous course of all things," as Isabel MacCaffrey translates Milton's line in her analysis of the ending of *Lycidas*.[27]

It is precisely in this matter of teleology that *Naturam* does not possess a dual structure, as has been argued: the succession of myths has been leading to this change of their naturalistic life in a greater life because, so the logical proposition goes, the many cannot be known except by the one. Nature cannot be defined without an end, and the end, no less abrupt than the one promised in the Gospel of Matthew, appropriately unifies the poem. More significantly, Milton's concept of teleology here puts him outside the realm of either Bacon or the "moderns" in their concept of nature. In fact, although Bacon and his descendants accept an end to all things, a kind of Sabbaoth too mysterious finally for human reason and therefore ultimately pointless in reality, they aggressively ruled out the Aristotelian conception of, and search for, a final cause. As Bacon wrote in 1623, "For the inquisition of Final Causes is barren, and like a virgin consecrated to God produces nothing."[28] Yet Milton is not really on the side of the professional "ancients"; indeed, of the two, he is much closer to Hakewill than to Goodman in his cosmology. Milton emphatically denies that nature decays because, as we have seen, he views her vitality, concretized in the poem in Ovidian myth and the classical landscapes, as a perennial performance. Like Bacon, he does not see nature as a system of laws only, a *natura naturata*, the enclosed machine of scholastics and Newtonians at their worst. Milton's very definition of nature does not exclude organizations and designs, nor the inevitable laws that follow the presence of structure, but it places its emphasis on functioning and the vitality of language and its mythologizing as part of that function and on the ends of such inventive activity: in short, a real *natura naturans*. As Milton wrote in the *De Doctrina*, "for nature cannot possibly mean anything but the mysterious power and efficacy of that divine voice which went forth in the beginning, and to which, as to a perpetual command, all things have since paid obedience" (CM XV, p. 93). Like Bacon, he shares wonder at the creation in that first week (the hexemeral basis of Bacon's *Instauratio Magna*) and the orderly processes of the Book of God's Works. Also in that most Baconian part of his poem, the *exordium*, Milton recognizes the dangers of the "enchanted glass" and the necessity for humility before approaching nature.

But whereas in Bacon, the mind finally is so enchanted and diseased that it cannot speak and must have a method, a *Filum labyrinthi*, a *Novum organon*, to do what human reason cannot, in Milton the mind can and does observe *and* speak. Furthermore, it contemplates not merely experience but being. In fact, in Milton's *Naturam* nature does not change either to decay *or* to progress. It is always the same, embodying good and evil, as Milton is careful to point out. There is a direction and purpose to each of the acts embodied in the translated Ovidian myths, and that purpose is the universal order of the Father toward which each act tends. But there is no direction necessarily for the total order, that is, within time; it simply is, and its vitality and is-ness is the source of myths and mythologizing. In other words, myths arise from delightful contemplation of being. And the delight, as it gives rise to language and myth, is in being as it is becoming, as it is metamorphosing into other being. In such contemplation of being, the only investigation can be through language and through myth, and the language does not imply control, the vexing and forcing of nature that Bacon found so necessary for experimentation. It does not imply utility. It does not even imply accuracy. Thus Milton is neither optimist nor pessimist. In *Naturam* classical myths adapted for his occasion and audience show a continuum finally and suddenly transposed to another level, but in themselves sufficient.

Of course the Ciceronian intentions of the *oratio* are always here, and what they are teaching is a figure of Nature as a source of being, inventing and reinventing herself. This is not to say that Milton does not share in his *Prolusions* the optimism and sense of achievement associated with Bacon, but the purposes, both social and political, are entirely different. In fact, in *Prolusion Three*, one of the prime sources used by editors to demonstrate Bacon's influence, the reader can actually learn the real source of Milton's attitude toward nature. In his attack on scholasticism in *Prolusion Three*, Milton calls for a program in his penultimate paragraph that sounds like the Baconian program no doubt quite familiar at Cambridge in the 1620s. Then concluding, Milton names the philosopher who should "be your teacher in all these subjects," obviously referring to his preceding catalogue. It is Aristotle, "that famous man . . . who possesses so much charm," who is distinguished from his brutish disciples and their "distressing logomachy." Aristotle "has left to us almost all these things, which ought to be learned," and among them the last subject in Milton's catalogue, "what is after all the most important matter": for the mind "to know itself and at the same time those holy minds and intelligences, with whom hereafter it will enter into everlasting companionship" (CM XII, p. 171). Thus, the traditionally assumed antipathy of Milton to Aristotle, natural enough in his years of logic and philosophy, simply does not obtain here. Milton's contemporary, Leibniz, also recognized a truer Aristotle, whose concept of nature as process, as generation and corruption, but also as "fundamental unity and continuity," Leibniz would describe as "heavy with the past and big with the future."[29] In fact, if J. H. Randall is correct, what Aristotle's nature implies is what Milton's *Naturam* describes: "a certain structure or pattern of acting, a structure to be investigated in the operating and functioning of that power."[30] For Milton's *Naturam* the mode of investigating this structure, *natura naturans*, was ancient myth transformed and dramatized for a special performance on a summer day in 1628 in Cambridge.

Thus each metamorphosis is for Milton a new baptism of reality, within time and the successive world of nature, adumbrating the transformation beyond the fire. It does not exist for itself alone, either in Christian typology or in Aristotle's world of function. As Martz observes, and as the Elder Brother has stressed, "in Milton's universe eternal flux exists only in chaos."[31] In the poem, flux exists for the life of the Father and his promise of greater life and rebirth. So, in Milton's total response to that succession of ordered life so vividly illustrated and enacted in the Ovidian and classical mythology, even the stars and the heavens, the most crucial functioning of nature, must be burned. In Milton's *peroratio* all of Nature, which cannot suffer decay or old age, must finally die in order to be transformed.

> And so finally into eternity
> the most ordered succession of all things
> passes, until at last flames will rage
> across the globe, fully surmounting the poles
> and rising to all the heights of huge heaven.
> In a pyre this world's body blazes.

Georgia State University

NOTES

1. From Warton on, the traditional dating of the Latin poem *Naturam* has been July 1628, the "trifles of that sort," written by Milton for "a certain Fellow of our College who had to act as Respondent in the philosophical disputation in this Commencement" (CM XII, p. 11) and published and distributed at the occasion, a copy of which Milton sent to Alexander Gill, the son of his headmaster at St. Paul's, with an accompanying letter, supposedly written July 2, the day after the commencement. Recently William Riley Parker in *Milton: A Biography*, 2 vols. (Oxford, 1968), II, p. 773, and John Shawcross in *ELN*, 2 (1965), 261–266, with compelling arguments, have questioned this dating. The only certain fact is that this poem, always followed by *De Idea Platonica*, was published in the *Sylvae* section of the collected poems in 1645 and again in 1673, a fact of some weight because, twice in his lifetime, at a significant interval, Milton deemed the poem worthy of his canon. Bush, *Variorum*, pp. 209–14, refutes both Parker and Shawcross but concedes that neither *Naturam* nor *De Idea* may have fitted the occasion, although he notes that there is nothing else in the published canon that does.

2. The younger Alexander Gill had been a friend of Milton's since childhood and, if we judge by extant works, was second only to Diodati in Milton's early friendship and admiration (CM XII, p. 7). The circumstances of Gill's reception of Milton's *Naturam* and his imprisonment shortly thereafter remind us that the ideal world revealed in the Renaissance *paideia* was no mere abstraction in its relationship to the real world where products like Milton's *Naturam* (which Gill may have taken with him to prison) were civilizing forces.

3. Parker, *Milton*, I, pp. 43–44.

4. Harris F. Fletcher, *The Intellectual Development of John Milton* (Urbana, 1961), II, p. 441. For the problems of dating the *Prolusions*, see Parker, II, pp. 774–75, and Shawcross, "The Dating of Certain Poems, Letters, and Prolusions Written by Milton," *ELN*, 2 (1965), 265–66.

5. Fletcher, *Intellectual Development*, p. 225.

6. Walter J. Ong, S. J., *Ramus, Method, and the Decay of Dialogue; From the Art of Discourse to the Art of Reason* (Cambridge, Mass., 1958), chapters V, VI, and VII.

7. Fletcher, *Intellectual Development*, pp. 256–58.

8. Cf. my essay, "Francis Bacon and the Negative Instance" (Durham: The Southeastern Renaissance Conference, 1970), p. 4.

9. Louis J. Martz, *Poet of Exile: A Study of Milton's Poetry* (New Haven, 1980), p. 79. For a useful summary of earlier studies of Milton and Ovid, see Kathryn A. McEuen, ed., *Prolusions* in YP I, pp. 218–19.

10. The Latin text can be found in CM, which I have used throughout the essay (I, pp. 260–66); the translation is mine.

11. Bush, *Variorum*, p. 214.

12. From the General Confession for Matins and Evensong in the Book of Common Prayer.

13. For this reference, see Bush, *Variorum*, p. 214. In all the cross-references listed here and elsewhere throughout the essay, cf. Bush's annotations in *Variorum*. All Biblical references are from the King James Bible.

14. *Works*, ed. James Spedding, Robert Leslie Ellis, and Douglas Denon Heath (London, 1858–74), III, p. 224. Also, see III, pp. 395 and 268. Cf. Ellis's long introduction to the philosophical works in I, pp. 21–67, and then his long introduction to the *Novum Organum*, pp. 71–102, for a discussion of the *pars destruens* and Bacon's method in general.

15. For a summary of Bacon and Milton, see the discussions in YP I, pp. 22–28, and the notes to the *Prolusions*, ed. McEuen, YP I, p. 247.

16. See the entry under "ergo" in A. Ernout-A. Meillet, *Dictionnaire etymologique de la langue latine* (Paris, 1959) and Freund, *A Copious and Critical Latin-English Lexicon* (New York, 1865).

17. One early place is in *De Idea Platonica*, 34. For the place of Isis in this archetype, see Hans Conzelmann, "The Mother of Wisdom," in James M. Robinson, ed., *The Future of Our Religious Past*, tr. Charles E. Carlston and Robert P. Scharlemann (New York, 1971), pp. 230–43.

18. E. Reiss, "An Instance of Milton's Use of Time," *MLN*, 72 (1957), 410–12.

19. *Aeneid* II, 324; X, 467–69, and *Georgics* III, 284. See my discussion of this *topos* in "Spenser's Georgics," *ELR*, 10 (1980), 204–06.

20. *The Prophetic Moment: An Essay on Spenser* (Chicago, 1971), p. 91.

21. Irene Samuel, "Milton on Comedy and Satire," *HLQ*, 35 (1972), 107.

22. "Tardior," 39; "leviori," 53; "minorem," 58; "ditior," 63; "certo," 34; "haud solite" and "ut olim," 39; "semper," 43; "eadem," 44; "pariter," 45; "solito," 51; "aequali," 54; "utque solet," 55; "olim," 63; and a carefully modulated pattern of "nec" and "neque" (42, 51, 53, 58, 60, 63) that almost amounts to a use of anaphora and contrasts with the key use of "at" and "sed" in the passage.

23. Bush analyzes similarities between the two poems *Naturam* and *Fair Infant* and concludes that the resemblances point toward the traditional dating, pp. 211–12.

24. Eliot's comments are in "Milton" (1947), reprinted in *Milton Criticism: Selections from Four Centuries*, ed. James Thorpe (New York, 1969), pp. 320–21. Note his references to Milton and Joyce.

25. C. A. Patrides, *Milton and the Christian Tradition* (Oxford, 1966), pp. 276–78. The conflagration is also a major motif in Hakewill.

26. Barbara Lewalski, "Time and History in *Paradise Regained*," in *The Prison and the Pinnacle*, ed. Balachandra Rajan (Toronto, 1973), p. 77. J. A. Bryant, Jr., in "Milton's Views on Universal and Civil Decay," *SAMLA Studies in Milton* (Gainesville, 1953), p. 6, suggests that Milton's views on nature in *Naturam* remain the same throughout his career. If so, then his conception of history as found in his last great works radically dif-

fers from his conception of nature, although it is significant that neither ends in a progressive betterment within time or even the hope for one such as Bacon's in Aphorism 92 of the *Novum Organum*.

27. *"Lycidas: The Poet in a Landscape,"* in *The Lyric and Dramatic Milton*, ed. Joseph Summers (New York, 1965), p. 91.

28. *Works*, IV, p. 365. For the Sabbaoth motif (as one example among many), see p. 362. For a useful summary of Bacon's epistemology in general, see F. H. Anderson, *The Philosophy of Francis Bacon* (New York, 1971). The dual structure of *Naturam* was discussed by O. B. Hardison, *"On Time* and Its Scholastic Background," *TSLL*, 3 (1961–62), 121.

29. Quoted in John Herman Randall, Jr., *Aristotle* (New York, 1960), p. 170. The previous quotation is from Randall's text.

30. Ibid., p. 174. A crucial work to consider in trying to understand and reconstruct Milton's reading of Aristotle is Aristotle's *De generatione et corruptione*. For a good summary of the relationships between Milton's conception of nature and Patristic and Scholastic sources, see William G. Madsen, "The Idea of Nature in Milton's Poetry," in *Three Studies in the Renaissance: Sidney, Jonson, Milton* (New Haven, 1958), pp. 183–283, especially his discussion of the laws of reason and nature, pp. 198–203, and differences between Nature and God, pp. 226–27. In this connection, see the reference to Mother Nature in *Prolusion Five* (CM XII, p. 199) where Milton's arguments for the concept of total form anticipate Raphael's in *Paradise Lost* and are completely Thomist.

31. Martz, *Poet of Exile*, p. 242.

THE AUDIENCES OF *AD PATREM*

William J. Kennedy

S CHOLARLY AND critical attention to *Ad Patrem* has focused mostly on its dating. The possibilities extend from Milton's last year at Cambridge (1631–32) to the months preceding the publication of *Poems* (1645).[1] Some argue for a late date because they find in it a superior craftsmanship resembling that of *Mansus* (1639) and *Epitaphium Damonis* (1640). Others find in it a slender art suggesting an earlier period, with its slighting reference to "juvenilia carmina" (115) precluding any date later than *Comus* (1634).[2] On purely critical grounds most studies of *Ad Patrem* support the latter conclusion by judging it an immature poem, anticlimactic and structurally deficient.[3] What no study has yet explored is its wit, irony, and even jocularity.[4] The problem of assigning it a precise date may be irresolvable, but the question of determining its tone is not. *Ad Patrem* is a highly self-conscious poem addressed to a father capable of appreciating the poem's sense of humor. An examination of the speaker's modes of voice and address and of the four audiences whom he summons can illuminate the poem's structure, tone, and comic resolution.

Milton's early poetry displays a good deal of humor.[5] In the Latin elegies the speaker seems to enjoy his own self-deprecation. The wry self-portrait in *Elegy VI* (1629) presents him with an empty stomach comparing himself grandly to Homer, drinker of water, as he begins composing *On the Morning of Christ's Nativity*. The ironic Ovidian wit of *Elegy VII* (1628) colors his representation of amorous high spirits. In the *De Idea Platonica* (1630) he defends Plato by satirizing Aristotle's literalist questioning of his archetypes, and then he teases him for exiling the poets from his republic. Milton's early English poetry reveals a similar sensibility. In *At a Vacation Exercise* (1628), for example, the speaker deflates his invocation to "native Language" with a sportive parody of scholastic logic. Even in *Comus* there are light touches: a single line like "How charming is divine Philosophy!" (475) slyly undercuts much of the brothers' naive confidence and deluded optimism. By composing *Ad Patrem* in a humorous frame of mind, the speaker is paying elegant tribute to his father's learned ability to enjoy the poem's hidden jokes.

The implied genre of *Ad Patrem* suggests that it is a family poem.

There are, however, few poetic models for the speaker's tribute to his living father. Classical Latin poetry, rich in tributes to sons and daughters, brothers, wives, and lovers, seldom evokes the father. Renaissance humanist poetry like Pontano's *De Amore conjugali* (1488) honors the family by paying tribute to the poet's wife and children. Examples that celebrate the father usually do so when he is dying or already dead. Marcantonio Flaminio (1498–1550), for example, dedicated a short hendecasyllabic "Ad Ioannem Antonium Flaminium patrem morientem." In it the speaker praised his father for having been himself a poet and man of letters, "eruditus / satis et satis eloquens" (2–3).[6] The epithet certainly applies to John Milton's father, whose own intellectual achievements earned his son's admiration, but Flaminio's poem is too brief to have offered anything more than a model for general commendation.

Closer to Milton's design is an ode by Ariosto in six stanzas on the death of his father. In it the speaker offers conventional signs of filial grief, "Has vivens lacrimas" (1) ("living, I offer these tears"), and conventional protestations of filial respect, "cum semper fuerim obsequens" (8) ("since I have always been obedient").[7] At the same time he ironically recognizes that his father, "extra nebulas instabilis plagis" (11) ("beyond the mists of our giddy region"), may be too wrapt in heavenly delight to pay his tribute much mind. For Milton the point of ironizing the speaker's relationship with his father would not be lost.

At a later date Ariosto would inspire Milton with other "things unattempted yet in prose or rhyme." In *The Reason of Church-Government* Milton acknowledged that chief among them was Ariosto's turn from Latin to vernacular, "to be an interpreter and relater of the best and sagest things . . . in the mother dialect" (YP I, p. 668).[8] In his *Epitaphium Damonis* Milton announced his own turn from Latin to English. In *Ad Patrem*, however, he was still very much committed to an older classical ideal. The poem tests that ideal with its own sprinkling of Attic salt. It unfolds not in the "mother dialect" of English but in the father tongue of Latin, the language of learning, history, and tradition that the speaker shares with his father, a language that the father spared no expense for his son to learn, as the speaker confesses in lines 78–85 of *Ad Patrem*.

Latin poetry requires of its fit audience not only an education, but also patience, labor, and a sympathy for taking "learned pains." Milton's father evidently had these qualities. As one would expect, he is the primary audience of this poem. The speaker addresses him directly in the vocative, from "pater optime" (6) to "chare pater" (111), and indirectly in the second person from "tibi" (6) to "te" (89). His expression of love and gratitude comes to focus on two issues: his sameness with his father and his difference from his father. Both father and son are dedicated to the muses, but whereas the former, an accomplished musician, pursues his art with an inferior regard for poetry, the latter, an accomplished poet, pursues his with uncertainty about his father's approval. In emphasizing these differences Milton is not so much ironizing the genre of *Ad Patrem* as he is opening it to other possibilities. He develops his poem as an example of mixed genre that incorporates tribute, autobiography, a defence of poetry, some satire directed against the rude masses, and a bit of pin-pricking at the bubble of his seriousness.[9]

The speaker resolves his differences from his father three-quarters through the poem when he addresses a second audience, "I nunc, confer opes quisquis malesanus avitas / Austriaci gazas, Perüanaque regna praeoptas" (93–94) ("Go now, gather riches, you unhealthy individual who prefers the ancestral treasures of Austria and the realms of Peru"). Both he and his father disdain worldly ambition. This shared aversion proclaims their similarity to each other rather than their estrangement from each other. It also proclaims the son's self-assurance.

Eleven lines later the speaker addresses still a tertiary audience. Grouped together as a "faedissima turba" (108), they personify his own demons, the spiritual anxieties that gnaw on him. They include sleepless worries, "vigiles curae" (105); complaints, "querelae" (105); envy, "Invidia" (106); and Calumny, "Calumnia" (107). At the poem's end he can dismiss them summarily because he has now resolved his doubts about his own intellectual abilities and about his dedication to poetry. He has also resolved the sense of strain separating him from his father. He therefore returns to his original audience, his "chare pater" (111), with renewed purposiveness as he draws toward the poem's conclusion.

In the final six lines he summons a fourth audience, his own literary productions, his "juvenilia carmina, lusus" (115), as testimonies of devotion to this father, and he urges them to preserve the latter's praise and good name as an example to a distant age. The request is a bit waggish. The speaker is calling upon one of his own creations, the poem itself, to be an enactment of the very talent that his father had earlier denigrated. Nowhere in the poem has the speaker indicated the nature of his father's objections to his poetic pursuits, but he has suggested that his father never brought any conventional Platonic arguments to bear against poetry itself: "Non odisse reor" (68) ("I don't think you have ever hated" [the muses]). The speaker's address to poetry becomes a hedge against his father's ever using those arguments. It reasserts this poem's encomiastic mode and exemplary moral purpose, "parentis / Nomen, ad exemplum, sero servabitis aevo" (120) ("you will preserve my parent's name as an example for a distant age"). The implied joke is that Plato himself approved of laudatory verse even after banning other types of poetry: "we can admit no poetry into our city save only hymns to the gods and the praises of good men."[10] The father himself has composed divine hymns; the son has composed this encomium. Since Plato has endorsed both activities, how could either the father or the son ever doubt their value?

The speaker's address to poetry also proclaims his dedication to the art. The tone is confident. Autobiographically it contrasts sharply with the sense of crisis that Milton expressed in his letter "To a friend" written in 1633. There, in response to the friend's charge that he has "given up [him] selfe to dreame away [his] Yeares in the armes of studious retirement," he admits that "I am something suspicio[us] of my selfe, & doe take notice of a certaine belatednesse in me" (YP I, pp. 319–21). Enclosed with that letter is *Sonnet VII*, "How soon hath time," which laments the speaker's having passed his "three and twentieth yeer," the age of ordination to the diaconate before ordination to the priesthood the following year.[11] With his father's approval, young John Milton eventually rejected a priestly career for a poetic one, but at the time of *Ad Patrem* he had yet no poetic achievement to lend credibility to his choice. He is sure enough of himself and his talent, however, to denigrate the present work as part of his "juvenilia" and to imply that better poetry will follow. *Ad Patrem*'s final address to poetry therefore affirms not only the speaker's validation of his art in his father's eyes, but also his own growing commitment to the craft.

The speaker has enlisted aid in his project. In the poem's opening lines he would desire ("cupiam") the Pierian founts to rush ("torquere") through his breast and allow their whole ("totum") stream to pass through his lips (1–2). He hopes that his muse might rise ("surgat") to the task forgetful of his earlier weak performances, his "tenues . . . sonos" (4–5). He knows that she is already thinking about his poor work ("exiguum meditatur opus," 7). Finally he summons her in a kind of indirect address by using the first person plural verb to imply her collaboration with him: "nec novimus ipsi / Aptiùs à nobis" (7–8) ("we know of no more fitting present from us"). The effect is tongue-in-cheek. It represents a high epic invocation here lowered to the order of an intimate family poem. One may note that none of Milton's poems before *Lycidas* — not even *In Quintum Novembris* or *Mansus* — begins with such an exalted call to the muse. *De Idea Platonica* does begin with an invocation, but it is clearly satiric and parodic. Here in a self-mocking way the speaker alleges that neither he nor his muse can repay his father's gifts, "donis / Respondere tuis" with mere words, "vacuis . . . verbis" (8–11).

Anaphorical repetitions of "donis" at the ends of lines 8 and 10, and of "Respondere tuis" at the beginnings of lines 9 and 10, establish the problem. Their almost comical awkwardness calls attention to the inadequacies of language. Words are evanescent and the speaker expresses doubts about his ability to master them. The speaker does not lose his faith, however. Even the metrics — two dactyls and a spondee in line 11, followed by two dactyls and a spondee, dividing the line into echoing halves — indicate his trust: "Esse queat, vacuis quae redditur / arida verbis" (11) ("still less could that poor [thanks] that is paid with empty words be equal" [to your gifts]). The speaker seems in fact to be winking at the convoluted syntax and awkward repetitions. He knows he can compose better verse.

The next line beginning with "Sed tamen" (12) confirms his ability. Again the speaker aligns himself with his muse in declaring their mutual wealth ("nostros census") on this very page that displays it ("ostendit pagina"). He iterates his claim in the following line: whatever wealth he shares with his muse ("quod habemus opem"), they both have numbered on this sheet ("chartâ numeravimus"). The last verb slyly underscores the speaker's semantic command by allowing for a play on its meaning. It implies not only an amount of wealth but also the setting it to number in poetic meter. With the muse's aid, and with a measure of wit and good humor, the speaker will embark on a defence of his art.

In addressing his father as the primary audience for the defence, the speaker urges him not to despise divine song ("divinum carmen," 17). The noun "carmen," which echoes from line 6 and forecasts ten other appearances that thread through the poem like a leitmotif, introduces another play on words. The phrase not only implies the divine origin of song but it also evokes the father's dedication to sacred music. Born about 1563 near Oxford, the elder John Milton moved to London at the age of twenty when his father, a convert to Roman Catholicism, disinherited him for his ties with the Anglican church. Though he enjoyed a good career as a scrivener with a profitable income and the benefits of real estate, he also pursued his talent as an accomplished musician.[12] He regularly associated with the best musicians of the day — William Byrd, John Mundy, Orlando Gibbons, and John Bull, who had developed English polyphonic vocal composition to a pitch of perfection between 1590 and 1620. Loyal to his own religious convictions, John Milton the elder applied their techniques to church music, and examples of his work that survive in William Leighton's *The Teares, or Lamentations of a Sorrowful Soul* (1613), Thomas Myriell's *Tristae Remedium* (1616), and Thomas Ravenscroft's *Whole Book of Psalms* (1621) indicate talent of a very high order.

John Milton junior plays on this aspect of his father's musical skill. Imputing sacred qualities to song, he cites those who hold music in reverence: the gods ("superi"), priestesses of Apollo ("Phoebades"), Sibyls ("Sibyllae"), and the sacrificing priest ("sacrificus") (21–26). The first citation significantly forecasts the motif of Orpheus that the speaker will develop in lines 52–55. Here the song is able to stir the trembling abyss of Tartarus ("tremebundaque Tartara carmen / Ima ciere valet," 21–22), lines whose extended dactyls recall phrases from Virgil's account of Orpheus in his *Georgics* IV, 469–82. The speaker's defence of song by referring his audience to the musician-poet is itself clever. When he combined music with poetry, voice with verse, Orpheus treated as a whole what the Miltons, *pere et fils*, audience and speaker, separated into parts. The other citations forecast later motifs too. The reference to Apollo evokes the motif of Phaethon which will recur implicitly in lines 35–40 and 61–76, and explicitly in lines 97–100, while the gilding of the sacrificial bulls' horns contrasts with the golden crowns of the heavenly saints which will be mentioned just a few lines later (32).

That representation of heavenly glory unfolds in a context that allows the speaker to use the first person plural "Nos" (30) to refer not to himself and the muses but to himself and his father. With this pronoun he designates their spiritual union in heaven after each has spent his lifetime on earth. The most marked feature of the ensuing lines is their echo of Christian Scripture. "Ibimus auratis per caeli templa coronis" (32), ("we will go through the broad spaces of heaven wearing golden crowns"), refers to Revelation iv, 4, where saints wear golden crowns: "et in capitibus eorum coronae aureae." Milton's lines are cast in the future tense — "cum repetemus Olympum" (30) ("when we will seek Olympus"). The leap into the future is significant, as though a reconciliation between father and son were possible only then. The predominance of light and fluent dactyls in these lines, however, preserves the speaker's high spirits and conveys them to his audience.

"Nunc" (36) dispels the speaker's dream of anticipated harmony. Retaining the light dactylic meter, he asserts that at this very moment Apollo is encircling the heavens: "Spiritus et rapidos qui circinat igneus orbes" (35) ("The fiery spirit who encircles our rapid spheres"). In the lines that follow the speaker reminds his audience that Apollo is more than the sun god. He is also the patron of the muses, a poet and musician who sings an immortal melody and ineffable song, "Immortale melos, et inenarrabile carmen" (37). His talents combine those of the speaker and his father. In addition, Apollo himself is a father. His son was Phaethon, and the former's ride through the skies in lines 38–40 recalls the path that the latter could not follow in Ovid's *Metamorphoses* II, 173ff.

With this motif the speaker begins to prepare the ground for a learned joke. As Ovid had recounted the myth, Phaethon was a heedless youth whose wishes Apollo honored at his own peril. Both Apollo and Phaethon, father and son, were foolish in different ways. The former was an "invito parenti" (II, 152) ("an unwilling parent"), while the latter was "infelix Phaethon" (II, 179) ("unhappy Phaethon").[13] Ovid, with his own insinuating doubts and qualifications, conditional clauses and interjections — "credunt" (II, 235) ("so they believe"), "fama est" (II, 268) ("so they say"), "si modo credimus" (II, 330) ("if we can believe it") — expected his audience to respond with bemused detachment.

The speaker of *Ad Patrem* seems sure that his own audience can appreciate his ironic reference to Ovid. If it honors his father's ability to recognize the allusion, it also honors his sense of humor in accepting its witty implications. If the joke redounds on the parent, it redounds to an even greater degree on the son. The example of Phaethon is the least likely one to prove his point. The popular sixteenth-century commentary on Ovid by Georgius Sabinus (1555) stressed the lesson for sons of heeding their parents' advice, and for parents of rescinding their own hasty promises for the sake of prudence: "duo sunt in hac fabula loci morales, obseruatione digni, alter admonet pueros, ne parentum iussa & praecepta contemnant, alter docet, non esse seruanda illa promissa quae non sunt his ipsis vtilia quibus promittuntur" ("there are two lessons worthy of observation in this tale; one teaches sons not to despise their parents' advice; the other teaches that promises not useful to the one to whom they are promised should not be kept").[14] Both speaker and audience have something to learn from this cautionary tale.

The speaker will refer to the Phaethon motif in the ensuing lines and will evoke it concretely at the end of the poem (lines 97–100). Now, however, he shifts his own discourse from classical myth to classical history. In lines heavy with spondees he evokes poetry's power and prestige in ancient courts: "Carmina regales epulas ornare solebant, / Cum nondum luxus, vastaeque immensa vorago / Nota gulae" (41–43) ("Songs used to adorn royal feasts when luxuriance and the bottomless pit of unsatiable gluttony were not yet known"). Here his concrete use of the past tense furnishes an argument against his father's abstract assertion of poetry's inferiority to music. The speaker quips that at other times and in other places poetry enjoyed the highest reputation. Indeed he tilts the argument in his own favor by representing poetic activity at the very peak of its grandeur. The ancient poet he cites is an epic one who "Heroumque actus, imitandaque gesta canebat" (46) ("sang of the acts of heroes and their exemplary deeds"). Against this high standard, music without words is an inferior art.

Here the speaker inverts his father's argument. Now bantering with him in sprightly dactylic rhythms, he risks insulting his audience's musical skill when he characterizes it as the inane modulation of voice, "vocis modulamen inane," empty of words, meaning, and eloquent numbers, "Verborum sensusque vacans, numerique loquacis," fit for rustic singers but not for Orpheus, "Silvestres decet iste choros, non Orphea cantus" (50–52). The citation of Orpheus, underscoring the brief earlier reference in lines 21–22, brings the argument to its climax, since the Orphic conception of poetry accords it the highest possible merit. By it Orpheus held rivers in check, gave ears to trees, and moved dead shades to tears (53–55). He accomplished all these effects not with the sound of his lyre but with the language of his verse: "Carmine, non citharâ" (54) ("by song, not by lyre").

The speaker next implores his father in a mock-serious tone heavy with thumping spondees: "Nec tu perge precor sacras contemnere Musas" (56) ("Do not proceed, I pray, to disparage the sacred muses"). This strategy evokes the comic implications of *De Idea Platonica*, in which the speaker chided Plato for exiling the poets since he was one himself. Here the strategy is to identify the father as a recipient of those very muses' beneficence. By their gifts he arranged sounds into apt measures and he learned how to vary his own voice, so that "Arionii meritò sis nominis haeres" (60) ("deservedly you would be heir to the name of Arion"). More importantly the speaker asserts a new claim: his father begot a son who now declares himself to be a genuine poet. He presents this assertion as gingerly as possible, first with a rhetorical question designed to ingratiate his audience, "quid mirum," and then with a proposition in two dependent conditional clauses, "si . . . Contigerit, . . . si . . . sequamur" (61–63). The complex syntax establishes the speaker's satisfaction with his fate, and the semantics of "contigerit" ("it will happily have befallen") confirms it. The verb usually implies good luck as well as irrevocability: he had been born that way and nothing will change it.

The second *si* clause asserts the dearness of his relationship with the father, but its momentous spondees cast a comic shadow of Phaethon over the speaker's presentation of himself: "charo si tam propè sanguine juncti / Cognatas artes, studiumque affine sequamur" (62–63) ("if so closely joined by a dear relationship we pursue cognate arts and a neighboring discipline"). Like Phaethon the speaker is appealing to his father for paternal beneficence. The affirmative statement that follows links the speaker with his audience under the patronage of Apollo. Dividing the line into parallel dactylic measures, the speaker says that the god wished to apportion himself between son and father by assigning poetry to the one and music to the other: "Altera dona mihi, dedit altera dona parenti" (65) ("he gave some gifts to me, other gifts to my father"). The result, rendered in dactyls that repeat the preceding line's metrics, is that the speaker and audience share the god between them. "Diuiduumque Deum genitorque puerque tenemus" (66) ("and father and son we possess the god divided between us").

A long period of nine dactylic lines reinforces this assertion with a particular application of the Phaethon figure to the speaker. It dèvelops a contrast between what the father did not command the son to do ("neque jubebas," 68) on the one hand, and on the other ("Sed magis," 73) what he does allow him to do. The litotes represents the father's willing suspension of authority over his son's career. Like Phaethon, the speaker enjoys this freedom. He praises his father for never having commanded him in the past ("jubebas") to follow the broad road to money, fame, and success. Shifting to the present tense, he thanks his father for not hastening him now ("rapis") into the legal or political profession, and for not condemning him ("damnas") to the noisy clamor of public life (71–72). Instead his father allows him access to a higher goal. He permits ("sinis") his son to walk beside Apollo as a blessed companion ("comitem beatum") far from the bustling crowd (74–76). The father has in effect apprenticed his Phaethon-like son to Apollo. Withdrawn in retirement, "secessibus altis / Abductum" (74–75), the son is already engaged in his own pursuit of poetry.

At this point the speaker assumes full responsibility for his argument when he shifts to the singular *mihi*: "Cùm mihi Romuleae patuit facundia linguae" (79) ("when fluency in the language of Romulus's descendants lay open to me"). Enumerating the components of his own intellectual wealth — his linguistic skills in Latin, Greek, French, Italian, and Hebrew and his learned competence in whatever arts and sciences he might wish to investigate — he acknowledges his father's detached contribution. Other sons have acquired wealth from their fathers, or else they are self-made men. This son is different. His wealth has come from his own application to study, but his father has made this application possible in the first place by dispensing of his own material wealth. The speaker acknowledges it with an emphatic vocative, "tuo pater optime sumptu" (78) ("at your own expense, dear father"). Even here, however, he does not surrender his humorous perspective. He caps his acknowledgment of

his father's generosity with a ludicrous image of Scientia personified as
a naked woman advancing toward him through parted clouds, bending
her face to be kissed: "Dimotáque venit spectanda scientia nube, / Nuda-
que conspicuos inclinat ad oscula vultus" (90–91) ("Knowledge comes to
be seen, the clouds parted, and naked bends down her striking face to
be kissed"). The speaker, however, reserves judgment on whether to accept or reject her: "Ni fugisse velim, ni sit libâsse molestum" (92) ("unless
I want to escape, unless it's annoying to kiss her"). As an indifferent suitor
to Lady Knowledge, he cuts an amusing figure.

The speaker's droll vision anticipates his introduction of a new audience. He now addresses one who pursues worldly riches for their own
sake, "quisquis malesanus avitas / Austriaci gazas, Perüanaque regna
praeoptas" (93–94) ("you unhealthy individual who prefers the treasures
of Austria and the realms of Peru"). The new vocative suggests satire and
even invective as it denigrates the motives of others who seek financial
profit. The mocking tone, however, remains low-key. Rhetorically the
speaker is using this new audience as a foil to reassert and confirm his
close relationship with his father. The key word is "malesanus" as it applies to the seeker of wealth. The father himself had compiled enough
money to educate his own son "suo sumptu." The difference between the
two audiences is that the father employed his income wisely while the
"malesanus" individual doesn't. The joke is on the worldly spendthrift.

A direct comparison follows. It explicitly evokes the motif of Phaethon, and it even includes a fleeting echo from Ovid's account of that
motif in the *Metamorphoses:*

> Non potiora dedit, quamvis et tuta fuissent,
> Publica qui juveni commisit lumina nato
> Atque Hyperionios currus, et fraena diei,
> Et circum undantem radiatâ luce tiaram.   (97–100)

[He gave no better gifts, even if they had been safe,
who entrusted public daylight to his young son,
and Hyperion's chariot and the reins of daylight,
and the tiara undulating all around with radiant light.]

The verbal echo from Ovid is "Publica," the adjective here modifying
"lumina" (98) and in the *Metamorphoses* II, 35 modifying "lux" in Phaethon's speech to his father: "O lux immensi publica mundi / . . . Pignora
da" (*Met.* II, 35–38) ("O public light of the wide world, give me assurances"). Summoning the entire Ovidian context, the reference once more
casts the speaker into Phaethon's role. For all his resourcefulness, he still
needs assurances from his father. The latter is already a public figure while

the son is only beginning his public career as a poet. The single word echoing from Ovid underscores the difference between mature conviction and youthful impetuosity.

Ironically the speaker's comparison of himself to Phaethon succeeds in rendering his father's gift more human and humane. By evoking it the speaker once again fashions a joke at his own expense. He acknowledges his father's generosity in allowing him to pursue his goals, but he also suggests the pitfalls of that generosity. More importantly he allows the comparison to become a foil to his own claim for filial success. That claim has been so outrageously high that only a shaft of good-natured wit can pierce its pretension. By referring to the unwary Phaethon the speaker shows that he can laugh at his own foibles. He then extends this laughter into the following lines when he draws the inflated conclusion ("Ergo ego") that he is part of a learned company, "doctae pars . . . catervae" (101) sitting among ivy and laurel (the spondaic line will recur with similarly self-conscious humor in *Mansus*, line 6: "Victrices hederas inter, laurosque sedebo").

With this comic resolution the speaker can now turn to yet a third audience, his *turba* of anxieties — sleepless worries, complaints, envy, and calumny (105–07). He dismisses them because they no longer trouble him: "In me triste nihil faedissima turba potestis / Nec vestri sum juris ego" (108–09) ("you have no harsh power over me, you vile mob, nor am I under your authority"). The dismissal illuminates the speaker's own pattern of growth. It has of course entailed trouble and conflict. Following Plato and Aristotle, Milton would later emphasize the point in *The Reason of Church-Government*: "if we look but on the nature of elementall and mixt things, we know they cannot suffer any change of one kind, or quality into another without the struggl of contrarieties" (YP I, p. 795). This "struggl of contrarieties" unfolds as one passes from the smaller to the larger, from what one is to what one is yet to become. "Everything we can know is viewed as transition from something into its opposite." The attainment of one's goal implies the abatement of conflict, but it is impossible to know whether or not one has really attained one's goal. Uncertainty remains unless one can banish one's cares and rest contented with one's achievements. The speaker's dismissal of his anxieties at the poem's end therefore signals at least a victory over himself, if not yet an entire victory in convincing his father about the value of his pursuing poetry.

That value the speaker will now assert after addressing his father as the poem's penultimate audience: "At tibi, chare pater" (111). Here the mode of address is hortatory and petitioning. The speaker is urging

his father to accept these memorial verses as a fitting tribute: "Sit memo-
râsse satis" (113) ("may it be enough for you that I have remembered").
Poetry's achievement is to withstand the flux of time. If the speaker still
entertains any doubts about his relationship with his father, he now prepares to resolve them by offering this poem as a lasting witness to his
father's memory. It will sublimate all the perceived differences between
father and son.

At the root of those differences have been competing claims about
the nature of art in general and poetry in particular. The speaker's final
address is to the poem itself as an emblem of the talent that has divided
him from his father, and that will now mend the quarrel between them:
"Et vos, O nostri, juvenilia carmina, lusus" (115) ("and you, O our amusements, songs of our youth"). By objectifying his own poetry both as "juvenilia carmina" and "lusus" on the one hand and as a potential guaran-
tor of his father's immortality and educator of posterity on the other, the
speaker reproves all charges against it. The poem's final lines dramati-
cally achieve the balance: "Forsitan has laudes, decantatumque parentis /
Nomen, ad exemplum, sero servabitis aevo" (119–20) ('perhaps you will
preserve these praises and the name of my father sung repeatedly as an
example to a distant age"). The period begins in doubt — "Forsitan" is an
emphatic dactyl in a predominantly spondaic line — but ends with a triumphant prolepsis: "sero servabitis aevo." Poetry, and especially a poem
like this one, has the unique capacity both to honor persons and to preserve that honor.

Some modern scholars assume that this envoy is a late addition to
the text composed just prior to its publication in *Poems* of 1645.[15] The
assumption may only complicate the question of the poem's dating, but
the grounds on which it rests are revealing. They suggest that an older
Milton in 1645 judged his youthful effort successful in withstanding the
flux of time and worthy of being included in his ambitious volume of
collected verse. The confirmed poet, reader, editor, and evaluator of
his earlier poetry, now turns his entire production into proof, witness,
testator — of still greater poetry yet to emerge.

This final play of perspectives, then, confers one last touch of wit
upon a poem that has abounded in wit and tonic good humor. With those
qualities the speaker succeeds in answering his own doubts about the value
of his art and his choice of a profession. At the same time he uses those
qualities to honor his father as the primary audience of his poem. To say
that the speaker has treated these concerns with humor and moderation
throughout the poem should not imply that he has at any point taken
them lightly. They have entailed not so much an Oedipal conflict be-

tween father and son as an admission of their mutually independent private selfhoods. In *De Doctrina Christiana* Milton would take pains to distinguish the Son of God from God the Father, even to the point of refuting the traditional interpretation of the theological doctrine of the Trinity. There he would argue that in no sense is the Son coessential or even co-equal with the Father. Each has his own substantial nature fully separable and independent from the other. In *Ad Patrem* the speaker enacts his recognition of separability and independence from his own father. Still, readers who refer to the poem for biographical information about Milton's vocational crisis and his father's approval or disapproval will find no substantial statement about either. Instead they will find dramatized an extremely close relationship between son and father founded on a mutual exchange of wit, humor, playfulness, banter, and jocundity.

The speaker achieves a serene resolution by addressing various audiences. He comes to see his differences from his father in terms of his differences from other audiences. In their light, disagreements with his father seem less severe. He shares with his father a view of art in general, if not poetry in particular, and a deep investment in their cultural tradition. One sign of this sharing is the speaker's ability to make learned jokes and his father's ability to understand them. With his father as audience, the speaker embarks upon a witty defence of his art. With others as audience, the speaker declares his estrangement from their values. He dismisses the "malesanus" seeker of wealth with a contemptuous "I nunc, confer opes." He dismisses the "turba" of personified anxieties with an inner conviction earned by self-knowledge. And finally addressing his own poetry as audience, he expresses his confidence both in its enduring powers and in his abilities to write better poetry yet to come. The audiences of *Ad Patrem* confirm the speaker's development as a person and as a poet. To their rhetorical ordering the poem owes its delightful vitality.

Cornell University

NOTES

1. For a survey of all the important conjectures see Bush, *Variorum*, pp. 232–40. Bush resolves the controversy in favor of the earliest date. He generally follows A. S. P. Woodhouse, "Notes on Milton's Early Development," *University of Toronto Quarterly*, 13 (1943–44), 66–101, esp. pp. 88–93, reprinted in *The Heavenly Muse*, ed. Hugh Mac-Callem (Toronto, 1972), pp. 47–49. For dating it at the time of *Comus* (1634), see William Riley Parker, "A Note on the Chronology of Milton's Latin Poems," in *A Tribute to*

George Coffin Taylor, ed. Arnold Williams (Chapel Hill, 1952), pp. 125–28. For dating it in 1638 see John Shawcross, "The Date of *Ad Patrem*," *Notes and Queries*, 204 (1959), 358–59.

2. All poetry quotations are from CM. For a new text based on the 1673 edition, with an excellent translation, see Fred J. Nichols, *An Anthology of Neo-Latin Poetry* (New Haven, 1979). Translations throughout this essay are my own.

3. The fullest study that makes these charges is Ralph Condee, *Structure in Milton's Poetry* (University Park, Pa., 1974), pp. 64–70. E. M. W. Tillyard judges it "the least good" of Milton's three major Latin poems, and "uneven in quality" in *Milton* (London, 1930), pp. 77–79, but Leicester Bradner ranks it with *Mansus* as Milton's best Latin poem in *Musae Anglicanae* (London, 1940), p. 116. James Holly Hanford thinks it is "characteristic" of the zeal animating Milton's Latin poetry in "The Youth of Milton," now in *John Milton: Poet and Humanist* (Cleveland, 1966), p. 42. Ernest Sirluck evaluates it in the context of Milton's vocational crisis in "Milton's Idle Right Hand," *Journal of English and Germanic Philology*, 60 (1961), 749–85.

4. Marguerite Little alludes to its "gentle irony" and "banter" in "Milton's *Ad Patrem* and the Younger Gill's *In Natelem Mei Parentis*," *Journal of English and Germanic Philology*, 49 (1950), 345–51. William Riley Parker sees it as "a smiling urbane attempt to persuade an old man to change his mind" in *Milton: A Biography*, 2 vols. (Oxford, 1968), I, p. 125. Little makes her assertion by analogy to Gill's poem; Parker makes his in the context of Milton's development. I make mine on the rhetorical principles articulated in my *Rhetorical Norms in Renaissance Literature* (New Haven, 1978).

5. For a persuasive recognition of that humor see Louis L. Martz, *Poet of Exile* (New Haven, 1980), pp. 31–59.

6. Quotations from *Renaissance Latin Verse: An Anthology*, ed. Alessandro Perosa and John Sparrow (Chapel Hill, 1979), p. 293. For the context of Neolatin poetry see my *Jacopo Sannazaro and the Uses of Pastoral* (Hanover, N.H., 1983).

7. Perosa and Sparrow, *Renaissance Latin*, p. 181.

8. All quotations from Milton's letters and prose in this essay are from YP.

9. For this splendid suggestion and a first-rate reading of *Ad Patrem* in its context, see Mary Ann Radzinowicz, *Towards Samson Agonistes* (Princeton, 1979), pp. 190–93.

10. Republic, 607A, tr. Paul Shorey, in *The Collected Dialogues of Plato*, ed. Edith Hamilton and Huntington Cairns (New York, 1961). Irene Samuel discusses the poem in its Platonic context in her definitive *Plato and Milton* (Ithaca. N.Y., 1947), pp. 46–49.

11. For a superb reading of the poem in this context see Edward Tayler, *Milton's Poetry: Its Development in Time* (Pittsburgh, 1979), pp. 126–33.

12. The fullest treatment is Ernest Brennecke, *John Milton the Elder and His Music* (New York, 1938). For the importance of music in Milton's early poetry see Jon Lawry, *The Shadow of Heaven* (Ithaca, N.Y., 1968), pp. 21–63. For music in Renaissance literature see James Hutton, "Some English Poems in Praise of Music," in *Essays on Renaissance Poetry* (Ithaca, N.Y., 1980), pp. 17–73.

13. Quotations from *Metamorphoses*, ed. Frank Justus Miller, Loeb Classical Library, 2 vols. (New York, 1916).

14. Georgius Sabinus, *Metamorphoses seu fabulae poeticae*, reprint of 1589 ed. published J. Wechel, Frankfurt (New York, 1976), p. 58.

15. See Walter MacKellar, *The Latin Poems of John Milton* (New Haven, 1930), p. 316.

MILTON'S ROMAN CONNECTION: GIOVANNI SALZILLI

James A. Freeman

M ILTON SCHOLARS have offered a simple (and probably true) answer to the question of why he praised Italian academies so highly. Although the intellectual accomplishments of these societies varied widely, they offered a hospitable social matrix which encouraged artists and thinkers. Milton cherished the New Testament idea of *koinonia*, of genuine community, and found it at a crucial time for his career in Florentine, Roman, and Neapolitan academies. I would like to explore the extrasocial activities of Italian *accademie* in the seventeenth century's first forty years to show how certain common practices influenced Milton. After detailing the typical academic conduct which may have guided his later work, I will turn to one specific case of indebtedness, the poetry of a Roman academic named Giovanni Salzilli.

I

By October of 1638 Rome had received pilgrims for so many centuries that it took little note when John Milton arrived. He had been preceded by Virgil, Ovid, Juvenal, Martial, Dante, Cellini, Du Bellay — an army of sensitive artists who reacted strongly to the city. Petrarch came to be crowned and Tasso came to die. Although we know Milton spent about four months there during two separate visits,[1] we also sense that he refused to be overwhelmed by the Eternal City. Indeed, he seems to have used the alchemy of his Protestant imagination to convert golden sights into lead bullets for battle against popery. The majesty of St. Peter's probably reappears in *Paradise Lost*, transmuted and debased, when Milton describes Pandaemonium, Satan's ornate war-temple. The organ concerts which were a remarkable part of Rome's carnival pageantry may prompt the musical simile he chooses to explain Pandaemonium's magical growth.[2] The Barbarini bee emblem, found on so many noble buildings, perhaps explains why Satan's fallen rebels milling outside Pandaemonium are compared to bees.[3] "Great and glorious *Rome*, Queen of the Earth," is what the Tempter offers to Jesus in *Paradise Regained*, but God's Son remains "unmov'd,"[4] just as, apparently, Milton did. While

87

in Geneva, traveling home, he glanced back over the Alps to his Italian experience and boasted in Camillo Cerdogni's scrapbook, "As I speed across the sea, I change only my location, not my mind."[5]

Despite these protestations, I suggest that Rome made more of a positive impression on Milton than he cared to admit. We may speculate how certain benign references in his later work were the result of what he saw. The mention of Psyche in *Areopagitica* or the allusion to Tobias in *Paradise Lost* (IV, 167ff.) gain psychohistorical importance if we remind ourselves of the pictures Romans were viewing during his visits.[6] One specific enterprise, however, proves that Milton could respond openly and warmly to riches in the city he otherwise calls the "chief Kennel" of *"Antichrist."*[7] His poem to Giovanni Salzilli wishes good health to a member of Rome's distinguished academy of the Fantastici and demonstrates that Milton already had incorporated into his own art certain habits common to academies.

Milton never tired of recommending to his countrymen that they establish academies like the Fantastici.[8] Learned gentlemen banded together in almost every Italian town, patterning themselves after Cosimo de' Medici's Platonic Academy in fifteenth-century Florence. Happily for Milton, academies reached their greatest popularity during the 1630s. Rome alone supported fifty-six *accademie.* In other cities on Milton's route, no poet, scientist, philosopher, or theologian lacked companions. Bologna is said to have nourished seventy academies, Venice forty-three, Naples twenty-nine, and Florence twenty—one of which, the Svogliati, Milton visited at least four times. Groups met to discuss a wide range of topics, to encourage projects such as a dictionary, and to disseminate their findings by open meetings and by publication. Their industrious camaraderie helped to conceal the fading of true genius during the seventeenth century. Bruno had disappeared in 1600, Guarini died in 1612, followed by Marino in 1625, Tassoni in 1635, and Chiabrera in 1637. As Milton turned north in 1639, Campanella died and Galileo was silent. For historians with hindsight, *seicentismo* had begun, with its Alexandrine commentaries on, or voluminous recapitulations of, ideas generated by men from previous centuries.

Certainly some academic behavior bordered then (as now) on the ridiculous. Names for groups were often cryptic or (literally) fantastic. Johan Jarkius lists other clubs in Rome like the Scatenati ("Wild Ones"), Incitati ("Stirred Ups"), and Intrecciati ("Tangled Ups").[9] Members too sometimes had to rechristen themselves with anagrams of their own names. In Florence, Milton's versatile friend Agostino Coltellini was known to his fellow Apatisti ("No-feelings") as Ostilio Contalgeni.[10] If baroque name-giving is a minor aberration, then the exhaustive scholarship that blanketed some topics is more questionable. Gianbattista Masullo of Naples's Oziosi ("Dawdlers") sounds like a parody of Teutonic, not Mediterranean, sensibility when he spends over two hundred pages to review different kinds of attraction. Why, he asks with *wissenschaftlich* eagerness, are moths attracted to light, remoras to ships, iron to magnets, and humors to emotion? For each of these "academic exercises" he dutifully cites opinions of 105 authorities ranging from Plato to Pico and Scaliger.[11] Even Milton's energetic friend Jacobo Gaddi, founder of several Florentine academies, laboriously tries to catalogue every top-rank writer of "philosophy, poetry, history, oratory and criticism."[12] A third propensity of academics subsidized absurd humor and encyclopedism. They freely gave and received elaborate compliments which, to northern ears, might have seemed remote from the impartial examination of ideas.

"But," as Christopher Hill notes, "Italian intellectuals still had much to offer — the new astronomy of Galileo, the neo-Hermeticism of Bruno and Campanella, the mortalism of Padua, the libertinism of Vanini . . . and of Malatesti."[13] These concerns percolate to the surface of many Miltonic works. Since twentieth-century readers no longer must save the appearance of his puritan reserve, we can admit that facetiousness, comprehensiveness, and adulation appealed to him. His own volcanic, even bawdy humor, his summas of education, grammar, theology, rhetoric, and history, and his encomia of people like Leonora Baroni (whom he associates with God, the world-mind, and a cure for madness) demonstrate how his soul was *naturaliter academica*. The personal satisfaction he experienced when men praised him should not be discounted, of course. Dati and Francini in Florence, Manso in Naples, Selvaggi and Salzilli in Rome all facilitated his ambition. Not since Cambridge and Ludlow had such a competent, appreciative audience surrounded him. At thirty, with little solid reputation at home, Milton no doubt glowed when some verse he recited was judged to be "extremely learned."[14]

While acknowledging Milton's emotional debt to academies, we can also point to intellectual tendencies which they reinforce. Lecture-and-discussion was the normal format of meetings; dialogue is Milton's characteristic mode of expression. In the two years before Milton arrived in Florence, Gaddi published three books of imaginary conversations.[15] All are virtuoso volumes and illustrate current techniques. The first book of *Adlocutiones* (1636) offers various addresses, some precious (every word of his "To Posterity" begins with the letter *P*), others vaguely familiar to readers of *Paradise Lost* (the exhortation to Florentine soldiers sounds much like that of Satan to his fallen troops in Hell). Gaddi's second book,

Elogia Historica (1637), allows listeners to eavesdrop on Latin chats with Tibullus, King Canute, Zoroaster, Alciati, Cardinal Bembo, Louis XIII of France, and Jerome Frascatoro, inventor of the ill-starred character Syphillis. Gaddi's third anthology of declamations appeared in 1638, perhaps in time for Milton's first visit. *Eliographus* also speaks out to kings, cardinals, critics, and notables like Amerigo Vespucci ("more fortunate than Columbus or Caesar"). The unifying concern for appropriate discourse justifies Milton's preoccupation in works like the *Prolusions, Lycidas,* and *Comus,* each of which, I think, would have pleased Italian ears. Later, the strong voices and varied accents of his political writing as well as the careful distinction of speakers in the long poems could easily have been defended by academic critics. Already a hero in literature and the plastic arts, the orator who altered his words and manner to sway an audience was given unprecedented support in academies.[16]

To be fair, we should note how intellectual virtues hint at vices which Milton could not excuse. First, the hierarchial organization of academies was bound to remind him of the king/priest/presbyter monolith that he detested. The rules ("leggi") for Naples's Oziosi required it to be led by a *Principe, Assistenti, Consiglieri,* and *Recivitore* who welcomed strangers. Florence's Svogliati ("Slackers") needed *Censori* and a *Bidello.* More to the point, perhaps, are titles which Coltellini's Apatisti adopted: *Protettore* and *Luogotenenti.*[17] The martial sound of such offices may echo in Hell, where Satan's army follows its "Leader" (*PL* II, 19) and those like Beelzebub who are "next in Order and Dignity" (Argument to Book I). Mammon directs the "Pioners" (I, 676) while Azazel carries the battle flag (I, 534ff.). On the other hand, good angels escape most of this prioritizing. Since Milton avoids the neat ranking which his generation learned from treatises like Thomas Heywood's ponderous *Hierarchie of the Blessed Angells* (London, 1635), he may be cautioning groups that organization in itself is no proof of merit. "Titles," Milton would agree with Satan, may be "merely titular" (V, 773–74).

Another characteristic of academies apparently divided his admiration. They discussed an extraordinary range of topics. Since Milton came to Italy in order to cultivate his mind ("animi causa," Argument to *Epitaphium Damonis*), he would have appreciated such sage and serious discussions as those held by members of the Florentine Academy during the years 1635–39. They held a memorial service for one who, twenty years before, had explained comets and telescopes; evaluated Torricelli's experiments; praised "Distributive Justice" in addresses which were later printed; described the qualities of a "Saintly Prince"; commented on secular paraphrases of the Psalms; heard a new treatise on music; pointed to recent scholarship on Galileo, Tacitus, and Guicciardini; and, as Milton headed back to his restless land, considered "the English schism."[18]

Yet such hydroptic thirst for learning may lead to frivolity. For example, Giuseppe Battista recalls that it was customary for the Oziosi to propose topics that would exercise the wit ("per esercizio d'ingegno") of members during Manso's time. Sandwiched between standard questions ("Is cowardice or rashness the more serious sin?" "Should death in tragedy be shown or narrated?") are sportive exercises like the useless ones which ancient Romans who lived under tyrants were obliged to focus upon: "Why does the dying swan sing?" "Why does Horace call swans *purpurei?*"[19] Intoxicating as such enterprises are, Milton sensed that they may deflect men's minds from godly topics. Raphael warns Adam, "Sollicit not thy thoughts with matters hid" (*PL* VIII, 167) after our Father begins to ponder astronomical theories. The damned angels conspicuously forget to "be lowlie wise" (VIII, 173) as they pompously "reason'd high / Of Providence, Foreknowledge, Will and Fate, / Fixt Fate, free will, foreknowledg absolute, / And found no end, in wandring mazes lost" (II, 558–61). Whatever Milton's true attitude toward learning, he seems to be aware of the dangers inherent in zealous polishing of the dark mirror of fallen intelligence which academies encouraged. The Great Consult may be his most serious indictment of mental presumption. Satan sits like the presiding officer of an academy, "High on a Throne of Royal State" (II, 1), and suggests the subject for debate: "by what best way, / Whether of open Warr or covert guile" (II, 40–41) may rebels injure God. The *paragone* of force versus fraud may be traced back to Homer but it gained special urgency during the Renaissance after Machiavelli's discussion of *forza / frode.*[20]

II

These general correspondences between academic preference and Miltonic practice encourage us to compare *Ad Salsillum* with Salzilli's own Italian works. Milton's forty-one lines add up to more than a get-well wish for his friend from the Fantastici. They begin by calling attention to the meter, recall that Salzilli, who had praised Milton's talent in a florid epigram, is now ill, and invoke Health and Phoebus to cure him so his songs may again cheer the muses and tame the flooded Tiber. This bare-bones outline misleads readers by concealing Milton's technical skill as well as by ignoring the links he forged to Salzilli's poems.

Although Thomas Warton praised only the second half,[21] I find a tight structure throughout which carefully considers sets of opposites, then presents a third quality to balance these conflicting elements. The *ter-*

tium quid unites artistic, geographic, and physical terms during the first twenty-two lines but, and here is proof of Milton's premeditation, unites clashing values in a larger mythological context during lines 23–41. The invocation to a muse introduces this binary method: her limp (that is, the scazontic meter) can be seen as Vulcan's ungainly shuffle (Catullus and Martial employed scazons for invective) or as the nymph Deiope's winsome dance. Decorum decides between these two evaluations: *scazontes* may be used in the correct place *(in loco)*. Next Milton modestly explains that Salzilli (a third quality) has elevated his humble muse from her ordinary place to a position among "great, god-like artists." Then the speaker identifies himself as another kind of reconciler: although a Londoner, he has bridged the distance from his "nest" in the windy north to Italy's fertile fields. Finally, Milton ends this preparatory section by contrasting Salzilli's mental and physical conditions: although genius has taught Salzilli's Roman mouth to speak as a Greek lyricist's, bile has corrupted his body so it cannot function.

The same mathematical framework of two opposing ideas which a third can moderate supports the concluding section. "Salus," enemy of "bilis," is called Hebe's "sister," perhaps so that Juno's servant Deiope, who begins the first section, may have a counterpart here in the second.[22] Apollo receives more attention, however, since he performs two functions. As Phoebus he elevated mere expression to poetry by coaxing "Lesbium melos" from "Romano ore"; as Paean he turns illness to health. Apollo's double relation to Salzilli/poet and Salzilli/patient extends beyond one man's country. If the young Roman recovers, his new strength will influence a whole mythic world: those fields of the first section, now catalogued as "Faunus' oakgroves, vine-bearing hills, Evander's territory," will rise above the physical world to enter a timeless realm where Numa already gazes forever upon Egeria. Milton ends his reasoned plea for Apollo's gifts by picturing two aspects of the Tiber: if Salzilli does not recover, "Tumidus Tibris" will rampage; if Salzilli does sing, the river will calmly flow to the salt sea. Apollo must choose between these possibilities, but Milton has injected such ugly examples of chaos that even a god who lives at ease should be persuaded to heal Salzilli's illness. Unless the roaring winds mentioned in the first section are to be duplicated in Italy's green and pleasant land by wild floods, the deity must act. Milton's poem thus admits the contrary but intertwined conditions of human life and art. Rather than acquiesce to mere description, it demonstrates that rational control can unite and dignify what otherwise will remain disparate and ordinary.

This emphasis upon two opposites, one of which must be chosen so that fecund order may prevail, recalls the dilemma of *Comus* and fore-shadows the idea of good intertwined with evil that typifies *Areopagitica* and the major poems. More than any of these other works, however, *Ad Salsillum* demonstrates by arrangement what mere statement probably could not. The poem's mythological references increase as it progresses, indicating that Italy not England is the land which facilitates imaginative composition. The speaker's muse, Vulcan, Deiope, and Juno huddle together in the first seven lines. They are associated, not with England, but with a technical question: will the poem's meter adequately convey meaning to Salzilli the Italian? Milton cleverly separates these deities from their counterparts in the second section. There throng Salus and her sister Hebe, inhabitants of Olympus who can be coaxed to Rome; Phoebus-Paean, destroyer of Pytho at Delphi who now has work in Italy; Faunus and Evander and Numa and Egeria from the legendary past of Rome the Great; and, from the present, Tiber and Portumnus.

Each mythological character has filiations to classical discussions and to Milton's other writings. In general, he recalls rather than invents. He knew that academic auditors appreciated learned restatements of familiar topics. The invention of Deiope's dancing adds vigor to Virgil's casual hint about Juno's most beautifully shaped follower and signals the cautious handling of most material common to Milton and Salzilli.[23] But two references would have struck the Italian as especially bold, that to the "pessimus ventorum" ("worst of the winds") and to Numa's ecstatic trance. Both passages can be called "molto erudita" since they spring from standard sources, but even the Renaissance habit of *retractatio,* or perfective imitation, cannot fully explain their novel force.

Blustery winds, for example, connote transitoriness, nothingness, war's destruction, or Yahweh's revenge in the Old Testament.[24] Similarly, the ἄνεμος of some twenty-eight New Testament passages threatens homes, ships, reeds, and fig trees. Its destructiveness is not specifically linked to God but can be tamed only by him.[25] Although Milton probably invokes many of these associations, the specific way by which he characterizes his wind points away from a simple source in the Bible.

More like Roman writers, Milton almost personifies the weather near England:

> pessimus ubi ventorum,
> Insanientis impotensque pulmonis
> Pernix anhela sub Jove exercet flabra.   (11–13)

[Where the worst of winds, from madly furious lungs, vigorously puffs its blasts under the sky.]

Cicero already had asked ironically why, since some philosophical schools thought of the sun and moon as deities, they did not extend godhood to the morning star, planets, fixed stars, the rainbow, clouds, seasons, storms, and rain squalls.[26] Athens boasted a monument to the eight winds which depicted each of them in handsome carvings around the upper register. The Aerides can still be seen today, but Milton never completed his pilgrimage to Greece. Closer to him while he wrote for his friend was the temple devoted to storms (Tempestates). Standing near the Capene Gate and a temple of Mars, this structure had been mentioned by Ovid and was erected by Lucius Cornelius Scipio, consul for 259 B.C.[27] But if the many physical representations of puff-cheeked winds common to Roman shrines and sarcophagi escaped Milton then the literary notices could not. Raging winds were standard ingredients of storm scenes which, in turn, were almost required elements of serious writing. Men as cultivated as Milton or Salzilli would have remembered at least some of these writers who delighted in telling how ferocious were the winds that whipped up various storms: Ennius, Pacuvius, Virgil, Livy, Ovid, Lucan, Statius, and Valerius Flaccus.[28] Historians like Tacitus eagerly amplified tempests.[29] Rhetoricians too urged their students to "describe a mighty storm" so that they might perfect their powers of memory, invention, and delivery.[30]

Although the brawling winds that appear in these and other Roman set-pieces provide a context for Milton's thought, they do not explain away his particular expression. If he had any one precedent in mind for his huffing "pessimus ventorum," I think it comes from Greek exemplars. Homer had introduced Typhoeus,[31] a monstrous dragon-son of Gaea and Tartarus, whom Hesiod describes:

A hundred snake heads grew from the shoulders of this terrible dragon, with black tongues flickering and fire flashing from the eyes under the brows of those prodigious heads. And in each of those terrible heads were voices beyond description: they uttered every kind of sound; sometimes they spoke the language of the gods; sometimes they made the bellowing noise of a proud and raging bull, or the noise of a lion relentless and strong, or strange noises like dogs; sometimes there was a hiss, and the high mountains re-echoed.[32]

Typhoeus' only act of generation is to sire the malevolent winds. Pindar picks up the emphasis on Typhon's cacaphony (the names Typhoeus and Typhon had become synonymous) and contrasts it to "the sweet triumphal hymns" that Phoebus may inspire in the town of Aetna. There the god-king Hiero honors poetry and takes away any fear of Typhon's volcanic bellowing. As patron of art and protector of his people, Hiero combines the functions of Phoebus and Zeus.[33] And in *Pythian* VIII,

15–20, Pindar once again recalls how Typhon was defeated and juxta-poses Apollo to Phoebus. These unflattering descriptions of a particular wind demon had already provided Milton with a significant reference in his Nativity ode and would supply other mentions in *Areopagitica* and in *Paradise Lost*.[34]

By harking back to a Greek original for the wind that opposed his progress to Italy, Milton suggests that his poem operates on several levels at once. The verse will endow the Greek character with Roman signifi-cance. Like Salzilli, who has sung "Lesbium melos" from his Italian throat, Milton the Briton has revived a Greek monster. Now this noisy brute (Apollodorus says that he gives out a "loud hissing sound")[35] threatens another worshipper of Phoebus — it breathes ("spirat") poison through-out Salzilli's body, impeding his poetry. Further, the contrary wind did not aid Milton's flight from his London nest to Italy's welcoming lands. I think it not too much to say that Milton here pictures himself as a sec-ond Aeneas who has braved a harsh trip to reach his esthetic homeland. The circumstances of his trip suggest a familiar Roman theme. Augustan writers often mention escape from some tainted world (Troy for Virgil, war-weary Italy for Horace). Despite fearful opposition, the brave voy-ager seeks purification in a distant but divinely-governed realm. Horace uses "Auster, the stormy wind, tyrant of the turbulent Adriatic,"[36] to sym-bolize difficulties that a pilgrim must overcome. To survive "warwaging winds,"[37] one must be convinced that his homeland is hostile or exhausted. The speaker of Epode 16 urges those who share his fear that the ravaged land will soon be occupied by wild animals and even more ferocious con-querors to set sail for some distant utopia, a fertile paradise where Eurus, the rainy southeast wind, does not flood the wheatfields. To reach these Happy Fields and Blessed Islands ("beata arva, divites insulas," 41–42) places that resemble the landscape around Salzilli, the emigrants must endure the buffetings of Notus, the south wind, or Africus, the violent southwest wind.[38] Milton's Britain had, from earliest times, been char-acterized by geographers as a place whose "overcast sky was always cloudy or rainy."[39] Whether or not he understood that there were war clouds on England's political horizon, he certainly knew that the country was largely unappreciative of his poetic efforts. Rather than succumb to the brutality that winds symbolized for Roman writers, Milton says that he has successfully evaded them and arrived in Salzilli's "beata arva."[40]

Italy is not free from danger to tradition since the Tiber may flood its banks and cover the tombs of kings. Yet if Salzilli recovers, he can charm the troubled water. This graceful compliment contains a second plea-sure for readers who had been teased into thought by the reference to

"the worst of winds." Almost everyone recognized that Numa had suc-
ceeded Romulus as king of ancient Rome. A peaceful, pious lawgiver,
he benignly balanced Romulus' talents as a warrior.[41] Likewise, Numa's
liaison with the nymph Egeria, who furnished him with advice, was famous, although treated with varying degrees of seriousness.[42] They met
near the Capene Gate, by the church of the Tempests, and suggested to
Milton a unique description:

> Ipse inter atros emirabitur lucos
> Numa, ubi beatum degit otium aeternum,
> Suam reclivis semper Aegeriam spectans.   (33–35)

[In the dim groves, where he spends a blessed eternity at ease, forever gazing
upon his Egeria, Numa himself will be astonished.]

Never before had their relationship been given such a mystical turn.[43]
Milton describes them lost in adoring contemplation much as Donne
speaks of the lovers in his "Ecstasy." Numa and Egeria inhabit some
sacred region which neither time nor flood nor wind can defile. Their
self-absorption both causes and rewards their blessed tranquility. Only
Salzilli's song can penetrate their trance and that sweet *cantus* will merely
augment it. Since Egeria was a Camena, or nymph usually associated
with the muses,[44] Milton repays his friend's compliment to his verse with
unusual felicity. Further, the Englishman once more honors Italy as a
land free from contingency, the achieved goal of his adventurous flight
from the impure locale treated in the poem's first half. The bold invention of Numa's perpetual joy suggests that near Rome one may find personal, political, moral, and aesthetic fulfillment. The fact that Milton
had reservations about many features of seventeenth-century Italy makes
such a statement an even warmer testament of friendship.

In addition, *Ad Salsillum* praises itself. Milton has endured contrary winds and created a poem to commemorate his achievement. His
word *impotens* (raging, furious, unbridled) applied to a north wind probably recalls the famous boast of Horace about his own poetry: "I have
completed a monument more enduring than bronze, more lofty than the
pyramids, a monument that no devouring rain nor raging north wind
("Aquilo impotens") . . . can destroy."[45] Horace's speaker continues in
phrases that have a particular significance for Milton since they promise
continued artistic development in Italy and new honor from the muses
since the Augustan will be the first to adapt Aeolic poetry to Italian
meters (or, in Milton's words, speak "Lesbium melos" from "Romano
ore"). By alluding to so many Greek, Latin, and modern Italian practices, Milton thus politely justifies Salzilli's epigram as well as his own
accomplishment.

Although *Ad Salsillum* can stand alone, it has relations to Milton's other work and to Salzilli's. A moment's reflection will show how its concerns are typically Miltonic: learned-but-flexible mythology, inclusive geography, decorous diction, a flight through space, trust in poetry, and hope for final reconciliation.

The relations to Salzilli's concerns demand some new thought since we know little of him as a man. Except for a letter from Tommaso Stigliani which proves Milton's friend survived his illness until at least 4 April 1644,[46] all the information we have comes from *Ad Salsillum* and a collection of fifteen Italian poems by Salzilli himself.[47] Eleven sonnets, three *canzoni*, and one *ottava* appeared in a collection by members of the Fantastici published in 1637. Since Salzilli's work is granted twenty-two pages, some 11 percent of the whole anthology, we may guess that their author was highly regarded. With only two omissions, he faithfully mirrors the interests of his fellow academics. Salzilli does not dwell on religious themes. Others in the volume urge readers to free Christ's tomb from infidels or honor the Resurrection or meditate on Mary and St. Agnes. Salzilli also sidesteps scientific verse. His colleagues, however, scold alchemy or wonder why the north wind does not freeze the Tiber. The bulk of Salzilli's verse is competent and predictably honors poetry, love, and unusual people.

The very first sonnet, "Calchi pur'[,] alma vil, serua de l'oro," radiates an academic trust which Milton shared: the noble soul seeks glory from poetry rather than wealth or social rank. (I will shortly return to this sonnet. Here it is enough to say the aesthetic disdain for a "vile soul, slave to gold, [which] indeed follow[s] misleading footprints" is common.) *Sonnet 3* bravely takes up arms in the battle of ancients versus moderns: "Our age has writers of verse and of prose who equal the ancients." Tasso, it claims, rivals Virgil and, with characteristic flattery, it continues that one "Mascardi" is now about to climb the heights of fame. Similarly, "Signor Giacomo N," who lives only in *Sonnet 10*, has come from near Milan so that Rome, the glorious authoress ("altrice gloriosa"), may nourish him. In the same vein, the long *First Canzone* praises "Poetry Triumphant" with that vigorous ingenuity one associates with idealistic young men. The speaker "follows a light clearer than gold" and thus turns to Phoebus for strength. Like Milton, Salzilli alludes to earlier poets who provide sea-marks beyond which he plans to sail. Homer, Ariosto, Tasso, and Guarini inspire true artists to surpass them. The speaker hints that he has at least caught up to them by using key words like the Virgilian "debellare" ("war down" of *Aeneid* VI, 853) and Petrarchan "l'aura" ("breeze" or "Laura"). Both he and Milton imply they address a select audience by using circumlocution to identify famous predecessors. Both, for example, summon Anacreon by mentioning only his birthplace, "La Teia Lira" ("the Teian lyre." Compare Milton's *Elegy VI*, 22: "Tëia Musa"). In short, each draws from the same European tradition to support his adulation for poetry.

Love poems likewise require their attention. Milton's six Italian poems of 1630 as well as *Elegies V* and *VII* complement Salzilli's amatory verse. The latter "reminds beautiful D____ that time flies" (*Sonnet 4*) or praises "Chaste Love"; the speaker of *Sonnet 7* hopes to escape "the bow and arrows of wanton love" so he may "steer [as Milton often does] beyond the stars . . . , transported from the clutch of Pluto to Jove's lap." Salzilli's love poems include conventional comparisons ("Lilla" outshines the dawn in *Sonnet 8*) and elegant compliments ("Love the wizard" ("Amor mago") mixes snow and flame in the lady's cheeks of *Sonnet 9*). Occasionally there are "baroque" statements: the "bella donna" of *Sonnet 5* "wrote to her lover with her own blood." In general, though, Salzilli displays more restraint than his coworker in the muses' field Martino Lunghi, who indiscriminately worships his lady's eyes, her hair and her hand as well as Thomas Aquinas and St. Luke.

Notable men inspire Salzilli and his colleagues. Other Fantastici extol achievement, especially if the doer is a possible patron: Louis XIII of France, Philip II of Spain (whose deeds "parallel" those of Hercules), or "Vladislao," king of Poland. Salzilli addresses only one public figure, Fulvio Testi, the secretary of state for Modena, but even this politician is congratulated in terms of art ("he takes upon himself the names of Ruggiero and Rinaldo," heroes in Ariosto and Tasso). Salzilli evaluates men by esthetic, not patriotic, standards. The unnamed horseman of the *ottave* may "boldly break the Saracen's face" during a joust, but his real distinction lies in his physical beauty upon which Salzilli dwells. While some Fantastici respond to art (one praises Guido Reni because "Aurora's colors were in his brush" and two others congratulate Ottavio Tronsarelli for his poems), none repairs to it so often. He shares a trust with Milton that some ideal force drives flowers, kings, and poets, infusing all with perfection. Milton's *Elegy V* praises spring since it invigorates animal spirits and human intellect; Salzilli's May Song secularizes the hymn by which Lucretius implored Venus to bless *De Rerum Natura*:

> Per te Maggio gentile
> Si placa il Cielo, e'l Mare,
> Per te con varie stile
> Ricca la Terra appare,
> Onde Ciel, Mare, e Terra in lor linguagio
> Narran le glorie sue, pomposo Maggio.

[For you, gentle May,
The sky calms itself, and the sea;
For you the rich Earth appears
In various guises.
Therefore, sky, sea and land in their language
Tell of your glories, magnificent May.]

The very typicality of Salzilli's thought on poetry, love, and unique individuals helps us understand academic taste and throws into high relief those unusual features which Milton noted.

For just as there are both general and specific connections between Milton and the academies, I find his broad sympathy with Salzilli to be complemented by some particular references. *Ad Salsillum* cleverly but politely incorporates certain ideas that Milton knew were important to his Roman friend. Both men speak to Phoebus Apollo. Salzilli's verse mentions him five times (an average of once for every three poems); Milton will in his lifetime allude to the patron of art some sixty times, mainly during this early period. Yet *Ad Salsillum* curiously invokes "Phoebe . . . sive tu magis Paean / Libenter audis" ("Phoebus, or Paean, if you prefer to be called by that name"). Since Milton nowhere else uses "Paean," we are probably justified in hearing an echo of Salzilli's first sonnet, which castigates the vile soul as it follows the misleading tracks of Aesculapius and Paean ("Calchi . . . D'Esculapio, e Peon l'orme fallaci"). After rejecting medicine as mere legacy hunting, the speaker abandons influence peddling in the noisy Forum. The sestet claims, wistfully and self-righteously, that his noble aspiration raises him to Mt. Pindus in Greece where one can reap abundant laurel and avoid Time, that tributary to Lethe which sweeps away other men's rich spoils. Such sentiments obviously appeal to Milton, who had rejected an ordinary vocation, repeatedly described flights to sublime places, feared Time, and hoped that art would protect her devotees. Further, *Ad Salsillum* gently comforts the speaker who longs for distant Greece: Salzilli already has reduplicated Sappho and Alcaeus in Italy. *Ad Salsillum* eases the fear of rivers like *Tempo* and *Lete* by reminding the speaker how art can tame the Tiber. Italy's pleasant places, which Milton enumerates, add up to more than one mountain in Thessaly. *Ad Salsillum* picks up the mention of Roman military practice in *Sonnet 1* to encourage its speaker: the heroes who received "spolie opime," "the choicest booty," cannot control the river which floods their tombs so well as a true poet. Perhaps Milton exaggerates the wild winds of his northern home to compensate Salzilli for illness often ascribed to the *malaria* of Rome's marshland.[48] At any rate, *Ad Salsillum* urges the author of *Sonnet 1* to think through to their logical conclusion the postulates he had advanced.

Another *hapax legomenon* suggests that Milton read more of Salzilli's verse. Sandwiched between mythical figures who appealed to both men (Urania, Hippogriff, Alphaeus, Arethusa, Amaryllis) is a "rich mer-'chant, killed in a duel." He tells how he wandered over seas as a "beggar" until "a quiet wind finally cast me up on my beloved Lido, now a rich man." Some insult led him to fight a strong foe who "quenched the last day of life." Summing up his career in an epigram worthy of the Greek Anthology, the Merchant says,

> With my strong breast,
> I endured waves and rocks,
> And then returned from far away.
> Now, in altered accent, I beg from Death.

The word "nest" (*nido*) unites this odd poem to *Ad Salsillum:* Milton speaks of leaving his "nidum," enduring fierce (not "quiet") winds and imploring Paean, enemy of Death, to heal his friend. Milton never again uses "nest" in Latin or English. He may have been struck by the irony of someone who survived hard voyages only to bring death upon himself because of "a sharp word." Lycidas' poetry earned friendship but could not prolong his life, even on a calm sea.

Thus *Ad Salsillum* proves how many filaments, obvious and subtle, bound Milton to Italy. In 1638 he might have turned to his travelling companion and, using the words of Shakespeare's Lucentio, bravely said,

> I am arrived [in] . . .
> The pleasant garden of great Italy,
> And by my father's love and leave am armed
> With his good will . . .
> Here let us breathe and haply institute
> A course of learning and ingenious studies.   (*Shr.* I, i, 3–9)

In 1639, having been encouraged by academic admirers like Giovanni Salzilli, Milton could fondly remember that the grand tour left every part of his social, intellectual, and artistic personality enriched.

University of Massachusetts

NOTES

1. David Masson still has the most complete account of this tour in *The Life of Milton: Narrated in Connexion with the Political, Ecclesiastical, and Literary History of his*

Time, I (London, 1881; rpt. New York, 1946). J. Milton French reprints vital documents in *The Life Records of John Milton*, I (New Brunswick, N.J., 1949).

2. John Arthos's fascinating study *Milton and the Italian Cities* (London, 1968), p. 60, mentions a "remarkable" concert with two organs during August, 1638, at Santa Maria sopra Minerva. *PL* I, 708–09 shows that Milton had at some time observed an organ carefully.

3. Masson, *Life*, I, p. 796 tells how 450 authors who had published between 1630 and 1632 were listed by a contemporary named Leo Allatius in *Apes Romanae*. Satan's "bees" may hark back to these *apes* whom the Pope encouraged.

4. *PL* IV, 45, 109. For poetry I use CM.

5. My translation of the lines Milton adapted from Horace, *Epistles* I. 11.27. See William Riley Parker, *Milton: A Biography*, I (Oxford, 1968), p. 181 and note.

6. Visitors to Rome may still enjoy illustrations of Apuleius' fable in Castel Sant' Angelo by Perin del Vaga or in Villa Farnesina by Raphael and his school. Paintings of Tobias are epidemic in Italy. Villa Borghese displays two, one by Giovanni Savoldo and another by Pier Francesco Toschi.

7. *Of Reformation* 2. In CM III, p. 55. Milton usually thinks of two Romes: the noble ancient city, now buried ("Romam sepultam." *Ep. Dam.*, 115) but still magnetic, and the modern city, impious because of its false religion ("Roma impia." *Prod. Bomb.* 4, 1).

8. Milton speaks most highly of academies in *Reason of Church-government* (CM I, pp. 809–10); *Of Education* (CM IV, p. 287); *Second Defence* (CM VIII, p. 123). My information about Italian academies comes from many sources. Masson and Arthos are listed above, other authorities below. Some additional works are: Camillo Minieri-Riccio, *Cenno storico intorno all'Accademia degli Oziosi in Napoli* (Naples, 1862), which uses many primary sources; G. Gabrieli, "L'Accademia in Italia: sguardo storico-critico comprensivo," *Accademie e Biblioteche d'Italia*, 5 (1928), 5–19, which has a good list of regional sources; Piero Rebora, "Milton a Firenze," *Il Sei-Settecento* (Florence, 1956), pp. 249–70, which breaks little new ground; James Holly Hanford, "Milton in Italy," *Annuale Mediaevale*, 5 (1964), 49–63, which gracefully recounts Milton's entire trip; William Riley Parker, *Milton*, 2 vols., which has an excellent bibliography; Eric W. Cochrane, *Florence in the Forgotten Centuries, 1527–1800* (Chicago, 1973), which displays the same learning of his earlier (but somewhat peripheral because of the dates) *Tradition and Enlightenment in the Tuscan Academies, 1690–1800* (Chicago, 1961).

9. Johan Jarkius, *Specimen Historiae Academiarum Eruditarum Italiae* (Leipzig, 1725), fols. 7ᵛ, 4ᵛ, 5ᵛ.

10. Coltellini regularly used his academic name. See the document reproduced in Edoardo Benvenuti, *Agostino Coltellini e l'Accademia degli Apatisti a Firenze nel secolo XVII* (Pistoia, 1910), p. 296. Also, Michele Maylender, *Storia delle accademie d'Italia* (Bologna, n.d.), I, p. 221.

11. Gianbattista Masullo, *Academicarum Exercitationum Liber Primus. Sive de Attractione* (Naples, 1622).

12. Jacobo Gaddi, *De Scriptoribus non Ecclesiasticis, Graecis, Latinis[,] Italicis Primorum Gradum in Quinque Theatris[,] scilicet Philosophico, Poetico, Historico, Oratorio, Critico* (Florence, 1648). This encyclopedia includes many eminent writers up to 1550 but ends with the letter S. If there is a second volume, I assume it has as interesting a selection as this one, which contains Callimachus, the Emperor Julian, and Thomas More.

13. Christopher Hill, *Milton and the English Revolution* (New York, 1977), pp. 56–57.

14. "Molto erudita" is what the minutes of the Florentine Svogliati record for his performance on 6/16 September 1638. The Milton entries were discovered only a century ago and reported to Alfred Stern, who reprinted them in *Milton und seine Zeit* (Leipzig, 1877), I, p. 499.

15. Jacobo Gaddi, *Adlocutiones, et Elogia Exemplaria, Cabalistica, Oratoria, Mixta, Sepulcralia* (Florence, 1636). "Ad Posteritatem" is on p. 17, "Ad Milites" on p. 38. *Elogia Historica, tum Soluta, cum Vincta Numeris Oratione Prescripta & Notis Illustrate* (Florence, 1637). *Eliographus[,] scilicet Elogia Omnigena* (Florence, 1638). Vespucci is on pp. 182–83.

16. Milton probably saw many representations of heroic orators. Roman coins of the Empire often showed the emperor exhorting his troops from a raised platform. These *adlocutiones* inspired such Renaissance artists as Ghirlandaio (Santa Trinità, Florence), Signorelli (Cathedral, Orvieto), and Botticelli (Vatican).

17. Carlo Padiglione, *Le leggi dell'Accademia degli Oziosi in Napoli ritrovate nella Biblioteca Brancacciana* (Naples, 1878), p. 10. Maylender, *Storia*, I, p. 221.

18. Salvino Salvini, *Fasti consolari dell'Accademia Fiorentina* (Florence, 1717), pp. 488–501.

19. Giuseppe Battista, *Le Giornate accademiche* (Venice, 1673), pt. 3, pp. 130, 151, 170, 182. There is a kind of comfort in knowing that certain academic questions remain unsolved. See H. Schoonhoven, "Purple Swans and Purple Snow . . . ," *Mnemosyne*, series 4, 31 (1978), 200–03.

20. *The Prince*, Chap. 18. I treat the force/fraud topic fully in *Milton and the Martial Muse: "Paradise Lost" and European Traditions of War* (Princeton, 1980). Except for being "rigged," Satan's discussion resembles many academic debates.

21. Thomas Warton's words are quoted in Henry John Todd, *The Poetical Works of John Milton* (London, 1801), VI, p. 343: "I know not any finer modern Latin lyric poetry, than from this verse [line 23] to the end. The close which is digressional, but naturally rises from the subject, is perfectly antique." Douglas Bush gathers together what little critical work has been done on *Ad Salsillum* in *Variorum*, pp. 263–67. Parker dismisses the poem in *Milton*, I, p. 173: "*Ad Salsillum* is a piece of poetical backscratching, rare with Milton but illustrating his quick response to Italian effusiveness." Even Ettore Allodoli (who might have better understood "effusiveness" because of his nationality) says in *Giovanni Milton e l'Italia* (Prato, 1907), pp. 22–23: *Ad Salsillum* "è da considerarsi piu come una esercitazione poetica accademica ben riuscita che come espressione sincera dell'animo di Milton" ("should be thought of more as a well-done exercise in academic poetry than as a sincere expression of Milton's heart").

22. So Douglas Bush suggests in *Variorum*, p. 264.

23. Juno describes Deiopea in *Aeneid* I, 72 as having "forma pulcherrima," "the most attractive figure," of all her nymphs. Aeolus succumbs to the bribe and immediately unleashes his winds against Aeneas.

24. Transitoriness: Job vii, 7; Psalm lxxviii, 39. Nothingness: Job xv, 2; Hosea xii, 1. War's destruction: Jeremiah xviii, 17. Yahweh's revenge: Isaiah xxvii, 8.

25. Homes: Matthew vii, 25. Ships: Acts xxvii, 14. Reeds: Luke vii, 24. Fig tree: Revelation vi, 13.

26. *De Natura Deorum* III, 20.51.

27. *Fasti* VI, 191–94.

28. Macrobius, *Saturnalia* VI, 2.28 gives Ennius credit for being the first to describe a storm in Latin.

Cicero, *De Oratore* III, 157 quotes with approval Pacuvius' storm description.

Virgil, *Georgics* I, 311–34: fall tempest affects all nature; *Aeneid* I, 55, 81–123: Aeolus' storm buffets Aeneas.

Livy XXI, 58.3–11: Apennine storm attacks Hannibal.

Ovid, *Metamorphoses* II, 474–572: storm kills Ceyx; *Fasti* III, 583–600: storm kills Anna, Dido's sister.

Lucan, *Pharsalia* V, 597–612: winds blast Caesar's ship.

Statius, *Thebaid* VII, 34–39: winds batter Mercury in Thrace.

Valerius Flaccus, *Argonautica* I, 608–50: "Hippotades" loosens his winds against Jason's newly-launched ship.

29. *Annals* II, 20: storm wrecks Roman fleet off coast of Germany.

30. Seneca, *Suasoria* III, 2. Perhaps the useless storm Satan raises in *PR* IV, 409–19 demonstrates that the attention to such topics by "all the Oratory of *Greece* and *Rome*" is misguided because biblical topics are expressed in "majestic unaffected style" (IV, 359–60).

31. *Iliad* II, 782–83 merely alludes to Typhoeus' being imprisoned underground as a result of Zeus' anger.

32. *Theogony* 826ff. I use the felicitous translation by Norman O. Brown (New York, 1953), p. 76, omitting his italics.

33. Pythian I.

34. Nativity ode, 226. *Areopagitica*, in CM IV, p. 338. *PL* I, 199 and II, 539. Also, *Prolusion IV*, in CM XII, p. 173.

35. *The Library* I, 6.3: συριγμὸν πολὺν.

36. Odes III, 3.4–5: "Auster, / dux inquieti turbidus Hadriae."

37. Odes I, 9.10–11: "ventos deproeliantes."

38. Line 22: "Notus aut protervus Africus."

39. Tacitus, *Agricola* XII: "caelum crebris imbribus ac nebulis foedum." Strabo IV. 5.2 makes the same observation.

40. Ovid has Aeolus' daughter castigate her unresponsive brother for becoming as savage as the winds he rules in *Heroides* XI, 9–14.

41. There are numerous accounts of Numa. Some of the most famous: *Aeneid* VI, 808–12; Livy I, 18, 19, 21; Cicero, *De Republica* II, 13.25–16.30; Sextus Aurelius Victor, *De Viris Illustribus* XXVII.15–XXVIII.3; Plutarch, *Numa;* Macrobius, *Commentary on "The Dream of Scipio"* XVII, 8.

42. Livy I. 19 claims that Numa invented Egeria to frighten his subjects. Ovid, *Metamorphoses* XV, 479–92 treats her with respect since she and the muses "blessed" Numa's activities. Juvenal jauntily dismisses her as Numa's *amica*, "girl friend," in Satire III. 12. Martial speaks of her as being the spirit of water, related to the muses in VI, 47.

43. Bush, *Variorum*, p. 266 reminds us of Keightley's suggestion: the "eternal contemplation" of Numa and Egeria that Milton seems to invent "may owe something to Lucretius I. 31–40, on Mars and Venus." It is possible, but Lucretius stresses the temporary nature of Mars' tranquility.

44. Camena was a synonym for muse. Milton himself understands the two words as interchangeable in *Sals.* 1 ("O Musa") and 7 ("camena nostra"). According to Aulus Gellius XVIII, 9.5, Livius Andronicus' translation of the *Odyssey* begins the practice.

45. Odes III, 3.1ff.: "Exegi monumentum."

46. Angelo Borzelli and Fausto Nicolini, eds., *Giambattista Marino: Epistolario. Seguito da lettere di altri scrittori del seicento* (Bari, 1912), II, p. 364, reprint the following note from Tommaso Stigliani:

Al signor Giovanni Salzilli, A Treviso
Suole Apollo abbandonare i suoi seguaci quando Venere
abbandona i suoi cultori. Per questa ragione, non puo
promettere di certo all'amico di mandargli una poesia
in lode di una duchessa.
Di Matera, 4 d'aprile 1644

[Apollo abandons his followers when Venus deserts hers. For this reason, one can't really
promise to send a friend a poem praising a duchess.]

Apparently Stigliani's heart-sickness dampened his creative powers just as did Salzilli's less
romantic ailment.

47. Lodovico Grignani, ed., *Poesie de' Signori Accademici Fantastici di Roma*.I was
not able to find this informative book in America, but the British Library has a copy
(#1062B.1) and Rome's Biblioteca Nazionale Centrale has another (#6.23.A.2). Masson
knew of it, but like his successors did little more than mention it. Since, after all these
years, Salzilli's companions in *Poesie* have no need for publicity, I do not document every
reference.

48. An anonymous contributor to *The Gentleman's Magazine*, 300 (1906), 507 makes
this suggestion. See "Milton in his Latin Poems."

MANSUS: IN ITS CONTEXT

Anthony Low

WHEN MILTON visited Naples in the winter of 1638, after his pleasant stay in Rome, he was shown a flattering hospitality by Giovan Battista Manso, marquis of Villa, who in earlier years had been the friend and patron of Tasso and Marino. "By him I was treated, while I stayed there, with all the warmth of friendship," Milton tells us in the *Defensio Secunda*, "for he conducted me himself over the city and the viceregent's court, and more than once came to visit me at my own lodgings" (CM VIII, p. 125). In the short preface to *Mansus,* the poem with which he repaid his host's considerateness to a yet-obscure foreigner, Milton says much the same thing: "He treated the author with the greatest kindness while he was in Naples, and did him many services out of humanity." Milton's preface also establishes the date of *Mansus:* "And so, before leaving the city, the visitor, in order not to seem ungrateful, sent him this poem."[1] For his part, Manso provided Milton with a Latin distich, rather drily characterized by Parker as a mark of "qualified admiration."[2] This brief poem, printed by Milton among the "testimonia" of his Italian friends that prefaced his *Poemata,* probably was one of those "written Encomiums" of which Milton speaks in *The Reason of Church-government,* which he received on the spot in Italy. The poem Milton wrote for Giovanni Salzilli in Rome, a month earlier, picks up several themes from Salzilli's compliment to Milton, evidently written first;[3] similar internal evidence suggests that Manso's distich preceded *Mansus.*

Manso and Milton had much in common. Both were urbane and civilized gentlemen; both were Christian humanists and lovers of the Latin classics; both loved to talk about literature with others of intelligence and understanding; both viewed poetry with utmost seriousness. There were differences too. Manso was old and Milton young; he was famous and Milton unknown; he lived at the center of civilization in his day and had befriended two of its best-known exemplars, while Milton came from the far northern periphery where, he often felt, the sun of culture as yet scarcely reached. The only really serious difference between the two men, however, was religious. Manso was a dedicated Roman Catholic, who was chosen to carry the miraculous blood in procession on the Feast of San Gennaro,[4] and who had supported Tasso in his last years when the poet was, as the saying goes, more Catholic than the Pope; Milton was a dedicated Protestant, well on his way to becoming a religious radical, who even in Italy lost few opportunities to express his views. In those days educated Protestants and Catholics often came together to enjoy friendly relations on a basis of mutual liking and cultural enthusiasm, but the warfare within western Christianity was too deep and active to be securely bridged. Certain subjects were better avoided. Even if well-intentioned men might be trusted not to quarrel or take official notice of views that might be illegal as well as distasteful, sudden denunciations of Papists or heretics by the less well-disposed could not be ruled out.

Milton, for example, was advised to avoid Rome after leaving Naples, although he had been received there hospitably not long before by Giovanni Salzilli, by Alessandro Cherubini, and even by the dreaded English Jesuits who had him to dinner. Certain merchants warned him that "in case of my revisiting Rome, the English Jesuits had laid a plot for me, because I had spoken too freely on the subject of religion: for I had laid it down as a rule for myself, never to begin a conversation on religion in those parts; but if interrogated concerning my faith, whatever might be the consequence, to dissemble nothing." Whether there was such a plot is unknown. Milton returned to Rome in spite of the warning, and was well received by Cardinal Barberini and by Lucas Holstein, the Vatican Librarian. Of immediate interest is that he could openly dine with the Jesuits at one time but later take seriously the threat of betrayal. Manso had apparently paid Milton every attention a young foreigner could hope for; yet he too was constrained by the religious issue. "On my leaving Naples," Milton says, "he gravely apologized for showing me no more attention, alleging that although it was what he wished above all things, it was not in his power in that city, because I had not thought proper to be more guarded on the point of religion."[5]

Such were the circumstances reflected in Manso's distich, and they amply account for his "qualified" praise:

> Ut mens, forma, decor, facies, mos, si pietas sic,
> Non Anglus, verùm herclè Angelus ipse fores.

[If your mind, form, grace, appearance, and manners were equaled by your piety, then, by Hercules, you would be no Angle, but truly an Angel.][6]

Obviously Manso is echoing the famous words of Gregory the Great when (as later reported in Milton's *History of Britain*), seeing some blond, young foreigners brought to Rome for sale, and inquiring their nationality in order to help them, he punned that they were not *Angli* but *Angeli*.[7]

Manso praises Milton's mind and manners as well as his youthful, northern good looks like those Gregory had admired; but what he adds with
one hand he takes back with the other. Having gotten to know something
about Milton's intelligence and wide learning, no doubt he expected him
to recognize the famous pun on which his distich is based, and also to
grasp some of the implications of the allusion, implied by the context in
which it was originally spoken. If Milton is analogous to the barbarous
English youths (in an early version Paul the Deacon calls them *pueri ve-
nales*, and Milton explains in his *History* that it was an old English custom to sell unwanted children), then Manso is analogous to Gregory, perhaps the greatest churchman since Peter himself, who had gone to the
forum to help these foreigners and who pitied them especially because
they were pagans in need of light. Moreover, the story continues, the
chance meeting led Gregory to send St. Augustine to convert Britain to
Catholic Christianity. Milton, too, Manso says, would be an angel, if only
his piety — which can only refer to his intransigent Protestantism — were
equal to his other virtues. The distich is civilized, accomplished, amusing, and it carries a sting. Yet Milton printed it in a place of honor, because, after all, he saw nothing to be ashamed of in being charged with
Protestantism, and he liked a good joke. The poem reflects a relationship
between the two men that is precisely what one might expect in the circumstances: they are antagonists over the issue of religion and expect never
to agree, yet they respect one another's intelligence, wit, and humanity.

What is true in miniature of the distich is true of *Mansus*, which
looks at many points as if Milton wanted to return an ambiguous compliment in kind as well as — and more fundamentally — to repay Manso
for his genuine kindness. Most editors and critics, after pausing to admire Milton's Latin, read the poem mainly for what it has to say about
Milton, in particular his Italian journey and plans for an epic. Parker,
for example, typically writes that the concluding lines are "so unexpected
and so charged with personal feeling that Manso may have puzzled over
their significance."[8] I doubt it. Both Milton and Manso were aware of
what the other was about; that is one source of what is at once a shared
literary joke, an unexpected, almost filial intimacy, and an emulous poetic power. As William Kennedy argues, the way to approach a Renaissance poem is first to consider its genre and broad rhetorical stance: in
particular, whom the poet addresses and how he may expect this audience to understand his words.[9] Milton had an ideal audience in Manso:
an extremely learned man, well read in the classical writers he himself
knew so well, and perfectly capable of understanding a nuance or inter-
preting an allusion. Manso was, after all, the founder of a Neapolitan

literary academy, himself a writer, and a man who could grapple with the difficulties of *Marinismo*. Milton also expected that at some point his poem would have a wider audience when it was published; in no other way could he eternize his host as promised. But that wider audience would, first, have many of the literary capabilities possessed by Manso, and second, be used to reading poems addressed to a friend or patron and prepared to read *Mansus* in the rhetorical context provided by its preface.

Because *Mansus* has several ends in mind — to repay a kindness, to immortalize a patron, to claim a similar immortality for poets, to continue a conversation, to answer a backhanded compliment, to bridge as well as to acknowledge the gap between poet and recipient — the poem is a familiar example of Renaissance *genera mixta*, in which no one genre obviously presides. Like all Milton's best poems before the last three, *Mansus* is an occasional poem and marks a stage in Milton's personal career, but it is no less universal for that. It is, as Bush writes, a "bread-and-butter epistle," yet one that thanks Manso not traditionally for his noble generosity or his fine table, as one might expect, or occasionally for his kindness as a tour guide, but rather for his wisdom in discerning true poets and his love in fostering them. It is, as Condee insists, a panegyric of sorts, yet (except for three or four words in the preface) one that has nothing at all to say about what are usually the foremost topics for praise — Manso's high rank, his noble family, his military prowess.[10] It is a novel variation on the poet-patron poem, yet one in which a young poet just coming into his force addresses an old patron who is not his except by momentary adoption, but the patron of two successful poets now dead, into whose fellowship Milton hopes to enter. It is (like Virgil's sixth Eclogue, which it so often echoes) a poem self-consciously about the making, nourishing, and transmission of poetry. Above all, however, and independent of specific generic considerations, *Mansus* is a subtle philosophical work that touches on poetry, friendship, fame, death, worldliness, the bond between fathers and sons, teachers and learners, and the nature of immortality, all partly in response to Manso's little distich and, one assumes, the conversations between the two of them during their several visits. For something in the meeting between Manso and Milton struck a chord, so that the occasion of their encounter in Naples became, like the deaths of Edward King and Charles Diodati, or the massacre of the Piedmontese, a landmark in Milton's life and poetic development. The evidence of the poem suggests that in *Mansus* Milton acts very like a son challenging a father who has threatened to reject him, and that he hopes through the sheer accomplishment of his poem and the persuasiveness of its nuances to impel recognition from this man who loved poetry, to bridge the gap

of sectarian difference between them, and, without actually establishing a literal poet-patron relationship with him such as Tasso and Marino
had enjoyed, nevertheless to achieve over the distance of geography and
belief something spiritually similar to that loving, filial bond.

Milton begins (1–6) by stating his intention to praise his host as a
patron and friend of poets, and therefore as a worthy successor to Gallus
and Maecenas. The names immediately evoke the presence of Horace and
Virgil, and Milton further underlines the connection he is beginning to
build with the classical past by means of verbal echoes, which such a
reader as Manso could be expected to recognize. Addressing him as well
known in the choir of Phoebus, "Manse choro notissime Phoebi," Milton
recalls Virgil's sixth Eclogue, in which Virgil pictures Gallus wandering
by the Permessus when "viro Phoebi chorus adsurrexit omnis" (66) ("all
the choir of Phoebus rose to do him honour").[11] Milton will add his praises
to those of other poets if his Muse has "sufficient breath." In this somewhat perfunctory expression of the modesty *topos*, Milton uses "Camoena"
for "Musa," employing a word (for a local Italian river goddess) that
recollects Horace and reinforces the connection while honoring Manso's
Latin descent. Although Milton seems to begin modestly and to intend
nothing but praise, he is already beginning to subvert the panegyric,[12]
by evoking (without naming) the two great Roman poets and suggesting
(without quite saying) that Apollo has granted Manso a rare honor not
only for his merits, but for his luck in being born, after a long interregnum, near two other great poets.

In the next section (7–23) Milton recalls that Manso was bound to
Tasso by a happy friendship: "Te pridem magno felix concordia Tasso."
The line, editors note, recalls Ovid's *Metamorphoses* VIII, 303: "et cum
Pirithoo, felix concordia, Theseus." While the immediate context is a list
of heroes, among them Theseus and his beloved companion Pirithous,
who are about to join the hunt for the Calydonian boar, in view of the
preoccupation of *Mansus* with friendship and death, often supported by
mythological allusions, one wonders if Milton did not intend Manso to recall not only the immediate context of Ovid's line but also the fate of the
famous pair. According to the poets, Theseus and Pirithous descended to
Hades together to carry off Persephone; Theseus escaped but Pirithous did
not. Horace concluded a well-known ode on the inevitability of death with
their example:

> infernis neque enim tenebris Diana pudicum
>   liberat Hippolytum,
> nec Lethaea valet Theseus abrumpere caro
>   vincula Pirithoo.   (4.7.25–28)

[For Diana releases not chaste Hippolytus from the nether darkness, nor has Theseus power to break the Lethean chains of his dear Pirithous.]

It is hard to tell how far to pursue the context of a Miltonic allusion. Certainly Manso would have recognized the Ovidian parallel and thus Theseus and Pirithous would have been namelessly evoked just as Horace and Virgil were earlier.

Not long after Tasso's death, the Muse entrusted Marino to Manso, "Musa Marinum / Tradidit"; and that poet took pleasure in being called Manso's foster-son: "ille tuum dici se gaudet alumnum" (9–10). The phrasing evokes a mother-muse (recalling *Lycidas,* 59, of the previous year) who turns her poet-child over to Father Manso for fostering. We shall see that this is only the first appearance of a suggestive pattern. When Marino died, Manso cared for his remains and commemorated him with a bronze bust. "Vidimus arridentem operoso ex aere poetam" (16) ("we see the poet smiling down from his carved bronze"). While similarity to Ovid's "viginti fulvos operoso ex aere" (*Heroides,* 3.31) is only verbal, further connections will appear later. But Manso's "pia . . . Officia," his pious offices for the dead, did not end in his tomb. "Cupis integros rapere Orco, / Quá potes, atque avidas Parcarum eludere leges" (18–19) ("As far as you can, you long to snatch them whole out of Orcus, and to elude the avid laws of the Fates"). Milton used a similar phrase to dismiss his poem in *Ad Patrem;* he will preserve his father's name to remote ages, "Nec spisso rapient oblivia nigra sub Orco" (118), if "black oblivion does not snatch you [the poem] down to crowded Orcus." For Milton, "Lethean Orcus" (*Ep. Dam.,* 201) represents not only death but oblivion. His usage is typically classical; an especially close parallel is Horace's ode on Pindar, which celebrates that panegyric poet's efforts to rescue heroes from oblivion. Pindar, Horace says,

> flebili sponsae iuvenemve raptum
> plorat et vires animumque moresque
> aureos educit in astra nigroque
> invidet Orco.   (4.2.21–24)

[(Pindar) laments the young hero snatched from his tearful bride, and to the stars extols his prowess, his courage, and his golden virtue, begrudging them to gloomy Orcus.]

The Parcae or Fates, of course, Milton pervasively associates with death in the early poetry.[13]

To perpetuate the memories of Tasso and Marino, Manso wrote biographies of both men and their families, "Amborum genus" (20). According to Virgil, when Aeneas first appealed to Evander for aid, he said they were descended from twin branches of one family, "genus amborum" (VIII, 142). Milton's echo of the phrase may evoke the quasi-paternal relationship between these allies. Pallas, Evander's son, became Aeneas's close friend before Turnus killed him in the Latin wars.

Milton begins the next section (24–48) by forcefully reintroducing himself as poet:

> Ergo ego te Cliûs et magni nomine Phoebi
> Manse pater, jubeo longum salvere per aevum
> Missus Hyperboreo juvenis peregrinus ab axe.   (24–26)

[Therefore I, Father Manso, in the name of Clio and great Phoebus, wish you health and long life, I, a young wayfarer, sent from the Hyperborean pole.]

"*Ergo ego* at the beginning of a line," writes Bush, "is an Ovidian mannerism."[14] Stepping into great Ovid's shoes, Milton declares himself a true poet just as he had shortly before in *Ad Patrem:* "Ergo ego jam doctae pars quamlibet ima catervae / Victrices hederas inter, laurosque sedebo" (101–02) ("Therefore I, however humble now among the company of the learned, shall sit in victory among ivy and laurel"). Boldly Milton evokes "the great name of Phoebus," the god who presides over poetry and this poem. For the first time, too, he names his muse. She is Clio, muse of history, as the Renaissance understood it: the recorder of notable and preferably virtuous deeds. Clio preserves in memory the names of the great and perpetuates their fame. She is golden, "aurea Clio" (*Patrem*, 14) because as E. R. Gregory explains, Renaissance etymologists derived her name from the Greek *Kleos,* meaning fame or glory.[15] Because Manso generously sought to rescue his poet friends from oblivion, Milton, in filial charity and communal solidarity, will do the same for him, young wayfarer though he is. He offers himself as a kind of foster-son to Manso, whom he addresses as "pater." This suggestion of a father-son relationship allows Milton to combine open respect and even love with subterranean rivalry, as a new-generation poet who is about to supersede, even as he praises and echoes, the old.

Virtuous Manso, Milton is confident, will not reject his offer:

> Nec tu longinquam bonus aspernabere musam,
> Quae nuper gelidâ vix enutrita sub Arcto
> Imprudens Italas ausa est volitare per urbes.   (27–29)

[Nor will you, who are good, despise a foreign Muse, who though scarcely nourished under the frozen Bear, has recently dared to make her rash flight through the cities of Italy.]

At first, one may see in this image a recollection of the allusion with which Milton closed *Ad Patrem,* when he compared his decision to embrace poetry to the rash determination of Phaethon in defiance of his father's advice. But a Virgilian echo suggests a further possibility. "Volitare per urbes" recalls "volitans iam Fama per urbes" (*Aeneid* VII, 104), as flying fame bears through the Italian cities the news proclaimed by an oracle that Latinus' daughter Lavinia will marry a noble stranger. Ariosto and other Italian poets had already echoed the phrase.[16] After all, Milton is performing a mission on behalf of Manso's fame, and his almost uncontrolled flight through Italy suggests not only youth and inexperience (again the modesty topos) but also the typically erratic flight of the untrustworthy goddess. As he was later to write in *Samson Agonistes,* Fame "with contrary blast proclaims most deeds, / On both his wings, one black, th' other white, / Bears greatest names in his wild aerie flight" (972–74).

Though the north is dim and shadowed, a parody of the Italian viewpoint, Milton too has heard swans singing on the silvery Thames. These swans, connected as editors note by a chain of references to Chaucer and Spenser, also recall the traditional iconographical link with Clio as a preserver of noble deeds.[17] And Virgil's promise in Eclogue IX, 27–29, typifies a related convention: "Vare, tuum nomen, superet modo Mantua nobis . . . / cantantes sublime ferent ad sidera cycni" ("Varus, thy name, let but Mantua be spared us . . . singing swans shall bear aloft to the stars"). So dark and cold is the England Milton portrays — lit only by northern constellations and relieved only by the silver of the Thames — that one might almost mistake it for Orcus or Hades. Yet, Milton insists, even in that frozen region there are worshippers of Phoebus. Punning etymologically, he suggests that no race can be wholly uncultivated, "incultum," if it is "sulcata" or furrowed by the Triones, the Plowing Oxen (Ursa Major). Fusing Herodotus with Callimachus, Milton recalls tales of northern maidens who made their way to Delos bearing gifts for Apollo. He embellishes the picture with further verbal echoes. The gifts for Phoebus include

> Flaventes spicas, et lutea mala canistris,
> Halantemque crocum (perhibet nisi vana vetustas).   (39–40)

[Golden ears of corn, baskets of yellow apples, the fragrant crocus, unless antiquity testifies in vain.]

The antique witness of which Milton speaks, and which he intends Manso to recall, includes the poems of Ovid and Virgil. Ovid too ends a line with "mala canistris" (*Metamorphoses* VIII, 675), when he describes the food set out by Baucis and Philemon for their divine guests, Jupiter and Mercury. In the *Georgics*, Virgil describes how to make a garden attractive to wild bees by inviting them with the flowers of fragrant crocuses: "invitent croceis halantes floribus horti" (4.109). Milton's lines not only shine with a beauty and a tranquility partly their own and partly borrowed from his sources, but by referring in the usual indirect way of this poem to Baucis and Philemon they powerfully recall themes of hospitality, piety, and recognition of disguised merit. Thus they also recall Manso's analogous percipience and the kind offices that he performed for Tasso and Marino and (what has to be suggested in such indirect depths but is consistent with the surface tenor of the passage) Milton's hope that Manso will recognize *him* for what he is. Meanwhile the indirect evocation of Virgil's bees, which are the climactic and transcendent symbol of *Georgics* IV, recalls the miraculous renewal and rebirth of the hive and of a world torn by storm, death, and civil feud. Just so the grain, the fruit, the flowers shine against the darkness and obscurity of the north, light and life emerging from darkness and oblivion, crops springing up from the culture of the *Triones*. This is not the last adumbration we shall see in *Mansus* of the resurrection theme.

Milton begins the next section (49–69) with Virgil's often-echoed words, "Fortunate senex" (49) ("fortunate old man"). The phrase sets the tone for a passage that, after some initial compliments, becomes a lovely pastoral in the midst of exile and hard georgic labor, suggesting poetic ease, darkened by tragedy, in the midst of life's long labors. The phrase calls up Roman and Stoic views still current in Milton's day of the happy man who lives in simple content on his country farm.[18] Wherever the "decus, et nomen" ("the name and fame") of Tasso and Marino may spread, there too Manso will be known. One suspects some irony in Milton's phrase, perhaps at the expense of this sort of worldly reputation, since it was first put by Virgil into the mouth of lying Sinon as he worms his way into the Trojans' confidence (*Aeneid* II, 89) — and it will reappear in Milton's poem on the notorious Salmasius.[19] Manso will live, too, in all men's mouths: "Tu quoque in ora frequens venies plausumque virorum" (52). Virgil is again evoked: "qua me quoque possim / tollere humo victorque virum volitare per ora" (*Georgics* III, 8–9) ("I must essay a path whereby I, too, may rise from earth and fly victorious on the lips of men"). I think Milton was to remember the immediately following lines in the invocation to *Paradise Lost:* "primus ego in patriam mecum, modo vita supersit, / Aonio rediens deducam vertice Musas" ("I first, if life but remain, will return to my country, bringing the Muses with me in triumph from the Aonian peak"). Virgil's vow certainly is relevant to Milton's situation in Naples, at a point in his career and with ambitions similar to Virgil's.[20] But the solemn note is undercut, since Milton echoes even more closely the disingenuous line "et venies tu quoque in ore virum" from an elegy of Propertius (3.9.32), a poet-patron poem in which the Roman elegist promises Maecenas that he will rise from the elegiac to the heroic if, as he does not expect, his patron first transforms himself into a proper hero to be written about. Thus he, and by implication Milton, turns the tables on his patronizing patron.

Because of his connection with Tasso and Marino, Manso will take flight, live in fame, and enjoy with them a traditional classical apotheosis: "Et parili carpes iter immortale volatu" (53) ("and with a like flight you will take the immortal way"). This classical and worldly fame, while not of a kind to be condemned, is nevertheless something about which Milton had already expressed reservations, calling the desire for it that he found in himself "That last infirmity of Noble mind." The irony implied by his allusions to Sinon and Propertius suggests a similar attitude now. We may note what kind of immortality Milton assigns to Manso here — purely classical and literary — because it will prove relevant to the ending of the poem. Also relevant to that ending is "plausumque" (52), which Milton inserts into his echo: Manso will live in men's applause as well as their mouths.

Milton's next lines are by far the most complex and subtle thus far in their use of classical allusion. They evoke a whole constellation of interlinked myths, echoing and supporting one another with true Miltonic resonance. Milton begins, as he often will in the major poems, with a simple analogy. Tasso and Marino preferred Manso's simple country farm (an image anticipated by "Fortunate senex") to association with great or princely patrons, just as Apollo, god of poets, preferred the simple cave of Chiron to King Admetus' house, even though Hercules himself had not long before deigned to be a guest there:

> Dicetur tum sponte tuos habitâsse penates
> Cynthius, et famulas venisse ad limina Musas:
> At non sponte domum tamen idem, et regis adivit
> Rura Pheretiadae coelo fugitivus Apollo;
> Ille licet magnum Alciden susceperat hospes;
> Tantùm ubi clamosos placuit vitare bubulcos,
> Nobile mansueti cessit Chironis in antrum,
> Irriguos inter saltus frondosaque tecta
> Peneium prope rivum: ibi saepe sub ilice nigrâ
> Ad citharae strepitum blandâ prece victus amici
> Exilii duros lenibat voce labores.   (54–64)

[It will be said that, of his own free will, Cynthius (Apollo) dwelt in your house and that the Muses were the attendants at your threshold. But not willingly did that same Apollo, a fugitive from heaven, come to the farmhouse of King Admetus, though he had received the great Alcides as his guest. When he wished to avoid the clamorous men who plow with oxen, he retreated to the celebrated cave of gentle Chiron, among pastures watered and leafy-roofed, beside the river Peneus. There, often, under a dark ilex, overcome by his friend's soft pleas, he would ease the hard labors of exile by singing to the sound of the cithara.]

Among several possible sources for Apollo's title, Cynthius, the most likely is Virgil's sixth Eclogue (3), the phrases of which echo so often through *Mansus*. In Virgil's poem a group of rural lads find Silenus sleeping in a cave, his veins swollen with yesterday's wine. Unexpectedly he wakens and sings a song appropriate to Apollo himself. He describes the creation of the world, the early myths, the story of Pasiphae's longing for the snowy bull, who rests "ilice sub nigra" (54) ("under a dark ilex"), suggesting Milton's "sub ilice nigrâ" (62). He sings of the Hesperidean maidens and the sisters of Phaethon, then (in words Milton echoed earlier) of Gallus, wandering by the Permessus, being greeted by the Apollonian chorus. Linus, shepherd of immortal song, has an Orphean voice that can "draw the unyielding ash-trees down the mountain-sides" ("cantando rigidas deducere montibus ornos," 71), an image Milton picks up as he describes Apollo's song: "Emotaeque suis properant de collibus orni" (68) ("the trees were moved and hastened down from their hills"). Virgil's poem, which pictures a powerful song emerging from an unlikely mouth, is partly about the transmission of poetry from one poet to the next. The ultimate source is Apollo: "Omnia quae Phoebo quondam meditante beatus / audiit Eurotas iussitque ediscere laurus, / ille canit" (82–84) ("All the songs that of old Phoebus rehearsed, while happy Eurotas listened and bade his laurels learn by heart — these Silenus sings"). Milton too has heard and made use of old songs.

The other Roman poet behind Milton's lines is Ovid. He too has a dark ilex, under which Phoebian Byblis, granddaughter of the god, was changed to a weeping fountain (*Met.* IX, 663–65). And while Chiron's cave was, as Milton says, well known, Ovid ended a line with the identical words: "Chironis in antrum" (*Met.* II, 630). A few lines later, we find phrases Milton used to describe the relationship between Manso and Marino. Apollo, having rescued his son Aesculapius from the burning body of his mother Coronis, has brought the child to Chiron for fostering. "Semifer interea divinae stirpis alumno / laetus erat mixtoque oneri gaudebat honore" (II, 633–34) ("Meantime the Centaur was rejoicing in his foster-child of heavenly stock, glad at the honour which the task brought with it"). Milton has "se gaudet alumnum" (10). Ovid also tells

of Apollo's exile from heaven, condemned to a year's labor as Admetus'
herdsman. He was punished for killing the maker of Zeus's thunderbolts;
the quarrel originated, of course, when Zeus killed Aesculapius, snatched
from death miraculously at his birth, for the crime of raising a mortal
man from the dead. So Apollo, serving out his exile for avenging the death
of his son Aesculapius, visits Chiron the foster-father of Aesculapius. And
he comes from the house of Admetus, where, as editors note, Milton
changed the order of the original myths to make Hercules a prior visitor.
There, no doubt, Apollo heard much about another resurrection, since
Hercules had raised Alcestis from the dead not long before and returned
her to Admetus. Ovid writes that, when Apollo brought Aesculapius to
Chiron, the centaur's daughter entered a prophetic trance, first predicting the death of the child for daring to give life a second time in scorn
of the gods, then predicting the end of her father Chiron, who, though
he has been gifted by the gods with immortality, will accidentally be shot
by Hercules with a poisoned arrow and beg the Fates for death (*Met.*
II, 633–75).

In an early poem, *In Obitum Procancellarii Medici*, Milton brought
together all the figures evoked in *Mansus* to illustrate the ineluctability
of death:

> Si destinatam pellere dextera
> Mortem valeret, non ferus Hercules
>   Nessi venenatus cruore
>   Aemathiâ jacuisset Oetâ . . .
>
>   . . . .
>
> Laesisset et nec te Philyreie
> Sagitta echidnae perlita sanguine,
>   Nec tela te fulmenque avitum
>   Caese puer genetricis alvo.   (9–12, 25–28)

[If man's right arm had power to repel fated death, fierce Hercules would not
have been laid low on Aemathian Oeta, poisoned by the blood of Nessus, . . .
nor would the arrow smeared with serpent's blood have stricken you, Philyra's
Son (Chiron); nor would you have been struck by the bolts and fire of your grand-
father, O boy cut from your mother's womb (Aesculapius).]

The interlinked pattern of deaths, resurrections, and deaths, augmented
by Milton's reversal of the traditional time-scheme, too obviously bears
upon the theme of death and immortality in *Mansus* to be accidental. The
mysteries of death and resurrection, loss and sympathy on which this passage touches by allusion cannot be simply paraphrased. But one implication is that Milton shares Manso's sorrow for his dead poet-sons, just as

Apollo and Chiron are linked by mutual grief for their lost son Aescu-lapius. Another is that restoration to life in this world or perpetuation in it for oneself or one's loved ones, though we may dearly long for it, is not natural and may if pursued too far even be impious. And Christian resurrection, though not immediately at issue at this point in the poem, as Sir Thomas Browne points out, "makes a folly of posthumous memory."

Apollo, exiled from heaven and undergoing hard georgic labors, ap-proximates fallen man in the Christian scheme of things. The Virgilian *duros labores (Aeneid* VI, 437; VIII, 291), which became a stock Roman value, are both the Christian man's task in life and his postlapsarian pun-ishment. So Lancelot Andrewes, in the apotheosis of Milton's *Elegy III,* is welcomed into heaven with the promise that he may now rest from hard labor: "Semper ab hinc duro, nate, labore vaca" (64). When Apollo pauses at the urging of his friend amid these labors, much as Milton would do with Edward Lawrence or Cyriack Skinner, the sound of his cithara, "Ad citharae strepitum" (63), recalls the courtiers of Alcinous, who relax "ad strepitum citharae" (1.2.31) in Horace's epistle urging a young friend to be a true Roman and work. William A. Sessions shows how the Vir-gilian ideal of long labors was taken up by Spenser as an English Prot-estant;[21] Milton's life and art fall into the same Classical-Christian tra-dition. But Milton, unlike Horace and like Homer, approved of such moments of pastoral ease, provided they were not unduly extended. And paradoxically, since his vocation is poetry, Milton's work and his ease are, like Apollo's (and Colin Clout's), not exclusive alternatives but two as-pects of the same central activity, represented in *Mansus* both by the georgic Apollo laboring among the *clamosi bubulci* and by the pastoral Apollo lightening the hard labors of exile by his song.

Behind Ovid's versions of the myths lies Pindar, whose work Milton undoubtedly knew well. The Pythian odes are permeated with the fig-ures and myths that Milton evokes in this passage. Pythia 3 tells the story of Aesculapius at length: his birth, his fostering by Chiron, his healing deeds, and his death at the hands of Zeus for a crime of which both Mil-ton and Manso would have disapproved: perverting his life-giving voca-tion for material gain, taking money to raise the dead. "Dear soul of mine," Pindar concludes from Aesculapius' fate, "never urge a life beyond / mor-tality, but work the means at hand to the end."[22] Men's lives are brief. "In the glory of poetry achievement of men / blossoms long; but of that the accomplishment is given to few." Again and again Pindar presents Chiron as a famous foster-father. One well-known son was Jason, cele-brated in Pythia 4. Appearing unknown before the pretenders to his throne, Jason introduces himself: "I think I can carry Chiron's discipline.

For I come from his cave / . . . where the Centaur's stainless daughters
brought me to manhood." Chiron fostered Achilles too and trained him
especially to honor the gods and his parents (Pythia 6). In Pythia 9, Pindar tells how Chiron and Apollo met at Chiron's cave to discuss Apollo's
love for Kyrene. In Nemea 3, he moves without transition from the deeds
of Hercules to Chiron's cave, where he praises the Centaur for training
his foster-sons so well: Jason, the "deeply wise," Aesculapius, whom he
raises in the "gentle-handed way of healing," and Achilles, whom he nurses
up to manhood and great deeds.

How much of this background did Milton intend Manso or other
readers to recall? One cannot be sure. Almost certainly he expected Manso
to recognize the verbal echoes of Latin poems thoroughly familiar to them
both (Milton may have worked from memory) and to recall the contexts.
Almost certainly he expected him to wonder (as editors have) why Milton varied the myth and made Hercules the earlier visitor — which might
have suggested the answer proposed here. Almost certainly he expected
him to recall that Hercules, Apollo, Admetus, Aesculapius, and Chiron
were interrelated figures whose paths crossed and touched recurrently
on the themes with which *Mansus* is pervasively concerned: hospitality,
fathers who foster sons and teach them Apollonian ways, fathers who
lose their sons to death, resurrection from death either heroic or impious,
and above all man's grief for lost loved ones and his longing to escape
death and oblivion, those dark and all-devouring ends to which, in the
classical view of things, he and his friends are inevitably fated. Men's lives
are brief, says Pindar; all, even the greatest, must descend to Orcus, says
Horace; only a lucky few may hope even to preserve their names and deeds
in poetry.

Of course, Milton knew of a Christian solution: resurrection and eternal life. But nowhere in *Mansus* does he comfort the old man with that
Christian consolation for himself or his two dead friends. There are urns,
busts, biographies, poems to memorialize the dead, but no mention of
heaven. The omission, unusual in even the most classical of Milton's
poems, is very likely due to the sectarian gulf that separated him from
Manso and his friends. Not that he begrudged them their prospect of
heaven: nothing in the tone of the poem suggests that. But the matter
of heavenly reward is one that, in the circumstances, calls for tactful silence. It is not for Protestant Milton to assure Catholic Manso of his salvation, though he may reveal his sympathy in other ways.

The last section of *Mansus* (70–100) falls into three parts. First Milton addresses Manso, "Diis dilecte senex" (70) ("Old man, loved by the

gods!"). Jupiter, Phoebus, and Mercury must have presided over his birth, for no one not dear to the gods from birth could have favored a great poet (72–73). The verb, *favere*, gives Manso credit for helping his friends; but the whole passage suggests that he was lucky to have had the opportunity of doing so.[23] Because he did, he enjoys a green and flourishing old age. He has added years to his life like Aeson, "Aesonios lucratur vivida fusos," and he preserves the honors of his brow unfallen, "Nondum deciduos servans tibi frontis honores" (75–76). Milton's final compliments, while they seem a logical conclusion to his encomium, raise several difficulties when put into context. In the *Metamorphoses*, Ovid tells how Medea restored youth to the dying Aeson, father of her husband Jason. Moved by Jason's pious offer to give up a portion of his own life for his father, Medea restores the old man in a metamorphosis that can only be called grotesque and unnatural and that amply confirms her reputation as a witch (VII, 159–293; and note the sequel, 294–349). Thus we have yet another ironic allusion to the unnatural prolongation of life.

Milton's reference to the unfallen honors of Manso's brow has called up the editorial annotation that he was, in fact, bald. Did Milton know that Manso wore a wig, which, we are told, he would good-humoredly put off and on for the amusement of his fellow members of the Society of the Blessed Virgin?[24] If he did, he phrased this, his last compliment to his benefactor, in such a way that no one would ever be sure; but one may hardly doubt that the old man did a double-take when he read these words; and, if Milton's English audience of 1645 could not appreciate the joke, it has been in the mouths of editors ever since Masson revived it. I do not mean to distort the poem; there is a subtle undercurrent of amusing grotesquerie, a shared joke, a continuation of the ironic allusions directed against the all-too-human desire to perpetuate in this world the life and fame of oneself and one's friends that Milton shared with Manso, all of which modifies but does not predominate over the major tone of genuine admiration and praise. This divided tone becomes more and more insistent and inescapable as *Mansus* moves toward its remarkable conclusion.

In the middle of the last section, Milton turns from Manso to himself. "O mihi si mea sors talem concedat amicum / Phoebaeos decorâsse viros qui tam bene nôrit" (78–79) ("O, if only my lot might concede such a friend to me, a friend who would understand how to honor Phoebean men!"). Milton's wish seems heartfelt. A natural reaction of his readers has been to respond: but you have such a friend, Charles Diodati; and then to wonder whether Milton had yet heard the grim news of Diodati's recent death back in England.[25] Probably not, I would guess, because the issue is digressive. Milton genuinely wishes for an understanding friend who will honor him as a poet, but he is thinking more in terms of and still addressing Manso rather than Diodati. (Though in *Epitaphium Damonis* the two are connected in Milton's thoughts.) When he himself comes to die, at some distant date, he wants to die like Tasso or Marino, old, successful, full of honors, and with someone like Manso to perform his last offices. But, pleasant as it may be to dwell for a moment on such a false surmise, Milton knows that Father Manso could never perform such a role for him. If he had such a Maecenian friend, he could complete his Virgilian course and crown his career with a British *Aeneid*, in which he might celebrate Arthur waging war beneath the earth and shattering the Saxon phalanxes under the British Mars: "Frangam Saxonicas Britonum sub Marte phalanges" (84). Milton did not, of course, need a Manso for financial support;[26] rather he longs for a literary confidant and a source of human encouragement in the long, strenuous path he has chosen.

Toward his conclusion, as Milton imagines himself dying under the kind ministrations of this imagined friend and going up to heaven, he seems to forget Manso as subject and audience and almost to lose control of his poem. "The flaws in 'Mansus,'" Condee writes, "lie in the incredible self-admiration Milton shows in the closing lines." "It would be difficult to defend [their] tone . . . especially the last line where Milton is so exalted by his own apotheosis that he bursts into applause for himself."[27] Bush, perhaps preferring to think that Milton could not have meant what he seems literally to say, loosely translates "plaudam mihi" (100) ("I shall applaud myself") as "I . . . shall know myself blessed."[28] But, though objectionable, the phrase seems clear. Let us consider how Milton leads up to it:

> Tandem ubi non tacitae permensus tempora vitae,
> Annorumque satur cineri sua jura relinquam,
> Ille mihi lecto madidis astaret ocellis,
> Astanti sat erit si dicam sim tibi curae;
> Ille meos artus liventi morte solutos
> Curaret parvâ componi molliter urnâ.
> Forsitan et nostros ducat de marmore vultus,
> Nectens aut Paphiâ myrti aut Parnasside lauri
> Fronde comas, at ego securâ pace quiescam.
> Tum quoque, si qua fides, si praemia certa bonorum,
> Ipse ego caelicolûm semotus in aethera divûm,
> Quò labor et mens pura vehunt, atque ignea virtus

Secreti haec aliquâ mundi de parte videbo
(Quantum fata sinunt) et totâ mente serenùm
Ridens purpureo suffundar lumine vultus
Et simul aethereo plaudam mihi laetus Olympo.   (85–100)

[When, at last, having passed through the full span of a life not silent, full of years, I shall leave to the ashes their rights, that friend would stand with flowing eyes beside my bed; it would be enough if I say to him, "Take me into your care." He would see that my limbs, slackened in livid death, were softly placed in a little urn. Perhaps he would fashion my countenance in marble and wreathe my locks with Paphian myrtle and Parnassian laurel; but I should rest in secure peace. Then too, if there is such a thing as faith, if the rewards of goodness are certain, I myself, withdrawn to the heavens of the gods on high, whither toil and a pure mind and fiery virtue lead, from some part of that secret world shall see (what is happening) here (so far as Fate permits) and with all my soul serene, smiling, with a face suffused with rosy light, and joyful, I shall applaud myself on ethereal Olympus.]

One solution to the problem is that there are at least two Miltons here. One dies, lies quietly in his urn, and is commemorated in marble: he is the classical Milton. The other, "ipse ego," ascends to heaven and looks down: he is the Christian Milton. Perhaps this second Milton, at once blushing and suffused with beatific charity, applauds the first. If he is not to gain Manso's "plausum virorum" (52) at least he can applaud himself from the balcony. And if we remember that Manso is Milton's audience, the comedy assumes an added dimension. Milton will not venture to describe the Christian fates of Tasso, Marino, or Manso, but he teases the old man by showing himself, the Protestant Milton, rising at once to heaven, whence he observes from the divine comic perspective earthly events, with a smile from more than the vantage of a marble bust or the bronze one from which Marino smiles (16). At last Christian immortality is allowed into the poem, and naturally it subsumes and transcends any possible immortality that might be achieved on earth, whether through monuments, or in the minds and mouths of men, or even by means of the long perpetuating power of poetry itself. A precedent for the comic last line is the last line of *Elegy III* on the death of Lancelot Andrewes, which in the midst of beatific bliss echoes a risqué Ovidian elegy (*Amores*, 1.5.26):[29] "Talia contingant somni saepe mihi" ("may such dreams often be my lot").

To say that the last line may be meant to amuse, and more specifically to tease the Catholic Manso, is not to say that Milton's whole conclusion is parodic. Like such contemporaries as Donne and Marvell, Milton could be both comic and serious at once. His "little urn" (90) appropriately recalls the little urn that Ovid imagines for himself when he anticipates death in his sad exile at Pontus (*Tristia*, 3.3.65). "Tempora vitae" (85) echoes the same phrase (also at line-end) in *Metamorphoses* III, 469. Narcissus, who has fallen in love with his reflection, is dying in that lonely company: a situation that reflects back complexly on Milton's. He too is alone save for his imaginary friend, but his allusion suggests that, unlike Narcissus, he can view his longing with some objectivity. When Milton suggests that his friend might fashion his countenance in marble, however, "nostros ducat de marmore vultus" (91), his implications are more surprising. He echoes what may be the best-known passage in the *Aeneid:* "excudent alii spirantia mollius aera, / (credo equidem), vivos ducent de marmore voltus" (VI, 847–48) ("Others, I doubt not, shall beat out the breathing bronze with softer lines; shall from marble draw forth the features of life"), but the duty of Romans (Anchises tells Aeneas in the underworld) is to rule the world, to aid the humble, and to war down the proud, "debellare superbos" (853). Editors note the immediate echo of line 848, but the breathing bronze of 847 also recalls Marino's bust. The allusion suggests once again that Milton does not give to earthly fame so much weight as first appears. Even on earth, he implies, let others fuss with monuments and wreaths, but he has more important concerns.

More echoes continue to undermine the solemnity. The pompous "Fronde comas" (93) echoes a Horatian epistle that describes the rise in Rome of a multitude of poetasters: "pueri patresque severi / fronde comas vincti cenant et carmina dictant" (2.1.109–10) ("boys and severe fathers alike, locks bound with leaves, dine and recite their verses"). The phrase, which like Horace's boldly begins its line, implies its own deflation, as its satire falls comically and impartially both on Father Manso and young Milton his would-be foster-son. "Si qua fides" is a stock phrase, but the accompanying "si praemia certa bonorum" (94) recalls both Aeneas' unfortunate oath to Dido that, if the gods regard goodness, she will have her reward (I, 603–05) and (yet once more) the protesting Sinon, who begs the Trojans by all the gods to trust him (II, 142–44). While Milton's protestations are just (who can disagree that faith, hard work, and goodness should lead to heaven?) they also evoke a long tradition of oaths that (as Gertrude said of the Player Queen) protest too much.

"Quantum fata sinunt," Milton's comment that he will look down from heaven "if fate permits," at first reminded me of Eve's similar remark when she urges Adam to eat the fruit quickly before fate leaves him irrevocably behind in the race up to godhood (*PL* IX, 883–85). But the immediate source (a rare instance of a neoclassical parallel not first suggested by the classics) is Vida's renowned *De Arte Poetica*. Vida is giving advice especially relevant to *Mansus:* if one author surpasses all others, then imitate him "so far as the fates will allow and Apollo grants you his favor" ("Quantum fata sinunt, et non aversus Apollo," 3.192). The next lines advise: "Haud tamen interea reliquûm explorare labores / Abstiteris vatum moneo, suspectaque dicta / Sublegere, et variam ex cunctis abducere gazam" ("I should scarcely discourage you, however, from exploring at the same time the productions of the rest of the poets and, by collecting noteworthy phrases from their works, drawing from all authors a diverse treasure").[30] Thus the allusion calls attention reflexively to the poem's allusiveness and, like the parenthesis in line 40, lightly jogs the reader's elbow.

Milton's last echo of the classics is the troublesome "plaudam mihi." He draws it from a Horatian satire, and its context is such as to puncture and amusingly counterpoint his surface solemnity:

> ut quidam memoratur Athenis
> sordidus ac dives, populi contemnere voces
> sic solitus: "Populus me sibilat, at mihi plaudo
> ipse domi, simul ac nummos contemplor in arca."   (1.1.64–67)

[As they tell of a stingy rich man of Athens, who, thus solitary, condemned the people's talk: "The people hiss me, but I applaud myself at home as soon as I contemplate the coins in my strongbox."]

Milton's phrase, grotesque to begin with, becomes impossible to take at face value, as exiled Ovid and lonely Narcissus are, so to say, metamorphosed into an isolated miser. And the turn in the comedy toward self-mockery again ensures that the joke is not wholly at Manso's expense, but is to be shared. If the closing structure of *Mansus* may be said to eclipse the worldly fame gained by Manso and his poet friends in the contrasting radiance of Milton's imagined Christian apotheosis, any resulting impression that Milton considers himself holier than his audience is negated by the increasingly outrageous implications of his self-referential allusions.

To sum up, if we consider what we know about Milton's relationship with Manso, in his words and Manso's little distich; if we consider whom Milton addresses throughout *Mansus* as his subject and especially as his audience; and if we look at the cumulative evidence of multiple classical allusions in the light of their original contexts—then, I think, we may conclude that *Mansus* is richer and more subtle than has usually been thought, at once more occasional and more universal. A worthy example of Milton's mature work, one of three major Latin poems written during a period in which he was proposing to turn from the pastoral and the elegiac to the heroic, it touches deeply on many serious philosophical themes having to do with poetry as a communal, restorative, and perpetuating activity, with friendship, with fatherhood and sonship, with religion and sectarianism, with life, death, and immortality. At the same time, Milton further complicates and modifies his tone by introducing clusters of underground grotesque and comic allusions. Some are directed toward Manso and repay him with interest in his own coin, turning upside down the father-son motif that Manso's own distich suggests, others toward himself and puncture what might otherwise be unbearably pretentious — but without detracting in the least from the poem's ultimate seriousness.

For the most part, the more deeply serious and even tragic allusions are classical in spirit as well as source and concern man's doomed state, his condition in this world as *pulvis et umbra,* as a short-lived creature who loves what fades and can hope for little more than the ease art gives to life or immortality for his deeds through monuments or, more rarely, poetry. In this world efforts by even the greatest men to escape death or to rescue others from it prove vain, though some comfort as well as pain may be found in the communal and filial-paternal bonds of poetry. For the most part, the comic allusions, though they too refer to classical sources, stem from a Christian spirit which, because it cheerfully hopes for a life beyond life, need care less about the forms of earthly fame. Such a Christian confidence, though it underlies the poem, is forbidden more direct expression by circumstances; so it issues obliquely, metamorphosed as a further source of comedy, less golden but still essentially friendly in its spirit of shared play, that emerges from the nervous contretemps of sectarian difference.

One may speculate that the doubleness of Milton's classical allusions is related to the doubleness of his occasional purpose: to meet Manso's offered challenge with a challenge of his own, yet at the same time to seek by means of his demonstrated sympathy not a break but a recognition and perhaps a kind of filial union. Since the human needs and the psychological patterns involved in this occasional encounter are in themselves universal, it may be judged that the specific occasion, as is so often the case with Milton, deepened and empowered rather than detracted from the universality of his poem. From a polemical or ideological perspective, on the level of church against church, Milton viewed the Protestant-Catholic gulf with utmost seriousness, but on a personal level, in an epistle, this split might dwindle to a petty impediment or even, transformed into comedy, become a potential means of reconciliation.[31]

After all, taken together, all Milton's allusions, whether seriously resonant or discrepantly comic, are possible only because he and Manso (with
any wider audience looking over their shoulders), if they cannot fully share
the religion they hold in common, yet can share a tacit bridging charity
and a love for humanistic endeavor both committed and urbane.

New York University

NOTES

1. I cite Milton's Latin poems from CM; translations of *Mansus* and his other poems
are mine unless otherwise noted.

2. William Riley Parker, *Milton: A Biography* (Oxford, 1968), II, p. 827, n. 34.

3. "Written Encomiums," CM III, p. 236; the Salzilli poems, see Bush, *Variorum*,
p. 263.

4. John Arthos, *Milton and the Italian Cities* (London, 1968), p. 102.

5. *Defensio Secunda;* CM VIII, p. 125.

6. CM I, p. 154.

7. Gregory's pun took on proverbial force; for an early version see Paulus Diaconus,
S. *Gregorii Magni Vita, Patrologia Latina,* ed. Jean-Paul Migne, LXXV, 50, which Sr.
M. Christopher Pecheux kindly located for me. Milton, citing Malmesbury and Bede, re-
tells the story in *History of Britain;* CM X, pp. 142–43.

8. Parker, *Milton,* I, p. 175.

9. William Kennedy, *Rhetorical Norms in Renaissance Literature* (New Haven,
1978), and his "The Audiences of *Ad Patrem*," in this volume.

10. Bush, *Variorum,* p. 268; Ralph Waterbury Condee, "'Mansus' and the Panegyric Tradition," *Structure in Milton's Poetry* (University Park, Pa., 1974), pp. 85–103.

11. Text and translation are from the Loeb edition of Ovid, ed. Frank Justus Miller.
I also use Loeb for Virgil (ed. H. R. Fairclough) and Horace's odes (ed. C. E. Bennett).
For Horace's satires and epistles I use the edition of Charles E. Bennett and John C. Rolfe
(Allyn and Bacon, 1949), my translations. Propertius is from *Elegies, Book III,* ed. W. A.
Camps (Cambridge, 1966).

12. Condee, "Panegyric Tradition," pp. 89–95.

13. See Bush's note on *Prod. Bomb.* 7; *Variorum,* p. 144. Needless to say, the present essay relies heavily on many parallels Bush cites.

14. Bush, *Variorum,* p. 252.

15. E. R. Gregory, "Three Muses and a Poet: A Perspective on Milton's Epic Thought,"
in *Milton Studies,* X, ed. James D. Simmonds (Pittsburgh, 1977), p. 41.

16. Bush, *Variorum,* p. 273.

17. Gregory, "Three Muses," p. 45.

18. On this tradition, see Maren-Sofie Røstvig, *The Happy Man* (Oslo, 1954).

19. In the *Defensio Secunda;* CM VIII, p. 56.

20. Bush does not note the further parallel in Virgil's line 8 (tu quoque – me quoque)
nor the victorious upward flight in Virgil's line 9 and *Mans.,* 53.

21. "Spenser's Georgics," *ELR,* 10 (1980), 202–38. See also Anthony Low, "Milton,

Paradise Regained, and Georgic," *PMLA*, 98 (1983), 152–69, written and published after this essay was completed, and *Work and Poetry*, forthcoming.

22. Translations by Richard Lattimore, *The Odes of Pindar* (Chicago, 1947).

23. Condee, "Panegyric Tradition," pp. 95–97.

24. David Masson, *The Life of John Milton* (London, 1859–80), III, p. 351; cited by Bush, *Variorum*, p. 278.

25. See Parker, Clavering, Shawcross, as cited in Bush, *Variorum*, p. 280.

26. Milton often speaks disparagingly of patrons, and nowhere else mentions Maecenas or Gallus.

27. Condee, "Panegyric Tradition," pp. 99–100.

28. Douglas Bush, ed., *The Complete Poetical Works of John Milton* (Boston, 1965), p. 155.

29. On *Elegy III* and double entendre by allusion, see Edward LeComte, "Sly Milton," *Greyfriar*, 19 (1978), 3–7.

30. Text and translation from *The De Arte Poetica of Marco Girolomo Vida*, ed. Ralph G. Williams (New York, 1976), pp. 96–97.

31. The potential for conflict between public beliefs and private friendship is well illustrated by letters between Milton and Carlo Dati, whose acquaintance Milton made during his visit to Florence. In 1647, Milton writes Dati that the "turbulent state of our Britain" has left him little time for "literary leisure." Still, he would have sent his poems to his "friends in Florence, to whose opinions I attach very much value," but some were in English and others, though in Latin, might "on account of the rather harsh sayings against the Pope of Rome . . . not be quite agreeable to your ears." Nevertheless, since Dati has asked, Milton will send them, hoping Dati will excuse him to his other friends in Florence "whenever I may be speaking of your religion in our peculiar way" (CM XII, p. 51; *Familiar Letter* 10, 21 April 1647). Dati replies, in a long, friendly letter filled with the gossip of classical erudition: "I am anxiously awaiting your poems in which I believe that I shall be afforded a large field for admiration of the fineness of your wit, except however in those which are in dispraise of my religion, which although offered by the lips of a friend, may indeed be excused, but not applauded. These will not be however an obstacle to my reception of the others" (CM XII, p. 311; Correspondence, Dati to Milton, 1 Nov. 1647). One may see how common love of the classics and of literature came to the aid of friendship.

TONGUES OF MEN AND ANGELS:
AD LEONORAM ROMAE CANENTEM

Diane Kelsey McColley

"THE PEOPLE have a general sense of the loss of Paradise," Milton is alleged to have said, "but not an equal gust for the regaining of it."[1] However apocryphal, the comment addresses an attitude that Milton challenged whenever he set pen to paper. "Gust" suggests taste, foretaste, trial, relish, zest; it recalls the "gusto di vera beatitudina" of Bembo's prayer to Love in the *Courtier*, which Hoby translates "a smacke of the ryghte blysse."[2] It suggests, too, a rush of wind, and so the insurgent breath of the Spirit who blows where he lists, whose aid and instruction Milton invokes, and whose province is "th' upright heart and pure" (*PL* I, 18).[3] Even though he called his longest poem *Paradise Lost*, the far larger portion devoted to dressing and keeping paradise than to losing it surely serves to create a taste for the regaining of it; his gustiest prose is purgative for the same purpose; and his most occasional poems invite us to savor and use the possibilities of paradisal goodness, not only beyond this world but in it.

The first of Milton's three epigrams to the celebrated Neapolitan singer Leonora Baroni, written probably in 1638 or 1639[4] and published in the *Poemata* of 1645, provides a *figura* of the artist's calling to stir up a gust for paradise. Like most of his poems it contains the germ of epic fruit. It makes dense use of the taste for paradox by which the Latin epigram flexed the wits of Renaissance schoolboys, but it is not an apprentice piece, Milton at thirty having already produced several masterly poems on related themes in his mother tongue and returned to Latin in honor of Roma, Leonora, and the cosmopolitan audience he too addressed.

As is usual with Milton and with epigrams, the compliment to Leonora contains frequent opportunities for interpretive choice, which any translation is bound to diminish. In the following one I have chosen some connotations which some readers may think secondary, yet which Milton as a habitual etymology-rescuer is sure to have included though not necessarily stressed. Three other versions are quoted in full in the notes.[5]

Ad Leonoram Romae Canentem

Angelus unicuique suus (sic credite gentes)
    Obtigit aethereis ales ab ordinibus.
Quid mirum? Leonora tibi si gloria major,
    Nam tua praesentem vox sonat ipsa Deum.
Aut Deus, aut vacui certè mens tertia coeli
    Per tua secretò guttura serpit agens;
Serpit agens, facilisque docet mortalia corda
    Sensim immortali assuescere posse sono.
Quòd si cuncta quidem Deus est, per cunctaque fusus,
    In te unâ loquitur, caetera mutus habet.   (CM I, p. 228)

To Leonora Singing in Rome

An angel protects each person (believe it, ye peoples)
    Heavenly winged from the celestial orders.
What wonder, Leonora, if to you comes greater glory:
    Your voice itself expresses God among us.
God, or at least a third mind leaving heaven
    Steals on his own through your throat and works his way;
Works his way, gently leading mortal hearts
    Sensibly to grow used to immortal sounds.
But if God is really all, and infused through all,
    In you alone he speaks, and keeps the rest in silence.

The epigram has not been much admired. William Cowper declined
to translate it because he found it inferior to the other two.[6] Its liberties
of diction and meter have annoyed strict classicists who wanted Latin
to stay dead, and its theological improbabilities seem to many uncharacteristically suborned to fanciful compliment. Whatever courtly lightness
of largesse appears in its hyperbolism, the matter of the artist's receptiv-
ity to the influx of God was so grave for Milton from first to last that
the poem deserves serious consideration as a part of the development of
his perceptions about inspiration and the right uses of art.

Several English poems had introduced strains that Milton uses Leonora's singing as an occasion to resume. "If such holy Song / Enwrap our
fancy long," he proposes in the Nativity ode, "Time will run back, and
fetch the age of gold"; though he adds that the Babe will have bitter work
to fetch us paradise. *Arcades* and *A Maske* musically set forth true and
false uses of art. In *At a Solemn Musick*, another musical occasion given
universal moment, he asks the "blest pair of *Sirens* . . . Voice, and Vers"
to present to our "high-rais'd phantasie" the "undisturbed Song of pure
concent" which Seraphim, Cherubim, and "just Spirits" forever sing,

>That we on Earth with undiscording voice
>May rightly answer that melodious noise;
>As once we did, till disproportion'd sin
>Jarr'd against natures chime, and with harsh din
>Broke the fair musick that all creatures made
>To their great Lord, whose love their motion sway'd
>In perfet Diapason, whilst they stood
>In first obedience, and their state of good.

Art presents heaven's music to our imaginations to teach us to rejoin it:

>O may we soon again renew that Song,
>And keep in tune with Heav'n, till God ere long
>To his celestial consort us unite,
>To live with him, and sing in endles morn of light.

The "till" is characteristic. Milton does not defer paradise, or enclose it "within." He thinks that we should "renew that Song" and "keep in tune with Heav'n" *soon* — that is, quickly and willingly — and that poetry and music may teach us how. He seems to have felt some pull toward conventional otherworldliness in an early draft that includes the line "snatch us from earth a while,"[7] but rejects the temptation for the wholesome hope "That we on Earth . . . May rightly answer." The "perfet Diapason" of the "state of good" to be regained resounds in *Paradise Lost* when Adam and Eve join all creatures in orisons of thanksgiving and praise.

The epigrammatic handling of the theme in *Ad Leonoram* involves a condensation of opposites of which "unicuique" and "ab ordinibus" provide the initial poles. There is constant play on the relations between singular and cosmic, earthly and celestial, sensible and intelligible beings and doings. Words that integrate contrasts include "angelus" and "gentes"; "praesentem," "secretò," and "sensim"; "mortalia" and "immortali"; "per cuncta" and "in te unâ"; "loquitur" and "mutus habet." At the same time, Milton packs into ten lines a sense of the scale of being and the range of faculties that is typical of paradisal sensibilities: "Deus," "angelus," that puzzling "mens tertia," "gentes," "in te unâ," and the silent but God-filled "caetera"; "mens," "corda," "vox"; "Roma," "coeli," "cuncta": all ring against each other in full diapason.

Unfallen beings in Milton's epics speak this way. Even when single singers, they keep in tune with heaven, holding God, angels, spheres, and all that earth nurtures imaginatively present in each occasional thought. Paradisal tongues, moved by love, constantly acknowledge the relations of all things, and regenerate speech rejoins this "concent." Adam and Eve yet sinless mention God, angels, each other, their children to be, beasts, trees, fruits, flowers, sun, moon, stars, fragrant air, and glistering dew; at their falls the sense of relation vanishes, Adam lets slip his roses and his responsibilities, and Eve "Intent now wholly on her taste, naught else / Regarded" (IX, 786–87).

The all-embracing mode of speech is the touchstone of true tongues and true art inspired by "that eternall Spirit who can enrich with all utterance and knowledge, and sends out his Seraphim with the hallow'd fire of his Altar to touch and purify the lips of whom he pleases" (CM III, p. 241). Leonora's singing, about which the poem says very little, is an example of such art; we accept its divinity on hearsay, but the poet's own language, linking contrasts and ranging the cosmos, embraces the universe and the empyreal heavens in harmonious numbers and returns to the single voice of his *figura* because it is often through single voices that God speaks.

Milton's praise of Leonora, his emphasis on the solo voice, and his theme of accustoming mortal hearts to immortal music fit the manner of Leonora's singing and the kind of music she sang. Warton quotes "M. Maugers . . . at the end of his judicious *Discours sur la Musique d'Italia*" (Paris, 1672):

Leonora has fine parts, and a happy judgement in distinguishing good from bad musick: she understands it perfectly well, and even composes, which makes her absolute mistress of what she sings, and gives her the most exact pronunciation and expression of the sense of the words. . . . She sings with an air of confident and liberal modesty, and with a pleasing gravity. Her voice reaches a large compass of notes, is just, clear, and melodious; and she softens or raises it without constraint or grimace . . . ; her looks have nothing impudent, nor do her gestures betray any thing beyond the reserve of a modest girl.

The ease born of disciplined talent must have moved the young poet who later sought "answerable style" from his "Celestial Patroness, who . . . inspires / Easie my unpremeditated Verse" (IX, 21–24); and the singer's modest and grave demeanor must have appealed to one who thought a poet "ought him selfe to bee a true Poem" and who had forsworn "those authors any where speaking unworthy things of themselves; or unchaste of those names which before they had extoll'd" to prefer above all "the two famous renowners of *Beatrice* and *Laura* who never wrote but honour of them to whom they devote their verse, displaying sublime and pure thoughts, without transgression" (CM III, p. 303). Further, Leonora was primarily a soloist: "She has no need of any person to assist her with theorbo or viol, one of which is required to make her singing complete; for she plays perfectly well herself on both those instruments." When, however, her mother and sister joined her in a concert, M. Maugers adds, their singing and playing "so powerfully captivated my senses, and threw me into such raptures, that I forgot my mortality, *et crus etre deja parmi les anges, jouissant des contentemens des bienheureux.*"⁸ Clearly, Milton had much the same impression.

Another reason for Milton's attention to the solo voice may be the nature of early baroque music, which uses both traditional polyphony and the newer monophonic style. Both the solo voice supported by harmonic accompaniment and the polyphonic interweaving of equal voices offered Milton ways of figuring paradisal "concent," and *Paradise Lost*, in keeping with his doctrine of individual faith and conscience rightly answering heavenly consorts, makes use of both kinds of voicing.⁹ In *Ad Leonoram* the solo voice is so prominent that all else is mute. Yet there is another solo singer present, the poet who celebrates the voice, and the heavenly choirs figure in his song.

A musician, though not a composer in music, Milton incorporates voice and verse in his poem thematically, in a verse about a voice; prosodically, in the metric flexibility of its free elegiac distichs and its abundant use of alliteration and onomatopoeia; and formally in its rhythm of alternation, resolution, and recapitulation. The crux at the repetition of "serpit agens" leads from the singular inspiration of Leonora's singing to its own leading of mortal hearts to immortal sound, and the sense of gentle but active leading is mimicked by the enjambments of the central quatrain in contrast to the end-stopped lines that surround it. The final couplet sums up the unambiguous paradox: God is all things, and is infused through all things, yet speaks through her alone.

The first distich alerts us to the relation of human and divine things never long absent from Milton's utterance:

> Angelus unicuique suus (sic credite gentes)
> Obtigit aethereis ales ab ordinibus.

Although the poem is not about the doctrine of guardian angels, and although as Robert West points out it is not clear that Milton (as distinguished from "gentes") believed that they were individually assigned,¹⁰ the opening lines set the stage by putting us immediately "parmi les anges." By the end of the seventeenth century, the study of angels was becoming sufficiently incompatible with scientific method, and representations of them had become so allegorical and subjective, that subsequent translators and annotators have tended to treat them as mere baroque embellishment. An early nineteenth-century translator paganizes Milton's spirits; David Masson calls his introductory premise "a fancy"; and West cautions that "no more can be made of it than a fanciful compliment to Leonora's voice."[11] Nevertheless, belief in the work of angels as guardians, messengers, and illuminators of the mind was a commonplace taken seriously by angelologists of Milton's time, with copious proofs from Plato, the Scriptures, and the Fathers and Doctors of the Church, even by Protestants who may have found the winged throngs of baroque ceilings excessively decorative. In *Paradise Lost* Adam and Eve are protected (though minimally) and instructed by several angels (though not one apiece), and Satan is offended that God has "Subjected to [Man's] service Angel wings, / And flaming Ministers to watch and tend / Thir earthly Charge" (IX, 155–57).

Angel lore in the first half of the seventeenth century was still as much a branch of natural history and its relation to moral philosophy as the study of herbs, stars, or exotic beasts, though its methods differed. Notable tracts were written about angels, systematically by the Jesuit-trained (though converted) John Salkeld, angelologist to James I; digressively by the playwright Thomas Heywood; and homiletically by Henry Lawrence, the "vertuous Father" of Milton's sonnet and a member of the Puritan parliament, who published his *History of Angells* the same year Milton published the *Poemata*.[12]

On the subject of guardian angels, Salkeld quotes Athenagoras' opinion that "although [God's] Maiestie with his vniuersall and common prouidence doth gouerne and prouide for all, yet the particular care of particular things is committed vnto the Angels"; and Anselm's that "euery soule that is sent into this life, is also committed to some particular Angell, who doth continually moue him to all good."[13] Heywood cites Plato's opinion that "children are no sooner born, but they haue one of those spirits to attend them" and later "teach, instruct, and gouern them."[14] Pertinently, Lawrence says that "every elect hath his proper and peculiar Angell deputed as his keeper and companion, yet so as extraordinarily many may be sent to his ayde . . . ; Our communion is exceedingly great with the Angells, both good and bad." By "writing on our fancies" they "represent objects to our understandings, and our wills which often take and moove us"; and we should "consider how great and intimate our converse is with them," for they are "channels and conduits through which God conveys himself to us."[15]

Milton reserves judgment in his *Christian Doctrine*, as West points out, concerning the assignment of a "proper and peculiar Angell" to each person, but he says that angels "guard over the meetings of the faithful" and are probably "put in charge of nations, kingdoms, and particular districts"; the angel he asks to "look homeward" in *Lycidas* is no doubt St. Michael, as patron of England as well as of Israel. He is primarily interested in their freedom of will, their voluntary obedience, and their "great pleasure in examining the mystery of man's salvation"; they are not omniscient, but are eager to learn; and "seven of them particularly patrol the earth: Zech. iv.10: *these seven are the eyes of Jehovah which go to and fro over the earth,* compared with Rev. v.6: *who are those seven spirits of God sent forth into the whole earth.*"[16]

In *Paradise Lost* Milton not only paints forth heavenly consorts but also shows the greatest angels on particular errands to Adam and Eve and holding intimate and serviceable conversation with them. He is careful to show that both men and angels have free will. Angels are God's messengers, but they do not impose or coerce human thought and feeling, and they have considerable liberty of invention and style. They are not to be worshipped and can even make mistakes, but they are glorious ministers, exemplary in their love of service to their fellow creatures.

Beginning in the late fifteenth century and culminating in the early seventeenth, artists, writers, and composers represented angels and humans engaged in intimate and dramatic communication. The most familiar of these in the visual arts are representations of the Annunciation to the Virgin, but artists also abundantly depicted angelic dealings with patriarchs, prophets, evangelists, and saints, especially those who could be taken as types of the inspired artist. The story of Tobias was a popular *topos* partly because the healing of Tobias's blindness by the archangel Raphael figures the artist's calling to purge and illuminate men's eyes. St. John on Patmos, whose revelation Christ "sent and signified . . . by his angel," is the model of the Christian visionary poet; in Adriaen van Wesel's carving the angel with his arm around John's shoulders gently touches his ear (see fig. 1). In Maerten van Heemskerck's *St. Luke Painting the Virgin* a winged spirit lights the painter's subjects with a torch, and Jan Gossaert's angel actually guides the painter's hand. Similarly, in Caravaggio's earlier, rejected painting of the popular topic of *St. Matthew and the Angel,* the angel guides the Evangelist's hand as he writes. In Rembrandt's painting the angel is ardently interested in the work; in Van Dyck's drawing he urgently interrupts it (see fig. 2). In Caravaggio's second painting and in Guido Reni's he aids the Evangelist's memory by enumerating the human geneology of Christ on his fingers. In paintings by Simon Vouet and Guido Reni an angel exhorts St. Jerome as inspired translator. Milton himself took the visions of Ezekiel, transported by the

Figure 1. "St. John on Patmos," by Adriaen van Wesel. Museum of the Brotherhood of Our Lady, 's Hertogenbosch.

Figure 2. "Matthew and the Angel," by Anthonie Van Dyck. Museum Boymans-van Beuningen, Rotterdam.

cherubim of divine knowledge, and of Isaiah, purged by the seraphim of divine love, as the types of his calling. Perhaps the most frequently shown angelic activity of all is music, both in Milton's poems and in the arts generally. In the liturgy, the cry of the seraphim becomes the Sanctus and joins in the Te Deum; the Annunciation to the shepherds begins the Gloria. *Angeli musicanti* not only adorn paintings and chancels but represent in them the harmony-in-diversity of heavenly life. In Botticelli's *Virgin of the Magnificat* an angel holds the Virgin's book and inkwell for her as she writes her poem, and in Crispijn van de Passe's an angel with a flaming torch leans over the Virgin who kneels before a four-part setting of her song (see fig. 3).[17] Van Eyck, Raphael, Cantarini, Gentileschi, and Strozzi (see fig. 4), among others, painted the story of St. Cecilia as composer and inventor of the pipe organ instructed by angels. These pictures associate God's messengers with inspired literary and artistic performance, as artists themselves, as stirrers up of creative energy by their fervent attention, as illuminators of the senses, the memory, and the imagination, and as channels and messengers of "that eternal Spirit, who can enrich with all utterance."

Angels, then, are a regular part of seventeenth-century life and are involved in the creative process, but the angels who spread protective wings over each person in the first lines of *Ad Leonoram* are not the inspirers of the elect singer:

> Quid mirum? Leonora tibi si gloria major,
> Nam tua praesentem vox sonat ipsa Deum.

Anyone can claim an angel; Leonora's voice sounds forth God.

Deus, capitalization notwithstanding, can be rendered "God," "the God," or "a god"; the English article forces the translator to choose. Jacob Strutt's very free 1814 translation paganizes and trivializes the lines: "Clearly thy voice a deity reveals; / Some mighty god, or tuneful spirit, steals, / (Warbling sweet strains) into thy swelling throat."[18] Charles Knapp's translation for the Columbia Milton uses both "a very present god" and "God" (I, p. 229). "A very present God," as David C. Bright has pointed out to me, gives "praesentem" its proper relation to "Deus" and brings to mind the "very present help" of Psalm xlvi. On the other hand, by requiring an article the construction retains a little of the pagan flavor of "a god." Walter MacKellar, Merritt Hughes, and Douglas Bush agree that Milton means the Christian God,[19] as the prevenient orders of angels would suggest, though Plato believed in guardian spirits too. Confronted with the language of both the Vulgate and Virgil, the reader must choose.

Figure 3. "Virgin of the Magnificat," by Crispijn van de Passe the Elder. Reproduced in F. W. H. Hollstein, *Dutch and Flemish Etchings, Engravings, and Woodcuts, ca. 1450–1700* (Amsterdam, 1949–76), no. 196.

Figure 4. "Ste. Cécile et l'ange," by Reinardo Strozzi. Musée des Beaux-Arts de Dijon.

The ensuing lines offer a more difficult choice:

> Aut Deus, aut vacui certè mens tertia coeli
> Per tua secretò guttura serpit agens.

Scholars have suggested numerous identifications of "mens tertia." In the *Variorum Commentary* Bush cites Leigh Hunt's "the intelligence of the third heaven (the heaven of love)" and Thomas Keightley's "the presiding power of the third sphere, i. e. that of Venus"; Masson's "some third mind, intermediate between God and Angel," which he finds "theologically vague"; and Hughes's comparison to I John v, 7, "For there are three that bear record in heaven, the Father, the Word, and the Holy Ghost."[20] Knapp translates it "the Third Intelligence," suggesting the presiding genius or angel of the sphere of Venus, third from the earth (CM I, p. 229).[21] Keightley thinks that "one can hardly suppose that he means the third person of the Trinity,"[22] but both Hughes and Bush do suppose so, no doubt taking Milton's unusual ideas about the Trinity into account.

Hughes calls Milton's notion a "fancy," however: "The idea that she was inspired by a guardian angel now changes to the fancy that she is inspired by the Holy Spirit."[23] Bush is most emphatic: "Since Milton seems clearly to be using *Deus*, especially in 9–10, for the Christian God, there would seem to be small doubt that *mens tertia* means the Holy Ghost. And whatever else he had in mind, he was surely thinking of 'the third heaven' of 2 Cor. xii, 2,4."[24] If we accept this association of "third mind" and "third heaven" we may find illumination in Calvin's comment that St. Paul's "third heaven" does not signify the planetary sphere of the pagan philosophers but "the blessed and glorious kingdom of God, which is aboue all the spheres . . . and aboue the whoole woorkmanshippe of the world."[25]

If "mens tertia" means the Holy Ghost, "vacui coeli" is hard to explain, though some readers might take some passages of *De Doctrina Christiana* I, vi as warrant for supposing that he might "proceed" in this way. The equivocality of the phrase, in fact, resembles Milton's unwillingness in the tractate to take a dogmatic view of the Holy Spirit, as in his comment that "the name of Spirit is also frequently applied to God and angels, and to the human mind. . . . Sometimes it means an angel. . . . Sometimes it means that impulse or voice of God by which the prophets were inspired. . . . Undoubtedly neither David, nor any other Hebrew, under the old covenant, believed in the personality of that 'good' and 'Holy Spirit', unless perhaps as an angel. . . . [Sometimes] the Spirit signifies a divine impulse, or light, or voice, or word, transmitted from above either through Christ, who is the Word of God, or by some other channel. . . . Further, the Spirit signifies the person itself of the Holy Spirit, or its symbol." Questioning passages usually cited as proof of the essential unity and equality of the Trinity, Milton adds, "in this kind of threefold enumerations the sacred writers have no view whatever to the doctrine of three divine persons," and cites 1 Timothy v, 21, "'I charge thee before God, and the Lord Jesus Christ, and the elect angels', where it might have been expected that the Holy Spirit would have been named in the third place, if such ternary forms of expression really contained the meaning which is commonly ascribed to them" (CM XIV, pp. 359–69, 399). We should be cautious, therefore, about overdogmatic interpretations of Milton's own theory of inspiration and particularly such ternary expressions as "mens tertia." With caution, I suggest a third possibility that seems more satisfactory than either the genius of the sphere of Venus or the Holy Spirit, without entirely negating these possibilities.

"Mens tertia" may mean a third mind or spirit in at least three senses. First, it may mean third in the sense of being neither *Deus* nor *Angelus*, taking *angelus* in its specific designation as a member of the lowest of the nine orders, the Angeli, as distinguished from the higher orders: Archangeli, Virtutes, Potestates, Principates, Dominationes, Throni, Cherubim, Seraphim. Second, it may suggest a member of the third and highest of the three hierarchies into which these orders were divided, and in particular one of those "elect angels" who in Scripture, as in the epigram, are alternatively called God and angels, for "the name of God is applied to them . . . when they represent the divine presence and person" (CM XIV, pp. 277–79). Third, it may designate such an angel as an intermediary between God and the inspired singer.

Concerning the hierarchical distinctions, Salkeld quotes Athanasius: "the worke of the super-celestiall Powers" is "a neuer interrupted Hymne, a neuer ceasing loue towards the diuine Maiestie," and "a continuall prayer for our saluation"; but "there is a difference of degree and science" between "the Thrones, the Cherubins, and Seraphins, who continually and without any mediator, or interpreter, doe learne of God," and the "inferiour Orders" who are instructed by them, "of which the Angels be the last of all in dignitie and perfection." In case one wonders whether the higher orders go forth on errands to mankind ("vacui coeli"), or how they can do so without interrupting their hymn to God, Salkeld replies, "The most secure opinion is, that of all sorts and orders of Angels (whatsoever their difference, degrees, or superioritie be) there may be sent messengers for their good, who are the heyres of saluation . . . ; but not yet ceasing therefore from their office of assistance [that is, presence before God]: for seeing that they doe injoy Gods presence and sight in euery place, they may easily be conceiued to execute their peculiar office in euery place."[26] Angels, though swift, are not ubiquitous; but God is everywhere, "per cunctaque fusus."

Perhaps, then, Leonora's visitant is not an ordinary angel out of the ranks ("ab ordinibus"), but one of the Seraphim sent "by that eternall Spirit who can enrich with all utterance," and more specifically one of the seven

> Who in Gods presence, neerest to his Throne
> Stand ready at command, and are his Eyes
> That run through all the Heav'ns, or down to th'Earth
> Bear his swift errands   (PL III, 649–52)

and might even by some holy rapture share their perpetual hymn by way of Leonora's singing.

A diagram illustrating the *Microcosmi Historia* of Robert Fludd schematizes the cosmos and its correspondences with the microcosm in an illuminating way (see fig. 5). The figure of a man, spreadeagled on the

Figure 5. Title page to volume 2 of *Utriusque Cosmi Maioris scilicet et Minoris Metaphysica, Physica, atque Technica Historia . . .* , by Robert Fludd (Oppenheim, 1619).

Ptolemaic model of concentric spheres governed by the planets and encompassed by the zodiac, is surrounded by three supercelestial spheres containing the nine orders of angels in their three hierarchies and showing their correspondences to the faculties of the mind. The inner sphere, or "hyerarchia infina," contains Angels, Archangels, and Virtues, and is the region of *Ratio;* the middle sphere contains Powers, Principalities, and Dominions, and is the region of *Intellectus;* the outermost or highest sphere is inhabited by Thrones, Cherubim, and Seraphim, and is the region of *Mens* and of *Epiphania* — something like Calvin's third heaven of "those who excell in knowledge."[27] Perhaps Milton's "mens tertia" comes from this sphere, the third heaven of *mens* and of epiphany, of the direct and ardent knowledge and love of God enjoyed and taught by the Cherubim and the Seraphim who continually behold his face singing "a never interrupted Hymne" and especially communicated by the seven who sometimes join the lower orders in traffic with mankind and so bring the heavenly powers full circle.

Whatever connotations we may choose, Milton may have left "mens tertia" deliberately open to interpretation, as he does the "something holy" that lodges in the breast of the singer in *A Maske* (245) and as he does in *Paradise Lost* by invoking both the Holy Spirit and the Celestial Muse. The richness of possibility thus preserved gathers both Hebrew-Christian and Christian-Humanist ideas about the relations of the mind of the poet and the mind of God, and at the same time presents no limitation to the Spirit or his conduits who inspire with diverse gifts in diverse ways.

The use of the plural "guttura" may glance at a passage from du Bartas that links the nine orders of angels with Urania, the "muse celeste":

> Sa face est angelique, angelique son geste,
> Son discours tout divin, & tout parfait son corps,
> Et sa bouche à neuf-voix imite en ses accords
> Le son harmonieux de la dance celeste.[28]

> [Her face is angelic, angelic her gesture,
> Her discourse wholly divine, and wholly perfect her body,
> And her mouth of nine voices imitates in its concent
> The harmonious sound of the heavenly dance.]

The ensuing lines contain the heart of the poem, and something else.

> Serpit agens, facilisque docet mortalia corda
> Sensim immortali assuescere posse sono.

Accustoming mortal hearts to immortal sound is the purpose of voice and verse, which are "of power . . . to set the affections in right tune" (CM

III, p. 238). But no one attuned to the metaphoric roots of words is likely to escape the feeling that a serpent lurks, and since Milton pronounced Latin in the Italian style,[29] the onomatopoetic subtle liquidity of the sibilants, played against the roundness and solidity of sound in the surrounding lines, creeps rustlingly, some would say hissingly, toward the punning "corda" and "sono," at the very moment when Milton is calling attention to our response to sound.[30] "Serpit agens" is on one level a perfectly benign phrase; on another, "serpit" suggests crawling, "agens" suggests acting, even feigning, and both suggest the subtlest beast of all the field. It would be hard to read these lines after the later epic without recalling several passages: "at [the Serpent's] Mouth / the Devil enterd, and his brutal sense . . . inspir'd," tempting either "with Serpent Tongue / Organic, or impulse of vocal Air"; in this manner, "Into the Heart of *Eve* his words made way, / Though at the voice much marveling," and later "his words replete with guile / Into her heart too easie entrance won" (*PL* IX, 188–89, 529–30, 550–51, 733–34). Why should the spirit who secretly inspires Leonora sound so much like the spirit who disguisedly beguiled Eve?

Inspiration is a tricky thing. Bad spirits can inspire as well as good ones. On the whole, Milton kept the voices of angels, men, and God strictly separate, in keeping with his firm belief in free will and responsibility. Nevertheless, he also believed in divine inspiration of sacred song, and fears failure "if all be mine, / Not Hers who brings it nightly to my Ear" (IX, 46–47). He is aware, too, that, as Sidney had said, "mans wit may make Poesie . . . infect the fancie with unwoorthie objects," that bad interpretation may abuse good art, and that the art of interpretation is difficult because the art of evil is to parody goodness. So there is a warning in the working of the poem: this art is good, yet bad art can also make its secret way into our hearts, and even good art can infect bad wits. It is not the art of God or his agents that is suspect, but art or a response to art that parodically perverts art's purpose of tuning mortal heartstrings to holy and joyful noise. Inspired art asks inspired interpretation; rightly inspired and interpreted, it leads to heaven, or at least to a gust for it. The test is what way the experience leads. By displaying and exercising in us this principal of interpretive choice by its use of sound, the poem teaches the capacity, like Leonora's, for "happy judgment in distinguishing good from bad music."

A similar choice attaches to "Sirena" in the third epigram. Like the sphere-born Sirens in *At a Solemn Musick*, this is a Platonic Siren, not a Homeric one luring men to wreck, yet there is something of a lure in the inevitable connotations. Present-day fascination with sin has produced an abundance of analyses of prefigurations, intimations, and effects of fallenness in Milton's work. Yet for Milton the Fall is a paradigmatic lacuna in the development of personhood and relation, "a parodic obliquity and anomaly" as Arthur E. Barker calls it,[31] a series of reductions followed by a series of recoveries. As Stanley Fish has so overwhelmingly exhibited, *Paradise Lost* can be read as a poem about the sins of the reader, flushing them from ambush;[32] and *Ad Leonoram* can be read that way too. But the purpose of diagnosis is purgation and health; Milton's poems are mainly about health. The Devil is a parodist, he tells us in the epic, best withered by laughter. So he is wittily insinuated into *Ad Leonoram* to be discriminated and dismissed. Thus purged, hearts are ready "immortali assuescere posse sono."

Readers have puzzled over the epigram's penultimate line as uncharacteristically pantheistic: "Quòd si cuncta quidem Deus est, per cunctaque fusus." The line connects with "aut Deus" and resolves the "either-or": everything is God. But it is more mystical than Milton usually allows. The discreteness of Creator and creation is the special brilliance of the Hebrew as opposed to the Greek account of origins and is essential to free will. On the other hand, Milton believed in creation *de Deo* rather than *ex nihilo* (*De Doctrina Christiana* I, vii), with free will a divine decree; Michael in *Paradise Lost* assures fallen Adam that God's "Omnipresence fills / Land, Sea, and Aire, and every kinde that lives, / Fomented by his virtual power and warmd" (XI, 336–38); and in the "New Heav'n and Earth," though individual entities will retain their identities, yet "God shall be All in All" (III, 341).

As a source, Keightley cites *Aeneid* VI, 724–27, but MacKellar thinks that "Milton may have been expressing a pantheism which was current at the time . . . in the Italian academies" and adds that "no particular significance should attach to Milton's words beyond the compliment to Leonora. Pantheism is not in harmony with the general tendency of his thought, and serves merely as a means of expressing an exaggerated tribute to a noted singer."[33] Hughes notes, similarly, that Virgil's "conception of the universe as animated by an omnipresent intelligence" in those lines was "often quoted by Italian Neo-Platonists in proof of pantheistic theories like that which Giordano Bruno supported by quoting them in *De la Causa, Principio e Uno.*"[34] Yet it was not Milton's practice to betray his thought for the sake of his art or to use either for frivolous purposes, though he might well subordinate a classical idea to a Scriptural one. Anchises' version to Aeneas, in the underworld, of creation and fall and the need for purgation is appropriate to the purging of lips necessary to the artist, but on the whole it is too dualistic for Milton, whose Christian sense of incarnation did not allow so much denigration of mortal clay, however dark a house it may sometimes be. A more consonant literary analogy for the line is the opening of the *Paradiso* of that "famous renowner of Beatrice":

> La gloria di colui che tutto move
>   per l'universo penetra, e risplende
>   in una parte più e meno altrove.

> [The glory of him by whom all things are moved
>   penetrates throughout the universe, and shines again
>   in one part more, and in another less.]

And the concluding line accords with Dante's and extends it: "In te unâ loquitur, caetera mutus habet." Leonora, for this occasion, is one of those parts in whom God shines more, as the young poet was fitting himself to be.

The conclusion fuses the themes of singularity and wholeness, but applied to a singer in Rome it might bring forth much the same objection that Ben Jonson made to Donne's *Anniversaries:* "If it had been written of the Virgin Marie it had been something."[35] Milton's epigram is slighter in form and perhaps in occasion, yet it belongs to the body of poetry of instructive praise that O. B. Hardison and Barbara Kiefer Lewalski have shown to be so significant a genre[36] and to which Milton devotes a long passage in the *Apology for Smectymnuus* (CM III, pp. 302–04). As Lewalski explains, Donne's exaltation of Elizabeth Drury and Marvell's of Maria Fairfax are more than extravagant compliments:

The human individual is symbolic . . . not as image or reflection of an ideal Platonic Form or Idea, but, more precisely, as image of God; on that ground the individual can be said to embody, restate, or incarnate divine reality or the entire Book of the Creatures in himself. . . . These are not praises judiciously evaluating the specific virtues and characteristics of the individual, as Ben Jonson's often are, but metaphysical praises of the possibilities of the human spirit acted upon by God. Yet these possibilities are never treated abstractly, but only as they may inhere in a particular person.[37]

Milton's epigram to Leonora participates in this sense of incarnation and epiphany, and so in the literature of compliment that offers models and stirs longing for the regaining of paradise, in which Donne and Marvell are Milton's colleagues and the particular role of the artist is his subject.

Before the loss of paradise, Adam and Eve come forth each morning and join "thir vocal Worship to the Quire / Of Creatures wanting voice" (IX, 198–99). George Herbert puts it that mankind is "Secretarie of [God's] praise"; all creatures "fain would sing" and tune their lutes, but "all their hands and throats / Are brought to Man, while they are lame and mute," and he who refrains "robs a thousand" of their song.[38] It is humankind's especial service and joy to give voice to the mute creation, and doubly the artist's to give voice to humankind with which to "renew that Song" once sung "in first obedience, and their state of good." When paradise has been fully regained in response to the work of "one greater Man" (I, 4), humankind and angelkind will sing together "in endless morn of light." Meanwhile, a gust for paradise—and for the strenuous joys of regaining it—may spring from our response to those single voices, helped perhaps by angels, in whom, as in this radiant little poem, God speaks.

Rutgers University

NOTES

1. William Riley Parker, *Milton: A Biography*, 2 vols. (Oxford, 1968), I, p. 615; J. Milton French, *Life Records of John Milton* (New Brunswick, 1949–58), V, p. 32; Henry J. Todd, *Some Account of the Life and Writings of John Milton* (London, 1826), I, p. 210n. Todd explains, "In a manuscript note, at the end of Toland's Life of Milton, communicated to me by Mr. F. G. Waldron, it is related that *Paradise Regained* was, in the poet's own opinion, the better poem, though it could never obtain to be named with *Paradise Lost*; and that Milton gave this reason for the general dislike, namely, *That the people had a general sense of the loss of Paradise, but not an equal gust for the regaining of it.*"

2. *Il Libro del Cortegiano del Conte Baldesar Castiglione* (Venice, 1528), sig. Piv; *The Courtyer of Count Baldessar Castilio . . .* done into English by Thomas Hobby (London, 1577), sig. Yi.

3. All quotations from *PL* and from the shorter poems are from CM.

4. Douglas Bush cites sources and agrees with those who question the traditional dating in Bush, *Variorum*, pp. 147–48.

5. The translation in *The Student's Milton* reads, "To each person (believe it, ye peoples) has been assigned his own angel from heaven's ranks. What wonder, Leonora, if a greater glory is yours? For your voice itself expresses in sound Deity present among us. Either God or certainly the Third Mind of Heaven come down to earth, steals mysteriously through your throat, steals and graciously teaches mortal hearts the power to accustom themselves insensibly to eternal sounds. For if all things be God, and He pervade them all, in you alone He speaks, in all the rest He is present but silent" (ed. Frank Allen Patterson [New York, 1931], p. 95).

Merritt Hughes translates, "Over everyone—so let the nations believe—his own particular angel from out the heavenly hierarchies spreads protecting wings. What wonder, Leonora, if a greater glory be yours? For the music of your voice itself bespeaks the presence of God. Either God, or certainly some third mind from the untenanted skies, is moving mysteriously in your throat — mysteriously moving and graciously teaching mortal hearts how they may gradually become accustomed to immortal tones. If God is all things and permeates all things, in you alone he speaks and possesses all His other creatures in silence" (*John Milton: Complete Poems and Major Prose* [New York, 1957], pp. 130–31).

The Columbia *Milton* suggests: "An angel each man — such be your belief, ye peoples — has as his lot, a winged angel from the heavenly ranks. Wherein, then, is it strange, if you, Leonora, have [even] greater glory, since your voice itself sounds forth God, a very present god? God, or at least, the Third Intelligence of emptied heaven [*i.e.*, the Third Intelligence, quitting heaven], makes its way unseen through your throat, aye, makes its way, and graciously teaches mortal hearts the power to grow accustomed insensibly to sounds immortal. But, if all things are God, and God is transfused through all, yet it is in you alone that He speaks: to all else that He possesses He vouchsafes no voice" (I, p. 229).

6. "I have translated only two of the three poetical compliments addressed to Leonora, as they appear to me far superior to what I have omitted"; Cowper, *Latin and Italian Poems of Milton Translated into English Verse* (London, 1808), p. 42.

7. Trinity College Manuscript, reproduced in Harris F. Fletcher, ed., facs. ed. of *John Milton's Complete Poetical Works*, I (Urbana, 1943), p. 391.

8. "And believed myself already among the angels, enjoying the pleasures of the blessed"; Thomas Warton, *Poems upon Several Occasions . . . by John Milton* (London, 1785), pp. 490–91n.

9. On Milton's knowledge and use of both polyphony and monody and on the influence of the Florentine *camerata* on English music in the early seventeenth century, see Sandra Corse, "Old Music and New in 'L'Allegro' and 'Il Penseroso,'" *MQ*, XIV (1980), 109–13. I am grateful to my graduate student at Rutgers, Christine Mumm, for pointing out the applicability of these styles to the voicing of *Paradise Lost*.

10. West, *Milton and the Angels* (Athens, Ga., 1955), p. 132.

11. *The Latin and Italian Poems of Milton*, trans. Jacob George Strutt (London, 1814), p. 57; Masson, quoted in Bush, *Variorum*, p. 149; West, *Milton and the Angels*, p. 132.

12. Salkeld, *A Treatise of Angels. Of the nature, essence, place, power, science, will, apparitions, grace, sinne, and all other properties of Angels. Collected ovt of the holy scriptvres, ancient Fathers, and schoole-diuines* (London, 1613); Heywood, *The Hierarchie of the Blessed Angells . . .* (London, 1635); Lawrence, *An History of Angells, being a theologicall treatise of our communion and warr with them* (London, 1645 and 1650). West cites and discusses these and other seventeenth-century works in *Milton and the Angels*.

13. Salkeld, *Treatise*, pp. 275 and 278.

14. Heywood, *Hierarchie*, p. 228; cf. pp. 219 and 210; and, for further classical references, Richard Hooker, *Of the Lawes of Ecclesiastical Politie, Eight Books* (London, 1622), p. 10.

15. Lawrence, *An History of Angells*, pp. 19–23.

16. *Christian Doctrine* I, ix, transl. John Carey, in YP VI, 343–46.

17. Van Wesel, *St. John on Patmos;* Museum of the Brotherhood of Our Lady, 's Hertogenbosch; van Heemskerck, *St. Luke Painting the Virgin*, Frans Halsmuseum, Haarlem; Gossaert, Kunsthistorisches Museum, Vienna; Caravaggio, *St. Matthew and the Angel* (1) destroyed, (2) Église St-Louis-des-Français, Rome; Rembrandt, Louvre, Paris; Van Dyck, Museum Boymans-van Beuningen, Rotterdam; Reni, Pinacoteca Vaticana, Rome; Vouet, *St. Jerome and the Angel*, Samuel H. Kress Collection, National Gallery, Washington, D.C.; Reni, *The Angel Appearing to St. Jerome*, The Detroit Institute of Arts; Botticelli, *Virgin of the Magnificat*, Uffizi, Florence; van de Passe, reproduced in F. W. H. Hollstein, *Dutch and Flemish Etchings, Engravings, and Woodcuts, ca. 1450–1700* (Am-

sterdam, 1949–76). My study of angels in the visual arts has been supported by a grant from the Research Council of Rutgers, the State University of New Jersey.

18. *The Latin and Italian Poems of John Milton*, trans. Jacob George Strutt (London, 1814), p. 57.

19. MacKellar, *The Latin Poems of John Milton*, Cornell Studies in English XV (New Haven, 1930), p. 111 (translation); Hughes, *Complete Poems*, p. 130; Bush, *Variorum*, p. 149.

20. Bush, *Variorum*, p. 149.

21. Heywood, *Hierarchie*, pp. 210 and 215, cites Plato's ranking of the "Soules of Coelestiall Bodies" as the third degree of intelligible nature (after God and Ideas), and says that the philosophers did not know the name of *Angel* but called them *Spirits* and *Minds;* and that the planetary governors were called *Intelligences* by the Sophists and *Cherubim* by the Hebrews.

22. Keightley, *The Poems of John Milton* (London, 1859), II, 421n.

23. Hughes, *Complete Poems*, p. 130n.

24. Bush, *Variorum*, p. 149.

25. Calvin, *A Commentarie vpon S. Paules Epistles to the Corinthians* (London, 1577), fol. 294^{v}.

26. Salkeld, *Treatise*, pp. 293–94, 318.

27. Fludd, *Utriusque Cosmi Maioris scilicet et Minoris Metaphysica, Physica, atque Technica Historia* . . . (Oppenheim, 1619), title page to volume 2. I do not wish to suggest that Milton subscribed to Fludd's occult eccentricities.

28. Guillaume de Saluste, Seigneur du Bartas, *L'Uranie. Ou Muse Celeste* (1623), lines 32–35.

29. According to Milton's pupil Thomas Ellwood, Milton told him, "if I would have the benefit of the Latin tongue, not only to read and understand Latin authors, but to converse with foreigners, either abroad or at home, I must learn the foreign pronunciation. To this I consenting, he instructed me how to sound the vowels; so different from the common pronunciation used by the English, who speak Anglice their Latin, that (with some few other variations in sounding some consonants, in particular cases; as C before E or I, like Ch. Sc before I, like Sh, &c.) the Latin thus spoken, seemed as different from that which was delivered, as the English generally speak it, as if it were another language" (*The Student's Milton*, p. xlvii).

30. Readers who think that alliterated *s* is always serpentine, however, should compare *Lycidas*, 176–80.

31. Barker, "Structural and Doctrinal Pattern in Milton's Later Poems," in Millar MacLure and F. W. Watts, eds., *Essays in English Literature from the Renaissance to the Victorian Age Presented to A. S. P. Woodhouse* (Toronto, 1964), p. 190.

32. Fish, *Surprised by Sin: The Reader in "Paradise Lost"* (London and New York, 1967).

33. MacKellar, *Latin Poems*, p. 246.

34. Hughes, *Complete Poems*, p. 131.

35. Notes of Ben Jonson's *Conversations with William Drummond of Hawthornden*, January, 1619, Shakespeare Society Publication 15 (London, 1842), p. 3.

36. Hardison, *The Enduring Monument: A Study of Praise in Renaissance Literary Theory and Practice* (Chapel Hill, 1962); Lewalski, *Donne's "Anniversaries" and the Poetry of Praise: The Creation of a Symbolic Mode* (Princeton, 1973).

37. Lewalski, *Donne's "Anniversaries,"* p. 47.

38. Herbert, "Providence," in *The English Poems of George Herbert*, ed. C. A. Patrides (London, 1974), p. 129.

HIGH PASTORAL ART
IN *EPITAPHIUM DAMONIS*

Janet Leslie Knedlik

N O   O N E can help comparing *Epitaphium Damonis* with *Lycidas*, but our tendency to measure the *Epitaphium* in terms dictated by the earlier English masterpiece has prejudiced evaluation of the Latin elegy. Even Douglas Bush's thoughtful summary in the *Variorum Commentary* reflects something of this tendency, when he remarks that "in *Lycidas* the beatific vision is the triumphant answer to the poet's questioning of God's ways to men . . . but in the Latin elegy that great argument is only touched upon, among many other themes, and the poem almost seems to ramble."[1] Yet the "onward pressure and unified complexity of the whole" which Bush praises in *Lycidas* have required strenuous scholarship to elucidate, for *Lycidas* is after all an audacious medley of pagan and overtly Christian elements and orchestrates into order a breathtaking range of tones and attitudes. Most would agree, on consideration, that in both *Lycidas* and *Epitaphium Damonis*, Milton conceives of his genre as one of daring modulation upon a varied Pan's pipe. For the Miltonic art-shepherd, it seems that dread voices, higher strains, or Virgil's own "paulo maiora"[2] rightfully alternate with an astonishing mixture of humbler notes, as the pastoral Tityrus touches "the tender stops of various Quills." If unifying force through depth — or the opening-out of interior vistas within serene stasis — is the distinguished Virgilian achievement (as in his Eclogue I, of Tityrus and Meliboeus), then the characteristic Miltonic mode achieves its unity rather through movement than through depth: a striking modulation of movement so that markedly disparate threads are woven into a single powerful progression. While *Lycidas* achieves this coherence by superbly, though variously, sustaining its complex movement toward a Christian justification for untimely death, the *Epitaphium*'s unity derives from the momentum of other themes and purposes. In evaluating the later Latin elegy, therefore, criticism must move well beyond that classic identification of the two poems by A. S. P. Woodhouse as sharing "the basic pattern of Christian monody, with pagan grief and despair freely expressed in the earlier movements, which act as a foil to the Christian conclusion, where these emotions are dispelled or transcended."[3]

Inevitable pairing and comparing of *Lycidas* and *Epitaphium Damonis*, then, have obscured appreciation of the *Epitaphium's* distinctive coherence and purposiveness. Part of that distinctiveness lies in a new kind of strategic restraint: Milton's decision not to use pagan elements as a foil to Christian elements through audacious intermixture as he had done in *Lycidas*, but rather to write a profoundly Virgilian elegy in which classical (and some Italian) precedents are allowed to maintain their integrity, even while they take on new overtones of Christian and Neoplatonic significance. Even the *Epitaphium's* closing vision of Damon, dwelling among the gods and heroes, is fastidiously classical and Olympian (except for the accent note of "Sion" in the poem's final line). Not only is the concluding vision steadfastly pagan in imagery and phrasing (rather than unveiling Christian revelation), but it is also steadfastly pastoral, so that at least some elements of classical pastoral are apotheosized rather than renounced in the elegy's conclusion, a second important aspect of the closing passage which has been overlooked in readings of the elegy.[4]

The fine purity of the *Epitaphium* — set over against the grand eclecticism of *Lycidas* — deserves appreciation. Milton eschews in the *Epitaphium* that superbly orchestrated violence to the classical genre which *Lycidas* proudly displays. He achieves instead a remarkable purity, poignancy, and passion through adaption of classical and Italian pastoral components into a Latin tribute to Damon in the great tradition — a tradition Milton now shares personally with his Italian friends — so that Damon might indeed be honored "secundo . . . post Daphnin," at least "inter pastores" (29–32). Working out of Virgilian precedent especially, Milton refuses to shatter pastoral convention as he had done repeatedly in *Lycidas*. Even the moving renunciatory gesture — "vos cedite silvae" (160) ("Depart, you forests")[5] — which plays an important role in the *Epitaphium's* progression is, after all, only one almost obligatory element of pastoral singing in a fully Virgilian manner, after Virgil's yearnings for epic in Eclogues IV and VI, and his farewell to pastoral in Eclogue X, "Gallus." So Milton works with convincing integrity in *Epitaphium Damonis* to make the inherited givens of the art-eclogue, as it was best known to and practised by his intended European audience (those *pastores* bred in Virgilian woods), emblematic in themselves of a Renaissance Christian poet's resolution of the issues this Latin elegy raises.

These issues are not the issues raised in *Lycidas*, dealing as *Lycidas* does with the question of God's justice to His servants in permitting their untimely deaths. Milton raises the issue of divine justice only once in the the *Epitaphium*, in the opening outcry of Thyrsis, and he does so with time-honored phraseology utilizing also a striking adaptation of Castiglione's *Alcon:* "Hei mihi! quae terris, quae dicam numina coelo, / Post-quam te immiti rapuerunt funere Damon" (19–20) ("woe is me! what deities on land or in the sky, Damon, may I call upon, now that they have mercilessly torn you away in death?"). The despairing question is no sooner uttered than it is answered with a resounding affirmation of the recognition of true worth in the afterlife (an affirmation which only grows stronger as the elegy progresses, rather than being veiled and then climactically revealed as in *Lycidas*):

> Siccine nos linquis, tua sic sine nomine virtus
> Ibit, et obscuris numero sociabitur umbris?
> At non ille, animas virgâ qui dividit aureâ,
> Ista velit, dignumque tui te ducat in agmen,
> Ignavumque procul pecus arceat omne silentum.   (21–25)

[In this way do you leave us? thus shall your virtue go down without a name, and be numbered among the obscure shades? But not at all would he who divides the spirits with his golden wand wish this, and into company worthy of you would lead you, and warn away all the ignorant silent herd.]

What justice is there now that Damon has been torn away so mer-cilessly? Thyrsis answers his own outcry with an immediate and certain intuition: that is, he sees at once that it is in the nature of things that Damon has found an end worthy and fitting for his excellent life, antici-pating the final vision, of which Thyrsis will be likewise certain — "nec me fallit spes lubrica" (198) ("nor does any false hope deceive me"). The innate superiority of Damon's soul will work for him an elevation above the common lot; Damon will not remain among "all the brutal and si-lent herd" of the dead in Hades. The inevitable gravitation of all things to their proper levels, the powerful attraction of like to like through mag-netisms which draw the pure soul upward in spite of the worst that may befall it — these affirmations undergird the *Epitaphium* and measure its difference in subject matter from the profound questionings resolved in *Lycidas*. The *Epitaphium*'s contrastive note of affirmation is underscored also when we compare the total absence of such consolation in the parallel passage of *Alcon* (and from Castiglione's elegy as a whole).[6]

No doubt at all occurs during the unfolding of *Epitaphium Damonis* as to Damon's apotheosis. Thyrsis' most piercing regret is that he was not at his friend's side to whisper at his death, "vale, nostri memor ibis ad astra," a line strikingly beautiful in Hughes's English as well: "Fare-well! remember me in your flight to the stars" (123). Divine order is not arraigned; disconsolate pagan grief is not expressed; the ecstatic conclud-ing vision is not therefore precisely the unveiling of "the idea of immortality . . . at last [in] its full Christian form," in which "mourning is banished in triumph and triumph includes consolation" (p. 270), as Woodhouse would make it when he identifies the structure of the elegy too closely with the patterns of *Lycidas*. The *Epitaphium*'s final vision is certainly no less triumphant than that of *Lycidas*, and is made even more intense by the absence of *Lycidas*'s closing frame. Yet, unlike the climax of *Lycidas*, the final ecstatic vision in the Latin elegy fulfills other purposes more central to this poem than the triumphant vindication of divine justice.

Epitaphium Damonis is unabashedly about Thyrsis, his grief, and the results of his grief. As the prose preface informs the reader, Thyrsis "se, suamque solitudinem hoc carmine deplorat" ("himself, and his solitude lamented in this song"). The elegy is surely an epitaph *for* Damon, breathing passionate tribute to Milton's friend Charles Diodati in its every part. But the work as a whole raises not the question of Damon's destiny or the justice of that destiny, but rather the question of the destiny of Thyrsis. Or better, as we have seen, the elegy passes from an initial brief questioning of Damon's death (19–25) to the far more riddling questions Thyrsis must now face, left behind alone in a darkened pastoral world. It is the situation of Thyrsis-without-Damon — "At mihi quid tandem fiet modò?" (37) ("But what is to become of me?") — that the elegy explores, both in personal autobiographical detail and in figural or universal typification. Throughout, loss of Damon is the loss of that without which Thyrsis' pastoral homeland seems barren and meaningless, so that Damon with his "salt" and wit (56) takes on a figural significance somewhat like that of the "She" of Donne's *First Anniversary* or the "halcyon" maiden of Marvell's *Upon Appleton House*, in a muted but effective eulogistic compliment to Diodati. Even in this seemingly nonclassical element, however, Milton is still working from hints in Virgil, in this case the treatment of Daphnis in Eclogue V, 56–65. In the figural patternings Milton develops in the *Epitaphium*, furthermore, the elegy will anticipate *Paradise Lost*, not as *Lycidas* does through its great argument of justifying eternal providence, but instead through the presentation of a process of valuing which grows upward through grief and loss of the highest and purest pastoral delights to the sterner disciplines and fuller compensations of epic heroism in a straitened world.

The underlying unifying principle of the *Epitaphium*'s progression of intermixing strains — all of them based on classical, principally Virgilian, adaptations — is the movement of the elegy toward an answer to a question asked only briefly in *Lycidas*: why should one cultivate one's mental pastures at all, when everything that made the labor seem worthwhile has vanished from the earth? The delightfully bleak refrain of the *Epitaphium* focuses insistently upon this central question, by reiterating that without Damon, Thyrsis has lost his love of pastoral labors: "Ite domum impasti, domino jam non vacat, agni" ("Go home unfed, my lambs, your master does not care about you"). This refrain is astonishingly irresponsible — not artistically irresponsible, as too many have suggested,[7] but irresponsible on Thyrsis' part. It transfigures precedent, and is a heedless gainsaying of the unanimous commitment to "shepherding" carried by both streams of pastoral tradition — the classical art-eclogue and the vernacular Christian pastoral tradition — which together enrich the English Renaissance pastoral.[8] At the end of his ten perfect eclogues Virgil can bid light-hearted farewell to the silvan pastoral world and turn to his epic venture, sending his young goats home fully fed: "Ite domum saturae, venit Hesperus, ite capellae" (X, 77) ("Go home well-fed, for evening comes, my goats"). But throughout the unfolding of Milton' second pastoral elegy we hear a disconsolate shepherd-poet whose pastoral artistry is being cut untimely short — by the advent of a death which demands far more from him than the conventional pastoral response of the splendid song of lament Thyrsis vows to render Damon, "unless" (as in Virgil) "me lupus antè videbit" (27) ("a wolf sees me first"). The *Epitaphium* is this promised pastoral tribute, but the elegy finds no abiding place here from the stinging goad of Damon's death and Thyrsis' resulting despair: "Go home unfed, my lambs, your master does not care about you."

Each time the refrain occurs, therefore, it reinforces the primary subject matter of the elegy: the interior mental dilemma of Thyrsis.[9] The refrain eloquently insists on Thyrsis' grieving distraction and disorientation in a world bereft of Damon. It pays intense tribute to Milton's friend by revealing that without his Damon, Thyrsis has lost the motivation needed to function either as the classical art-shepherd cultivating his pastoral songs (and hence growing up, like Virgil in his eclogues, toward epic), or as a poet-pastor laboring for the flock of "the English Church and Nation" (Woodhouse, p. 266).

An equally dramatic use of classical pastoral precedent is Milton's careful adaptation of the pastoral procession from Virgil's "Gallus" (and elsewhere), a procession which in *Lycidas* indecorously includes St. Peter and the personification of Cambridge University. In the *Epitaphium*, the members of the procession are strictly classical. Only the functioning of the procession within the elegy departs from convention: except for the "Sicilian muses" of the opening lines, Nature in *Epitaphium Damonis* does not mourn for Damon, as she mourns for the dead (or for the love-stricken) in classical elegy (and in *Lycidas*). Milton avoids the "pathetic fallacy" used throughout *Lycidas* because to draw Nature into human grief would jeopardize the way the Latin elegy presents growth in Thyrsis' sense of values. Nature, or at least Nature-without-Damon — and the whole panoply of pleasures which she affords — is precisely what Thyrsis must re-evaluate in terms of Damon's death. Hence Nature in the *Epitaphium* must remain neutral; she remains herself and apart from the painfully human process of upward growth the shepherd must endure if he is to know and value Nature rightly. The procession becomes, therefore, a parade of innocent natural enticements and solaces for Thyrsis' bereavement, but a parade which represents only those pleasures that Nature affords when she is deprived of Damon and all Damon represents. While Thyrsis' rejection of the merry games and willing shepherdesses is not a renunciation of pastoral Nature as a whole, as the elegy later shows, yet it is a recognition that the true soul of natural created life is not physical leisure and amusement but rather the higher values of rapport and intimacy between pure souls together pursuing the highest loves. It is a lesson Milton will have Adam learn when he watches the "sons of God" take wives from among "a Beavie of fair Women" amidst feast and music, "love and youth not lost, Songs, Garlands, Flours." To Adam's naive joy Michael returns:

> Judg not what is best
> By pleasure, though to Nature seeming meet,
> Created, as thou art, to nobler end
> Holie and pure, conformitie divine.   (XI, 603–06)

As the procession of would-be comforters unfolds, Thyrsis entertains not even the momentary impulse of the protagonist in *Lycidas* to sport with Amaryllis in the shade, but turns deaf ears to pastoral amusements and natural beauty (69–92) — the same deaf ears he has been turning to his moping sheep and to the less vocal call of his fields and grape vines (58–67). Nowhere does Thyrsis see hope of the fit company and sweet society of a kindred soul which, of course, made Eve a second paradise for Adam, "dearer [herself] then all":

> Quis mihi blanditiásque tuas, quis tum mihi risus,
> Cecropiosque sales referet, cultosque lepores?   (55–56)

[Who then will bring back to me your pleasant company, who will bring back your Attic salt, your culture and wit?]

Only Mopsus, learned in "avium linguas, et sydera" ("the tongues of birds and stars"), comes anywhere near the mark, in diagnosing Thyrsis' grief as love pangs (75ff.) with the same ironic truth as that of the *Pearl*-poet, who describes the grieving dreamer as "fordolked of luf-daungere." Thyrsis is indeed suffering for love — not with the momentary love-sickness of Virgil's Gallus, but with the enduring yearning of a soul that grows upward in the fashion of Neoplatonism from the pure love of friends to love of the highest beauty and truth. More exactly, the intensity of the mental bereavement Thyrsis suffers during the unfolding of the *Epitaphium* documents the extent to which his soul has been kindled not by Saturn's slanting leaden rays (79–80) but by the fiery darts of the Celestial *Amor*, who inspires upward "Nec tenues animas, pectúsque ignobile vulgi" (193) ("no narrow spirits, or the common ignoble herd").

The elegy is heavily laden with the vocabulary of "worth," of purity and aspiration and the magnetisms they exert upon the soul. After all, Thyrsis was drawn — "traxit" — away from Damon's company not by "error" (113) but by "dulcis amor Musae" (13) ("love of the sweet Muse"), and he was brought home by another love, "pecoris relicti cura" (14–15) ("care of the flock left behind"). The unquestioned superior value of Damon — and all the grace and wit and purity that he represents as Thyrsis bemoans the solitude in which he is left (36–56) — becomes the touchstone for the elegy; the touchstone against which Thyrsis is testing all the values of pastoral life as he has known it. Thyrsis readily rejects the merely physical delights of pastoral nature when they present themselves in forms divorced from their originally indwelling higher values. On the other hand, the fittingness of the pastoral tribute to friendship enshrined in Virgilian art has been retained and approved already by Thyrsis as worthy of Damon (27–34), although the prospect of so commemorating his friend holds no comfort or real direction for the grieving shepherd.

But what of that other pastoral world of Italy — the one where Thyrsis was held by love of the sweet muse so that he was lamentably absent from his friend's deathbed? When Thyrsis tries to renounce this world — "Ecquid erat tanti Romam vidisse sepultam?" (115) ("was it so important to see buried Rome?") — he is stricken in conscience:

> Quamquam etiam vestri numquam meminisse pigebit
> Pastores Thusci, Musis operata juventus,
> Hic Charis, atque Lepos; et Thuscus tu quoque Damon.   (125–27)

[Although even now I will never regret remembering you, Tuscan shepherds, youths skilled in the Muses; here were Grace and Wit; and you too, Damon, are a Tuscan.]

Weighed repeatedly in terms of the pure value of Damon himself, and in the harsher terms of the reality of Damon's death (140–52), Thyrsis arrives at a qualified valuation of the Italian journey. There too, as in Damon, Thyrsis found the true soul of pastoral, beauty informed by grace and the preserving salt of wit. He cannot but honor in memory all in Italy truly worthy of Damon. Nonetheless, while in Italy Thyrsis closed in the tender kids (another pastoral emblem, like Virgil's full-fed goats and Milton's unfed lambs, for poetic creativity, 141), he was naively unaware that Damon had died — even, one must suppose, unaware that he could die. Now, home in England again and sitting by his accustomed oak, Thyrsis realizes that he must give ultimate value only to such things in his pastoral world as are not only intrinsically worthy of Damon (as all true beauty in Art and Nature must be), but which are commensurate also with the fact of Damon's death and with a world of cruel limitations, a world in which Damon can and must die. The stage is being set for the advent of the highest trophies of the pastoral world, those aspects of pastoralism which in themselves most directly embody transcendent values and hint of and communicate the original Life from which all pastoral delights derive: most obviously the cups of Manso, but actually the last three movements of the elegy — epic, Italian cups, apotheosis — as a whole. But at this point the weighing and testing process moves toward its most wrenching recognition and decision.

Reenacting through the oblique vision of his high pastoral art the innocence and naivete of Thyrsis in the pastoral paradise of Italy, Milton traces (140–52) the hypothetical conversation of intimate friends who will meet on earth never again. Damon would speak, Thyrsis fondly had imagined, of his herbs and simples, his healing arts, while Thyrsis of course dreamed of sharing with Damon the progress and accomplishments of his poetic art. Thyrsis' concluding comment, much later (180), that he had been saving all these things to give to Damon, makes it clear that part of what Thyrsis had been planning to tell Damon concerned his Virgilian aspirations to epic and the stirrings of a more powerful artistic capacity than the slender pastoral reed can bear (155–68). It had been part, therefore, of Thyrsis' pastoral experience, while in Italy and still ignorant of Damon's death, that the poetic novitiate of the rural muse itself should tend upward to higher artistic enterprise.

Here, as in the remainder of the elegy, it becomes evident that for Milton true pastoral embodies its own self-transcendence (grace is immanent and yet transcends created nature). *Humilis* is, after all, the tabernacle and mode of the Christian *sublimis*. Pastoral too is a lowly tabernacle redolent of glory: though humiliated through sin and death, though subordinated and disciplined now of necessity, yet it is destined for eternal glorification. Milton by the time of the *Epitaphium* (had he learned this through his Italian reading, thought, and conversation, crystalized by the crisis of Diodati's death?) handles his pastoral materials in view of what he may not have apprehended at the time of *Lycidas*: that banquet to be made (as in *Paradise Lost*) of the classical hierarchy of pastoral and epic genres, transfigured through the alchemy of Christian incarnational paradox.

The volitional climax of *Epitaphium Damonis* arrives when the doubly illusory pastoral dream of Thyrsis in Italy is rudely broken off in the present reality of Damon's death. That careless innocence Thyrsis has been remembering is now gone forever. It was illusory then; it is doubly untrue remembered (yet one remembers). Thyrsis' new and dear-bought knowledge emerges as a mental environment in which the highest previous pastoral pursuits of medicine and song encounter needs they are insufficient to assuage:

> Ah pereant herbae, pereant artesque medentûm
> Gramina, postquam ipsi nil profecere magistro.   (153–54)

[Ah! perish the herbs, perish the arts of the doctors, their grasses, since they can do nothing for their master.]

But what of Thyrsis' pursuits ("Ipse etiam")? And there follows (after the renunciation of Damon's medical arts) the seemingly parallel renunciation by Thyrsis of pastoral poetry: "vos cedite silvae." Yet this striking Virgilian echo which renounces pastoral in favor of epic is not, as it might seem, that personal vocational response of Thyrsis to the reality of Damon's death, toward which the elegy has been building. Instead, this farewell to pastoral and the following description of Milton's project for an epic are the components of a lengthy explanatory "parenthesis" — introduced by anacoluthon in line 155 and extending all the way to line 180 ("these things I was saving for you Damon"). Rather than renouncing pastoral after Damon's death, Thyrsis had savored the thrilling anticipation of following in the footsteps of Virgil before he knew of Damon's death; indeed had been waiting to share this growth with Damon. Now, however, those naive Italian hopes are tried and tested, as Thyrsis recalls them here, against the harsh disappointment of Damon's death. Any suggestion of untoward self-centeredness at this point is forestalled by a rare expression of Miltonic diffidence: "I fear I am vain ("turgidulus"), yet I will relate it" (160). Well might he fear; even a carefully distanced memory of a Virgilian epic boast is the single Virgilian adaptation no Renaissance poet might undertake lightly.

The actual renunciation Thyrsis makes, his actual adaptation to the loss of Damon and to the resulting insufficiency of naive pastoral dreams, follows: it is the poignant acceptance of human limitations bravely adopted after the epic venture has been remembered: "quid enim? omnia non licet uni / Non sperâsse uni licet omnia" (171–72) ("What then? One human being is not allowed everything, nor can one hope to be allowed all things"). This recognition sets the tone that is finally and fully in keeping with Damon's death. It is also a stance in keeping, however, with Damon's life, and with Damon's apotheosis, the ultimate vision of which will soon enter as the last triumphant answer to the question of why Thyrsis ought still to cultivate his art—if he can do so on terms worthy of Damon and commensurate with a shattered pastoral world in which Damon is dead. The truly painful choice that this elegy embraces, and announces to the world (through the interior mental valuing process of Thyrsis reflected on a succession of pastoral landscapes), is Milton's resolution to cleave to his epic vocation even though Damon be lost, and to chasten and discipline his high poetic aspirations to a lonely service of the native flock of one northern island. Again, in the most personal and seemingly nonclassical section of the elegy, we see Milton's brilliant grounding of his elegy in Virgilian precedent, for Britain is after all the land Virgil had described as "far sundered from all the world" in Eclogue I, 66, in which Meliboeus laments being cast out of Arcadia forever, and banished even perhaps as far away as that very northern island. The allusion is one Milton's Italian friends surely might have recognized and savored.

This, then, is the volitional climax of the *Epitaphium*'s progression: the straitened heroism of Thyrsis as he reaffirms, in the face of unexpected additional deprivation and depression, a decision entertained in Italy in anticipation of Diodati's sharing it. This is even, I think, the true epitaph for Damon—not simply the elegy itself, fine as that is and crafted to place Damon in the company of Daphnis and Bion, but also the gesture sent after the too-soon departed friend: Thyrsis' resolution to pursue his epic even after all of life has lost its savor. In these lines he proves that he has benefited and is benefiting still from knowing his friend, even in his death—or most of all in his death.

Milton cleaves closely to the classical art-eclogue in his powerful close as well, and I want to bypass Manso's cups to consider the heavenly vision of Damon at this point, rendered in terminology drawn from classical myth and pagan religion. Comparison of *Epitaphium Damonis* and *Lycidas* has led to placing undue theological emphasis on the celebration of Diodati's virginity in the closing movement of the Latin elegy. This reference to virginity need not be overtly Christian, although unquestionably the idea of 144,000 virgins in Revelation provides a scriptural basis for the vision of Diodati.[10] Milton, however, goes out of his way to avoid emphasizing the potential Christian meaning of the passage, because he is using Damon's virginity to different ends. His classical diction emphasizes instead the high pastoral paradox he is laboring to elucidate, based upon his sophisticated utilization of the generic metaphors provided by epic and pastoral in themselves:

> purum colit aethera Damon,
> Aethere purus habet, pluvium pede reppulit arcum;
> Heroúmque animas inter, divósque perennes,
> Aethereos haurit latices et gaudia potat
> Ore Sacro.   (203–07)

[The pure ether Damon inhabits — Damon possesses the ether, himself pure — he spurns with his foot the rainbow. Among the spirits of heroes and the immortal gods he drinks the ethereal potions and quaffs joy with his sacred lips.]

Like draws to like: because Damon was pure in this life he now inhabits the pure ether. Damon pursued purity during his pastoral existence — he loved "purpureus pudor, et sine labe juventus" (212) ("the blush of modesty, and a youth without stain"): a not-unknown classical virtue, after all. The subtly implanted Neoplatonic contrast of the refracted light of this world as against the white light of eternity in the wonderful classical rainbow image only helps maintain the figural significance of Damon's chosen path of preferring the One to the Many. But most importantly, in keeping with his former purity and its inherent self-denials, Damon now drinks deeply of the joys of Olympus "Heroúmque animas inter, divósque perennes." "With the immortal gods and the souls of heroes," therefore, Damon participates in the orgiastic wedding feast of bliss; Damon who, like *Comus'* Lady, walked not after Bacchus nor knew the pleasures of the marriage bed, will taste the joys of an apotheosized pastoral world of idyllic delight under the vine-wrapped *thyrsus* of the god of wine and ecstasy. Even the single overtly biblical note in the poem (given the liturgical echo allowed in line 111), the adjective "Sion" in the last line, reinforces the imagery of pastoral apotheosis, evocative as it is of the pastoral redemption of Millennial Israel: "But ye, O mountains of Israel, ye shall shoot forth your branches, and yield your fruit to my people of Israel; for they are at hand to come" (Ezek. xxxvi, 8) or "the mountains and the hills shall break forth before you into singing, and all the trees of the field shall clap their hands" (Isa. lv, 12).

Epitaphium Damonis concerns itself with what is worthy of and for Damon, in order to ask what is worthy of and for Thyrsis if he is to con-

tinue to be the true peer of Damon. Damon's apotheosis is splendid, but
expected. The equally splendid apotheosis of pastoral into an heroic context in the closing movements of the *Epitaphium* is not so expected. Damon's apotheosis turns out to be based on his pursuit of a singular purity,
a purity involving denial of certain pastoral pleasures in the ardent pursuit of a higher value. Damon's death has been showing Thyrsis how little
such pleasures mean in themselves, without indwelling grace and wit.
Finally, Damon's apotheosis in the last lines shows that pursuit of the
highest goods, even at the cost of temporal renunciation, is indeed the
very stuff of which heroes and epic heroism are made. Nor is pastoral
renunciation to be regretted when it is compensated by a heavenly fulfillment incomparably greater, yet in the same mode.

The apotheosis of pastoral is linked thematically and figurally to that
of Damon and shows that for Milton, already here as later in *Paradise
Lost,* pastoral is the mode of paradise; Eden is the figure of pure delight
whether in Nature or in Supernature. Pastoralism is not renounced, therefore, in the wholesale way Ralph W. Condee argues in his otherwise splendid essay on the structure of *Epitaphium Damonis.*[11] Rather it is trans-
valued, as in *Paradise Lost;* through loss its temporal values are tested
and sorted out from its eternal ones. The shepherd Damon pursued purity through the self-discipline of chastity and found heroic apotheosis.
To willingly forego immediate pastoral gratification for the higher call
of its heavenly original is the mode of heroism. Thyrsis will follow Damon
(like draws like) by pursuing beyond pastoralism his pastoral responsibilities: willingly foregoing earthly delights not evil in themselves and
giving up the gratification of temporal European fame for the native call
to vernacular epic:

> Mi satis ampla
> Merces, et mihi grande decus (sim ignotus in aevum
> Tum licet, externo penitúsque inglorius orbi)
> Si me flava comas legat Usa, et potor Alauni.   (172–75)

[I will have ample reward and think my honor great — even though unknown
then through the ages and utterly inglorious throughout the external world, if
blond-haired Ouse reads me, and he who drinks of the Alne.]

Thyrsis, like Damon, is being drawn upward throughout the progress of the elegy by the same magnetisms that had inspired their young
shepherds' souls in youth: the exchanges of grace and wit, the love of the
sweet muse, and the care of the flock. These loves will continue, the concluding movements affirm, to inflame the soul of Thyrsis to aspire even
to the severe self-discipline of the British epic. Though he will have no

one to whom he can pour out his heart or with whom he can share the rigors of his lonely task, no companionship or ease and only limited temporal incentive and reward, yet his sustaining motivation will derive like Damon's from the original source of all true loves and aspirations, of all truly heroic enterprises. While loss of Damon has made Thyrsis temporarily neglect his sheep, Damon's example finally enjoins him to a task in which all their shared loves of grace and mind and muse and flock are joined. Thyrsis' dedication of himself to epic, therefore, along with the affirmation of the royal themes of regeneration and divine love depicted on the cups of Manso, constitute a strong return to the "extraesthetic" world of responsibility.[12]

It is beautiful and right that the highest answers to the question "why should I nurture my increase in so sorry a world?" should come to Thyrsis (as to Adam and Eve) out of the pastoral world itself, so recently invaded by death. The fruits of the Italian journey and his own growth toward epic — "these things I was saving for you beneath the tough-barked laurel, these things and more also" (180–81): the cups of Manso. As the poem moves toward its unqualified visionary close, and as the desolate refrain is left at last behind, Thyrsis draws consolation and encouragement from those glimpses afforded to every mortal *from within the pastoral experience itself:* glimpses of incarnate worth and joy. In fact, the worth of the Italian cups for Thyrsis is a fine figural emblem of the similar solace and encouragement Milton drew from the presence for him in all classical literature of those suggestions of higher truth heralding the inevitability of the Christian revelation. The charming tradition of the pastoral trophy is a terrestrial version of celestial reward, and for a Christian poet to strengthen such patterns of meaning is only to realize what has been implicit all along. On a larger, generic scale, implicit in the traditional Virgilian pattern of poetic growth from pastoral to epic is the universal reality that the pastoral vision must be shattered in time so that growth into the heroic order of things may occur. Yet, artistically and theologically, the best of pastoral in its exquisite perfection is never left behind, for its essence is to embody in humility those very consummations that inspire and sustain heroic endeavor on the highest levels.

In the *Epitaphium* as an artistic whole, Milton sets before us a high instance of how the "reductive outlook" of the pastoral mode can explore through its ironic simplicity the complex relationship between art and life. To deny art and labor altogether — "Go home unfed, my lambs, your master does not care about you" — is never a real alternative for Thyrsis. Held before us by the delightful pastoral artifice of Milton's refrain, it is a stance as incompatible with pastoral as it is with epic vocation. With magnificent Virgilian irony, the poet Milton complains of disillusionment with art through the illusory vehicle of art itself. Pastoral verse can capture the moon's deception (140). In fact, Milton reenacts both pastoral innocence and (surpassing Virgil?) the inadequacy of pastoral innocence through the artistic verity of a pastoral poem raised to its highest potential.

As the final three movements of *Epitaphium Damonis* are modulated to their poignant completion by the skilled fingers of a disciplined singer whose pastoral pipe will hang abandoned hereafter (its apprenticeship never forgotten), the pastoral protagonist Thyrsis has made his choices, reaffirmed his values, and reordered his energies. He has tested and sorted out his memories, retaining his allegiance to the highest and purest values of his pastoral beginnings. He sees before him the ecstatic pastoral vision of the heavenly future. Between these foci of delight stretch out the years of his plain and present heroic task. Artistically, therefore, Milton's Latin pastoral elegy has maneuvered more than a score of poignant Virgilian motifs into a strikingly transfigured sequence of meaning that fully realizes their inherent classical suggestiveness without destroying their original classical purity. Philosophically and thematically, the elegy has arrived at as satisfying and coherent a resolution of its central issue as ever *Lycidas* does, although its theme is different: what must motivate and sustain artistic growth, when temporal motivations have disintegrated? All that remains is for twenty years of heroic effort in a bittersweet world to teach the poet the utter simultaneity of epic and pastoral, as it is celebrated in *Paradise Lost:* that moment-by-moment apotheosis of pastoral within the heroic which must mix past and future, "memory and desire," in the "here, now, always" of the paradise within.

Seattle Pacific University

NOTES

1. Bush, *Variorum*, p. 288.

2. Sicilian muses, let us sing of "somewhat greater things," Virgil announces in the opening line of his "Messianic" Eclogue IV on Pollio.

3. Woodhouse, "Milton's Pastoral Monodies," *Studies in Honor of Gilbert Norwood*, ed. Mary E. White (Toronto, 1952), p. 288.

4. Relevant here are comments (nowhere explicitly related to *Epitaphium Damonis*) by John R. Knott, Jr., in *Milton's Pastoral Vision* (Chicago, 1971), p. 81: "The consolation of the pastoral elegy typically promises the restoration of harmony between man and an idealized natural world that has been brutally interrupted by death. . . . With the collapse of the pastoral fiction, reality breaks in on the poet, forcing the recognition that decay

and disorder are a part of life. The equilibrium thus lost can be recovered if the fiction of a pastoral world is superseded by a higher fiction of a pastoral heaven beyond the possibility of change."

5. The translations are my own (with a special debt to Merritt Hughes); the Latin text of *Epitaphium Damonis* is taken from CM. Virgil's eclogues are cited from the *Loeb Classical Library* text.

6. For comparison of the two works, see Thomas Perrin Harrison, "The Latin Pastorals of Milton and Castiglione," *PMLA*, 50 (1935), 480–93.

7. On behalf of Milton's elegy, I would echo the indignation of Ralph W. Condee against critics who have patronized Milton's use of this refrain on pp. 578–79 of "The Structure of Milton's 'Epitaphium Damonis,'" *SP*, 62 (1965).

8. See Helen Cooper, *Pastoral: Medieval into Renaissance* (Totowa, N.J., 1977).

9. Ralph Condee shows how the refrain may change its meanings as the immediate dramatic context shifts during the elegy. I would emphasize instead the fundamental formal stasis of a refrain, which lends it whatever power it may possess to acquire shadings of meaning. In its formal stasis, this refrain directly encapsulates the shepherd's depression and aimlessness with regard to his poetic vocation. Throughout the *Epitaphium*, Milton is relying heavily on that tradition in which the pastoral landscape externalizes states of mind; a fascinating study of this topic showing the Italian debt in *Paradise Regained*, is Stewart A. Baker, "Sannazaro and Milton's Brief Epic," *CL*, 20 (1968), 116–32.

10. See Woodhouse, *Pastoral Monodies*, pp. 270–72, for an argument which presses the Christian aspect of the passage without noting Milton's verbal reticence.

11. This excellent study, discussed in notes 7 and 9 above, errs, I believe, in misinterpreting that self-transcendence implicit in so much pastoral (I am speaking of Virgil's reiterated eagerness to launch into epic in his eclogues or the haunting apotheosis of Daphnis, for example) as being in Milton a weariness with the genre and a need to "clearly and passionately surmount the tradition" (p. 578).

12. This is Woodhouse's expression, and he laments the seeming lack of such a "return" in *Epitaphium Damonis*, while he finds it implicit in *Lydicas*'s closing frame (p. 272).

IMITATION
IN *EPITAPHIUM DAMONIS*

Gordon Campbell

C HARLES DIODATI, the closest friend of Milton's youth, and possibly the only intimate friend he ever had, died in London in August 1638, while Milton was in Florence. It is not known precisely when or where Milton learned of Diodati's death, but it is likely that he was still in Italy when the news reached him.[1] Milton's Italian hosts had received him warmly, and some of them must have offered words of sympathy and comfort to the distressed young traveler. On his return to England Milton decided to write a poem which would commemorate the death of Diodati and the kindness of Milton's Italian friends. He composed *Epitaphium Damonis*, arranged to have it privately printed, and sent copies to his friends in Italy and England.[2] He wrote the poem in Latin, that being the only language which would be readily understood by both English and Italian recipients.

Milton chose to cast his memorial poem in the form of a pastoral lament, written in hexameters rather than in the more usual elegiacs. Pastoral laments were immensely popular in the Renaissance, and the form was particularly appropriate for a poem commemorating Diodati, whose two surviving letters to Milton — both written in Greek — are filled with exuberant pastoralism. A characteristic passage in the first letter joyously anticipates a shared holiday: "and the air and the sun and the river and trees and birds and earth and men will celebrate the holiday with us, and laugh with us, and join in the dance with us." And in the second letter Diodati exults in the glories of the countryside: "the days are long, the pathways are in bloom, and embellished and teeming with leaves, on every branch there is a nightingale or goldfinch or other songbird seeking delight with its chirpings. . . . If only I could acquire a noble companion, that is to say well-educated, with a good memory for all things, I should be more prosperous than the king of Persia."[3] Diodati yearns for Milton, his noble companion (ἐσθλὸν ἑταίρον; the idiom is Homeric), and in *Epitaphium Damonis* Milton yearns for Diodati, his faithful companion ("fidus . . . comes," 37–38).[4] The pastoral idiom of Milton's poem is not an escape from the effusion of real passion.[5] It is on the contrary a reflection of the language which Diodati used to describe his intoxication with nature when writing to his friend Milton.

The accidental survival of Diodati's letters enables us to understand the appropriateness of the pastoral idiom of Milton's poem and also affords a tantalizing glimpse of the private level of allusion in the poem, the chain of discourse which only Diodati would have understood. The account of Diodati's apotheosis, for example, includes the assertion that his "divinum nomen" will be "Diodotus" (210). The tradition of a new name in heaven is both Christian (the "new name" written in the white stone of Revelation ii, 17) and classical (Romulus, for example, became the god Quirinus), and Milton blends these traditions and adds a play on Diodati's name. Ordinarily one would assume that etymological wordplay embedded in the *consolatio* of a lament would be unremittingly solemn, for within the Christian tradition such paronomasia was sanctioned by Jesus' unsmiling play on Πέτρος ("Peter"), and πέτρα ("rock") in Matthew xvi, 18. Milton's use of wordplay at this point *is* solemn, but Diodati's letters show that the wordplay in Milton's poem also serves as an affectionate recollection of Diodati's practice in his letters. In the first letter Diodati transliterates Milton's name into Greek, but translates his own name, which appears as Θεόσδοτος, which is a poetical form of Θεόδοτος, the word he uses in the second letter;[6] both words mean "god-given." Thus Milton's play on "Diodotus" which like Θεόδοτος means "god-given," can be seen to have both public and private significance. Milton's choice of the Hellenic form *Diodotus*,[7] rather than the Latinate form *Deodatus* which appears in the *Argumentum* that precedes the poem, may have been intended to facilitate comparison with Diodotus the teacher of Cicero.

In *Epitaphium Damonis* Milton styles himself as Thyrsis, and Diodati as Damon. One should resist the temptation to attach too much significance to the choice of names, as both are exceedingly common in Renaissance pastoral. It is possible that Milton's choice of the name Thyrsis for himself reflects Theocritus' use of the name for the mourner of Idyll I, especially as that poem is Milton's single most important model. But Milton's choice of the name Damon for Diodati cannot be readily explained; it may be a private allusion to an understanding shared by Milton and Diodati. The idea that Milton chose the name Damon with a view to suggesting the friendship of the Pythagoreans Damon and Phintias seems unlikely, since Milton did not choose to call himself either Phintias or Pythias.[8] Damon was a popular name in Greek, and although it did not appear in pastoral verse prior to Virgil (Eclogues III and VIII), it had since become commonplace. Both names were popular, but to my knowledge the use of Damon for the name of the mourned, and Thyrsis for the name of the mourner, occurs in only one other poem, Pietro (or Basilio) Zanchi's *Damon*, in which a character called Lycidas asks Thyrsis why he is so sad, and Thyrsis responds with a lament for Damon.[9] The fact that Zanchi's Damon was Baldassare Castiglione[10] (whose Alcon is thought to have influenced Milton's poem)[11] makes the coincidence, if such it be, a pleasing one.

The title of Milton's poem sets it firmly in a Greek tradition, for the poem is described as an *epitaphium*. The Greeks of antiquity distinguished between *elegos, epikedeion,* and *epitaphios*. Milton's poem is usually termed an elegy, and although it is not written in the elegiac metre, its concern with an individual death rather than a public event such as the death of soldiers in battle certainly aligns it with the tradition of elegy. Recently the poem has been classed as an epicedion,[12] but this seems inaccurate, as in late antiquity (when a clear sense of the form emerged) the term *epicedion* referred to a public lament containing more praise than grief.[13] Since Milton did not choose to call his poem *Elegion Damonis* or *Epicedium Damonis*, his choice of the term *epitaphium* should not be ignored.

In ancient Athens an *epitaphios logos*, or funeral oration, was delivered over the graves of those who had fallen in battle. Thucydides (II. 35–46) claims to record the most famous of these speeches, Pericles' address at the end of the first year of the Peloponnesian War. Milton was of course familiar with this speech, and in alluding to it in *Animadversions* (1641) brought the word "epitaphian" into English (from Lucian's Greek)[14] as he abused the prelates for "making sad Orations at the Funerall of your deare *Prelacie*, like that doubtie Centurion *Afranius* in *Lucian*, who to imitate the noble *Pericles* in his *Epitaphian* speech, stepping up after the battell to bewaile the slaine *Severianus*, falls into a pittiful condolement, to think of those costly suppers, and drinking banquets, which he must now taste of no more; and by then he had done, lack't but little to lament the deare-loved memory, and calamitous losse of his Capon, and whitebroth."[15] Milton writes with the confidence of one who had recently composed a successful *epitaphion* which, like that of the noble Pericles, lamented a terrible loss. Of the surviving Hellenic *epitaphia* the one which most resembles Milton's poem is Hyperides' oration (delivered in 322 B.C.) on his intimate friend the general Leosthenes.[16] Hyperides' sense of personal loss is central to the oration, which unlike any other surviving Hellenic *epitaphion* affirms the hope of personal immortality, and speculates that its subject's earthly defense of the worship of the gods will be honored with the personal care of Hades. Although Milton could not have read the oration itself (it was discovered on a papyrus in Thebes [in Egypt] and first published in 1858), he certainly would have been familiar with the commendation of this *epitaphion* in Longinus' *On the Sublime* for its epideictic qualities as manifested in Hyperides' skilful deployment of *topoi.*[17] Milton's poem displays precisely this virtue, for the highly conventional idiom of pastoral becomes in Milton's hands a vehicle for intense personal emotion.

In Hellenistic terms the term *epitaphios* was extended beyond the early sense of a prose funeral oration to include poetic laments, and in these poems (and in the Latin poems modeled on them) the features which made Hyperides' *epitaphios* unique among surviving Hellenic examples have become commonplace, for these poems articulate a sense of personal loss at the passing of an individual, and affirm the hope or the certainty of personal immortality. Two of the most famous poems of the Hellenistic period incorporate the term *epitaphios* into their titles: Bion's *Epitaphios for Adonis,* and the *Epitaphios for Bion,* which was traditionally attributed to Moschus. Both poets were imitators of Theocritus, and in using the word *epitaphium* in his title Milton claims his place in the tradition of imitators of Theocritus. In the opening lines of his poem Milton asserts his position as an imitator with a series of references to Theocritus. He begins by invoking the nymphs of Himera, a Sicilian spring and river mentioned by Theocritus (V. 124, VII. 75) and a name associated with Stesichorus, the traditional inventor of bucolic poetry and the author of a lament for Daphnis. Milton then reminds the nymphs of the death of Daphnis, whom Theocritus had commemorated in Idyll I, of Hylas, whose fate Theocritus had described in Idyll XIII, and of Bion, who had been mourned in the *Epitaphios Bionos.* In taking pains to identify himself as an imitator of Theocritus, Milton deliberately provokes comparison with Virgil, the greatest imitator of Theocritus.

The relation of the *Epitaphium Damonis* to the tradition of pastoral lament is a complex one. The sources of many of the phrases and incidents in Milton's poem have been established by the cumulative efforts of his editors and critics. It is apparent that Milton's wide reading in the literature of antiquity and in the Latin literature of the Renaissance enabled him to cull many phrases which caught his poet's eye and reshape them for incorporation into his own poem. This habit of adapting elements of the poems of his predecessors — especially Virgil and Theocritus — raises the question of how the reader is to respond to the recognition of an ancient phrase. On some occasions the original provenance of the adapted phrase is so well known that one wonders to what extent Milton's deployment of the phrase constitutes an allusion to its original context. The example of this problem most familiar to students of Milton is the last line of his *Elegia III*, "Talia contingant somnia sæpe mihi" ("May such dreams often befall me"). Within the context of Milton's poem the line presents no problem, as it is clearly a pious wish for the recurrence of a sacred vision. But the phrase irresistably recalls its original in Ovid's *Amores*, "proveniant medii sic mihi saepe dies" (I.v.26) ("may it be my good fortune to have many a midday like this one"), in which Ovid is indulging in a lover's fantasies. And once this phrase is recognized, other phrases in Milton's poem betray their Ovidian origins. "Nec mora, membra cavo posui refovenda cubili" (35) ("Without delay I stretched out on the hollow bed in order to refresh my limbs") seems to recall the same romp with Corinna (I.v.2), and lines 53–55 of Milton's poem also seem to draw on this erotic poem (I.v.9). Are we supposed to recognize these borrowings? I suspect that the answer is yes, and that our recognition of the original context is supposed to make us appreciate Milton's ennobling of fine phrases that had hitherto been used in a context unworthy of them. But one cannot be certain, for the echoes of Ovid may reflect nothing more than Milton's youthful enthusiastic reading of that poet, and may not be part of the design of the elegy. At the age of seventeen Milton may not yet have been wholly the master of his craft.[18]

Epitaphium Damonis is quite another matter, for by 1639 Milton, then aged thirty, was an accomplished poet who had already written some of the finest poems in the English language. Like the early Latin poems, the *Epitaphium Damonis* recalls the phrases of earlier poets, but in this poem Milton's use of phrases which conjure up their originals in antiquity is clearly deliberate and carefully controlled. Before examining some of these phrases it may be salutary to pause for a moment to remind ourselves that the same technique was used by the greatest poets of antiquity.[19] According to an anecdote in the elder Seneca, Ovid borrowed phrases from Virgil "non supripiendi causa sed palam mutuandi, hoc animo ut vellet agnosci" ("not stealing them, but borrowing openly with the intention of being recognized"; *Suasoriae* III, 7). And in the most famous example of such borrowing Virgil himself incurred a puzzling debt to Catullus (or perhaps directly to Callimachus, whose poem Catullus was translating). In *Aeneid* VI Aeneas descends to the underworld and meets Dido, who had committed suicide in despair at the infidelity of Aeneas. Acutely aware of his responsibility for Dido's death, Aeneas pleads that he did not leave her shores voluntarily: "Invitus, regina, tuo de litore cessi" (VI, 460). In Catullus' translation of Callimachus' "Coma Berenices" (LXVI, 39) he makes the lock of Berenice's hair say "Invita, o regina, tuo de vertice cessi" ("It was not of my will, o queen, that I left your head";

the Greek line has not survived). Virgil has transformed mock-heroic into heroic, and the sheer daring of such a transference has left generations of his admirers breathless with horror that Virgil could contaminate such a fine moment with a piece of frivolity. It seems likely to me, however, that Virgil was attempting to use the same technique that Milton was to use in *Elegia III*, and that we are to admire the dexterity with which Virgil has transformed a clever line from a court elegy into a pained and hesitant expression of anguish.

The clearest example of this kind of creative imitation in Milton's *Epitaphium Damonis* is the refrain which Milton uses seventeen times, "Ite domum impasti, domino jam non vacat, agni" ("Go home unfed, my lambs, your master has not time for you now"). The refrain does not draw its phrasing from any of the refrains in the pastoral laments of antiquity, but rather from Virgil's Eclogue VII: "ite domum pasti, si quis pudor, ite juvenci" ("go home well fed, my heifers, go, for shame").[20] Virgil's Thyrsis thinks that the cattle should feel ashamed, either for occupying the time which their master wishes to devote to sexual activity, or (possibly) for exhibiting voyeuristic tendencies (like the goats in Eclogue III, 8) in wanting to remain while their master makes love.[21] Milton has chosen for his model a line which in its original context is coarse, and has adapted it to a solemn setting. How should the sympathetic reader react to the echo? Both Virgil and Milton have invested a light but well-turned phrase with a measure of dignity, and in both cases recollections of the original context give the reader pause. In both cases the *frisson* that accompanies recognition seems to be functional, in that the echoes suggest something of the nature of the relationship portrayed in the imitative passages. In Virgil's case his use of Catullus underlines the erotic element in the relation between Dido and Aeneas, and in Milton's case the effect is similar. The line which Virgil gave to Thyrsis is an expression of passion, and something of this passion survives in Milton's phrase. Milton had chosen to commemorate Diodati in a form invented by Theocritus and developed by Virgil. In the pastorals of these ancient writers the shepherds share the morals of their sheep, and are at times enthusiastically homosexual or bisexual. In Milton's England active homosexuality was deemed a sin, and it would be wrong to describe Milton's relation with Diodati in these terms.[22] But their friendship was not less passionate for not being physical. The erotic echo in Milton's refrain is meant to convey to the reader something of the passion which Milton felt for his dearest friend.

Milton also uses echoes of the poems of antiquity to animate the natural landscape of *Epitaphium Damonis*. On the surface Milton's poem is naturalistic, in that there is no overt use of the pathetic fallacy. When

Dati and Francini are said to have taught the name of Thyrsis-Milton to their beech trees ("suas docuerunt nomina fagos," 136), Milton seems to be saying that his friends have sung his praises among the trees. The personification of the trees implicit in this line becomes explicit only when we recall that Milton's line is based on similar passages in Virgil in which the woods are personified and instructed in song. Thus at the beginning of Eclogue I, for example, Meliboeus enjoins Tityrus to teach the woods to re-echo the beauty of Amaryllis ("formosam resonare doces Amaryllida silvas"),[23] and nature is seen to respond. And the response of nature in Virgil's poem enlivens the landscape of Milton's poem.

This phenomenon can also be observed in Milton's depiction of sheep: "ovium quoque tædet, at illæ / Mœrent, inque suum convertunt ora magistrum" ("I am weary even of my sheep, and they are sad and turn their faces to their master," 67–68). Again there is a naturalistic explanation: the sheep are turning to their master in a spirit of sadness because they have been neglected and want to be fed (cf. "The hungry Sheep look up, and are not fed" in *Lycidas*, 125). This interpretation is strengthened by the appearance of the refrain in the next line, for the refrain emphasizes that the shepherd is neglecting his hungry sheep. Echoes of Theocritus and Virgil, however, enrich the lines by suggesting that the sheep are mourning. "Mœrent" can mean "they are mourning," and this is precisely what the herds in Theocritus I are said to do (74–75); as in Milton's poem, only the animals are responsive to death in Idyll I. In Virgil's Eclogue X, the whole of the natural landscape is seen to respond, and even the cliffs weep (15). The sheep are shown to be gathered around the shepherd ("stant et oves circum," 16); the implication is that they too are in mourning. Milton's evocation of this passage ensures that his readers will understand his sheep to be in mourning.

One of the most striking features of Milton's imitations of phrases from the literature of antiquity in this poem is that the phrasing often derives from a Latin imitation of a Greek passage, while the substance derives from the Greek original. In line 43 of *Epitaphium Damonis*, for example, Milton asks "Quis fando sopire diem, cantuque solebit?" ("Who will now lull the day to sleep with conversation and song?"). Editors cite Virgil, Eclogue IX, 51–52: "saepe ego longos / cantando puerum memini me condere soles" ("I recall as a boy how I would sing through the long summer days and put the sun to bed"). To these lines one might reasonably add Horace's "condit quisque diem collibus in suis" (the farmer on his hillside "sees the day to bed"; *Odes* IV.v.29). Both passages resemble Milton's, and recollections of both probably shaped his phrasing, but neither is commemorative, and neither is describing a shared experience. For these elements one must turn to what I take to be Virgil's source, an epigram by Callimachus which Milton would have known both from the Greek Anthology (vii.80) and from Diogenes Laertius (ix.17):

εἶπέ τις, Ἡράκλειτε, τεὸν μόρον, ἐς δ᾿ ἐμὲ δάκρυ
ἤγαγεν, ἐμνήσθην δ᾿ ὁσσάκις ἀμφότεροι
ἥλιον ἐν λέσχῃ κατεδύσαμεν

[One told me of your death, Heraclitus, and brought me to tears, and I remembered how often we had sent the sun to rest with our conversation.]

The tone and substance of the epigram establish it as Milton's original.

A similar example is Milton's assertion that Diodati will be remembered "secundo / . . . post Daphnin" ("second after Daphnis," 30–31). The parallel passage in Virgil is Eclogue V, 49, where Menalcas proclaims Mopsus "alter ab illo." "Illo" refers to the "magistrum" of the previous line, whom I take to be Daphnis. Milton would have known that the phrase "alter ab illo" does not mean "second to Daphnis," but rather "successor to Daphnis."[24] Milton's ultimate source is not Virgil, but Virgil's source, Theocritus I.3, where Thyrsis tells the unnamed goatherd that he will take second prize to Pan: μετὰ Πᾶνα τὸ δεύτερον ἆθλον ἀποισῇ. Milton's "secundo" is Theocritus' δεύτερον, not Virgil's "alter."

A particularly revealing example of the interplay between Milton's Greek and Latin models is his reworking of a simple but effective contrast in Virgil's Eclogue VII. In that poem Corydon describes grass that is softer than sleep ("somno mollior herba," 45), and by way of contrast Thyrsis, Corydon's opponent in the singing contest, describes grass that is dying of thirst ("moriens sitit . . . herba," 57). Milton uses the second of these phrases early in the Epitaphium Damonis by recalling how in England Diodati would stay by his side when the crops were dying of thirst ("siti morientibus herbis," 40), and retards the completion of the expected contrast for ninety lines, whereupon the "mollior herba" appears to describe the soft grass on which Milton was lying in the poplar grove by the cool waters of the Arno ("gelidi cum stratus ad Arni / Murmura, populeumque nemus, quà mollior herba," 129–30). But as Milton imitates Virgil, so in the same phrase Milton reaches back to Theocritus by linking the soft grass with a grove of trees and cool water. In Idyll V (another singing contest) Lacon assures Comatas

ἅδιον ᾀσῇ
τεῖδ᾿ ὑπὸ τὰν κότινον καὶ τἄλσεα ταῦτα καθίξας.
ψυχρὸν ὕδωρ τουτεὶ καταλείβεται· ὧδε πεφύκει
ποία, χἀ στιβὰς ἅδε.　　　　　　　　　　　　　　　(31–34)

[You will sing in greater comfort under the olive, beneath those trees. There is cool water falling nearby, and a grass bed]

The source of Milton's contrast is Virgil, but the context of his use of a Virgilian phrase evokes Theocritus. And the matter does not end there, for "morientis" is also used of Diodati (122), and the immediacy of the present participle recalls the similar effect in Theocritus I, where the statement of the death of Daphnis is put in the present tense: Daphnis Θνάσκει ("dies," 135).

It is apparent that many of the phrases in *Epitaphium Damonis* are enriched by the echoes of their original contexts. But what is the significance for Milton and his poem of this practice of imitation? Longinus provides a starting point in his discussion of *mimesis* (the Greek technical term equivalent to *imitatio*) by introducing a metaphor whereby Plato is said to be "breaking a lance"[25] (διαδορατιζόμενος) with Homer in imitating him. Longinus admits that to initiate a contention with Homer may be overambitious, but insists that it is not profitless and that it is not a disgrace to be defeated by one's predecessors.

In ancient pastoral, contention between poets takes the form of a singing contest (Virgil, Eclogues III and VII, Theocritus, Idylls V, VI, VIII, and IX). Milton incorporated the convention of the singing contest into his own poem: "Et potui Lycidæ certantem audire Menalcam" ("And I could listen to Menalcas contending with Lycidas," 132). The primary reference is presumably to the literary recitals of the Florentine academies at which Milton had read his own poems; in September 1638, for example, Milton had read a poem in Latin hexameters to the members of the Svogliati, who thought it "molto erudita."[26] Such occasions were not contests, and it is interesting that Milton should choose to represent them as such. In a sense, *Epitaphium Damonis* is Milton's entry in a singing contest in which the other contestants are Virgil and the Hellenistic pastoral poets; in imitating Milton was competing. There are signs that Milton continued to hold this view throughout his creative life. It seems significant that the epigraph to the *Poems* of 1645, "Baccare frontem / Cingite, ne vati noceat mala lingua futuro" ("Wreathe my forehead with bacchar, and let not an evil tongue injure the destined poet") should be the words of a Thyrsis (the name which Milton assumes in *Epitaphium Damonis*) in a singing contest (Virgil, Eclogue VII, 27–28). Virgil's Thyrsis is already a rising poet[27] ("crescentem . . . poetam," or in some versions of the text, "nascentem . . . poetam"; VII, 25), but he sees himself as a future *vates*; this native Latin word has religious and prophetic associations which *poeta*, a Greek loan word, does not.[28] Milton's epigraph explains that he is already a *poeta*, and is destined to become a *vates*.

Milton's sense that imitative poetry is in competition with its original is most prominently expressed in *Paradise Lost*, in which the imitation of Homer and Virgil is almost continuous, and in which Milton stridently asserts the superiority of his entry in the singing contest over his Greek and Roman rivals. His subject, he claims, is

> Not less but more Heroic than the wrauth
> Of stern *Achilles* on his Foe pursu'd
> Thrice Fugitive about *Troy* Wall; or rage
> Of *Turnus* for *Lavinia* disespous'd,
> Or *Neptun*'s ire or *Juno*'s, that so long
> Perplex'd the *Greek* and *Cytherea*'s Son.   (IX, 14–19)

In *Epitaphium Damonis* Milton is prepared to take second place to Theocritus ("secundo . . . post Daphnin"); in *Paradise Lost* he is no longer willing to admit the superiority of his competitors. The *poeta* has become a *vates*.

Milton had often intimated that he would become an epic poet, and one of the central intimations is the passage in *Epitaphium Damonis* (162–68) in which he describes his plans for a British epic which was never to be written. This passage has upset some readers of the poem (notably Tillyard), because it seems to have nothing to do with Diodati. Considered in the light of Milton's competition with Virgil, a competition that involves imitation, the passage becomes more understandable. In *Georgics* III, 8–48 Virgil predicts that he will write a great poem about Caesar — Virgil describes it as a temple — and Milton is imitating this prophecy. As it happens the poem which Virgil projected was not the one which he eventually wrote, and by gentle historical irony the same was to be true of Milton. At the beginning of *Paradise Lost* Milton again chose to recall Virgil's projected epic, for his assertion that the Spirit prefers "before all Temples th'upright heart and pure" seems to contain a clear recollection of Virgil's *templum* for Caesar. The special place of Virgil in Milton's sense of his vocation as a poet can scarcely be overstressed, for Milton often presents himself as a Christian Virgil, and his imitations of Virgil in *Epitaphium Damonis* and *Paradise Lost* very naturally often add a Christian dimension. There was an important precedent for this in *Christos Paschon*, which modern scholars dismiss as a slavish imitation of Euripides, but which Milton described with respect as a tragedy in the preface to *Samson Agonistes*. In that play, to take but one example, Medea's lament for the children she is about to kill is given to Mary as she weeps for Jesus.[29] It is evident from Milton's poems, including *Epitaphium Damonis*, that he approved of such imitations.

Epitaphium Damonis is an imitative poem, and in that quality inheres its greatness. This claim may seem paradoxical to some readers, although recently critics have grown increasingly interested in literary imitation as it was practiced in the Renaissance.[30] Imitation of great poets was a normal exercise in the schools of Milton's day — witness for example his youthful *Apologus de Rustico et Hero,* an academic imitation of a fable by Mantuan. As Milton matured as a poet, he developed and transformed his youthful skills in the art of imitation, to the extent that many of his greatest poems — *Lycidas, Epitaphium Damonis,* and *Paradise Lost* — are imitations of the great poems of antiquity. From imitation by rote, Milton progressed to that kind of creative imitation which assimilates and transforms its sources. As Longinus had explained, one of the roads to excellence "is the imitation and emulation of the great prose writers and poets of the past" (*On the Sublime* XIII, 2). Addison realized that Milton had taken this road: "*Milton,* though his own natural Strength of Genius was capable of furnishing out a perfect Work, has doubtless very much raised and ennobled his Conceptions, by such an Imitation as that which *Longinus* has recommended." By such means, Addison observes, "one great Genius often catches the Flame from another, and writes in his Spirit, without copying servilely after him" (*Spectator* 339). In *Epitaphium Damonis* Milton has caught the flame of Theocritus and Virgil. In 1645 Milton placed *Epitaphium Damonis* at the end of his collection of poems. It is appropriate that his greatest Latin poem should have been accorded this important position, for it looks, Janus-like, back on Milton's achievement as a Latin poet and represents the culmination of his labors in that form, and looks forward to his achievement as the writer of the greatest English Epic.[31]

University of Leicester

NOTES

I am grateful to Mr. Roger Collins, Mrs. Kirsty Shipton, and the editors of this volume for their comments on an early draft of this paper.

1. William Riley Parker, "Milton and the News of Charles Diodati's Death," *MLN,* 72 (1957), 486–88.

2. Letter to Carlo Dati, YP II, p. 763.

3. The Greek texts are printed in *The Life Records of John Milton,* ed. J. M. French, 5 vols. (New Brunswick, N.J., 1949–58), I, pp. 98–99, 104–05. The translations are my own, as are all translations of the ancient poems.

4. Quotations from Milton's poems are taken from CM. The translations of his Latin poems in my text are usually those of Mary Campbell, as printed in my edition of Milton's *Complete Poems* (London, 1980).

5. Cf. Ralph W. Condee, "The Structure of Milton's 'Epitaphium Damonis,'" *SP*, 62 (1965), 577–94.

6. Milton calls Diodati "Theodotus" in an affectionate phrase in *Familiar Letter* 6 (CM XII, p. 18).

7. Several editors (H. J. Todd, M. Y. Hughes, J. Shawcross) silently emend "Diodotus" to "Diodatus."

8. The suggestion was first made by A. S. P. Woodhouse, in "Milton's Pastoral Monodies," in *Studies in Honour of Gilbert Norwood*, ed. M. E. White (Toronto, 1952), pp. 265–66. "Pythias" is an ancient *falsa lectio* which survived in Renaissance England; see for example Richard Edwards' play *Damon and Pithias* (1571).

9. Basilio Zanchi, *Poemata* (Rome, 1550), fols. 65^r–67^v.

10. See W. Leonard Grant, *Neo-Latin Literature and the Pastoral* (Chapel Hill, 1965), p. 316.

11. T. P. Harrison, "The Latin Pastorals of Milton and Castiglione," *PMLA*, 50 (1935), 480–93. See also Lawrence V. Ryan, "Milton's *Epitaphium Damonis* and B. Zanchi's Elegy on Baldassare Castiglione," *Humanistica Lovaniensia*, 30 (1981), 108–23, published after this essay was accepted.

12. Grant, *Neo-Latin Literature*, pp. 306–30.

13. For a taxonomy of ancient (and modern) laments see Margaret Alexiou, *The Ritual Lament in Greek Tradition* (Cambridge, 1974), pp. 102–28.

14. Lucian, *How to Write History*, 26.

15. *Animadversions*, Section IV; YP I, p. 701.

16. See *Minor Attic Orators*, ed. J. O. Burtt, Loeb edition (London, 1954), II, pp. 531–59.

17. D. A. Russell, ed., "Longinus," *On the Sublime* (Oxford, 1964), pp. 162–63, commentary on XXXIV, 2.

18. For a different view of the matter see Michael West, "The *Consolatio* in Milton's Funeral Elegies," *HLQ*, 34 (1970–71), 235; see also Edward Le Comte, "Sly Milton: The Meaning Lurking in the Contexts of his Quotations," *Greyfriar*, 19 (1978), 3–7.

19. See the essays collected by David West and Tony Woodman in *Creative Imitation and Latin Literature* (Cambridge, 1979), especially D. A. Russell's fine survey "De Imitatione," which provided the original stimulant for many of the ideas developed in this essay, and the examples discussed in this paragraph. See also Donald Lemen Clark's chapter on imitation in *Rhetoric in Greco-Roman Education* (New York, 1957), pp. 144–76, and Davis P. Harding, *The Club of Hercules: Studies in the Classical Background of Paradise Lost*, Illinois Studies in Language and Literature Vol. 50 (Urbana, 1962), pp. 8–23.

20. Eclogue VII, 44. Milton's line may owe a slighter debt to Eclogue X, 77.

21. See Robert Coleman, ed., Vergil, *Eclogues* (Cambridge, 1977), p. 219, commentary on VII, 44.

22. For an opposing view see J. T. Shawcross, "Milton and Diodati: An Essay in Psychodynamic Meaning," in *Milton Studies*, VII, ed. Albert C. Labriola and Michael Lieb (Pittsburgh, 1975), pp. 127–63.

23. Cf. Eclogue II, 3–5 (where the trees are beeches) and VI, 83, and Propertius I.xviii.31–32.

24. Coleman, *Eclogues*, p. 165, commentary on 48–49.

25. Russell, commentary on XIII, 4; p. 118, n. 17.

26. French, *Life Records*, I, p. 389.

27. See Louis Martz, "The Rising Poet," in *The Lyric and Dramatic Milton*, ed. Joseph Summers (New York, 1965), pp. 8–9.

28. Coleman, *Eclogues*, p. 214.

29. Alexiou, *Ritual Lament*, p. 64.

30. Since this paper was accepted for publication, several studies of Renaissance imitation have appeared, including G. W. Pigman III, "Versions of Imitation in the Renaissance," *Renaissance Quarterly*, 33 (1980), 1–32, and Richard S. Peterson, *Imitation and Praise in the Poems of Ben Jonson* (New Haven, 1981).

PORTRAITS OF AN ARTIST:
MILTON'S CHANGING SELF-IMAGE

Albert C. Labriola

---

*E*PITAPHIUM DAMONIS shows Milton at a crucial juncture of his life. Having returned from the Italian journey, he laments the separation from his Florentine friends while he mourns the death of his closest boyhood companion, Charles Diodati. At the same time he acknowledges the influence of both Diodati and the Florentines on his development as a poet. But toward the end of the poem, in announcing plans for a *magnum opus*, he brings to a close the early phase of his development and undertakes with uncertainty and anxiety the role of epic poet. In relation to his past and in anticipation of his future, Milton presents a view of himself to which he will refer time and again throughout his career.

In speaking about the effect of Diodati's death on him, Milton expectedly recapitulates the depth and degree of their friendship. Within that relationship Diodati was a correspondent, interlocutor, and confidant. Milton is unwilling to dissociate his friend from these roles because he had entrusted to Diodati, since childhood, periodic glimpses of himself. Despite his friend's death Milton unfolds a self-image deriving from the Italian journey of 1638–39. As a result, *Epitaphium Damonis* continues the relationship reflected in Milton's earlier verse-letters to Diodati (*Elegiae Prima* and *Sexta*) and *Familiar Letters* (Nos. 6 and 7) to his friend.

While disclosing his self-image, Milton also reassesses his friendship with Diodati. Because of the Italian journey that friendship acquired even more significance than it had before. In classifying Diodati as a Tuscan, whose lineage is traceable to the city of Lucca, Milton is being neither fatuous nor frivolously complimentary. He is affirming that by ethnic affiliation, if not virtual birthright, Diodati is included among the *cognoscenti*, savants, or *literati* who share certain literary and aesthetic values flourishing in seventeenth-century Italy. Though not attributable to ancestry, Milton's connection with this enlightened culture was affirmed by his proficiency in the Italian language and his reception in Italy. In 1647, eight years after his return from Italy, Milton received a letter from

179

Carlo Dati, a Florentine intellectual whom he had befriended, praising
him as one "who writes and speaks in so correct and polished a fashion
in our beautiful idiom." Having written in Tuscan, Dati expresses the
hope that Milton "will find pleasing the sound of that which [he] speak[s]
and possess[es] so well" (CM XII, p. 297). In a letter written one year
earlier, Dati is similarly complimentary, remarking that the Tuscan language is "so dear and familiar . . . that in [Milton's] mouth it appears
not as a foreign tongue" (CM XII, p. 313).

If the tone of *Epitaphium Damonis* seems self-congratulatory, it also
acknowledges gratitude to Diodati. Retrospectively Milton avers that since
childhood his intellectual friendship with Diodati had reflected the coterie
society he entered at Florence. Thus, Milton's expression of "eternal loss"
("aeternum . . . damnum," 111) is more than conventional lamentation
over the death of a friend.[1] It marks the end of a relationship that began
in or before grammar school, during which his literary aspirations were
developed and creative energies aroused. His disappointment at the death
of his friend cannot be overestimated, for Diodati, more than anyone,
was to have heard and shared in the emotional texture of Milton's success
in Italy. Especially in its exuberant passages, *Epitaphium Damonis* recounts how and what Milton intended to tell Diodati about the Italian
journey, a context for a new understanding of their friendship. If at times
the poem sounds like conversation, the implied listener is Diodati.

Renewal of friendship with Diodati would have eased the transition from intellectual camaraderie with the Florentines to virtual solitude at home. As *Epitaphium Damonis* also explains, Milton intended
to inform his friend of tentative plans for a *magnum opus*, an Arthuriad,
so that their relationship would have provided a supportive context for
his literary aspirations. In other words, a sympathetic confidant, like Diodati, would have continued at home what intellectual encouragement
and emotional gratification Milton had received abroad. Not to be overlooked is Milton's assertion in *Epitaphium Damonis* that while traveling
in Italy he continually remembered Diodati and anticipated their reunion.
By invoking Diodati and the Florentines and recalling their admiration
of him, Milton validates his aspirations, authenticates his achievements,
calls attention to the process of his maturation as an author, and reaffirms the literary and aesthetic values that have guided him. As a gesture
by which he articulates these constituents of his literary ego, *Epitaphium
Damonis* demonstrates how self-perception and self-image are the necessary, if not compulsive, means toward acquiring or renewing self-worth.
Commendatory verses by Francini and Salzilli, which Milton included
in the 1645 edition, are further evidence of his continuing use of acco-

lades received in Italy as testimonials. So indelibly imprinted on his psyche was this self-image that Milton considered it an essential part of his auto-biography, especially several years later when he affirmed his dignity against detractors during the polemical controversies.

Milton's lament in *Epitaphium Damonis* — "But what at last is to become of me?" ("At mihi quid tandem fiet modò?" 37) — is deeply poignant as well as conventional. Separated by distance from the Florentines, whom he was never to see again, and deprived of Diodati's friendship, Milton was exceedingly forlorn. In describing himself as "wandering through solitary places" ("loca sola pererrans," 8), Milton gives evidence of acute alienation from most of his countrymen. Responding to one of the letters in which Carlo Dati praised his mastery of Italian, Milton in 1647 complains that "those whom habits, disposition, studies, had so hand-somely made my friends, are now almost all denied me, either by death or by most unjust separation of place, and are so for the most part snatched from my sight that I have to live well-nigh in a perpetual solitude."[2] Indeed, this view is comparable to what is expressed in *Epitaphium Damonis*: "But we men are a painful race, a stock tormented by cruel fate, with minds mutually alienated and hearts discordant. A man can hardly find a comrade for himself in a thousand; or, if one is granted to us by a fate at last not unkind to our prayers, a day and hour when we apprehend nothing snatches him away, leaving an eternal loss to all the years":

> Nos durum genus, et diris exercita fatis
> Gens homines aliena animis, et pectore discors,
> Vix sibi quisque parem de millibus invenit unum,
> Aut si sors dederit tandem non aspera votis,
> Illum inopina dies quâ non speraveris horâ
> Surripit, aeternum linquens in saecula damnum.   (106–11)

In their expression of Milton's admiration of the Florentines, the letter to Dati and *Epitaphium Damonis* are likewise comparable. Together they establish Florentine society as the norm in relation to which Milton's own country falls short or, from another perspective, the ideal toward which Britain should strive.

Epitaphium Damonis enables Milton to understand more fully his earlier inclinations toward friendship and his desire to enter a literary society, impulses voiced time and again in the *Familiar Letters*. Along with the letters written before its publication, *Epitaphium Damonis* charts the development of Milton's self-image. In writing, for instance, to Thomas Young in 1625 (*Familiar Letter*, No. 1), his preceptor at St. Paul's, Milton explains that he is "in London amid city distractions, and not,

as usual, surrounded by books." He promises another letter when he returns "to the haunts of the Muses" (p. 7), no doubt a reference to the country environment where he pursued private study. Most significant is an
expression of gratitude for Young's instruction and encouragement of Milton's literary education. Despite their separation Milton avows that Young
is a continuing presence in his intellectual life: "as that most vehement
desire after you which I feel makes me always fancy you with me, and
speak to you and behold you as if you were present, and so (as generally
happens in love) soothe my grief by a certain vain imagination of your
presence, it is in truth my fear that, as soon as I should meditate a letter
to be sent you, it should suddenly come into my mind by what an interval of earth you are distant from me, and so the grief of your absence,
already nearly lulled, should grow fresh, and break up my sweet dream"
(p. 7). Almost to the smallest detail such a view anticipates Milton's frame
of mind in *Epitaphium Damonis*, alternating between the joy of recounting the numerous successes of the Italian journey and the sadness of realiz-
ing that Diodati, with whom his literary aspirations were shared since
childhood, is not simply absent but dead.

If the letter to Young is one of the earliest anticipations of Milton's
frame of mind in *Epitaphium Damonis*, other letters provide similar in-
sights into the process of self-definition occurring in the pastoral elegy.
To Alexander Gill in 1628 (*Familiar Letter*, No. 2) Milton acknowledges
having received his poem praising a military victory: "I know not truly
whether I should more congratulate Henry of Nassau on the capture of
the city or on your verses; for I think the victory he has obtained nothing
more illustrious or more celebrated than this poetical tribute of yours.
But, as we hear you sing the prosperous successes of the Allies in so sono-
rous and triumphal a strain, how great a poet we shall hope to have in
you if by chance our own affairs, turning at last more fortunate, should
demand your congratulatory muses!" (p. 9). The patriotic celebration of
Britain suggested in the letter to Gill was a topic that Milton later considered for his own *magnum opus*. In *Epitaphium Damonis* Milton describes plans for an Arthuriad, recounting the settlement of Britain by
Trojans, Greeks, and Romans, illustrious forebears of the British, and
heralding Arthur as the prototype of British heroism. Not only in *Epitaphium Damonis* but in the *Commonplace Book*, Milton outlined plans
for such a work. In *Mansus*, written while Milton was on the Italian journey, the tone of his literary aspiration is also evident. He expresses a desire for patronage similar to what Manso provided Tasso and Marini, exclaiming: "O, if my lot might but bestow such a friend upon me, a friend

who understands how to honor the devotees of Phoebus — if ever I shall summon back our native kings into our songs, and Arthur, waging his wars beneath the earth, or if ever I shall proclaim the magnanimous heroes of the table which their mutual fidelity made invincible, and (if only the spirit be with me) shall shatter the Saxon phalanxes under the British Mars!"[3]

Coupled with similar comments in *Epitaphium Damonis*, studied within the larger context of the two poems, and understood in relation to the Italian journey, this passage from *Mansus* really advocates a connection between Rome and Britain. The grand work Milton was contemplating, tracing the lineage of Britons to Graeco-Roman antiquity, would have depicted martial heroism and celebrated the role of the poet in reviving that cultural ideal. As the letter to Alexander Gill makes clear, the poem and its author, respectively means and agent of perpetuating the heroic past of a culture, would have acquired fame and reputation. Accordingly, the concept of heroism characterizing Milton's early intent in writing an epic pertains, as well, to the poet.

In this respect poems like *Epitaphium Damonis* and *Mansus* and the letters recounting the Italian journey also seek to promote affinity between Britain and seventeenth-century Florentine literary society. Advocated in that literary society was Milton's own conception of the poet as hero, the very same view reflected in *Epitaphium Damonis*. As it relates to Diodati, Milton's poem is a mixture of the elegiac and heroic, lamenting Diodati's premature death and short-lived career while celebrating his apotheosis, a reward for having pursued the heroic vocation of poet. Applied to Milton, the elegiac tone is an expression of grief that his maturation as a poet, a process to which his friendship with Diodati had substantially contributed, may be interrupted or impaired because of his friend's death. The heroic tone is reflected in Milton's acknowledgment that his progress in pursuing the vocation of poet, to that point in his career, has been acclaimed and rewarded. After he had sent not only *Epitaphium Damonis* but also some of his Latin poetry to Carlo Dati, Milton received a long letter from his Florentine friend, who solicits memorial verses in behalf of a mutual friend who died, Francesco Rovai. In recalling their friend, Dati characterizes him as an exemplary member of the Florentine literary society Milton had entered. At the same time the characterization of their mutual friend is a tonal blend of the elegiac and heroic since Dati implies that the values reflected in the brief career of Rovai and his readiness to achieve his potential liken him to Diodati and to the young Milton:

I take courage to beseech you to honor with your verses the glorious memory of Signor Francesco Rovai, egregious Florentine poet, dead before his prime, and I think well known to you. The worthy gentlemen, Nicholas Heinsius and Isaac Vossius of Holland, my friends and very singular patrons and famous men of letters of our age have done the same. Signor Francesco was noble of birth, gifted by nature with the highest genius, and enriched by art and by the indefatigable study of the finest sciences. He understood Greek very well, spoke French, wrote brilliantly in Latin and Tuscan. He wrote tragedies and was praiseworthy in lyric poetry in which he praised heroes, and deprecated the vices, particularly in those seven Canzoni made against the Seven Deadly Sins. He was polite, courteous, beloved of princes, of uncorrupted manners, and most pious. He died young, without having published his works; his friends are preparing for him sumptuous exequies which will be deficient only in that I have been charged with the funeral oration. (CM XII, pp. 297–99)

As the means by which Milton unfolds his self-image, *Epitaphium Damonis*, other Latin poems about the Italian journey, and pertinent correspondence highlight a transition in his career — from pastoralism to a later phase of his maturation. Explaining in *Familiar Letter*, No. 10 (1647), to Dati why he sent *Epitaphium Damonis* to the Florentines, Milton remarks: "I had carefully caused it to be sent, in order that, however small a proof of talent, it might, even in those few lines introduced into it emblem-wise, be no obscure proof of my love towards you" (p. 49). The emblematic lines describe the poetical contests at Florence in which Milton participated: "Ah, what a man was I when I lay beside cool, murmuring Arno, where the soft grass grows by the poplar grove, and I could pluck the violets and the myrtle shoots and listen to Menalcas competing with Lycidas. And I myself even dared to compete, and I think that I did not much displease, for your gifts are still in my possession, the baskets of reeds and osiers and the pipes with fastenings of wax":

> O ego quantus eram, gelidi cum stratus ad Arni
> Murmura, populeumque nemus, quà mollior herba,
> Carpere nunc violas, nunc summas carpere myrtos,
> Et potui Lycidae certantem audire Menalcam.
> Ipse etiam tentare ausus sum, nec puto multùm
> Displicui, nam sunt et apud me munera vestra
> Fiscellae, calathique et cerea vincla cicutae.   (129–35)

Within the conventional framework of the pastoral elegy, the gifts of baskets and pipes refer to accolades Milton received, such as inscribed books or verses commending his talent, including those printed in the 1645 edition. The singing contests and the names of the contestants, Menalcas and Lycidas, are derived from the pastoral tradition represented in the Eclogues of Virgil and the works of earlier poets, notably the Sicilian elegists.

No less an example than Virgil underwent the same transition, recounted in introductory verses to the *Aeneid*, lines attributed to him: "I who once piped a song on a slender reed; who, quitting the woods, then caused the nearby fields to obey the ever greedy tiller of the soil — a work pleasing to farmers; I now sing the dread weapons of Mars."[4] E. R. Curtius comments on these lines in the following way: "Here Virgil's epic is linked with his bucolic and didactic poetry. This biographical sequence of Virgil's works was regarded by the Middle Ages as a hierarchy grounded in the nature of things — a hierarchy not only of three poetical genres, but also of three social ranks (shepherd, farmer, soldier) and of three kinds of style. It extended to the corresponding trees (beech — fruit-tree — laurel and cedar), locales (pasture — field — castle or town), implements (crook — plow — sword), animals (sheep — cow — horse). These correspondences were reduced to a graphic schema of concentric circles, known as *rota Virgilii* (Virgil's wheel). In Renaissance England bucolic is still regarded as preparatory to epic (Spenser, Milton)."[5]

Though Curtius does not mention *Epitaphium Damonis* (or, for that matter, any works by Milton), in it are found all five images — shepherd, beech tree, pasture, crook, sheep — associated with the earliest phase of the *rota Virgilii*. All five images, moreover, are in emblematic lines about the Italian journey, including Milton's assertion that the "beech-trees learned my name from Dati and Francini" ("nostra suas docuerunt nomina fagos / Et Datis, et Francinus," 136–37), evidence of widespread reputation during his stay in Italy and for many years after his departure. To highlight the transition or maturation from an earlier to a later phase of his career, Milton uses images of pipes and piping: "And myself — for I do not know what grand song my pipe was sounding — it is now eleven nights and a day — perhaps I was setting my lips to new pipes, but their fastenings snapped and they fell asunder and could carry the grave notes no further. I am afraid that I am vain, yet I will relate it. Give way, then, O forest" ("Ipse etiam, nam nescio quid mihi grande sonabat / Fistula, ab undecimâ jam lux est altera nocte, / Et tum forte novis admôram labra cicutis, / Dissiluere tamen rupta compage, nec ultra / Ferre graves potuere sonos, dubito quoque ne sim / Turgidulus, tamen et referam, vos cedite silvae," 155–60).

After having detailed his intent to write an Arthurian epic, Milton comments: "And then, O my pipe, if life is granted me, you shall be left dangling on some old pine tree far away and quite forgotten by me; or else, quite changed, you shall shrill forth a British theme to your native

Muses" ("O mihi tum si vita supersit, / Tu procul annosa pendebis fistula pinu / Multùm oblita mihi, aut patriis mutata camoenis / Brittonicum strides," 168–171). The granting of life to which Milton refers may be contrasted with the death of Diodati. Equally important, Milton is questioning the depth of his talent — whether he has the ability to become an epic poet. After he had begun an Arthurian epic, the pipe became unfastened in a matter of days, and the endeavor was terminated. An inability to sing as an epic poet is the silence he dreads. However gratifying they were, Milton's willingness to forget his past achievements as a pastoral poet is evidence of commitment to another "life," that of an epic poet whose goals are loftier and whose fame is more widespread and durable. *Epitaphium Damonis* thus balances nostalgic affection for his past against uncertainty and anxiety about future intentions and epic aspirations. In his works there is no better example of *pictura poesis* as a means of self-perception and a manifestation of self-image.

Curtius's emphasis on the *rota Virgilii* calls attention to a prevalent medieval and Renaissance view that Virgil was the model in relation to whom poets planned their careers and measured their progress. As a corollary to the introductory verses to the *Aeneid,* Curtius (p. 231) quotes from the concluding lines of the *Georgics* (IV, 559–66): "Thus I sang of the tending of fields and flocks and trees, while great Caesar hurled war's lightnings by high Euphrates and gave statutes among the nations in welcome supremacy, and scaled the path to heaven. Even in that season I Virgil, nurtured in sweet Parthenope, went in the flowery way of lowly Quiet: I who once played with shepherd's songs, and in youth's hardihood sang thee, O Tityrus, under the covert of spreading beech." Apart from their indication of a transition in Virgil's career, these lines anticipate a major emphasis in the *Aeneid:* the *pax Romana* achieved by a warrior who became a lawgiver. As Curtius observes, "Virgil is deeply imbued with the spirit of the Augustan Age of Peace and its ethical ideals" (p. 173). Supporting this observation is an element of prophecy, if not divine intrusion, in the *Aeneid* when Jupiter foretells the Augustan peace. Thus sanctioned, the era of Augustus is to be viewed as the zenith of that culture. To the extent that Aeneas, the founder of the Roman state and an embodiment of moral strength, foreshadows many of the traits of its most illustrious ruler, Augustus, the concept underlying their heroism is clearcut. As Milton, like Virgil, left behind the role of pastoral poet, he had an analogous view of the historical and mythical elements that would be amalgamated in the grand work toward which he was striving. According to the Tudor myth England was founded by Aeneas' grandson, from whom Arthur was supposed to have descended. Called Augusta or

Albion, England cyclically manifested the fullness of its glory — among other examples, in the reigns of Henry V and Elizabeth I. Because Milton would have traced British culture to its Graeco-Roman antecedents, in his epic Arthur, like Aeneas, would have exemplified moral strength; and Elizabeth, like Augustus, wold have been treated as an exemplary ruler. Though he never wrote an Arthurian epic, much of the material to have been in it was included in *The History of Britain.*

In many ways the epic contemplated by Milton had already been undertaken by Spenser, whose *Faerie Queene* incorporates in its allegory a mythical view of British history, which Guyon and Arthur study in the library of the Castle of Alma (Book II, Canto 10). But Milton's plans for an epic bear the imprint of a changing political situation and his own personal adversity. As a result, his concept of the heroic or cultural ideal to be celebrated in literature was substantially transformed. In the process of the transformation, Milton's view of himself as an epic poet and a Renaissance Virgil, if he ever made such an identification, was likewise altered. Though the transformations to which I refer took place over many years, there is a shorthand account of them in the proems of *Paradise Lost.* Too well known to be rehearsed here, the proems chart Milton's developing self-image in a twofold context: classical and Judaeo-Christian. He continued to liken himself to epic poets of classical antiquity and to stress the prophetic nature of his work. Thus, Tiresias and Phineus, two blind prophets whom he mentions in the proem of Book III of *Paradise Lost*, become classical antecedents of his own gift of prophecy. His identification with Phineus is also recounted in the *Familiar Letters.* Writing in 1654 to Leonard Philaras, an Athenian who inquired about his blindness, Milton describes his condition in clinical detail. Though Philaras viewed Milton's blindness as a privation, Milton perceived it in a more complex way. He alternated between lamenting his handicap and valuing his blindness as a gift from God, singular status that he was accorded as an instrument of Providence. In the letter to Philaras (*Familiar Letter*, No. 15, p. 69), Milton supplements the remarks on his blindness with a reference to "the Salmydessian seer Phineus" in the *Argonautica,* which he quotes:

> All round him then there grew
> A purple thickness; and he thought the Earth
> Whirling beneath his feet, and so he sank,
> Speechless at length, into a feeble sleep.

When, in the same letter to Philaras, Milton accommodates this classical antecedent to the Judaeo-Christian tradition, he projects a self-image reliant on direction and purpose being imparted to him and associated with gradual awareness of Providential intent: "what should prevent one from resting likewise in the belief that his eyesight lies not in his eyes alone, but enough for all purposes in God's leading and providence? Verily . . . He looks out for me and provides for me, as He doth, leading me and leading me forth as with His hand through my whole life" (p. 71). Here, Milton's state of mind resembles that of the speaker in *Sonnet XIX*. Even more graphically, it is similar to that of Samson who awaits a clearer understanding of his changed role and redirected life. At the same time that he manifests faith and confidence in the higher but still obscure design of Providence, Samson reflects patience and fortitude in withstanding adversity. Such virtues, contrasted with those of an Arthurian hero, are celebrated in the proem of Book IX of *Paradise Lost*.

Events in his earlier life, some of which are recounted in *Epitaphium Damonis*, anticipate, explain, and influence in Milton a changing self-image, which is reflected in *Familiar Letter*, No. 15 (to Philaras), articulated in *Sonnet XIX*, allegorized in *Samson Agonistes*, and recounted in the proems of *Paradise Lost*. Separation from his Italian friends, the death of Diodati, and the inability to complete work prematurely undertaken (not only an Arthurian epic but also an earlier endeavor, *The Passion*) cause the young Milton, like Samson, to experience alienation, disquieting self-doubt, aimlessness, and unachieved aspiration. Like Samson, interruption or seeming failure after having undertaken a course of action diverted Milton from a long-standing goal that had been encouraged by the expectations of others and rewarded by their approval. From the very relationships that provided encouragement and approval, Milton and Samson were severed. Nor did they establish other human relationships from which this kind of solace could be derived. Dependence on others was gradually replaced by a readiness to be led by Providence. The resultant state of mind was a form of contemplative repose that counterbalanced anxiety, of faith in Providence that eased the anguish of self-doubt. As with Samson, Milton's alienation from others was more complete because of blindness. Correspondingly, his attentiveness to direction imparted to him from the godhead was heightened. If Samson "saw" anew his role as liberator and was moved to act compliantly, analogously Milton undertook the vocation of epic poet a second time. As a God-directed author, if not prophet, Milton writes of a higher heroism, but his greatest reward, like that of Samson, was to have been called and chosen to live it. What Samson with his "eyes fast fixt" may have learned about his relationship with God, Milton experienced to a comparable degree in his own lifetime.

Milton's earlier view of, and literary venture into, epic heroism was not discarded, but adjusted. For what Milton initially set out to do had already been done: first by Virgil who created a hero of moral strength different from the Homeric prototype; second by Spenser who redefined the Virgilian concept of moral strength in relation to several Christian virtues. Both epic poets, the one of classical antiquity, the other of the English Renaissance, also celebrated the illustrious heroism of their respective national histories, exemplified by Aeneas and Augustus, Arthur and Elizabeth. Whereas Virgil and Spenser extolled the eras in which they lived as recurrent manifestations of values of earlier periods, Milton deplored the evil of the Stuart monarchy. Fittingly, in his letter to Dati (*Familiar Letter*, No. 10), the same one mentioning the emblematic lines of *Epitaphium Damonis*, Milton tells of "that most turbulent state of our Britain, subsequent to my return home [from Italy], which obliged me to divert my mind shortly afterwards from the prosecution of my studies to the defence anyhow of life and fortune. What safe retirement for literary leisure could you suppose given one among so many battles of a civil war, slaughters, flights, seizures of goods? Yet, even in the midst of these evils . . . know that we have published not a few things in our native tongue" (p. 51).

In a letter to Philaras (1652), written after the overthrow of the Stuart monarchy, Milton retrospectively views his career while anticipating the personal and political imprint characterizing his later poetry. Responding in *Familiar Letter*, No. 12, to a request from Philaras that he participate in the liberation of Greece, Milton urges his friend to undertake the very endeavor for which he seeks outside aid. In praising his friend, a "native of Attic Athens, who [has] besides, after happily finishing a course of literary studies among the Italians, reached such ample honours by great handling of affairs" (p. 57), Milton alludes to Philaras' cultural ancestry and to his Italian humanistic education. In effect, Philaras becomes a projection of Milton's self-image, for by implication Milton is harking back to his own early studies, alluding to his Italian journey, and developing a concept acknowledging the interdependence in classical antiquity, while advocating the revival in one's own era of rhetorical skills, exemplary traits of character, and political freedom. By implication also, he is speaking about the English Commonwealth as a model for seventeenth-century Greece and about himself as a reformer whom Philaras might emulate. Just as he perceived continuity yet adaptation from his earlier self-image, delineated in *Epitaphium Damonis*, to his more recent role in the state, so also Milton seeks to persuade Philaras that humanism is related to politics, that a poet can effect social and governmental reform.

From such a perspective he emboldens Philaras, whom he extols as one "in whom singly at this day the Arts of the old Athenians and all their celebrated excellencies appear, after so long an interval, to revive and rebloom" (p. 57). About himself Milton avers that "whatever literary advance I have made I owe chiefly to steady intimacy with their writings from my youth upwards"; furthermore, "were there in me, by direct gift from them, or a kind of transfusion, such a power of pleading that I could rouse our armies and fleets for the deliverance of Greece, the land of eloquence, from her Ottoman oppressor — to which mighty act you seem almost to implore our aid — truly there is nothing which it would be more or sooner in my desire to do. For what did even the bravest men of old, or the most eloquent, consider more glorious or more worthy of them than, whether by pleading or by bravely acting, to make the Greeks free and self-governing?" Continuing, he remarks that "some one should, if possible, arouse and rekindle in the minds of the Greeks, by relation of that old story, the old Greek valour itself, the old industry, the old patience of labour. Could some one do *that* — and from no one more than yourself ought we to expect it, looking to the strength of your feeling for your native land, and the combination of the same with the highest prudence, skill in military affairs, and a powerful passion for the recovery of the ancient political liberty — then, I am confident, neither would the Greeks be wanting to themselves, nor any other nation wanting to the Greeks" (pp. 57–59).

Written in the midst of the polemical controversies, such an enjoinder projects a self-image more fully developed because of Milton's experience in politics, though anticipated in *Epitaphium Damonis* and influenced by the Italian journey fifteen years earlier. While in Florence Milton acquired a copy of Benedetto Bonmattei's text on the Tuscan language. In expressing his admiration and gratitude, Milton celebrates the importance of exactitude and correctness in spoken and written language to the well-being of a culture and to the political freedom of its people. In writing to Bonmattei (*Familiar Letter*, No. 8) in 1638, Milton cites examples from classical antiquity:

Nor is it to be considered of small consequence what language, pure or corrupt, a people has, or what is their customary degree of propriety in speaking it, — a matter which oftener than once involved the salvation of Athens: nay, while it is Plato's opinion that by a change in the manner and habit of dressing serious commotions and mutations are portended in a commonwealth, I, for my part, would rather believe that the fall of that city and its low and obscure condition were consequent on the general vitiation of its usage in the matter of speech. For, let the words of a country be in part unhandsome and offensive in themselves, in part debased by wear and wrongly uttered, and what do they declare but, by no light indication, that the inhabitants of that country are an indolent, idly-yawning race, with minds already long-prepared for any amount of servility? On the other hand, we have never heard that any empire, any state, did not flourish moderately at least as long as liking and care for its own language lasted. Therefore, Benedetto, if only you proceed to perform vigorously this labour of yours for your native state, behold clearly, even from this, what a fair and solid affection you will necessarily win from your countrymen. (P. 33)

Among other things Milton's letters to Philaras and Bonmattei supply a partial context in which to view his developing self-image. The political freedom Milton advocated in the Commonwealth was related to the longstanding cultural tradition that he studied as a youth, in which he participated during the Italian journey, and that he celebrated in *Epitaphium Damonis*. As the apologist for the Commonwealth, he chose to view liberation from the Stuart tyranny as an endeavor recalling the political ideals of the Athenian city-state and reviving the heroic traits of character of that culture and its people. The larger historical framework in which he viewed the Commonwealth enabled him to define his own role more precisely and to perceive his controversy with royalist sympathizers as another example of an earlier struggle between freedom and oppression. As the articulate and persuasive advocate of political freedom, Milton had a complex self-image. In the letter to Philaras, for instance, he affirms that by invoking classical models of political freedom he will provide the norm by which his countrymen will view themselves, so that the traits of character and conduct of the ancient Athenians will become the hallmarks of Englishmen in the seventeenth century. Such an outlook is an adaptation of his epic aspirations announced in *Epitaphium Damonis*, in which the Arthuriad he briefly describes would have related Britain to both classical Greece and Rome. On a more fundamental level, in the letter to Bonmattei, Milton highlights the importance of language as a sign of its user's character, as the cause of the heroic temperament of a people, and as the means by which a cultural and political ideal may be achieved and maintained.

In the same letter to Bonmattei, Milton demarcates a continuum from classical antiquity to his own era, virtually the same continuum charted in the letter to Philaras. To Bonmattei he asserts: "Nor has Attic Athens herself, with her pellucid Ilissus, nor that old Rome with her bank of the Tiber, been able so to hold me but that I love often to visit your Arno and these hills of Faesule" (p. 35). By alluding to the rivers, Milton invokes the mythic, cultural, and literary significance of *locus* or place. Furthermore, Milton enjoins Philaras (in *Familiar Letter*, No. 12) to revive in Greece what he himself sought to establish in Britain: a political community grounded in a well-defined cultural tradition that Milton has known since his youth and interpreted and applied to himself, his era, and his country.

As Milton's political service became more prolonged, his earlier view of himself in *Epitaphium Damonis* was adapted to the circumstances in which he found himself. When other letters written during the Interregnum are briefly examined, Milton's self-image comes into clearer focus. To Henry Oldenburg, agent for Bremen to the English government, who had indicated that Milton was spending too much time in political controversy, Milton writes in 1654: "what can be nobler or more useful in human affairs than the vindication of Liberty?" Elaborating further, he states that "An idle ease has never had charms for me, and this unexpected contest with the Adversaries of Liberty took me off against my will when I was intent on far different and altogether pleasanter studies" (*Familiar Letter*, No. 14, p. 65). In *Familiar Letter*, No. 28 (1659), Milton states to Jean Labadie, minister of Orange and Protestant reformer:

my feeling is that I have real fame only in proportion to the good esteem I have among good men. That you also are of this way of thinking I see plainly — you who, kindled by the regard and love of Christian truth, have borne so many labours, sustained the attacks of so many enemies, and who bravely do such actions every day as prove that, so far from seeking any fame from the bad, you do not fear rousing against you their most certain hatred and maledictions. O happy man thou! whom God, from among so many thousands, otherwise knowing and learned, has snatched singly from the very gates and jaws of Hell, and called to such an illustrious and intrepid profession of his Gospel! (Pp. 105–07)

To Oldenburg in 1659 (*Familiar Letter*, No. 29) Milton speaks of the "lately confederated enemies of Liberty and Religion" (p. 111); to Richard Jones (*Familiar Letter*, No. 30) whom he commends for seeking out the "path of virtue" Milton forewarns in 1659 that "arduous and difficult . . . is the slope of virtue only" (p. 113). Finally, in a similar vein though written after the Restoration, Milton explains in 1666 to Peter Heimbach, councilor to the Elector of Brandenburg, how "virtues are nourished most and flourish most in straitened and hard circumstances" (*Familiar Letter*, No. 31, p. 115). These comments respond to a letter from Heimbach that celebrated "the marriage-union" in Milton "of so many different virtues" (p. 115).

In these letters written during the Interregnum or soon after the Restoration, Milton admires in others the traits of character and conduct most akin to his own and most compatible with his self-image. In speaking to and about his correspondents, he is provided with another opportunity to describe himself. In these same letters, written while *Paradise Lost* was being composed or revised, there is a remarkable affinity between Milton's projected self-image and his portraiture of heroism in the epic. If, from that perspective, the passages in the letters quoted immediately above are carefully reread, they become virtual character studies of Abdiel and Noah, among others, in *Paradise Lost*. As a controversialist who rebuts the sophistry and casuistry of Satan, Abdiel in his advocacy of the "testimonie of Truth" (VI, 33), for which he has "born / Universal reproach" (VI, 33–34), is a counterpart of Milton. In the political argument between Abdiel and Satan, framed as another version of the contest between freedom and tyranny, Milton compresses his experience in the polemical controversies. And in the portrait of Noah, who conjoins such virtues as "Justice and Temperance, Truth and Faith" (XI, 807) while remaining "fearless of reproach and scorn" (XI, 811), Milton depicts "The one just Man" (XI, 818), a biblical counterpart of himself. Because of political service and personal adversity, Milton's self-image and concept of heroism were shifted from the Arthurian emphasis mentioned in *Epitaphium Damonis* to the biblical basis recounted in his later poems.

In Adam's dream-vision of which he is a part, Noah is one of God's chosen spokesmen contending against adversaries. Such a contest reenacted in and through time provides the continuum of cyclical history and a catalogue of heroes in relation to which Milton locates himself. At times ascendant but on other occasions oppressed (respectively, during the Interregnum and after the Restoration), the "testimonie of Truth" enlists spokesmen whose character and conduct reflect several heroic virtues tested by adversity. This view of history and the concept of heroism are exactly what Milton sought to impart, for instance, to Philaras (in *Familiar Letter*, No. 12), whose native Greece in the seventeenth century was oppressed by Ottomans and whose ancient libertarian heritage might be resurrected if indeed a spokesman were summoned into action. From Milton's perspective the difference between seventeenth-century Greece and the English Commonwealth is the measure between an effete and servile culture susceptible to oppression and an enlightened community in which language is related to liberty and heroism in numerous and significant ways, which are anticipated in *Epitaphium Damonis* but more fully developed because of later experience.

An important disclosure of the poet's psychic life and literary ego, *Epitaphium Damonis* is an early instance of Milton's autobiographical impulse, a habit of self-examination reflected time and again throughout his works, in writings as diverse as the *Familiar Letters* and *Samson Agonistes* or *Paradise Lost*. Viewed as forms of autobiography, such writings show a speaker perceiving himself, an artist for whom in most cases *pictura poesis* is really self-image. Manifested in the vision, voice, and feeling of these writings, the process of self-perception is better understood in relation to the context in which it began and continued to unfold, a context in which education, literary endeavor, heroism, and cultural and political ideals are essential ingredients.

Duquesne University

NOTES

1. The Latin text of *Epitaphium Damonis* is cited from CM; the translation from *John Milton: Complete Poems and Major Prose*, ed. Merritt Y. Hughes (New York, 1957), p. 135.

2. *Familiar Letter*, No. 10. CM XII, p. 47. Ed. Donald Lemen Clark and trans. David Masson. Henceforth the *Familiar Letters* will be cited parenthetically in the essay according to the numbering and English translation of this edition. Later research has moved toward a renumbering and redating of some of the letters, but such technical aspects of the study of the *Familiar Letters* do not bear on my argument.

3. *Mansus* is quoted from the English translation in *John Milton: Complete Poems and Major Prose*, ed. Merritt Y. Hughes, p. 130.

4. Cited in Ernst Robert Curtius, *European Literature and the Latin Middle Ages*, trans. Willard R. Trask (1953; rpt. New York, 1963), p. 231.

5. Curtius, *European Literature*, pp. 231–32. For extensive commentary on the *rota Virgilii*, see Domenico Comparetti's *Vergil in the Middle Ages*, trans. E. F. M. Benecke (1895; rpt. New York, 1929), esp. pp. 56–58 and nn. 21–26, which cite the commentaries of Aelius Donatus and Servius. See also L. P. Wilkinson, *The Georgics of Virgil: A Critical Survey* (Cambridge, 1969), p. 274 and nn. 15–16. For a study of the *rota Virgilii* and its application to Spenser, see W. L. Renwick, *Edmund Spenser: An Essay on Renaissance Poetry* (London, 1925), esp. pp. 34–64; and Merritt Y. Hughes, *Virgil and Spenser* (Berkeley, 1929), esp. pp. 317–22. In *Vergil and the English Poets* (1919; rpt. New York, 1966), pp. 92–147, Elizabeth Nitchie comments on Spenser and Milton in relation to the Virgilian model. Louis L. Martz's "The Rising Poet, 1645," in *The Lyric and Dramatic Milton*, ed. Joseph H. Summers (New York, 1965), pp. 3–33, interprets Milton's first published volume as a deliberate imitation of the Virgilian model. Having studied Milton's arrangement of the poems in the 1645 volume, Martz concludes that Milton, after the manner of Virgil, has matured beyond the earlier stages of his poetic career and is ready to embark on his role as epic poet. Acknowledging that *Epitaphium Damonis* is the final poem in the 1645 edition, Martz observes that the Latin pastoral elegy "thus marks the end of an era that the whole volume serves to celebrate and commemorate, while the whole volume has been arranged to convey a sense of the predestined bard's rising powers" (p. 12). For a recent study of the Virgilian model and its application to Spenser and Milton, see Richard Neuse, "Milton and Spenser: The Virgilian Triad Revisited," *ELH*, 45 (1978), 606–39.

IDEOLOGY IN THE *POEMATA* (1645)

Thomas N. Corns

N EARLY ALL of Milton's extant Latin poems were published together in the twin volume, *The Poems of Mr John Milton, Both
English and Latin, Compos'd at several times* (London, 1645).[1] Some
had been printed earlier or had been read publicly,[2] and it is reasonable
to assume that at least the epistles had circulated to some extent in manuscript. My concern, however, is less with the individual items than with
the combined impact of the Latin element in the volume.

Poems (1645) concludes a three-year period of hectic press activity
by Milton. His first divorce tract, *The Doctrine and Discipline of Divorce* (London, 1643), had occasioned so hostile a response from his erst-
while Presbyterian allies[3] that he had felt constrained to expand it to a
second edition (London, 1644), to augment it with the corroboration of
earlier reformed divines (*The Judgment of Martin Bucer* [London, 1644]),
to explore more fully the biblical texts on which his thesis rested (*Tetra-
chordon* [London, 1645]), to answer specific attacks (*Colasterion* [Lon-
don, 1645]), and, as a contingency, to defend the freedom of speech of
heterodox Puritans (*Areopagitica* [London, 1644]). In passing, and quite
separately from the great debate within English Puritanism between
Presbyterians and those who, like Milton, disputed their right to deter-
mine doctrine, he also produced his blueprint for education reform, *Of
Education* (London, 1644). After this often courageous and often brilliant flurry of controversial prose came *Poems* (1645).

It is a curious volume in its context, totally distinct from all that Milton had recently committed to the press. Of course, it differs from the
rest in that it is polyglot poetry, not vernacular prose. But also the book
itself differs physically and in its circumstances of publication from the
others. It is a smallish octavo: all other Miltonic items of the period are
quartos. The former is the customary format for creative writing and de-
votional literature, whereas quarto was typically used for controversy and
current affairs.[4] *Poems* (1645) bears the name of printer, Ruth Raworth,
and bookseller, Humphrey Moseley; the others, for the most part, are
anonymous except for the author's name or initials. There is evidence that,
in this, they conform to the practice of radical propagandists of the
mid-1640s, who protected their printers and distributors, while inviting

prosecution themselves. *Poems* (1645) is even endorsed on its title page "Printed and publish'd according to Order." The order referred to is presumably the 1643 Order of Parliament that required, among other things, that texts for publication be cleared by a licenser, the very order which Milton had attacked the previous year in *Areopagitica*. There is no reason to suppose that Milton submitted any other work of the period to "the hasty view of an unleasur'd licencer . . . perhaps far his inferiour in judgement."[5] Instead of the stark text under the courageous affirmation of Milton's authorship, *Poems* (1645) entered the world with an elaborate statement of its pedigree and associations. Moseley, its bookseller, was soon to establish himself (if, by 1645, he had not already done so) as the major publisher of creative writing in London. It is clear from the advertisements he published that his house produced mainly poetry, plays, and prose romances, with a few theological works, none of which are of the radical kidney of Milton's divorce tracts.[6] Moseley adds a sensitive and insightful preface, in which he complains of the domination of the press by controversial prose, an ironic sentiment in the context of Milton's recent publication record.[7] Moreover, the volume prints prominently the commendations of respectable figures.

Against the background of Milton's recent achievement, what an incongruous and puzzling volume *Poems* (1645) must have seemed to its original readers. I have argued elsewhere that the poetry volume may have served to redefine contemporary responses to his controversial prose.[8] Milton had attracted a number of attacks which sought to identify him with the archetypal sectary of Presbyterian propaganda, ignorant, propertyless, and low-born. The publication of his poems challenged that destructive image and asserted his liberal, humanistic scholarship. I want now to explore the corollary of that thesis, namely, how an awareness of his contemporary standing as prose controversialist in radical causes transforms our appreciation of his *Poems* (1645) and, in particular, of the Latin poetry it contains.

Milton is, of course, at pains to stress that many items are the work of his adolescence. The title page emphasizes that they were "Compos'd at several times," and many poems bear a note of his age at the time of composition. Nevertheless, the discrepancies between the ideological position of many poems and his own known position in 1645 are marked and bewildering.

Consider his elegies on Nicholas Felton, bishop of Ely (*In Obitum Praesulis Eliensis*) and Lancelot Andrewes, bishop of Winchester (*Elegia Tertia*), composed in the mid-1620s. Each offers a vision of prelatical apotheosis. Felton is made to describe the blessed experience of his elevation:

> Erraticorum syderum per ordines,
>   Per lacteas vehor plagas,
> Velocitatem saepe miratus novam,
>   Donec nitentes ad fores
> Ventum est Olympi, et regiam Chrystallinam, et
>   Stratum smaragdis Atrium.
> Sed hic tacebo, nam quis effari queat
>   Oriundus humano patre
> Amoenitates illius loci, mihi
>   Sat est in aeternum frui.   (*Eli.*, 59–68)

[Through the ranks of the wandering stars I was borne, and through the Milky stretches, marvelling oft at my new-found swiftness, until we came to the shining portals of Olympus, and to the palace of crystal, and the halls paved with emeralds. But here I will hold my peace, for who, if born of human sire, would have the strength to set forth in full the loveliness of that place? *I* count it enough to enjoy that place forever.]

Lancelot Andrewes's eschatalogical prospects are similarly prosperous. The poet, to assuage his grief at the bishop's death, is vouchsafed a vision of his entry into heaven:

> Dumque senex tali incedit venerandus amictu,
>   Intremuit laeto florea terra sono.
> Agmina gemmatis plaudunt caelestia pennis,
>   Pura triumphali personat aethra tubâ.
> Quisque novum amplexu comitem cantuque salutat,
>   Hosque aliquis placido misit ab ore sonos;
> Nate veni, et patrii felix cape gaudia regni,
>   Semper ab hinc duro, nate, labore vaca.   (*El.* 3, 57–64)

[While the aged [bishop] moved onward, a reverend figure, so gloriously robed, the flower-strewn earth was all aquiver with joyous sounds; heaven's hosts beat out strains with their jewelled wings, and the air, pure and undefiled, rang with notes of an exultant trump. Each [member of the heavenly choirs] greeted with embraces and with songs his new comrade, and one sent forth from calm and peaceful lips these sounds: "Draw near, my son; in gladness garner the joys of your Father's kingdom; henceforth always, my son, be free from rugged toil."]

Between writing such respectful panegyric and committing it to print, Milton's admiration for episcopacy as an institution and for the saintliness of bishops had moderated. In 1641–42 he published his five antiprelatical tracts, disputing the biblical justification for episcopal church government and asserting that bishops had retarded the English reformation. The venerable Andrewes, as apologist for episcopacy, was a particular target for assault. Milton criticizes in detail his defense of episcopacy, cockily dismissing his "rude draughts": "And surely they bee rude draughts indeed, in so much that it is a marvell to think what his friends meant to let come abroad such shallow reasonings with the name of a man so much bruited for learning" (*Church-government;* CM III, p. 201). Bishops, as a group, are popish decadents, cramming "plump endowment[s]" into their "canary-sucking, and swan-eating" mouths (*Of Reformation;* CM III, p. 19). With a curious irony, Milton's antiprelatical invective follows his elegies into an eschatological perspective, though the bishops' part in the vision is much changed:

But they contrary that by the impairing and diminution of the true *Faith,* the distresses and servitude of their *Countrey* aspire to high *Dignity, Rule* and *Promotion* here, after a shamefull end in this *Life* (which *God* grant them) shall be thrown downe eternally into the *darkest* and *deepest* Gulfe of HELL, where under the *despightfull controule,* the trample and spurne of all the other *Damned,* that in the anguish of their *Torture* shall have no other ease then to exercise a *Raving* and *Bestiall Tyranny* over them as their *Slaves* and *Negro's,* they shall remaine in that plight for ever, the *basest,* the *lowermost,* the most *dejected,* most *underfoot* and *downe-trodden Vassals* of Perdition. (CM III, p. 79)

Many items among the Latin poems of the 1645 volume similarly fossilize a religious and political sensibility which is at odds with Milton's views at the time of publication. Consider his obsequious celebrations of 5 November. Of course, in 1645, Milton had not yet assumed his regicidal stance of 1649. Any republican sentiment would have been reckless and very unusual so early. Even though the parliamentary cannon were trained on the king's standard, the pretence remained that the Civil War was being fought against wicked councilors, and was to persist at least until 1647. Milton's line in the antiprelatical tracts had been to attack the bishops as an offense to the rights of kings, though, as Carey has pointed out, Milton's more intimate and hostile attitude to kingship can be established through an examination of the imagery he uses.[9] Nevertheless, the glowing terms in which he chooses to praise James I in his Latin poems set him apart from a tradition of radical Puritanism stretching back to the 1610s. Milton praises the late king in his role as peacemaker: "Pacificusque novo felix divesque sedebat / In solio" (*Q. Nov.,* 5–6) ("James, bringer of peace, blessed, rich, was seated on his new throne"). It is not to be expected that the youthful Milton ("Anno aetatis 17") is to berate James I as he will in 1649 as one who "in stead of taking heart and putting confidence in God by such a deliverance from the Powder Plot . . . was hitt into such a *Hectic* shivering between Protestant and Papist all his life after, that he never durst from that time doe otherwise then equivocat or collogue with the Pope and his adherents" (*Eikonoklastes;* CM V, p. 196). Still, praise for the irenic James would seem strange coming from a young Puritan even in the 1620s when the poem was written, for he had remained "felix divesque" by holding aloof from the Thirty Years' War between reformed Europe (led by his son-in-law, the Elector Palatine) and the forces of the Counter-Reformation. English radical Protestantism had, throughout, advocated direct intervention in the conflict, and James's refusal to become openly involved seems to have been unpopular.[10] Milton's eulogy, then, puzzles even in the immediate context of its creation. Why should he have chosen to praise James as peace-bringer (or passive accomplice in the demise of reformed Europe, as to some it surely seemed)? Maybe the young Milton was really quite reactionary; or perhaps the opportunity to produce well-turned panegyric overwhelmed his sense of its ideological implications. Anyway, the poem appears strange in the context of his later prose polemic.

Another Latin poem set against the background of the Thirty Years' War is curiously silent on the dangers of the conflict to reformed religion. *Elegia Quarta* is addressed "Ad Thomam Junium praeceptorem suum, apud mercatores Anglicos Hamburgae agentes, Pastoris munere fungentem" ("To Thomas Young, His Teacher, Serving Now as Chaplain Among the English Merchants Resident in Hamburg"), at a time when, it would seem, Milton feared that Young would be caught up in the fighting as the conflict spread to the Baltic. The poem has been interpreted as an expression of solidarity between radical Puritans.[11] This, I think, is erroneous. Though Milton berates England as ungrateful in that Young could not find an appropriate living there, the poem contains no suggestion I can identify that he had been barred from preferment because of his Puritan leanings. He was, of course, a Puritan, and was to emerge in the 1640s as a major Presbyterian divine. However, his theological position need not have precluded employment, and in 1628 he was advanced to a fairly good living in Stowmarket.[12] *Elegia Quarta* is a decidedly reactionary poem. Milton's concern with the Thirty Years' War — as much a touchstone of radical commitment as, say, the Spanish Civil War in the 1930s — extends no further than anxiety for his former tutor: "Te tamen intereà belli circumsonat horror, / Vivis et ignoto solus inópsque solo" (83–84) ("Round you, nevertheless, resounds meanwhile the horrid din of war: you live alone, poor, in an unfamiliar land"). On the threat to reformed religion he is silent.

Just as some of the Latin poems are remote in political and religious sensibility from the maturer Milton of the 1640s, so, too, others express an Ovidian and perhaps courtly eroticism explicitly denied in his divorce tracts. Sometimes the sexuality is oblique, as in the stunning personification of "scientia" in *Ad Patrem:*

> Dimotáque venit spectanda scientia nube,
> Nudaque conspicuos inclinat ad oscula vultus,
> Ni fugisse velim, ni sit libâsse molestum.   (90–93)

[Sweeping the clouds apart, Science comes, to be viewed, and, naked, she inclines her bright face to my kisses, unless I should wish to flee, unless I should find it burdensome to taste her kisses.]

Mythological allusion in the Latin poems is facetiously and lasciviously erotic. *Elegia Quinta,* on the coming of spring, describes the frolicking gods. Phoebus urges Aurora to leave "thalamos . . . seniles" (49) ("the aged couch") of her spouse to sleep with him. The Earth, meanwhile, lusts for Phoebus (57ff.). "Jupiter ipse alto cum conjuge ludit Olympo" (117) ("Jupiter himself frolics with his consort on towering Olympus"); this notion of sexual play seems markedly un-Miltonic. Pan "luxuriat" (125) ("runs riot"), threatening even Cybele and Ceres. Faunus chases an Oread who hides, but not very well, because she, too, is lustful: "fugit, et fugiens pervelit ipsa capi" (130) ("she flies, yet, as she flies, she would fain have herself be caught"). The witty pointing of the phrase offers an amused endorsement of such carnality.

Other poems project a lyrical persona directly engaged in libidinous pursuits. In *Elegia Prima,* addressed to Charles Diodati, the poet describes his habitual practice of spying on the physical merits of young women from a hiding place in a thick grove, an observation which supports the would-be worldly-wise comment, "Gloria Virginibus debetur prima Britannis" (71) ("'Tis to the maids of Britain that first glory [in beauty] is due!"). *Elegia Septima* rehearses an uncontrollable physical passion conceived by the poet for a woman he has merely glimpsed: "Protinus insoliti subierunt corda furores"(73) ("Straightway unwonted frenzies entered my heart"). A slave to carnal Cupid, he entertains the aspiration that the girl may be tractable to seduction: "Forte nec ad nostras surdeat illa preces" (90) ("mayhap she would not be deaf to my prayers"). He concludes nursing the happy misery of his wild passion (99).

Of course, there is no reason to assume a genuinely autobiographical content in either poem. The voyeurism of *Elegia Prima* seems inherently unlikely, and the psychologically implausible frenzy of *Elegia Septima* is quite unsupported by any other documentation. Most likely, they are fictions selected to provide material for neatly turned expressions of the poetic sensibility young Milton wished to project.

However, the erotic element in his Latin poems sits very incongruously among his other publications of the 1640s. Milton was later to idealize the "Rites / Mysterious of connubial Love" (*PL* IV, 742–43), but in the divorce tracts his expressed opinion is decidedly austere. Sexuality is represented as a trivial, incidental, and distasteful element in heterosexual relations. What counts is the ethereal union of fit conversing souls: sex is but "the work of male and female" (*Doctrine and Discipline of Divorce*; CM III, p. 386), "the quintessence of an excrement" (CM III, p. 393). Passion for the unknown women of his Latin poems reflects exactly the sort of sexual sensibility that the divorce tracts reprehend, and the amorality posited in his Latin mythologizing is remote from the severity of his prose works.

How then are we to interpret collectively the Latin poems of 1645? Three points are pertinent. Milton always cherished the product of his own pen. For example, he retained copies of his university prolusions and his earliest Latin correspondence, which he published together shortly before his death. He protested with unrestrained vehemence at misquotation by his opponents in controversy,[13] and *Areopagitica* exudes his indignation that anyone should presume to intercept his writing. That he should have preserved and published his earliest poetry is not surprising, though it does not explain why he waited till 1645 to give the press a volume which was more or less complete by 1640.

Secondly, Milton's polemic had attempted to establish the persona of the cultured man of letters drawn involuntarily into controversy. His comments about how uncomfortable he found it to write prose and how well his poems had been received by "the privat Academies of *Italy*" (*Church-government*; CM III, p. 235), committed him to substantiate this carefully constructed image of himself with some token of his humanistic creativity. *Poems* (1645), this elegant, little volume from an ultrarespectable and perhaps rather conservative publisher of noncontroversial writing, fascinatingly counterpoints his prose production and confronts the image of him as low-class sectary which his enemies had labored to engender.

Finally, not only was Milton concerned with how he was perceived by others, he was also obsessed with his own developing genius. Perhaps

more than any major English poet before Wordsworth, he was profoundly
self-regarding. Concern with "the growth of a poet's mind" is at the heart
of *Ad Patrem* and *Lycidas*, and even in *Paradise Lost* he retains an intense interest in the genesis of his inspiration. Of course, by the mid-1640s
he must have been well aware of major changes in his outlook, his aspirations, and his ideological position. After all, men whom he had defended
in 1642 were by 1644 his enemies and were to remain so. Milton knew
he was changing, and, I suggest, in his Latin poems he has documented
that transformation. Consider the lines which he appends to his elegies
(whether they refer just to *Elegia Septima*, as the Columbia editors seem
to suggest, is uncertain):

> Haec ego mente olim laevâ, studioque supino
>   Nequitiae posui vana trophaea meae.
> Scilicet abreptum sic me malus impulit error,
>   Indocilisque aetas prava magistra fuit.
> Donec Socraticos umbrosa Academia rivos
>   Praebuit, admissum dedocuitque jugum.
> Protinus extinctis ex illo tempore flammis,
>   Cincta rigent multo pectora nostra gelu.
> Unde suis frigus metuit puer ipse Sagittis,
>   Et Diomedéam vim timet ipsa Venus.

[All this once on a time, with warped and twisted mind, and with all true zeal
laid prostrate I wrote, setting up idle trophies of my worthlessness. So utterly,
forsooth, mischievous error wrenched me astray, and drove me onward, and my
untaught youth proved but misguided teacher, until the shades of Academe prof-
fered to me the Socratic streams, and untaught me, (and loosed) the yoke I had
let fall (upon my neck). Straightway, from that moment, the fires were quenched,
my heart has been unyielding, belted with deep ice. Hence the lad fears the cold
for his beloved shafts, and Venus herself dreads might that matches the might
of Diomedes.]

Hill comments, "When he published his Cambridge elegies in the *Poems*
of 1645 Milton carefully apologized for 'these vain trophies of my profli-
gacy'. Everything he wrote about himself around this time and later must
be related to his desire to differentiate himself from those who meant
license when they cried liberty."[14] Though I would endorse this as a general statement, as an account of the coda to *Elegia Septima* it is uncon-
vincing. If Milton had worried about disclosing the sensuality of his youth,
then his best remedy would have been his wastebin. Quite simply, he
need not have published these poems. Rather, I suggest, he offers them
to us as documents in his evolution, capturing, like a snapshot album,

moments in his poetic and intellectual growth, and eternalizing the process by which his sensibility was transformed.

University College of North Wales

NOTES

1. It was registered for publication in October 1645, but Thomason dated his copy 2 January (i.e., January 1646).
2. *De Idea Platonica* was most probably printed earlier, though no copies survive; see *The Poems of John Milton*, ed. John Carey and Alastair Fowler (London, 1968), p. 66. *Epitaphium Damonis* was printed by itself in 1640. Milton refers to readings of his poetry before Italian academies in *Church-governement*, CM III, p. 235.
3. William Riley Parker, *Milton's Contemporary Reputation* (Columbus, 1940), pp. 73–75.
4. Statements about the norms of contemporary publishing practice are based on work in progress, a statistical account of the Thomason Collection of Civil War tracts.
5. *Areopagitica*, CM IV, p. 325. All quotations and translations of Milton's prose and poetry are from CM.
6. See, for example, Moseley's list bound into Bodleian Library Don f. 144, and reproduced in Edmund Waller, *Poems 1645* (London, 1971).
7. He complains that *"the slightest Pamphlet is now adayes more vendible then the Works of learnedst men"* (a3ᵛ).
8. "Milton's Quest for Respectability," *Modern Language Review*, 77 (1982), 769–79.
9. John Carey, *Milton* (London, 1969), p. 63.
10. Godfrey Davies, *The Early Stuarts 1603–1660* (1937; rpt. Oxford, 1945), pp. 21–22, 53–54.
11. For a discussion, see Bush, *Variorum*, pp. 79–80.
12. *DNB*, 63, 392.
13. See my "New Light on the Left Hand: Contemporary Views of Milton's Prose Style," *Durham University Journal*, n.s. 62 (1980), 177–81.
14. Christopher Hill, *Milton and the Puritan Revolution* (1977; rpt. London, 1979), pp. 451–52.

AD JOANNEM ROUSIUM:
ELEGIAC WIT AND PINDARIC MODE

Stella P. Revard

AD *JOANNEM Rousium,* first written to accompany the replacement volume of the 1645 poems sent to the librarian of the Bodleian at Oxford, was not published by Milton until 1673 when he reissued
the poems of the 1645 volume, adding several earlier pieces and the tract
Of Education, as well as this ode to John Rouse. The ode that originally
served as proem to introduce the 1645 poems to Rouse appears as envoy
to the 1673 volume, the last poem in the book and the next to the last
piece; *Of Education* concludes the volume.[1] The fact that Milton chose
to publish the poem and to place it as the penultimate work (after the
Latin elegy to Damon) seems to indicate not only that he valued it but
also that he regarded it as a kind of valedictory piece, fitting to conclude
the section of Latin poems and to sum up the contents of his first and
earliest poetic output. Its final placement at the end of the Latin poems
is doubly fitting, since it is also one of the last Latin poems that Milton wrote.

Although *Ad Joannem Rousium* has been almost universally praised
by the critics who have written of it, the ode has excited interest mostly
for its biographical detail or for its poetic form. Both E. M. W. Tillyard
and Louis Martz comment on the agreeable portrait of the young poet
and personal tone of his lines. The poem possesses, as Tillyard remarks,
a "mixture of stateliness and of half-humorous and urbane elegance,"
or as Martz says, a combination of learned wit and a carefree air.[2] Other
critics, however, are more intrigued by Milton's poetic versatility than
by his elegant air or self-portraiture. *Ad Joannem Rousium* represents
for them a unique experiment in the formal pindaric ode and as such
looks forward to the experiment with other choral meters in *Samson Agonistes.*[3] In *The Reason of Church-government,* Milton expresses admiration for Pindar and Callimachus and their magnific hymns.[4] It is curious
then that the only poem of this period to use pindaric strophe, antistrophe,
and epode is not a hymn or choral piece but a personal poem in the style
of the elegiac letters included in the 1645 volume. Tillyard was one of
the first to point out that *Ad Joannem Rousium* is more elegiac than pin-

daric in tone and to question why Milton had used pindaric strophes for this personal proem or envoy that resembles the introductory or conclud- ing poems that the elegiac or lyric Latin poets attached to their volumes.[5] Hence it would appear that the ode is something of a critical puzzle, ad- mired for its disparate elements, but elusive in its intellectual design, its stately pindaric manner at odds with its elegiac wit.

Yet we can scarcely doubt that John Milton, who had newly dem- onstrated his mastery of English and Latin verses in the 1645 volume, knew exactly what he was doing in combining elegiac and pindaric ele- ments within this ode. Here is more than an experiment in a Greek met- rical form translated into Latin or a formal verse letter to a friend. As with his early elegies, Milton uses the personal letter to make some se- rious statements about himself as a poet and the function of poetry in the world. Though ostensibly the poem does no more than recommend a replacement volume to the care of the librarian at Oxford, it contains some of Milton's more interesting statements concerning the relationship of poetry to society, particularly a society beset with serious civil prob- lems, which felt it had better things to do than cultivate the muses. How- ever genial Milton's manner with Rouse, however casual his banter on the subject of the lost book, his remarks about the poet and his role in society must be taken seriously. And the fact that Milton employs now elegiac, now pindaric tones must be taken as part of that sober purpose. As the Renaissance often viewed them, Roman elegiac poets — Ovid, Propertius, Tibullus — and their fellow lyric poets — Horace, Catullus — stand in a different relationship to their society and their times than does the committed pindaric bard. The former (the Renaissance thought) look upon poetry as a pleasant peaceful pastime, to be cherished in quiet, whatever the din of civil disturbance raging about them. The pindaric bard — and Pindar stands as the original of the type — though cherishing the muses no less, takes a more active civil role, speaks directly to his so- ciety and seeks to cure, not to retreat from its ills. Milton, of course, is aware of these different types of poet and their different stances toward society. When he assumes first the elegiac, then the pindaric voice, we can see him now taking on one, now the other role. To trace how Mil- ton progresses from the elegiac to the pindaric poet in this ode is to watch him bid farewell to one kind of poetry and to commit himself to another. At heart, then, *Ad Joannem Rousium* is a poem about John Milton and his role as a poet.

Milton begins the ode sounding very much like a Roman Catullus or Propertius, adopting the convention of addressing his own book.

Gemelle cultu simplici gaudens liber,
Fronde licet geminâ,
Munditiéque nitens non operosâ,
Quam manus attulit
Juvenilis olim,
Sedula tamen haud nimii Poetae.   (1-6)

[Book of twin parts, happy in a single cover
but with a double leaf,
shining with an unstudied elegance
once given it
by a youthful hand—
a zealous hand but not yet that of an assured poet.][6]

He describes the two-part book of English and Latin poems almost as though it were a Roman-type book, a scroll whose ends were to be polished with pumice and so shine neatly ("munditiéque nitens"). His description calls to mind phrases, that Catullus and Propertius used in the proems to their volumes when they likened the polishing of the scroll's end to the polishing of their verses. Catullus speaks of his book being smoothed off with dry pumice stone ("arida modo pumice expolitum," Proem 1, 2) and Propertius begs that his verse run smoothly, polished with fine pumice ("exactus tenui pumice uersus eat," Proem 3, 1.8).[7] Like them, Milton takes pleasure in the appearance of his nicely bound book and compares by implication the unstudied elegance of the binding with that of the verses themselves. He addresses it affectionately by name: "parve liber" (13) or "libelle" (37) ("little book"). Catullus also refers fondly to his "lepidum novum libellum" ("pretty new little book"). He too is about to present it to a friend, Cornelius, whom he commends as the writer of a three-volumed history of the world. Milton may well have thought of Catullus' friendly dedication of his verses to the learned Cornelius when he dispatched his book to Rouse, whom he calls a custodian of learning in the third strophe ("AEternorum operum custos fidelis," 54). Catullus apologizes for his verses as trifles and contrasts himself, perhaps ironically, with his laboriously learned friend.

Cui dono lepidum novum libellum
Arida modo pumice expolitum?
Corneli,tibi; namque tu solebas
Meas esse aliquid putare nugas,
Jam tum cum ausus es unus Italorum
Omne aevum tribus explicare chartis,
Doctis, Juppiter, et laboriosis!   (1-7)

[To whom do I give my pretty new book,
freshly smoothed off with dry pumice-stone?
To you, Cornelius: for you used to think
that my trifles were worth something,
once, when you took courage, alone of Italians,
to set forth the whole history of the world in three volumes,
learned ones, by Jupiter, and laboriously done.]

Here is another convention that affects Milton. Roman poets express on
the one hand negligence and indifference toward their verse, yet on the
other great pride and boundless ambition. Catullus concludes his proem
with a plea to the muse that his verses, which he has only now called
trifles, may last more than an age: "quod, o patrona virgo, / Plus uno
maneat perenne saeclo" (9–10). Propertius has similar ambitions, attrib-
uting to poetry the power to lift him from the earth to the heights: "quo
me Fama leuat terra sublimis" (Proem 3, 1.9). Adopting the apologetic
voice of the Latin elegist, Milton is both modest and ambitious. The very
fact that he is sending his book to Rouse argues ambition, for he urges
Rouse to guard it with the great works of Latin and Greek poetry held
by the Bodleian (70–72). He describes himself in the opening strophe,
however, as young and eager, but not yet too much a poet. His poetry,
moreover, is carefree and playful, composed while he wandered now in
Italian, now in English fields, alluding both to the places where he wrote
many of the poems and the languages in which he wrote.

> Dum vagus Ausonias nunc per umbras
> Nunc Britannica per vireta lusit
> Insons populi, barbitóque devius
> Indulsit patrio, mox itidem pectine Daunio
> Longinquum intonuit melos
> Vicinis, et humum vix tetigit pede.   (7–12)

[– while he sported with wandering freedom
now in Ausonian shades, now in English fields,
unconcerned with the public world, and, following his own devices,
he indulged his native lute or then with Daunian quill
sounded a foreign air to his neighbors,
his feet scarcely touching the ground.]

In these lines Milton is looking at the poet he was during the 1620s and
1630s when he composed the elegies, lyrics, and pastorals of the 1645
volume, a private poet, concerned with his own poetic world of mead-
ows and forest shades, a *persona* close to the ones he adopted for *L'Allegro*

and *Il Penseroso*. Depicting himself as a sportful young elegist whose foot scarcely touched the ground, Milton ignores, of course, the poetic personality of the Nativity ode and the serious pastorals, *Lycidas* and *Epitaphium Damonis*. He does so deliberately, I believe, for he wants his reader to look upon him for the moment as a gentleman-poet without serious public, religious, or personal cares, a young Ovid or Propertius or even Virgil.

The Roman gentleman-poet of the first century B.C. wrote a special kind of occasional poetry for a select circle of friends, young men of his own class and so-called learned ladies or courtesans.[8] He concentrated on lyric, elegy, pastoral and avoided the more serious genres, epic or tragedy. When challenged to write a more serious verse, he pleaded his youth, his particular disposition for elegant light private poetry, putting off to mature or old age the commitment to sing of arms and the man. Among the elegiac poets Tibullus, Propertius, Ovid, all offer apologies for preferring elegy to epic, and the lyric poet Horace offers a similar defense of ode. Two of these apologies for elegy (by Ovid and by Propertius) are worth looking at more closely in that they have particular application to Milton's self-portrait in strophe 1. In the introduction to the third volume of the *Amores*, Ovid draws a picture of himself as a young poet that much resembles Milton's. He recounts how he was strolling through the woodland shades one day, contemplating what form his verses should take, when he was accosted by two ladies. The first was Elegeia, the second Tragoedia. Although he is addressed by both, and attracted first to the one, then the other, in the end he is won by Elegeia and her graceful blandishments. She represents to him youthful charm and diversion, the society of young men and women, and the delights of the woodland countryside about him. Thus, though he does not entirely dismiss Tragoedia but puts her off till a later age, he decides to remain in his poetic retirement. Propertius recounts a similar conflict, which for him results in a different outcome, for he completely dismisses the call of the more serious muse. Nevertheless, he feels compelled in each of his three books of elegies to justify his service to elegy (1.7; 2.10; 3.3; 3.5). He confesses that he has been entreated by the more martial muses, but, as he explains in 2.10, he deems that it is fitting for young men to sing of Venus and love, for old men to sing of wars and tumults. Moreover, in 3.3 he states that Phoebus expressly forbade him to aspire to epic poetry, recommending elegy as more suitable to his poetic temperament. In both 3.3 and 3.5 Propertius alludes to the two springs of the muses; the higher, Hippocrene, is for epic poetry, but the lower, Aganippe, which he imagines in a lush woodland grotto, is for elegy. His delight, as he tells us, is in these lower springs of Helicon and in the beauty of the muses before they have ascended to the epic heights.

> me iuuat in prima coluisse Helicona iuuenta
> Musarumque choris implicuisse manus;   (3.5, 19–20)

[It pleases me to have worshipped in Helicon in my early youth, and to have entwined my hands in the dances of the Muses.][9]

Milton's view of the young poet has much in common with what we have observed in Propertius and Ovid. The young poet whom Milton describes in strophe 1 is a private person, uncommitted to public responsibility ("insons populi"); like the Roman elegists he wanders in pastoral retreats playing and indulging his own art. The word "lusit" (8), which literally means "he played," carries with it the connotations of free sport, amusement, pastime, and even dalliance and banter. "Indulsit" (10), two lines later, reinforces these meanings; the poet indulged his native lyre or lute ("barbitóque . . . patrio"), yielding to the pleasant sport of poetry, just as Ovid yielded to the graceful Elegeia. This idyllic woodland world of youth and spring and poetry is presided over in Milton as in Ovid and Propertius by the light pastoral muses, whose country retreat at Oxford is the counterpart of the elegist's Helicon or Parnassus. There Milton describes their fountains near the birthplace of Father Thames and there also he describes the sacred band of poets devoted to them:

> Thamesis ad incunabula
> Caerulei patris,
> Fontes ubi limpidi
> Aonidum, thyasusque sacer.   (18–21)

[to the cradle
of blue Father Thames,
where the clear fountains
of the Aonides are, and the sacred dance.]

The Oxford muses who lead the band of poets resemble the muses who refresh Propertius in the woodland cave and are his comrades in dance. Although Milton in *Ad Rousium* neither names the springs of the Aonides nor distinguishes between the higher and lower poetry they inspire, in *Ad Patrem*, written some years earlier, he refers to the higher Pierian fountains and calls upon the muses to spur him to a poetry more sublime than that he has hitherto written (1–5). The poetry of his youth was inspired by the lower springs of the muses and written in imitation of those "smooth Elegiack Poets," who, as he tells us in *The Apology for Smectymnuus*, delighted him both for "the pleasing sound of their numerous writing, which in imitation I found most easie . . . and for their matter . . . I was so allur'd to read, that no recreation came to me better welcome" (CM III, p. 302). In describing the muses at Oxford, Milton is alluding to those deities of a poetry that as a youth he enjoyed reading and composing, muses no longer flourishing in a land beset with civil disturbance. Oxford as a military headquarters during the Civil War encouraged little intellectual or poetic activity. Now, moreover, the time for graceful private elegy seems past; as Milton reflects in *The Reason of Church-Government*, higher poetry — epic or tragedy — "shall be found more doctrinal and exemplary to a Nation" (CM III, p. 237). To write such poetry a new kind of poet must appear, who, ascending to Hippocrene, shall recall the muses to their homes.

Yet, even while he occupies himself with the serious question of the displaced muses, Milton remains throughout much of this ode the genial elegist. This is certainly the case in those sections of the poem (antistrophes 1 and 2) where he enjoys a friendly joke with Rouse concerning the unfortunate book that lost its way after being dispatched to Oxford. He asks who seduced the book by fraud and how it went astray from its brothers, treating the incident as a piece of mock epic.

> Quis te, parve liber, quis te fratribus
> Subduxit reliquis dolo?
>
> . . . .
>
> Quin tu, libelle, nuntii licet malâ
> Fide, vel oscitantiâ
> Semel erraveris agmine fratrum,
> Seu quis te teneat specus,
> Seu qua te latebra, forsan unde vili
> Callo teréris institoris insulsi,
> Laetare felix.   (13–14, 37–43)

[Little book, who thievishly abstracted you
and left your brothers?

. . . .

Yet, little book, although because of a messenger's
dishonesty or sleepy carelessness
you once wandered from your brothers' company —
and may be now in some cave
or den where you are rubbed by the coarse hard
hand of a stupid huckster —
you may rejoice in good fortune.]

Addressing the book directly and treating it like a lost child, Milton affects a solicitous concern for its welfare and spins out an entertaining anecdote about the messenger's motives for "losing" the book and the person of the man now holding it. The direct address, the playful concern, and above all the invention of anecdote link Milton to the Latin elegists who first exploited this kind of situation in verse. Ovid and Propertius both have elegies that concern lost or returned tablets, which they address with affected concern or outrage and which they make the subject of imaginative anecdotes. Although neither elegy (Ovid, *Amores* 1.12 and Propertius 3.23) offers an exact parallel to the situation in Milton's ode, both have several parallels in treatment. The elegies concern either the loss of tablets or their return by the lady to the lover, and the situation is, therefore, emotionally charged. Ovid's lady sends the tablets back with a message that displeases him, and he threatens to throw them away and then speculates what might happen to them if he "loses" them. He tells them to lie in the street where they will be crushed by the weight of a passing wheel, exclaiming that it would be better for a judge to read such tablets or that they should lie in a miser's accounts.[10] The tablets sent by Propertius' lady do go astray, and as Milton laments the loss of his book, Propertius laments the lost tablets. He speculates about what was written on them and where they now lie. The tablets and the love messages, perhaps the love verse, are dear to him, and he fears that they have fallen into the hands of an avaricious merchant who will write his bills on them.

> me miserum, his aliquis rationem scribit avarus
> et ponit duras inter ephemeridas!
> quas si quis mihi rettulerit, donabitur auro: (3.23, 19–21)

[Alas! and now some greedy merchant writes his bills
upon them and places them among his unfeeling ledgers!
If any will return them to me he shall have gold for his reward.]

In both the elegies and in the Rouse ode a relatively trivial event (the loss of tablets or a book) is treated with mock seriousness; an object is addressed and regarded as a person (in Propertius and Milton, a cherished person), and an incident involving that object is imaginatively created for the reader. In all three poems, the imagined incident is unsavory. Ovid creates a miser, Propertius a greedy merchant, and Milton a stupid huckster who now possesses the cherished tablets or book. All three poets, moreover, expect the reader to share in their mock outrage and, of course, be entertained by their poetic inventiveness. But there is still another "person" who is addressed besides the book or tablets and the reader: the friend for whom the poet writes and from whom the tablets come or to whom the book is sent.

Like the Latin elegies, Milton's ode is a personal poem written to a "learned friend," a *doctus amicus*, as Milton calls Rouse in the first anti-strophe (16). The learned friend of Latin elegists such as Ovid and Tibullus and Propertius was not male, however, but female. This *docta puella* inspired the poet, who dedicated his lines to her and described her in his poems, the word, *docta*, applying not only to her learning and wit, but also to her experience as a courtesan. Cynthia, the *docta amica* of Propertius, is perhaps the most famous of these "learned" friends.[11] When Milton gives Rouse the title, "learned friend," which Propertius had so endearingly bestowed on Cynthia, it may be that he is sharing with an Oxonian, well-versed in Latin literature, a subtle joke that it is not to a Cynthia but to a "friend" of a different sort that he entrusts his verses. At any rate, he asks Rouse for the kind of special care and protection that the Roman elegists often invoked. They did not entrust their poetry to a vulgar audience, but to a circle of young men and women who were learned and sympathetic to the muses. In the final epode Milton instructs Rouse to shelter his book from the mob and to preserve it for the learned and judicious readers to come.

> Et tutela dabit solers Roüsi,
> Quò neque lingua procax vulgi penetrabit, atque longè
> Turba legentum prava facesset;
> At ultimi nepotes,
> Et cordatior aetas
> Judicia rebus aequiora forsitan
> Adhibebit integro sinu.   (78–84)

[And provided by the watchful protection of Rouse;
there the babbling tongue of the populace will not penetrate
and the crowd of vulgar readers will be far away.
But our remote descendants
in a wiser age
will perhaps see things with impartial mind
and juster judgment.]

Milton concludes his ode, as he opens it, with the genial tone of the private elegist, hoping for a wise audience to appreciate his book and offering thanks for the favor of Rouse (Roüsio favente") who has preserved it.

Yet, despite the familiar accents of the opening strophe and antistrophe and the light banter in antistrophes 1 and 2 in recounting the book's possible misadventures, Milton, beginning with strophe 2 and more firmly in strophe 3, modulates the tone of his personal ode, and the strain we then hear is of a higher mood. The elegiac poet and his learned friend retreat to the background and the heroic bard advances. The muses under the protection of the god Apollo take their places, not now in wood and stream, but in the temple guarded by the priest whose person Rouse now assumes. The little lost book is regretted no longer; its more fortunate brother now dispatched to Rouse will insure its immortality. Milton turns from deploring its low fate, imprisonment in some cave or den, to imagine its escape from Lethe and flight to heaven.

                                    profundam
              Fugere Lethen, vehique Superam
              In Jovis aulam remige pennâ;   (44–46)

    [that you may escape the depths of Lethe
    and may be carried on oaring wing to the high court of Jove.]

With his little book our poet also mounts on high, forsaking the lower springs of Helicon and seeking Hippocrene, which he alludes to as the Pegasean stream ("amne Pegaséo," 36). Assuming the pindaric mantle, he makes strophe and subject stride hand-in-hand.

One of the most striking characteristics of the pindaric style is the abrupt shift in tone, often accompanied by a sudden heightening.[12] In some of his earlier poetry and particularly in the monody *Lycidas*, Milton had displayed this characteristic. For instance, in *Lycidas*, with the entrance of Phoebus Apollo, Milton turns abruptly from the bitter complaints of the Swain to the sublime words of the god (76–84). In *Ad Rousium* the shift is from the elegant banter of the first two strophes to the serious outcry: how may the muses be saved in a land inhospitable to poetry. This outcry in strophe 2, moreover, is framed as a question and placed directly parallel to the question asked in antistrophe 1. Both questions begin with the interrogative "quis" ("who"), but the first "who" refers to a man, the second to a god or god-sprung man. The first queries in a half-amused way who led the book astray; the second demands with righteous anguish who will restore a nation lost to learning and strayed from the muses. This evocation of the muses follows directly after the idyllic description of the muses' retreat at Oxford. There Milton creates two effects. The first is playful and elegiac, the second solemn and pindaric. No sooner have we been shown the pleasant clear fountains of the muses and the cradle of blue Father Thames than with solemn resonant tones Milton evokes the sacred dance that the Bacchic throng engage in with the muses. The mood is suddenly heightened.

                        thyasusque sacer
              Orbi notus per immensos
              Temporum lapsus redeunte coelo,
              Celeberque futurus in aevum.   (21–24)

[and the sacred dance
which has been famous in the world
while the firmament has turned through vast stretches
of time and will be famous for ever.]

This cosmic dance moves as though in tune with the movement of heaven and eternal time; those who join in it are not mere pastoral deities and earthly men. The word "sacer," used to describe the band of poets, is important, for it tells us that the poet is not a private man amusing himself and indulging his art, but a man divinely elected. The word "sanctus" ("holy") used in line 30 to describe the power of the poet and the word "sacris" ("sacred places") used to denote the holy sanctuaries of poetry's god, Apollo, reinforce the notion that the poet is a man with a holy vocation.

The idea that the poet is ordained by the gods is manifest throughout Pindar's poetry. Apollo, god of poetry, and Zeus, the father of the muses, figure prominently in the Pythian and Olympian odes as guardians of society and patrons of poetry. Unlike the lyric and elegiac poets of Rome who regarded poetry as a private pastime and felt that the poet should not concern himself directly with political issues, Pindar felt that the poet must be a voice that addressed kings and nobles. He should act as a stabilizing force in a society that centered on him and listened to him. Pindar's claims for the poet are, of course, the epic claims, the very ones that Propertius declines and Ovid puts off. The muses are important to Pindar not merely as inspirers of his verse (the elegiac poets too called on the muses for inspiration), but as guardians of religious order and social welfare. In practical terms Pindar recognized that poetry is the organ for future fame, that the poet through the muses grants glory and preserves the memory of great men, whether statesmen, heroes in battle, or athletes, insuring that their deeds do not go down in darkness.[13] But even as poetry commemorates the past and passes down history to the future, it binds men together, promoting joy and soothing sorrow. Pindar even goes so far as to measure a good society by its service to the muses. In Olympia 11, for example, he praises the West Wind Locrians as honorable and straightforward, hospitable to strangers and not devious in their dealing, summing up his praise by saying that they have not forgotten their service to the lovely arts of the muses (Olympia 11.15–19). For Pindar how the muses are served is the touchstone for judging the good of a society.

Holding poetry as the measure of social good, Pindar feels that the true poet has certain obligations. As the servant of the muses he is elected by god and not man, and his chief function is to speak the truth. The

old poets, possessing higher principles than their modern successors, sang
for delight and for the sake of the Muse, not for money (Isthmia 2.1–10).
Further, as Pindar tells us in another ode, the muse when she sings truth
will grow greater: "αὔξεται καὶ Μοῖσα δι᾿ ἀγγελίας ὀρθᾶς" (Pythia 4.279)
("And the Muse through a straightforward report will increase"). In Pindar's view the good of poetry flourishes with truth, for truth is the ultimate concern of the good poet. In Nemea 8 he gives us a brief sketch of
the ideal poet and his selfless commitment to the Muse.

> χρυσὸν εὔχονται, πεδίον δ᾿ἕτεροι
> ἀπέραντον, ἐγὼ δ᾿ἀστοῖς ἁδὼν καὶ χθονὶ γυῖα καλύψαι,
> αἰνέων αἰνητά, μομφὰν δ᾿ ἐπισπείρων ἀλιτροῖς.   (Nemea 8.37–39)

> [Some pray for gold,
>   others for land without limit,
> but I pray to hide my limbs in the earth as one who gladdened his
>   fellow-citizens,
> praising that which deserves it and laying blame on the workers of evil.]

Although this concept of the poet as the servant of the muse is common among the Greek poets of the archaic world and is handed down
to such Roman poets as Virgil, it is a concept that Milton associated with
Pindar.[14] In the sonnet "Captain or Colonel, or Knight in Arms," it is
Pindar's name and reputation he calls upon when he bids, as he does also
in the Rouse ode, "Lift not thy spear against the Muses Bowre" (9). In
Lycidas, moreover, he assumes the voice of the poet-priest, and like
Pindar before him, lays praise and scatters blame with even hands. The
middle sections of the Rouse ode call to mind the poetic voice heard in
Lycidas and some of the questions raised about the responsibilities of
poetry. In calling for a new kind of poet to purge the land, Milton echoes
a plea that Phoebus and Peter first urged in the earlier poem. With the
authority of the Apollonian bard and the conviction of the Christian
pastor, he cries out:

> Modò quis deus, aut editus deo
> Pristinam gentis miseratus indolem
> (Si satis noxas luimus priores
> Mollique luxu degener otium)
> Tollat nefandos civium tumultus,
> Almaque revocet studia sanctus
> Et relegatas sine sede Musas
> Jam penè totis finibus Angligenûm.   (25–32)

> [But what god or demigod,
>   remembering with pity the ancient character of our race—
> if we have made enough atonement for our past sins,

our degenerate idleness and effeminate luxury—
will put an end to the wicked broils of civil war,
and with his sacred power will bring back our nourishing studies
and the banished Muses who have been left
with scarcely any refuge in all England?][15]

Milton's opening line appears to echo the beginning of Olympia 2, imitated by Horace in antiquity and by Cowley in the seventeenth century.[16] The poem, which celebrates Zeus, Heracles, and Theron, the king of the Sicilian city Acragas, involves the search for a "saving hero"; its first line appeals to the lordly-lyred hymns for a suitable subject:

> Ἀναξιφόρμιγγες ὕμνοι,
> τίνα θεόν, τίν᾽ ἥρωα, τίνα ἄνδρα κελαδήσομεν;
>
> (Olympia 2.1–2)

> [Lordly-lyred songs,
> What god, what hero, what man shall we celebrate?]

The god is the highest god, Zeus; the hero is his son, Heracles; and the man is King Theron, the descendant of the royal Theban line. The ode singles out these three who have won great prominence after trial and goes on to recount the fortunes of the house of Thebes, famous for its great but unhappy progeny (Cadmus, Semele, Oedipus), a house which has survived despite adversity and now enjoys happiness in its descendant, Theron. Thebes survived, Pindar tells us, because of Thersander, grandson of Oedipus and son of Polyneices, a hero who turned back the ill fortune of his family and overcame the plagues, wars, and civil tumults that beset his ancestors. With the favor of the gods, Pindar concludes, bad fortune can turn to good, and a person, a family, a nation be saved.

The celebration in Olympia 2 of the saving god, hero, and man has special application to Milton's ode, which also appeals to a god or a hero ("deus, aut editus deo") to succor the land, an England spoiled like Thebes with civil tumult and plague. Indolent and luxury-loving, the English have become degenerate and brought dissension and misery to their race. Unable to save themselves, they need a god or hero, a Heracles or a Thersander, to help put an end to war. Yet this appeal for a god-sprung or god-elected man need not be restricted to a Heracles, who was begotten by Zeus, but may include the man raised or elected by god, as the poet is.[17] In a nation troubled by war, the springs of poetry have been polluted by foul Harpies. It is the responsibility of a poet elected by god and armed with an Apollonian quiver to slay these birds of prey: to castigate the unworthy and restore the muses to their places.

Immundasque volucres
Unguibus imminentes
Figat Apollineâ pharetrâ,
Phinéamque abigat pestem procul amne Pegaséo.   (33–36)

[Who with the shafts of Apollo
will transfix the foul birds that threaten us
with their claws and drive
the plague of Phineus far from the Pegasean stream?]

The appeal for the Apollonian quiver introduces at this point in the ode the authority and power of the god of poetry, who may endow his followers with all his gifts: not only mastery over the lyre but might to slay Pytho or the foul birds that pollute the springs of poetry. In *Lycidas* Phoebus appears in person to remind the poet of his divine appointment and his higher responsibilities (to forsake sport with Amaryllis in the shade, to speak truth and seek the approbation of Jove). In *Ad Joannem Rousium* the reference to Apollo confirms that the poet alone can purge the land. Pindar consistently holds the same view, as he celebrates again and again the special connection that the poet has with Apollo and the muses. From them, as he tells us in Pythia 1, he takes his golden lyre, which has the power to soothe the eagle, Zeus's own bird, and even cause savage Ares to drop his arms. In Olympia 2 Pindar compares the god-appointed poet to the eagle that soars above ravens, which vainly caw at him from below. The words that the poet uses Pindar compares to shafts, held in a quiver under his arm, which he directs at men of understanding. In his view the poet is a man with special powers that have been given him by the god and that he must use as the god directs him. Like Pindar Milton believes that God protects and guides the poet. In *Paradise Lost* his invocations of the muse in Books III and VII urge that special protection, and his prayer in the Rouse ode that with poetry's mantic power the menacing birds may be driven off looks forward to the plea to the muse in Book VII also to drive off threatening foes: "the barbarous dissonance / Of *Bacchus* and his revellers" (PL VII, 32–33).

The appeal for Apollonian power in strophe 2 affirms not only the importance of poetry to the land but also the importance of the "libellum," the little book that was lost but now stands replaced by the volume sent to Rouse. The book in antistrophe 2 even assumes a kind of heroic personality, having survived its trial in the underworld (the cave or den) and escaped Lethe to mount on high and join the gods. It too in a sense is chosen or elected by Rouse, who in strophe 3 begs for it to complete the just number, and we might even apply the word "editus" to it, used for the hero of strophe 2, since the book now is, as the Latin word implies, not only born, but spread abroad and published to the world. Further, it will be received into a library that has, as Milton tells us, more precious treasures than the temple at Delphi and will be taken into the hands of Rouse, whom Milton now compares to Ion, Apollo's son.

> Téque adytis etiam sacris
> Voluit reponi quibus et ipse praesidet
> Æternorum operum custos fidelis,
> Quaestorque gazae nobilioris,
> Quàm cui praefuit Iön
> Clarus Erechtheides
> Opulenta dei per templa parentis
> Fulvosque tripodas, donaque Delphica
> Iön Actaea genitus Creusâ.   (52–60)

[You he desires to place in the hallowed
sanctuaries over which he himself presides,
the faithful custodian of immortal works,
the guardian of treasure more illustrious
than the golden tripods and Delphic offerings
which were entrusted to Ion
in the rich temple of his divine father —
Ion the son of Erechtheus' daughter, Actaean Creusa.]

Rouse now appears not merely as the *doctus amicus* of earlier strophes, but as a priest who guards a sacred heritage at Oxford, itself described as a rich and holy sanctuary. These allusions to Apollo and Delphi serve not only to reaffirm the sacred nature of the poet and his book, but also to call to mind some clear pindaric associations. Delphi was renowned in antiquity for its Pythian games as well as for its oracle, and Pindar composed twelve odes commemorating Pythian victories, the most famous of these being Pythia 1, written in praise of Apollo and his lyre and in honor of Hieron, king of Sicily, who presented many treasures to the temple at Delphi, among them the famous statue of the charioteer, yet to be seen there. In the Pythian odes and generally throughout his poetry Pindar was fond of reminding his audience that Apollo was served by athlete and poet alike, who strive in his honor, both seeking as their ultimate success the approbation of the god.[18] Both also consecrate gifts to the god, the athlete gold and tripods as thank-offerings, the poet his poem. In comparing the book-treasures of the Bodleian, the monuments of poets, to the golden treasures and tripods of Delphi, given by kings and athletes, Milton is also inviting, like Pindar, comparison between different kinds of monuments and, like the earlier poet, he grants the advantage to poetry. In Nemea 5 Pindar affirms the superiority of the living ode over monuments in stone or metal, opening his poem with a resounding disclaimer of the latter:

Οὐκ ἀνδριαντοποιός εἰμ᾽, ὥστ᾽ ἐλινύσοντα ἐργάζεσθαι ἀγάλματ᾽ ἐπ᾽ αὐτᾶς
βαθμίδος
ἑσταότ᾽. (Nemea 5.1–2)

> [I am not a maker of statuary, one who works on
> an image standing quiet on its step.]

This boast is shared by later poets, such as Propertius who declares that his elegy is more lasting than the Pyramids and the house of Jove or Horace who proclaims his ode more durable than bronze.[19] It is a sentiment handed down to Shakespeare in the Renaissance who in sonnet 55 begins: "Not marble nor the gilded monuments / Of princes shall outlive this powerful rhyme" (55, 1–2), and one reaffirmed by Milton who in his own poem included in the second folio states that Shakespeare has in his poetry built for himself a "live-long Monument" (8). In the Rouse ode, Milton once more echoes this age-old boast, offering a graceful compliment to the librarian at Oxford, whom he calls a faithful custodian of immortal works, and assuring a place for his own book among the high names of those authors who were the lights of the Greek and Roman people: "inter alta nomina / Authorum, Graiae simul et Latinae / Antiqua gentis lumina, et verum decus" (70–72).

It is significant, however, that Milton goes beyond the graceful compliment to Rouse as a custodian of learning to compare him with Ion, Apollo's son. In so doing, he reinforces the Apollonian associations introduced earlier at the same time that he makes use of a typical pindaric device, the likening of a principal person in an ode to a hero of myth. Pindar works these comparisons sometimes directly, sometimes indirectly, as, for example, he compares Hieron directly to Philoktetes in Pythia 1 (50–52), but in Olympia 1 indirectly connects him with Pelops by alluding to the favor the gods grant both these men. Milton's comparison of Rouse to Ion is indirect, for Milton seems only to compare the treasures over which the men preside. Yet, in evoking the son of the god and recounting his ancestry, Milton means, of course, for us to look upon Rouse like Ion as a priest specially born and ordained to guard the sacred possessions of the god in a sacred place. Moreover, he is doubtless aware that the story of Ion, son of Apollo born of a mortal woman, has a close parallel in the account of Iamos, told by Pindar in Olympia 6. Iamos is born of Evadne, a mortal woman who like Creusa is wooed in secret by Apollo.

Like his Euripidean counterpart, he is reared privately, ordained by his father to seercraft and appointed guardian of an oracle, the one at Olympia. Milton probably uses the story of Ion from Euripides' play because, as Merritt Y. Hughes has suggested, he wishes to evoke the magnificent description of Apollo's temple at Delphi included there.[20] Olympia 6 however, also begins with a striking evocation of architectural splendor where Pindar compares the building of a palace to the construction of splendid verse, a comparison implicit, of course, in Milton's likening of Delphi's golden treasure to Oxford's poetical one.[21]

Apollo's sacred home at Delphi is once more alluded to in antistrophe 3 when Milton recounts the journey of the little book to Oxford. As in antistrophe 2, the adventures of the book are colored with epic associations, but now the book is less the hero enduring trial in the underworld than it is the athlete coming victoriously to the "diam domum" ("brilliant" or "divine house") of the god, having fulfilled his Pythian ordeal.

> Ergo tu visere lucos
> Musarum ibis amoenos,
> Diamque Phoebi rursus ibis in domum
> Oxoniâ quam valle colit
> Delo posthabitâ,
> Bifidóque Parnassi jugo:
> Ibis honestus,
> Postquam egregiam tu quoque sortem
> Nactus abis.   (61–69)

[So you shall go to see
the lovely groves of the Muses,
and shall go again to the noble home of Phoebus,
where he dwells in Oxford's valley
in preference to Delos
or twin-peaked Parnassus.
You shall go with honor,
since you depart in assurance
of a notable destiny.]

In the formulaic style of epic Milton three times dismisses the book on its journey, addressing it directly as before, "ibis" ("you shall go"); with this direct address his tone is once more fond and affectionate, his mood lighter than in the two preceding strophes. Clearly, the country muses of valley and stream, with whom he sported as a young poet, have been recalled to Oxford. The book will visit their pleasant groves, but it will also see the temple of Apollo and confer with the god who now prefers Oxford to Delos or the peak of Parnassus. The allusion to the birthplace of Apollo and the full range of his dwelling places, from temple to grove to highest mountain, tells us that all kinds of poetry and learning (pastoral and elegiac and epic) are nourished in Oxford. It may be that Milton associates Oxford also with those safe retreats of the muses, described by Pindar in several of his odes, the never-never land beyond the fringes of the world, such as the home of the West Wind Locrians in Olympia 11 or the land of the Hyperboreans in Pythia 10. In the society of the West Wind Locrians, neither strangers nor muses meet with cold hospitality, and in the land of the Hyperboreans, lyres and flutes sound; choruses of girls sing; all bind their hair with golden laurel; and neither old age nor disease, battle nor scandal, afflict any.[22] There, Pindar tells us, the muses are safe, and accordingly never absent themselves from the festivals. There may also be a reference here to the retreat that Horace describes in the first ode of his second book, a retreat to a cave of poetry, where in the company of Dione and the light lyre the poet may be free from danger and find safe harbor.

It is significant, however, that it is for his book, not for himself, that Milton wishes "placidam . . . requiem" (75–76), ("peaceful rest"). In so wishing, he seems moved by the desire, as he says at the beginning of the final epode, that his labors should not have been empty or in vain. "Labores," a word with Herculean associations, may refer, as Merritt Hughes seems to think, to the tracts that Milton sent to Rouse along with his volume.[23] I think it is more likely to refer to his whole effort as a writer and so casts the poet once more, as in strophe 2, into the role of the active hero, a role which he at times shares with his own book. Now, certainly the book is traveling to a hero's reward — to an illustrious lot and true glory ("egregiam . . . sortem," 68, and "verum decus," 72). Both *sors* and *decus* are words drawn from the epic vocabulary. Moreover, the "sedesque beatas" to which kind Hermes leads the book are the blest abodes, the sacred isles to which the heroes were led. Several times in his odes Pindar refers to the isles of the blest, most particularly in Olympia 2, where he describes Achilles and Cadmus, who have experienced hardship and trial in real life, attaining there a final rest and reward. The rest that Milton invokes for his little book is not only the rest won for heroes after trial, but the "requiem" and "decus" (the Greek δόξα) that the athlete experiences, having been victorious in the race "where that immortall garland is to be run for, not without dust and heat."[24] Both Milton's book and Pindar's athlete-hero enjoy Apollonian rewards.

In the final epode the ever-changing Rouse is now linked with Hermes, who, as he guides the souls of the dead to the blest abodes, will guide the book to Oxford. Not only marshal of shades, Hermes is also the patron of learning and god of pastoral poetry, and in these final lines Milton looks to Rouse as just such a tutelary spirit of good favor:

> sedesque beatas
> Quas bonus Hermes
> Et tutela dabit solers Roüsi.   (76–78)

> [and for the blessed abode
> provided by kind Hermes
> and the watchful protection of Rous.][25]

Milton also looks to the future where his descendants in a wiser age, with impartial mind and judgment, may come to know his poetry. Yet, though the tone of these lines is almost a return to the graceful elegance of the opening strophe, and the evocation of future Oxford idyllic, the poet does not forget the harsh realities of his own age where the tongues of the multitude are insolent ("procax," 79), the crowd wicked ("prava," 80), and envy or spite ("livore," 85) is not yet buried. Perhaps his book of gentle elegies and pastorals will be appreciated by a sane and healthy posterity, but the present age calls for a poet quite different from the man who wrote those lines. He must heed the call for a god-elected bard. Milton's farewell to his little book, entrusted to Rouse's favor, is also a tacit recognition that he has bid fair peace to the world of forest shades; another world calls forth the epic poet to fresh woods and pastures new.[26]

Southern Illinois University at Edwardsville

NOTES

I wish to thank the School of Humanities and the Graduate School of Southern Illinois University at Edwardsville for support of my work on Pindar and the elegiac poets by granting released time for research and travel funding. I wish to thank Carl Conrad, Professor of Classics at Washington University, St. Louis, also; much of what I know about Pindar and the Latin elegiac poets I owe to his insight and learning.

1. I have consulted editions of the 1645 poems and the 1673 volume at the Bodleian Library and British Library and the original manuscript of *Ad Joannem Rousium* at the Bodleian Library, Oxford.

2. E. M. W. Tillyard, *Milton* (London, 1961), pp. 71–72; Louis L. Martz, "The Rising Poet, 1645," in *The Lyric and Dramatic Milton*, ed. J. H. Summers (New York, 1965), pp. 4–5.

3. Edward K. Rand, "Milton in Rustication," *SP*, 19 (1922), 115; S. E. Sprott, *Milton's Art of Prosody* (Oxford, 1953), p. 131; F. T. Prince, *The Italian Element in Milton's Verse* (Oxford, 1954), p. 148 n.; Edward Weismiller, "The 'Dry' and 'Rugged' Verse,"

The Lyric and Dramatic Milton, p. 128; John T. Shawcross, "The Prosody of Milton's Translation of Horace's Fifth Ode," *Tennessee Studies in Literature*, 13 (1968), 88 (analyzes the metrics of the Rouse ode); also see Bush, *Variorum*, pp. 324–31.

4. CM III, p. 238. Citations of Milton's prose and poetry will be from CM, the prose cited by volume and page number, the poetry by line number.

5. Tillyard, *Milton*, pp. 171–72.

6. "Ad *Joannem Rousium* Oxoniensis Academiae Bibliothecarium," CM I, pp. 316–25. The prose translation is by Douglas Bush, ed., *The Complete Poetical Works of John Milton* (Boston, 1965), pp. 179–81.

7. *The Poems of Catullus*, ed. W. B. McDaniel (New York, 1931), p. 1; Propertius, *Elegies I–IV*, ed. L. Richardson, Jr. (Norman, Oklahoma, 1977), p. 93.

8. Both Ovid and Propertius refer to the audience of young men and women for which they wrote. See, for example, Ovid, *Amores*, 2.1, 5–10, 37–38, ed. E. J. Kenney (Oxford, 1961). Of course the role of gentleman-poet might, while pretending aesthetic disinterest, mask telling commentary on the life and politics of Rome.

9. See Propertius 3.2, 15–16: "at Musae comites et carmina cara legenti, / nec defessa choris Calliopea meis." Also see Margaret Hubbard, *Propertius* (London, 1974), pp. 72–82.

10.   Ite hinc, difficiles, funebria ligna, tabellae,
　　　　　　　　tuque, negaturis cera referta notis!
　　　　　　　　. . . . . . .
　　　　　　　　proiectae triviis iaceatis, inutile lignum,
　　　　　　　　vosque rotae frangat praetereuntis onus!
　　　　　　　　. . . . . . .
　　　　　　　　aptius hae capiant vadimonia garrulla cerae,
　　　　　　　　quas aliquis duro cognitor ore legat;
　　　　　　　　inter ephemeridas melius tabulasque iacerent,
　　　　　　　　in quibus absumptas fleret avarus opes.
　　　　　　　　　　　　　　　　　(*Amores*, 1.12, 7–8, 13–14, 23–26)

[Go away from here, troublesome tablets, funereal pieces of wood, and you, wax crammed with writing that will tell me no!
. . . .
Lie there, thrown down at the crossing of the ways, useless wood, and may the weight of the passing wheel break you to pieces!
. . . .
It would be fitter for such tablets to receive the imprint of
　　　　　　prattling bail-bonds
for some attorney to read in harsh tones;
It would be better that they should lie among day-books
and tables over which a miser weeps for money spent.]

(All translations, unless otherwise noted, are mine.)

11. See Propertius 1.7, 9–11:

　　　　　　　　Hic mihi conteritur vitae modus, haec mea fama est,
　　　　　　　　hinc cupio nomen carminis ire mei,
　　　　　　　　me laudent doctae solum placuisse puellae.

　　　　　　　　[So the time of my life is passed. This is my renown,
　　　　　　　　this the fame I wish to go forth for my song;
　　　　　　　　let them praise me only that I pleased a learned girl.]

12. Sixteenth- and seventeenth-century editors and commentators frequently commented on the features of Pindar's style, often citing the views of ancient writers such as Horace, Pliny, and Quintilian. See, for example, the commentary by Erasmus Schmidt in his excellent 1616 edition of the odes (Pindar, *Odes*, ed. Erasmus Schmidt [Wittenberg, 1616], pp. 1–2. A useful summary of classical and Renaissance views on Pindar is found in Thomas Pope Blount, *De Re Poetica* (London, 1694), pp. 65–68, 171–74.

13. For the power of poetry to preserve the memory of great deeds, see the following odes of Pindar:

ἁ δ᾿ ἀρετὰ κλειναῖς ἀοιδαῖς
χρονία τελέθει.   (Pythia 3.114–15)

[brave deeds in glorious songs
last for a long time]

μεγάλων δ᾿ ἀέθλων
Μοῖσα μεμνᾶσθαι φιλεῖ.   (Nemea 1.11–12)

[The Muse loves to recollect great contests]

ἀοιδαὶ
καὶ λόγοι τὰ καλά σφιν ἔρν᾿ ἐκόμισαν.   (Nemea 6.30a–30b)

[Songs and stories have brought down noble deeds to us]

Pindar, *Carmina*, ed. C. M. Bowra (Oxford, 1935).

14. See my article, "Milton's Muse and the Daughters of Memory," *ELR*, 9 (1979), 432–41.

15. Although most translators render line 25 as a question, it is possible to translate it as an optative: "Would that some god or demi-god might."

16. J. H. Finley cites a number of parallels in Horace to Milton's appeal to an unnamed god or hero, as well as several places where Horace, like Milton, chastises his people for their slackness and invokes the return of peace (John H. Finley, "Milton and Horace," *Harvard Studies in Classical Philology*, 48 [1937], 54n.). Relevant passages cited by Finley include *Odes* 1, 2.25–52; *Epodes* 7, 17–20; *Odes* 1,2.47; 1, 35.33–40; 2,1.25–36; 4, 15.9–20 (Horace, *Carmina*, ed. T. E. Page [London, 1964]). Ode 1, 12 of Horace is a special case since its opening line is a direct imitation of Pindar's Olympia 2: "Quem virum aut heroa vel acri tibia sumus celebrare, Clio? / quem deum?" As Renaissance commentators frequently pointed out, Horace has reversed the pindaric order and instead of appealing in descending order to god, hero, and man, he calls in rising order upon man, hero, and god. Milton, like Pindar, appeals first to God.

17. The Latin word *editus*, the participle of *edo* signifies sprung from or born from and also elevated or standing out. It could also be applied to writings and proclamations and signify published, proclaimed, spread abroad. Milton, I believe, is using all three senses. I wish to thank Carter Revard for drawing my attention to the third of these meanings and its possible application to the book.

18. For a discussion of Pindar's linking of poetic and athletic performance, see John H. Finley, Jr., *Pindar and Aeschylus* (Cambridge, Mass., 1955), pp. 28–31, 74; Thomas Hoey, "Fusion in Pindar," *HSCP*, 70 (1965), 243; Charles Paul Segal, "Pindar's First and Third Olympian Odes," *HSCP*, 68 (1964), 224.

19. See Propertius 3.2, 18–20, 22, 25–26:

carmina erunt formae tot monumenta tuae,
nam neque pyramidum sumptus ad sidera ducti,
nec Iovis Elei caelum imitata domus

. . . .

mortis ab extrema condicione uacant

. . . .

at non ingenio quaesitum nomen ab aeuo
excidet: ingenio stat sine morte decus.

[My songs will be so many monuments to your beauty,
for neither the expense of leading the Pyramids to the stars,
nor the house of Jove at Elis, representing the sky.

. . . .

are exempt from the final terms of death

. . . .

But the fame gained by my wit shall not ever
pass away, but my wit stand glorious without death.]

Note the use of "decus" to end line 26. Milton employs the same word in a final position at the end of line 72 and the third antistrophe. Also see Horace, 3 *Odes* 30.1–5.

Exegi monumentum aere perennius
regalique situ pyramidum altius   (1–2)

[I have made a monument more lasting than bronze
and higher in royal structure than the pyramids.]

Milton's use of the word "monumenta" (51) to apply to books probably follows Propertius and Horace; and see Virgil, *Georgics* III, 12–14, *Aeneid* VIII, 312.

20. John Milton, *Complete Poems and Major Prose*, ed. Merritt Y. Hughes (New York, 1957), p. 148n.

21. See Pindar, Olympia 6, 1–3:

Χρυσέας ὑποστάσαντες εὐτειχεῖ προθύρῳ θαλάμου
κίονας ὡς ὅτε θαητὸν μέγαρον
πάξομεν.

[Like those raising up golden pillars for the forecourt
of a well-built chamber, let us construct a wondrous
palace.]

22. Milton uses the term "Hyperborean" in *Mansus* (26) to describe England.

23. Hughes, *Complete Poems*, p. 148n. For recent information about books and pamphlets that Milton sent to Rouse, see Gwen Hampshire, "An Unusual Bodleian Purchase in 1645," *The Bodleian Library Record*, 10 (1982), 339–48.

24. In this celebrated sentence from *Areopagitica* (CM IV, p. 311), Milton thinks like Pindar of the pursuit of virtue as an athletic contest, taking his metaphor from the games about which Pindar wrote.

25. "[T]utela solers Roüsi" may echo *Georgics* IV, 327, "custodia sollers."

26. As Gordon Campbell mentions in his essay in this volume, Milton chose the epigraph for the 1645 poems from Virgil, perhaps alluding to his own "vatic" ambitions: "Baccare frontem / Cingite, ne vati noceat mala lingua futuro" (*Eclogues* 7, 27–28) ("Bind the brow with foxglove, lest an evil tongue harm the future bard").

MILTON'S LATIN AND GREEK VERSE: AN ANNOTATED BIBLIOGRAPHY

John B. Dillon

INTRODUCTION

MILTON'S LATIN poems, totaling some eighteen hundred lines of varying length, constitute a sizeable portion of his "minor" verse. For the light that they shed on his life and thought they have been studied extensively; less often, though increasingly in recent years, they have also been treated as productions worthy of literary analysis, either by themselves or within the larger context of the development of Milton's poetic art. They have been edited repeatedly and often annotated. All have been translated into English, most of them many times over. A few have also been translated into other tongues. They have a concordance. Studies exist on their stylistic and metrical aspects and on their literary relationships. But much of this work appears in writings of broader scope and is thus not immediately identifiable in the general Milton bibliographies as pertaining specifically to the Latin verse. Under these circumstances students of the Latin poems (and they are not the only students of Milton similarly handicapped) may feel the need for a relatively comprehensive guide to significant editions of these pieces, to their translations and illustrations, and to historical and critical comment on them.

The present bibliography is intended to meet that need. Topically arranged and furnished with what it is hoped will be useful annotations, it covers all of Milton's known writings in quantitative Latin verse. It also covers his few metrical essays in Greek. The latter, with one trifling exception, Milton printed together with his Latin poems, thus authorizing the concept here adhered to of a corpus of his verse in these two languages. Included are not only the pieces collected in the *Poemata* of 1673 and such other Latin poems as are normally printed in separate editions of Milton's poetry but also a number of verse scraps not usually thought of in this context. These are the surviving portion of an epigram on Justinian inscribed in Milton's copy of the Harington translation of Ariosto's *Orlando Furioso*,[1] two adaptations of Juvenal from the prose works, the adaptation of a line from Callimachus in Milton's letter of 1639 to Lukas

Holste, his adaptation of a line from Horace entered later in that year in the album of Count Camillo Cerdogni,[2] and the metrical translations in his marginalia on Euripides.[3] Not included are pieces not now generally believed to be Milton's, though at times ascribed to him; whereas ideally a bibliography such as this should treat the *dubia et spuria* as well, considerations of time and space have in this instance precluded their coverage.[4]

Few bibliographies can hope to be absolutely complete. This one makes no pretence in that direction. Rather, it is a selective record, encompassing, insofar as editions (including manuscript material) and comment are concerned, only those items that seem to make an actual contribution either to the history and the constitution of the text or to an understanding and appreciation of the poems themselves. Material not dealing specifically with the Latin and Greek verse, no matter how useful it might be for background purposes, has been excluded, although exceptions have been made for two testimonies on Milton's pronunciation of Latin and for a very few discussions of matters in Milton's prose works that bear directly upon poems intimately associated with them. I have also included one piece on Milton's youthful works that despite its silence on this point may safely be assumed to take the earlier Latin poems into account; this step has necessitated the inclusion as well of what may be an equally informed response.[5] But as the Latin and Greek poems have been comparatively understudied it is not reasonable to make such assumptions in every instance, and other contributions lacking specific references to these pieces have been excluded. Material appearing to be wholly derivative has been ignored, as have also been mere citations not adding to our knowledge of the passages or poems referred to. My practice in marginal cases has been to include the item in question.[6]

Translations and illustrations, both of course forms of interpretation, are cited comprehensively insofar as these have come to my attention.[7] Some of the translations are in fact adaptations and are so indicated. I am not aware of any imitations.[8] Material dealing with the reception and influence of the Latin poems has been included; simple references to them, and to the Greek verse, have not been. This is a bibliography, not an allusion book. I have, however, included a number of *obiter dicta* when these appear both to derive from an actual reading of the poems and to possess some degree of critical utility, however slight.[9] Though the primary reason for their appearance here lies in their nature as evaluative criticism, the recording of some of the less enthusiastic appraisals may also serve to offset certain Miltonolatrous remarks occasionally encountered in discussions of the poet's *fama posthuma*.[10]

It has been said that as a source for scholarly comment Milton is virtually inexhaustible. The amount of writing devoted to him to date does nothing to disprove this observation. In attempting to map out this small part of it as it now exists I had necessarily to overlook many potentially relevant items cited in the several sources drawn on for identifying likely titles.[11] It was, for example, not feasible to inspect all unpublished doctoral dissertations and master's theses, book reviews, encyclopedia articles, and popular biographies of Milton that might contain material on his Latin and Greek verse. Items not seen and not clearly identifiable, either from their title or from some other description, as meeting the previously outlined criteria for inclusion have been omitted. Since, however, this is an *annotated* bibliography, requiring for its completion a reading of almost everything listed in it, and since I have been scrupulous to track down items cited in what I have read, it does at least include the historical consensus on the core of pertinent materials falling within its purview (and of course it contains a good deal more than that).[12]

A few words on mechanics. This bibliography, unlike Gaul, is divided into four parts, of which the first is devoted to works of reference, including other bibliographies. The second treats material dealing with more than one of the Latin and Greek poems, although treatment of material pertaining solely to certain groups of poems (the *Elegiae* as a whole; the gunpowder epigrams; the epigrams *Ad Leonoram*; *Naturam non pati senium* and *De Idea Platonica*; the Greek pieces in the *Poemata*; "*Carmina Elegiaca*" and "*Asclepiads*"; pieces from the *Defensiones*) is deferred until the following part. Within this second part are sections listing editions noteworthy for their textual contributions, for their annotations, or for both; translations, including some with accompanying texts that are not particularly remarkable and some without texts but outfitted with annotations of varying degrees of utility; illustrations; and comment. In order to make this last section (by far the largest) more manageable, I have created out of it two subsections for material devoted entirely or almost entirely to linguistic matters, including diction and prosody, and to Milton's "sources" and his relationship to them as expressed in his work.[13] The third part deals with matter relating only to individual pieces or to the groups thereof indicated earlier in this paragraph; the fourth deals with the reputation and influence of the Latin poems.

The items listed under each rubric are ordered chronologically, usually by date of first publication. To save space, items are listed only once. Compensatory cross-referencing, essential in a larger work on this plan, has here been held to a minimum. Separate entries have normally not been given to different editions of the same work; major revisions are noted comprehensively, whereas copublications and largely or totally unaltered reprints are cited only as a convenience and by no means exhaustively. Doctoral dissertations subsequently published as books are cited in the latter format only. Unless otherwise indicated, volume and page references are to the first edition. Titles of well-known books are sometimes cited in abbreviated form, as are frequently the names and locations of publishers. Authors of works originally anonymous are, if known, identified by name within square brackets; other suppletions are indicated by the same sign. A table of abbreviations will be found at the end of this introduction.

Conceived of and executed with the present volume in mind (and not begun until the latter had come to assume a certain degree of substance), this compilation has been subject to temporal restrictions whose effects will be readily apparent. The chief of these is the lack of indexing by poem. The organizational scheme used, requiring as it does the reading of over half the work in order to identify all listed material on most of the poems, is increasingly dysfunctional the larger a bibliography becomes. When it became clear that the unexpectedly large amount of incidental criticism was expanding this one to the point where an *index locorum* might be appropriate, there was no longer sufficient time to reexamine for this purpose the many items already annotated in only a rather general fashion. Since a selective index, no matter how carefully qualified, would be bound to be misleading, the idea of including an *index locorum* had, regretfully, to be dispensed with. There is, however, an *index nominum*. Again, a certain amount of stylistic inconsistency is traceable to the same source. In the end, formal perfection had to give way to the demands of substance in this essentially occasional work. Considering the detail of many of the annotations and the reasonably high degree of completeness achieved within the stated guidelines,[14] these compromises may not prove too unsatisfactory.

Many people have assisted in the course of this labor. Professors Albert R. Cirillo, John T. Shawcross, and John A. Via graciously responded in writing to questions put to them, as did also Mr. Rodney G. Dennis, Curator of Manuscripts at the Houghton Library, and Ms. Laura Gorretta, Assistant University Archivist at Case Western Reserve University. Ms. Christine L. Roysdon of the Linderman Library, Lehigh University, and Mr. G. Marvin Tatum of the Olin Library, Cornell University, generously devoted valuable time to a search for one temporarily elusive dissertation. Courteous and efficient service was rendered by personnel at the Bodleian Library, the New York Public Library, and libraries at Brown, Cornell, Harvard, and Yale universities. Ms. Cheryl Spiese and her associates in the Interlibrary Loan Office at the State University of New York at Binghamton gave many hours of knowledgeable assistance; without their aid and that of their counterparts at numerous lending institutions this bibliography would not have been possible. Two anonymous readers offered occasional suggestions for improvement; Professor Anthony Low, whose painstaking services as an editor call for special recognition, offered many more. The remaining errors and infelicities are of course my own.

State University of New York at Binghamton

NOTES

1. The Miltonic authorship of this item is, to my mind at least, uncertain. But its acceptance into the canon by Carey (no. 39 in the bibliography; subsequent references in this form omit the words "in the bibliography"), whose edition is the only separate one of Milton's poems to include any of these verse scraps, has led to its inclusion here (in addition to this piece, somewhat misleadingly called "Note on Ariosto," Carey also prints the two adaptations of Juvenal here referred to as *De virtute* and *Sylla*). John T. Shawcross, *Milton's Spelling: Its Biographical and Critical Implications* (Ph.D. diss., New York University, 1958), pp. 270–71 (cf. also his article, "What We Can Learn from Milton's Spelling," *HLQ* 26 [1962–63], 351–61, p. 358), has shown that Milton is in all probability not the author of a number of the English-language Ariosto marginalia and has also cast serious doubt on his authorship of others in the same tongue (all of which were accepted by the editors of volume 18 of the Columbia *Works* [no. 32]). But inasmuch as English spelling practices have limited applicability to a Latin text, as Shawcross himself accepts as Milton's one foreign-language marginalium in this volume ("Marginalia, Milton's," no. 7, V, pp. 73–74), and as the inscription's reported location in the volume suggests that it may not have been entered at the same time(s) as most of the marginalia, these findings are not in themselves sufficient to exclude from the canon a verse accepted by several scholars and explicitly rejected by none.

2. Despite some pronouncements to the contrary, the Horatian matter in the Cerdogni album inscription is not a mere quotation but rather a recasting of the original generalization (*Ep.* 1.11, 27) to suit one specific instance, John Milton. Similarly, in the case of the line from Callimachus (*Hymn.* 6, 58) the original aorist form of the verb, which indicates a single action, has been altered to the imperfect, the thought being thereby accommodated to the continued activity of Milton's subject, Cardinal Barberini. These changes affect the sense and are thus to be differentiated from alterations that simply accommodate the syntax of an original to that of a sentence in which it is embedded (cf., e.g., the passage from Virgil near the beginning of *Ep. Fam.* 9 [the letter to Holste]); the latter process is of course only a form of quotation. In view of the common practice of including in the poetic corpus Milton's *"In Salmasii hundredam"* (*Salmas.* 1; an adaptation of Persius, *Prol.*, 8–14), analogous consideration of these other verse adaptations seems eminently justifiable.

3. Although their Columbia editors (no. 32, XVIII, p. 604) cite only that of *Rhesus*, 1–5, in this regard, several of these translations seem to be verse. Which (if any) really are is a matter requiring further study.

4. The more standard of these are conveniently discussed by Bush (no.6), pp. 337–40, to whose references may be added the following on the Mazarin *Epitaphium:* L. B. Hessler, "Attributed to Milton," *TLS*, 28 June 1934, p. 460; T. O. Mabbott, "The Miltonic Epitaph on Mazarin," *N&Q*, 167 (1934), 349–50; J. Milton French, "The Miltonic Epitaph on Mazarin," *N&Q*, 168 (1935), 445. Of the several verse translations of the *Ad Christinam*, two that seem to have sunk below even the scholarly horizon are those by Jacques Delille, "Cromwel à Christine, Reine de Suède, en lui envoyant son portrait" (*Almanach des Muses*, 1801, p. 129; rpts. in Delille's *Poésies fugitives et morceaux choisis*, rev. ed. [Paris: Giguet et Michaud, 1802], pp. 214–15, and in his *Oeuvres* [e.g., 2d ed., Paris: Lefèvre, 1833, p. 862, with spelling "Cromwell"]; based in part on Voltaire's 4-line verse tr. of the end of the poem in the *Dictionnaire philosophique*, s.v. "Cromwell"), and by Charles Symmons (no. 113; 1st ed., pp. 371–72; 2d ed., pp. 430–31; 3d ed., pp. 316–17). For discussion of William King's *Miltonis Epistola ad Pollionem*, sometimes naively thought to be *by* Milton, cf. Bradner (no. 189), pp. 258–59 and 264. The verses in the *Nova Solyma* now ascribed to Samuel Gott are discussed by Begley (no. 150), by Mackail (no. 152), and in other reviews of Begley listed in Stevens (no. 9), pp. 266–67. A Latin verse inscribed in a copy of *La Vieux Natura Breuium* (1584) now in the New York Public Library has sometimes been thought to be by John Milton the poet; cf. Hunter (no. 131), pp. 22–23, and Parker (no. 233), p. 1122. Verse translations (and others appearing to be prose) of passages from various Greek poets embedded in Milton's prose works are listed in the Columbia edition (no. 32), XVIII, 604–07; until these are definitely established as Milton's own it seems best to treat them as *dubia*.

5. Nos. 133 and 137, respectively.

6. Also ignored are statements whose only claim to originality lies in gross factual inaccuracy (e.g., that *Ep. Fam.* 7 and *Prod. Bomb.* 1 are in hexameters, that the Gunpowder Plot poems [*sic*] are an attempt to write in the heroic mode, or that the Latin poems were translated by John [!] Cowper at the urging of one of his female admirers), as well as one reference work apparently existing in but a single copy and long ago superseded by Cooper's *Concordance* (no. 2; the item in question is O. W. Wheeler's *Verbal Index to the Greek [Latin and Italian] Poems of Milton*, a manuscript of 69 folios reported by Stevens [no. 9], p. 2, as being in the Boston Public Library). But I have included a few possible slips and minor (and perhaps unintentionally different) reformulations of something already said by someone else, plus of course conjectures which, however improbable they may be, were put forth seriously by their authors.

7. Verse translations of individual poems or of parts thereof may be published practically anywhere; because they so frequently go unreported they pose an especially difficult problem. In view of the long-standing pastime of turning Latin verse into one's own vernacular it is reasonable to suppose that further discoveries may await here. A number of my few additions to the Milton bibliographic record fall into this category.

8. Thomas Godfrey's "Pastorals, I" (in his *Juvenile Poems on Various Subjects*, ed. Nathaniel Evans [Philadelphia: Printed by Henry Miller, 1765], pp. 22–25) is, *pace* John T. Shawcross (no. 14, p. 18), hardly an imitation of the *Epitaphium Damonis*. A more likely candidate for consideration in this regard is Francis Wrangham's piece beginning, "When first the siren Beauty's face" (in his *Poems* [London: n. p., "1795"], pp. 70, 72, 74), which is some respects is very close to the *Elegia septima*. Militating against it, however, are the conventionality of the theme and the lack of any clear allusion to Milton (whose influence

is also not immediately apparent in the elegiac couplet translation by George Caldwell on facing pages 71, 73, 75).

9. Thus I have included Edward Phillips's comment on *Mansus* (no. 384), which has been held to be possibly a recognition of the pastoral element in that poem. But I have not included similar comments in the early lives of Milton and elsewhere whose only contribution seems to be an appreciation (usually, second-hand) of the poem's "elegance." The Svogliati *Minutes* entries cited as no. 102 strike me as marginal at best, but the *molto erudita* comment is perhaps sufficiently critical to warrant inclusion.

10. E.g., the statement by Douglas Bush (no. 6, p. 9; emphasis mine) that "Critical opinion, which has naturally been preoccupied with Milton's English poetry, has *always* stressed the artistic skill of his best Latin verse." Apart from the obviously biased remarks of Claude de Saumaise (no. 60), this generalization overlooks, *inter alia*, comments made by a number of other classicists expressing their critical, if not exactly laudatory, opinion (cf. nos. 61, 152, 168, 193).

11. Bush's *Variorum Commentary* "Index" (no. 6, pp. 341–61) furnished an initial working list, supplemented extensively by entries in Stevens, Fletcher, and Huckabay (nos. 9, 10, and 12, respectively). In the absence of an adequate Milton bibliography for the seventeenth and eighteenth centuries (a seventeenth-century bibliography by John T. Shawcross is, however, now under way) the following were sometimes helpful: Kreuder (no. 492), Parker (no. 191), Plunkett (no. 487), Riffe (no. 489), Sherburn (no. 485), and the two Critical Heritage volumes by Shawcross (nos. 13 and 14). For the period after Huckabay the primary sources were the Milton and the Neolatin listings in the Modern Language Association of America's *International Bibliography* for the years 1968 through 1980, supplemented by the Milton section in *The Year's Work in English Studies* from volume 49 (for 1968) through volume 59 (for 1978), by the Neolatin section in *The Year's Work in Modern Language Studies* from its inception in volume 32 (for 1970) through volume 41 (for 1979), and by skimming recent issues of some journals. A number of citations of items published in Japan (and some material for annotations) were provided by Miyanishi (no. 15); other studies covering Milton scholarship and/or Milton's literary reception in various countries yielded no pertinent titles not already identified through the sources listed above. Further checking while the present volume was undergoing review permitted an updating through 1981, and a very few items appearing in 1982 have also been included.

12. Among the items *not* included are the following mostly out-of-the-way ones, cited here, along with the reasons for their omission, in order to save others the trouble of seeking them out in connection with Milton's Latin and Greek verse: William Massey's *Corruptae Latinitatis Index* (London, 1755; noted by Shawcross [no. 14, p. 17] as criticizing Milton's Latin) — Milton items are entirely from the *Defensio prima* (none from *Salmas.* 1); J. B. Salaville's translation of the *Defensio prima* (*Théorie de la royauté d'après la doctrine de Milton*, Paris, 1789, etc.; issues after the first ascribe this piece to Mirabeau) and I. P. V. Troxler's translation of the same work (*Die Schutzrede von Johann Milton für das Englische Volk*, in his *Fürst und Volk, nach Buchanan's und Milton's Lehre*, Aarau, 1821) — both of these (Troxler used the second issue of the *Théorie* as an aid in his own work) omit most of the personal polemics, including *Salmas.* 1; Anon., "On Milton's *Lycidas* and Smaller Poems," *The Literary Magazine* (Philadelphia), 6 (1806), 95–96 (noted by Fletcher [no. 10, p. 10] as containing remarks on the Greek verses and Dr. Burney) — the matter on the Greek verses is taken directly from Burney (no. 375; author is not the famous Dr. Burney but a son of the same name); the series of articles called "Milton's Pronunciation of Latin," *N&Q*, 90 (1894), 146, 253, 489; 91 (1895), 436 — starts with Ellwood's testimony (no. 62) and continues as a debate on the proper pronunciation of classi-

cal Latin, without at all illuminating Milton's own pronunciation; Andrew J. George, ed., *The Shorter Poems of John Milton* (New York and London, 1898; translations of *Ell.* 1 and 6 and *Ep. Dam.* sometimes said to be new ones by George) — the translations are Cowper's (no. 45); Kenjiro Kuroda, "Milton's Juvenilia," *Ehime University Reports*, 1, no. 3 (Dec. 1952), 243–73 — *Ad Patrem* quoted in part but article is entirely on Milton's early poetry in English.

13. Also listed in these subsections (but cross-referenced at the appropriate place in Part III) are a very few items devoted to the *Elegiae* as a whole but kept here for the convenience of persons interested specifically in linguistic matters or in source studies. An early attempt to create a further subsection on dating was unsuccessful — too much of the writing on this topic is either bound up in discussions of broader scope or limited to but a single poem.

14. This is of course an impressionistic judgment, and I would qualify it with a repetition of Calvin Huckabay's remark (no. 12, p. vii) that "frequently I discover items that I have missed, and they are not always recent items." In view of the incidental nature of much of the comment on these pieces, this situation is unavoidable. Readers are invited to bring omissions to my attention.

SIGLA

I. WORKS BY MILTON

Apol.	*Apologus de Rustico & Hero*
Asclep.	"*Asclepiads*"
Barberini	Adaptation of Callimachus in *Ep. Fam.* 9
Carm. El.	"*Carmina Elegiaca*"
Coelum	Adaptation of Horace in the Cerdogni album
De virtute	Adaptation of Juvenal in the *Defensio secunda*
Effig.	*In Effigiei Ejus Sculptorem*
El. 1, etc.	*Elegia prima*, etc.
Ell.	*Elegiae*
Eli.	*In obitum Praesulis Eliensis*
Ep. Dam.	*Epitaphium Damonis*
Ep. Fam.	*Epistolae Familiares*
Idea	*De Idea Platonica quemadmodum Aristoteles intellexit*
Inv. Bomb.	*In inventorem Bombardae*
Justinian	Verse on Justinian
Leon. 1, etc.	*Ad Leonoram Romae canentem* [1], etc.
Mans.	*Mansus*
Naturam	*Naturam non pati senium*
Patrem	*Ad Patrem*
Phil. Reg.	*Philosophus ad regem quendam* . . .
Poemata	Poems in the 1673 *Poemata*
Postscr.	"Postscript" appended to *El.* 7
Procan.	*In obitum Procancellarii medici*
Prod. Bomb. 1, etc.	*In Proditionem Bombardicam* [1], etc.
Ps. 114	[Greek] *Psalm CXIV*
Q. Nov.	*In quintum Novembris*
Rous.	*Ad* Joannem Rousium *Oxoniensis Academiae Bibliothecarium*
Salmas. 1	"*In Salmasii hundredam*"
Salmas. 2	"*In Salmasium*"
Sals.	*Ad Salsillum poetam Romanum aegrotantem*
Sylla	Adaptation of Juvenal from *The Readie & Easie Way*

II. JOURNALS CITED MORE THAN ONCE

ELH	*ELH: A Journal of English Literary History*
ELN	*English Language Notes*
ELR	*English Literary Renaissance*
GM	*Gentleman's Magazine*
HL	*Humanistica Lovaniensia*
HLQ	*Huntington Library Quarterly*

JEGP	*Journal of English and Germanic Philology* (*)
MLN	*Modern Language Notes* (**)
MLQ	*Modern Language Quarterly*
MLR	*Modern Language Review*
MP	*Modern Philology*
MQ	*Milton Quarterly*
N&Q	*Notes and Queries*
PMLA	*Publications of the Modern Language Association of America* (***)
PQ	*Philological Quarterly*
PRR	*Poetical Register and Repository of Fugitive Poetry*
RenP	*Renaissance Papers* (Southeastern Renaissance Conference)
RES	*Review of English Studies*
SCN	*Seventeenth-Century News*
SEL	*Studies in English Literature, 1500–1900*
SELit	*Studies in English Literature* (Japan)
SP	*Studies in Philology*
TLS	*The Times* (London). *Literary Supplement*
UTQ	*University of Toronto Quarterly*

(*)   From volume 58 (1959): *JEGP: Journal of English and Germanic Philology*

(**)   From volume 77 (1962): *MLN*

(***) From volume 43 (1928): *PMLA: Publications of the Modern Language Association of America*

BIBLIOGRAPHY

PART I: REFERENCE AND BIBLIOGRAPHY

A. *General reference*

1. Gilbert, Allan H. *A Geographical Dictionary of Milton.* Cornell Studies in English, vol. 4. New Haven: Yale University Press, 1919.

   Good coverage of the Latin poems; glosses often include sources and parallels.

2. Cooper, Lane. *A Concordance of the Latin, Greek, and Italian Poems of John Milton.* Halle: Max Niemeyer, 1923.

   Covers *Poemata, Salmas.* 1 and 2, and *Carm. El.* and *Asclep.*

3. Skeat, W[alter W.] "A Reader's Guide to Milton." In Beeching (no. 27), 1938 and subsequent eds., and in Helen Darbishire, ed., *The Poems of John Milton* (London: Oxford University Press, 1961), pp. 607–76.

   A glossary; annotations of matter in the Latin poems highlighted by the rubric *"Lat.-P."* in boldface, followed by poem and line references.

4. Le Comte, Edward S. *A Milton Dictionary.* New York: Philosophical Library; London: Peter Owen, 1961.

   Separate entries for each of the *Poemata* plus *Carm. El.* and *Asclep.* (a joint entry; critical comment on *Carm. El.*). Other noteworthy entries: *Effig.* (verse tr. by Le Comte); *Phil. Reg.* (Comenius parallel); *Q. Nov.* (list of parallels with the Satan of *Paradise Lost*).

5. French, J. Milton, ed. *The Life Records of John Milton.* Rutgers Studies in English, vol. 7. New Brunswick: Rutgers University Press, 1949–58; rpt., Stapleton, NY: Gordian Press, 1966. 5 vols.

   Discussions on dating and circumstances of most of the Latin and Greek poems, locatable through the index to each volume; quotations translated into English prose, sometimes by French himself. Records (I, p. 122) Harris Fletcher's view on the dating of the gunpowder epigrams (modified in no. 211). Additions and corrections in vol. 5.

6. Bush, Douglas. "The Latin and Greek Poems." In M. Y. Hughes et al., eds. *A Variorum Commentary on the Poems of John Milton.* New York: Columbia University Press, 1970–. I, pp. vii–361.

   Copious commentary on the *Poemata, Salmas.* 1 and 2, and *Carm. El.* and *Asclep.* Headnotes and line-by-line annotations on each poem have selected comment since Todd (no. 22) as well as Bush's own views and a massive collection of verbal and conceptual parallels, primarily from classical and Renaissance Latin authors. Occasional comment by Geoffrey Bullough, B. A. Wright, and A. S. P. Woodhouse.

7. Hunter, William B., Jr., et al., eds. *A Milton Encyclopedia*. Lewisburg, PA: Bucknell University Press, 1978–. 8 vols. to date.

Arranged alphabetically by key word (but titles of M.'s works by first word, articles ignored). No article on the Latin and/or Greek poems as a whole, but separate articles by Ralph [Waterbury] Condee on *Ell*. (s.v. "Elegies") and *Ep. Dam*. and by E. Richard Gregory on the gunpowder epigrams (s.v. "Gunpowder"), on *Leon*. 1–3 (s.v. "Leonora"), and on *Apol.*, *Carm. El*. and *Asclep.*, *Effig.*, *Eli.*, *Idea*, *Mans.*, *Naturam*, *Patrem*, *Phil. Reg.*, *Rous.*, and *Sals*. Other pertinent articles: "Diodati, Charles" (by Albert C. Labriola; *El*. 6); "Milton and Christian Humanism" (Albert R. Cirillo; *Patrem*; s.v. "Humanism"); "Inspiration" (Michael J. Lieb; *Ell*. 5 and 6); "Ode" (Elaine B. Safer; *Rous.*); "Pastoral Poetry" (John R. Knott; *Ep. Dam.*); "Milton's Translations from the Psalms" (Margaret P. Boddy; *Ps. 114*); "Rous(e), John" (John T. Shawcross; *Rous*. MS); many other entries on persons referred to in the poems, on editors, translators, illustrators, and critics, and on Milton bibliography and scholarship (most of these by Shawcross). A number of the more general articles (e.g., those on "Diction" and "Versification") omit consideration of the Latin and Greek poems; companion articles (e.g., "Versification, Latin") are lacking.

See also: nos. **32, 76**.

B. Bibliography

8. Thompson, Elbert N. S. *John Milton: Topical Bibliography*. New Haven: Yale University Press, 1916.

Very selective. "Latin and Italian Poems" on pp. 29–30.

9. Stevens, David Harrison. *Reference Guide to Milton from 1800 to the Present Day*. Chicago: University of Chicago Press, 1930; rpt., New York: Russell & Russell, 1967.

Last year covered is 1928. Supplemented by Fletcher (no. **10**) and continued by Huckabay (no. **12**). Topical arrangement.

10. Fletcher, Harris Francis. *Contributions to a Milton Bibliography 1800–1930*. University of Illinois Studies in Language and Literature, vol. 16, no. 1. Urbana: University of Illinois Press, 1931.

Supplements Stevens (no. **9**). Chronological arrangement; rough subject index. Evaluative annotations.

11. Hanford, James Holly. *Milton*. New York: Appleton-Century-Crofts, 1966. 2d ed., compiled by Hanford and William A. McQueen, Arlington Heights, IL: AHM Publishing Corp., 1979.

One of the Goldentree Bibliographies. Selective but generous listing, arranged topically. The 2d ed., McQueen's revision and updating of the original (which was compiled with the assistance of Charles W. Crupi), includes items published through 1977.

12. Huckabay, Calvin. *John Milton: An Annotated Bibliography 1929–1968.* Duquesne Studies, Philological Series, vol. 1. Pittsburgh: Duquesne University Press, 1969.

    Massive continuation of Stevens and Fletcher (nos. 9 and 10). Called "Revised Edition" as it represents a revision and expansion of Huckabay's *John Milton: A Bibliographical Supplement 1929–1957* (same publisher, 1960). Topical arrangement.

13. Shawcross, John T., ed. *Milton: The Critical Heritage.* London: Routledge & Kegan Paul; New York: Barnes & Noble, 1970.

    Selection of Milton criticism to 1731, with useful bibliographical information for the period in the introduction (which has comment on evaluations of the Latin poems), headnotes, and appendices.

14. Shawcross, John T., ed. *Milton 1732–1801: The Critical Heritage.* London: Routledge & Kegan Paul, 1972.

    Companion volume to no. 13, on the same plan and with similar bibliographic merits. Introductory survey again has matter on the Latin poems.

15. Miyanishi, Mitsuo. *Milton in Japan, 1871–1971.* Tokyo: Kinseido, 1975.

    Historical study with considerable attention to scholarship and a chronologically arranged bibliography (pp. 165–290) of Japanese publications on Milton.

16. Johnson, William C. *Milton Criticism: A Subject Index.* Folkestone: Dawson, 1978.

    Alphabetically arranged guide to matter cited in the indices of 150 books on Milton.

See also: no. 6 ("Index" serves as a bibliography), **487, 489.**

PART II: EDITIONS, TRANSLATIONS, ILLUSTRATIONS, AND COMMENT
(GENERAL AND MULTIPLE)

A. *Editions*

17. Milton, John. *Poems of Mr.* John Milton, *both English and Latin, Compos'd at Several Times.* London: Ruth Raworth for Humphrey Moseley, 1645. Reproduced in nos. **28** and **35**, and in *John Milton: Poems, 1645; Lycidas, 1638* (Menston: Scolar Press, 1970).

    Includes first ed. of the *Poemata* (foliated separately and so issued, as well as together with the English and Italian poems). *Effig.* under the portrait.

18. Milton, John. *Poems, &c. upon Several Occasions . . . With a small Tractate of Education.* London: Printed for Thomas Dring, 1673. Poems reproduced in no. **35**.

    Includes 2d ed. of the *Poemata* (separately paginated but foliated continuously with the English and Italian poems; errata for the whole before English poems, p. 1).

19. Anon., ed. *Poems upon Several Occasions . . . The Third Edition.* London: Printed for Jacob Tonson, 1695.

   Poemata lack *Phil. Reg.* and *Effig.* Some editorial emendation.

20. Newton, Thomas, ed. *Paradise Regain'd . . . Samson Agonistes. And Poems Upon Several Occasions.* London: J. and R. Tonson and S. Draper, 1752.

   Companion volume to Newton's ed. of *Paradise Lost* (same imprint, 1749; 2 vols.) and frequently republished with it as vol. 3 of *The Poetical Works.* Emendations of the *Poemata* by Newton along with scanty explicative and textual notes.

21. Warton, Thomas, ed. *Poems Upon Several Occasions, English, Italian, and Latin.* London: Printed for James Dodsley, 1785. 2d rev. and enl. ed., London: Printed for G. G. J. and J. Robinson, 1791.

   Remarks on the Latin poems in the preface; Latin and Greek poems (including, as do most editions after this, *Salmas.* 1 and 2) copiously annotated. Some notes by John Bowle, George Steevens, and Joseph Warton. Additional material in the 2d ed.

22. Todd, Henry John, ed. *The Poetical Works of John Milton.* London: J. Johnson, etc., 1801. 6 vols. 2d ed., "with considerable additions," 1809 (7 vols.); 3d ed., London: C. and J. Rivington, 1826 (6 vols.); 4th ed., 1842 (4 vols.).

   Variorum edition; Latin and Greek poems always in the last volume; *Life* in the first. 2d ed. (with many new notes by Todd) standard for most purposes.

23. Mitford, John, ed. *The Poetical Works of John Milton.* The Aldine Edition of the British Poets. London: William Pickering, 1832; often reprinted. 3 vols.

   Latin and Greek poems in vol. 3. Many brief notes by Mitford (largely philological) plus others from nos. 21 and 22. Notes omitted in the rpt. in Mitford, ed., *The Works of John Milton in Verse and Prose* (London: Pickering, 1851). "Life" (no. 125) in vol. 1.

24. Keightley, Thomas, ed. *The Poems of John Milton.* London: Chapman and Hall, 1859. 2 vols.

   Latin and Greek poems (the former heavily annotated by Keightley with some notes from his predecessors as well) in vol. 2.

25. Masson, David, ed. *The Poetical Works of John Milton.* London: Macmillan, 1874. 3 vols. The "Cambridge edition," as opposed to the 2-vol. "Golden Treasury edition" of later in the same year. Rev. ed., 1882 (3 vols.; a "Second Edition" of the 1874 "Golden Treasury" ed.; rpt., 1893, 1896, 1903). Rev. ed., 1890 (3 vols.; "Cambridge edition" but on the general plan of the 1882 ed.; rpt., 1894 and 1896).

First ed. has introductions to the Latin and Greek poems in vol. 2, texts and notes in vol. 3, and some matter on the *Ep. Dam.* (correcting the notes) in the preface in vol. 1 (pp. ii–v). Eds. of 1882 (in 12mo.; sometimes called "little Masson") and of 1890 (in 8vo.; "big Masson") have introductions and texts in vol. 1, notes in vol. 3. Latter ed. expands earlier material and adds whole or partial translations of many of the poems (some verse, some prose; most of these are from no. 135) plus *Carm. El.* and *Asclep.* (not translated; in notes, III, pp. 371–73). Monumental.

26. Moody, William Vaughn, ed. *The Complete Poetical Works of John Milton.* Boston: Houghton Mifflin, 1899; several times reprinted.

    Poemata (minus *Apol.* and the Greek pieces, which together with *Salmas.* 1 and 2 are printed in the Appendix) outfitted with critical headnotes and translated by Moody. Tr. revised by E. K. Rand for the 1924 ed.

27. Beeching, H. C., ed. *The Poetical Works of John Milton.* Oxford: Clarendon Press, 1900; frequently reprinted. "New Edition," New York: Oxford University Press, 1938; frequently reprinted.

    Cooper's *Concordance* (no. 2) based on the edition of 1900; "New Edition" has Skeat's "Reader's Guide" (no. 3). Unannotated; 1935 New York ed. has Cowper's translation of the Latin poems (no. 45); "New Edition" has translations from the Columbia edition (no. 32). Lacks *Carm. El.* and *Asclep.*

28. Anon., ed. *Milton's Poems 1645: Type-facsimile.* Oxford: Clarendon Press, 1924.

    Facsimile of no. 17, with expansion of some of the ligatures in the Greek poems and textual notes by [H. W. Garrod].

29. Grierson, H[erbert] J. C., ed. *The Poems of John Milton.* London: Chatto & Windus, 1925. 2 vols.

    Latin and Greek poems (for the first time arranged chronologically) in vol. 1; preface has comment on the dating and arrangement of the poems in the 1645 and 1673 *Poemata.* Lacks *Carm. El.* and *Asclep.*

30. MacKellar, Walter, ed. *The Latin Poems of John Milton.* Cornell Studies in English, vol. 15. New Haven: Yale University Press, 1930.

    Introductions to the poems, text, prose translations, and copious annotations. Includes Greek poems. *Carm. El.* and *Asclep.* (not translated) in an appendix.

31. Patterson, Frank Allen, ed. *The Student's Milton.* New York: F. S. Crofts and Co., 1930. 2d ed., 1933; frequently reprinted.

    Text preceded by Nelson Glenn McCrea's prose translations of the Latin and Greek poems. 2d ed. adds "Notes on the Poetry," taking into account the Latin poems (also covered in the "Additional Textual Notes"). Lacks *Carm. El.* and *Asclep.*

32. Patterson, Frank Allen, et al., eds. *The Works of John Milton*. New York: Columbia University Press, 1931–40. 18 vols. plus 2-volume *Index*.

Poemata, ed. by W[illiam] P. Trent in collaboration with Thomas Ollive Mabbott and with a prose translation by Charles Knapp, in vol. 1, pt. 1 (textual notes, with the editor's text and prose translation of *Carm. El.* and *Asclep.*, pp. 578–98). *Salmas.* 1, ed. by Clinton W. Keyes with a prose translation by Samuel Lee Wolff, in vol. 7 (pp. 428–29). *Salmas.* 2 and *De virtute*, ed. by Eugene J. Strittmater, in vol. 8 (pp. 56 and 92; facing-page translations are Burnett's [no. **469**]). *Barberini*, ed. by Donald Lemen Clark, in vol. 12 (p. 44; translation on p. 45 is Masson's [no. **135**]). *Sylla, Coelum*, Euripides marginalia, and *Justinian*, ed. by Mabbott and J. Milton French with prose translations "by Nelson Glenn McCrea and others," in vol. 18 (pp. 267, 271, 304–20, and 330, respectively), which also has additional textual notes on the Latin poems by Mabbott and French (pp. 641–43; controversy on *Asclep.* in nos. **447–451** ended here). *Index*, by Patterson with the assistance of French Rowe Fogle, is a powerful reference guide to M.'s writings (incl. the Latin ones as translated in this edition).

33. Hughes, Merritt Y., ed. *John Milton: Paradise Regained, The Minor Poems, and Samson Agonistes*. New York: The Odyssey Press, 1937; several times reprinted.

Latin and Greek poems arranged chronologically, with prose translations (reprinted in no. **37**) and copious annotations.

34. Fletcher, Harris Francis, ed. *The Complete Poetical Works of John Milton*. Boston: Houghton Mifflin, 1941.

A revision of no. **26**, with succinct headnotes and occasional footnotes to the Latin and Greek poems, some modifications in the Moody-Rand translation, and new prose translations of the Greek poems, *Apol.*, and *Salmas.* 1 and 2. Lacks *Carm. El.* and *Asclep.*

35. Fletcher, Harris Francis, ed. *John Milton's Complete Poetical Works Reproduced in Photographic Facsimile*. Urbana: The University of Illinois Press, 1943–48. 4 vols.

Critical ed. based on reproductions of texts in nos. **18, 17, 390, 464, 478, 435**, (all these in vol. 1) and **460** (in vol. 4, along with variant page of no. **18** containing *El.* 4, 17–40; these, in "Additions and Corrections for Volume 1," on supplementary pages 104-A and 344-A for that volume).

36. Garrod, H. W., ed. *Poemata*. In Helen Darbishire, ed. *The Poetical Works of John Milton*. Oxford: Clarendon Press, 1952. 2 vols., several times reissued. Vol. 2.

Textual introduction with list of metrical irregularities (pp. xvii–xx), text (incl. *Salmas.* 1 and 2, *Carm. El.*, and *Asclep.*; pp. [229]–288), and textual commentary (pp. 364–71).

37. Hughes, Merritt Y., ed. *John Milton: Complete Poems and Major Prose.* New York: The Odyssey Press, 1957; frequently reprinted.

   Latin and Greek poems arranged chronologically, with translations from no. 33 and considerably revised and expanded annotations. *Sylla*, with prose translation, on p. 880 (in the prose). Lacks *Salmas.* 2.

38. Bush, Douglas, ed. *The Complete Poetical Works of John Milton.* Boston; Houghton Mifflin, 1965. Reprinted as *Milton: Poetical Works* (London: Oxford University Press, 1966 and later printings).

   Latin and Greek poems arranged chronologically, with annotations and prose translations by Bush (trs. of *Ell.* 5 and 6 and *Ep. Dam.* revised from no. 52).

39. Carey, John, ed. "The Minor Poems and *Samson Agonistes*." In John Carey and Alastair Fowler, eds. *The Poems of John Milton.* London: Longmans, 1968; rpt., 1972 (also New York: Norton); and in Carey, ed., *John Milton: Complete Shorter Poems* (London: Longman Group, 1971).

   Latin and Greek poems arranged chronologically, annotated and with prose translations by Carey. Includes *Justinian, De virtute*, and *Sylla*.

40. Shawcross, John T., ed. *The Complete Poetry of John Milton.* Garden City, NY: Doubleday, 1971.

   Revision of no. 54 with the addition of texts of the foreign-language poems; hence called "Revised Edition." Notes to and datings of the Latin poems sometimes altered from previous ed.

41. Hodge, Robert, ed. "The Shorter Poems." In John Broadbent and Robert Hodge, eds. *Samson Agonistes, Sonnets, &c.* Cambridge: Cambridge University Press, 1977.

   Contains *Ell.* 1, 5, 7, *Rous.* (1–12, 25–36 only), *Ep. Dam.*, with verse translations by Hodge and critical and explanatory notes. Introduction has general comment on erotic aspects of M.'s earlier Latin verse plus specific comment on *Ell.* 1, 5, 6, 7, *Rous.*, *Ep. Dam.* (verse translation of *El.* 6, 12–14, and 55–71).

42. Nichols, Fred J., ed. and tr. *An Anthology of Neo-Latin Poetry.* New Haven: Yale University Press, 1979.

   Edition and prose translation of *Patrem* and *Ep. Dam.*, with brief critical summaries and notes on the poems (pp. 632–51, 718–21 [notes]).

43. Campbell, Gordon, ed. *John Milton: The Complete Poems.* London: J. M. Dent & Sons; New York: E. P. Dutton & Co., 1980.

   Poemata only. Text a corrected rpt. of B. A. Wright's Everyman's Library edition (London: Dent, 1956 and subsequent printings). Introduction and notes by Campbell. Introd. has brief comment on the Latin poems (specific comm. on *Ell.* 4 and 5, *Procan., Q. Nov., Mans., Ep. Dam.*); notes have prose trs. of the *Poemata* (Latin poems tr. by Mary Campbell, Greek poems by Gordon Campbell).

B. Translations

44. [Wilson, Harbord], presumed translator. Verse translations of parts of *Idea* and *Patrem*. In a copy of no. 17 in the University of Illinois Libraries.

Cited by Fletcher (no. 211), I, p. 192. Presumably from exercises in double translation. Early 18th century.

45. Cowper, William, tr. In William Hayley, ed. *Latin and Italian Poems of Milton Translated into English Verse . . . by the late William Cowper, Esqr.* Chichester: Printed by J. Seagrave for J. Johnson and R. H. Evans, London, 1808. Standard modern edition in H. S. Milford, ed., *Cowper: Poetical Works*, 4th ed. with corrections and additions by Norma Russell (London: Oxford University Press, 1967).

Translation written in 1791–92 and preserved in the original form, with corrections by Hayley and by Cowper (some of the latter as late as 1798) and with some translations not printed by Hayley (nos. 373, 468), in British Library Add. MS. 30801. Excerpts, with substantive differences, in Hayley's *Life* (no. 111). Omits *Q. Nov.*, the gunpowder epigrams, *Leon.* 1, Greek poems, and *Salmas.* 1 and 2. Notes by Cowper and by Hayley (as well as some from nos. 21 and 22); some of these reprinted in Hayley, ed., *Cowper's Milton* (Chichester: W. Mason for J. Johnson and Co., 1810), III, pp. 393–429 (Hayley's preface reprinted here in vol. 4 as "Appendix Number 1"); Milford-Russell ed. omits notes not printed with the text. Illustrations by Flaxman (no. 57).

46. Anon., tr. *Das Leben Miltons von Wilhelm Hayley, Esq.* Winterthur: in der Steinerischen Buchhandlung, 1797.

Anonymous translation of no. 111 (1796 ed.). Reported by Norma Russell, *A Bibliography of William Cowper to 1837* (Oxford: Clarendon Press, 1963), p. 180, as having prose trs. of Hayley's excerpts from no. 45 based in part upon the Latin originals.

47. Fellowes, Robert, tr. In Charles Symmons, ed. *The Prose Works of John Milton*. London: Printed by T. Bensley for J. Johnson, etc., 1806. 7 vols.

Verse translations of *Barberini* (I, p. xvi) and of *Salmas.* 2 and *De virtute* (VI, pp. 379 and 391).

48. Strutt, Jacob George, tr. *The Latin and Italian Poems of Milton*. London: Printed by D. S. Maurice for Josiah Conder, 1814.

Verse translations of *Poemata* only (minus the Greek pieces). Scanty notes.

49. [Kervyn de Lettenhove, G.], tr. *Oeuvres choisies de Milton: traduction nouvelle avec le texte en regard*. Paris: Charles Gosselin, 1839.

Prose translations of *El.* 1, *Mans.*, *Ep. Dam.*, and *Leon.* 2.

50. Skeat, Walter [W.], tr. *Milton's Lament for Damon and His Other Latin Poems*. London: Oxford University Press, 1935; rpt., Norwood, PA: Norwood Editions, 1977.

Verse translations of the *Poemata* (minus the epigrams [incl. *Apol.*] and the Greek pieces). Translation of *Ep. Dam.* a revision of that in no. 392. Preface and introductions by E. H. Visiak.

51. Skeat, W[alter W.], and A. Vesselo, trs. In E. H. Visiak, ed. *Milton: Complete Poetry and Selected Prose.* [London]: The Nonesuch Press [1938]; New York: Random House, 1938. Pp. 755–819.

    Verse translations by Skeat a revision of those in no. **50**; verse translations by Vesselo of *Prod. Bomb.* 1–3, *Inv. Bomb.*, *Leon.* 1–3, *Apol.*, *Salmas.* 1 and 2, *Phil. Reg.*, and *Effig.* Notes on the Latin and Greek poems adapted by Visiak from material provided by Skeat (pp. 840–44); translator's note by Skeat (pp. 856–57).

52. Bush, Douglas, ed. *The Portable Milton.* New York: The Viking Press, 1949; often reissued.

    Has Bush's prose translations of *Ell.* 5 and 6 and *Ep. Dam.* (revised in no. **38**). Introduction has comment on these poems.

53. Wolfe, Don M., et al., eds. *Complete Prose Works of John Milton.* New Haven: Yale University Press, 1953–82. 8 vols. in 10.

    Verse tr. of *Salmas.* 1 by Donald C. Mackenzie (IV [pt. 1], p. 487); verse trs. of *Salmas.* 2 and *De virtute* by Helen North (IV [pt. 2], pp. 580 and 599). Translations of *Barberini* and *Sylla* (I, p. 355; VII [rev. ed.], p. 405) are Masson's (from no. **135**).

54. Shawcross, John T., ed. *The Complete English Poetry of John Milton.* New York: New York University Press; Garden City, NY: Doubleday (Anchor Books), 1963.

    Literal prose translations (practically line-by-line) of the Latin and Greek poems in chronological order, with collations in the "Textual Notes." Numerous footnote annotations. Latin and Greek texts added in no. **40** ("revised ed.").

55. Desarmenien, Jeanne, tr. "Milton et Poussin," by Mario Praz. In Jacques Blondel, ed. *Le Paradis Perdu 1667–1967.* Paris: Lettres Modernes, 1967. Pp. 177–201.

    Translation of the original version of no. **184**. Prose translations of *El.* 1, 61–62, *El.* 5, 119–30, *Ep. Dam.*, 217–19, and *Procan.*, 41–44 (footnotes, pp. 187–90).

56. Crehan, T., ed. *The Minor Poems of John Milton.* Exeter: A. Wheaton & Co., 1976.

    Introduction has Crehan's prose translations of *El.* 5, 55–60 and *El.* 7, 51–60, plus brief treatment of the Latin poems of the Cambridge period.

See also: nos. 5, 25, 26, 30, 31, 32, 33, 34, 38, 39, 40, 41, 42, 43, 113, 120, 123, 135, 138, 140, 146, 147, 154, 188, 209, 212, 218, 218a.

C. Illustrations

57. Flaxman, John. In no. 45 (1808 ed.).

Two untitled illustrations, engraved by Abraham Raimbach: Bishop Andrewes and angels before the sleeping Milton (*El.* 3, 53–64; facing p. 18 [in the copy in the Cornell University Libraries, facing p. 12]); Doris and her nymphs delivering Milton's letter (*El.* 4, 1–8; facing p. 20). Reproduced in Marcia R. Pointon, *Milton & English Art* (Toronto: University of Toronto Press, 1970), p. 78. Originals in the Henry E. Huntington Library and Art Gallery, San Marino, CA. Flaxman's frontispiece (original also in the Huntington) has no bearing on the Latin poems *per se.*

58. Harvey, William. In *The Poetical Works of John Milton*. London: Tilt and Bogue, 1843. 2 vols. II, pp. 281, 302, 303, 308, 341.

Five untitled illustrations: Milton in his study, writing a letter (*El.* 1); flying Cupid having shot his bow (*El.* 7); Turkish (?) cavalry massed behind a firing cannon (*Prod. Bomb.* 1, etc.); imaginary funeral monument for Gostlin (*Procan.*); books and a burning oil lamp (*Rous.*).

D. Comment

1. Linguistic Aspects

59. [Milton, John]. *Of Education.* [London]: n. p., 1644.

Recommends pronunciation of Latin in the Italian fashion, especially as regards the vowels (pp. 3–4; no. 32, IV, p. 281).

60. Saumaise, Claude de. *Ad Ioannem Miltonum responsio, opus posthumum.* Dijon: Philibert Chavance, 1660; rpt., London: Thomas Roycroft, 1660.

Attack on M. as *pessimus poeta* (pp. 5–6 [London ed., p. 5]), concentrating on matters of prosody and diction in the Latin poems. Written *ca.* 1652.

61. Heinsius, Nicolaas. [Letter to Isaac Vossius, 28 February 1653]. In Pieter Burman, ed. *Sylloge epistolarum a viris illustribus scriptarum.* Leiden: S. Luchtmans, 1727. III, pp. 667–71.

M.'s Latin poems inelegant; their prosody frequently faulty. This part of the letter is reprinted in no. 5, III, p. 320.

62. Ellwood, Thomas. *The History of the Life of Thomas Ellwood.* London: Assigns of J. Sowle, 1714; rpt., 1715 and 1765. Standard modern ed. by C. G. Crump (London: Methuen, 1900).

Describes M.'s "foreign" pronunciation of Latin (Crump, pp. 89–90).

63. Wordsworth, C[hristopher]. "On Some Faults in Milton's Latin Poetry." *Classical Review*, 1 (1887), 46–48.

Alleges a number of errors in prosody and grammar.

64. Fiske, John. "Life and Writings of Milton." *Cosmopolitan*, 34 (1902–03), 41–53. Rpt. as "John Milton" in his *Essays Historical and Literary* (New York: Macmillan, 1902), II, pp. 37–67.

Appreciative estimate of M.'s diction (*Essays*, II, p. 44).

65. Rand, E. K. "*J* and *I* in Milton's Latin Script." *MP*, 19 (1921–22), 315–19.

    Study of no. 435 (believed by Rand to be in M.'s hand) suggests that consonantal *i* in M.'s Latin should never be printed with a *j*-form. Answered in no. 67.

66. Godolphin, F. R. B. "Notes on the Technique of Milton's Latin Elegies." *MP*, 37 (1939–40), 351–56.

    M.'s metrical and rhetorical practices in light of those of Ovid, Tibullus, and Propertius (emphasizing the latter two).

67. Kelley, Maurice. "'J' and 'I' in Milton's Script." *MLR*, 44 (1949), 545–47.

    Modifies Rand's position (no. 65) in light of M.'s scribal practices in the Commonplace Book.

68. Cawley, Robert Rals[t]on. *Milton and the Literature of Travel*. Princeton: Princeton University Press, 1951.

    Archaizing and stereotypic geographical references in the earlier Latin poems (pp. 73, 116, 139).

69. Fletcher, Harris F[rancis]. "A Possible Origin of Milton's 'Counterpoint' or Double Rhythm." *JEGP*, 54 (1955), 521–25.

    M.'s Latin prosody discussed (pp. 523–24).

70. Groom, Bernard. *The Diction of Poetry from Spenser to Bridges*. Toronto: University of Toronto Press, 1955.

    Compound epithets in M.'s English and Latin verse (pp. 76–77).

71. Kimmich, Paul Edward. *John Milton's Technical Handling of the Latin Elegy*. Ph.D. diss., University of Illinois, 1958.

    Analysis of *Ell.* from standpoint of metrics, diction, etc.

72. Aylward, Kevin J. *Milton's Latin Versification: The Hexameter*. Ph.D. diss., Columbia University, 1966.

    M.'s hexameters (incl. those in *Ell.*) generally in line with late Renaissance prosodic theory and thus in some respects different from classical practice as analyzed today. Specific comparisons of M.'s versification with the practices of Virgil and Ovid.

73. Duckworth, George E. "Milton's Hexameter Patterns—Vergilian or Ovidian?" *American Journal of Philology*, 93 (1972), 52–60.

    In *Ell.* M. more Ovidian than most Roman poets; in the hexameter poems M. follows Virgil in the *Eclogues* to a degree but still shows many Ovidian features.

74. Dillon, John B. "*Surdeo*, Saumaise, and the Lexica: An Aspect of Milton's Latin Diction." *HL*, 27 (1978), 238–52.

    Defends M.'s use of *surdeo* (*El.* 7, 90) and *Belgia* (*El.* 3, 12).

See also: nos. **92, 114, 329, 450.**

2. Sources and Relationship Thereto

75. [Milton, John]. *An Apology Against a Pamphlet.* London: Printed by E. G. for John Rothwell, 1642.

M. notes his imitation of "the pleasing sound" of "the smooth Elegiack Poets" (p. 15; no. 32, III, pt. 1, p. 302).

76. Osgood, Charles Grosvenor. *The Classical Mythology of Milton's English Poems.* Yale Studies in English, vol. 8. New York: Henry Holt and Company, 1900.

A source study and dictionary. Discussions of material in the *Poemata* locatable through the index.

77. Cory, Herbert E. "Spenser, the School of the Fletchers, and Milton." *University of California Publications in Modern Philology*, vol. 2, no. 5 (1912), pp. 311–73.

Comparison of *Q. Nov.* with P. Fletcher's *Locustae* and with Spenser's *Faerie Queene*; England as treated in *Mans.* a "Spenserian Fairyland," with Spenser's Arthur in the background (pp. 347–49).

78. Rand, E. K. "Milton in Rustication." *SP*, 19 (1922), 109–35.

Critical survey of M.'s transmutation of the ancients in his Latin poems.

79. Riley, Edgar Heisler. *The Virgilian Element in the Works of Milton.* Ph.D. diss., Cornell University, 1925. 2 vols.

Ch. 2, "The Latin Poems" (I, pp. 15–43; primarily *Q. Nov.*, *Mans.*, and *Ep. Dam.*); appendices on unquestionable, probable, and possible traces of Virgil, addenda (covering *Carm. El.* and *Asclep.*), and additions to the first two appendices (II, pp. 248–89, 376–93, 449–68, 523–25, 525–26; page refs. to material on Latin poems only).

80. Hartwell, Kathleen Ellen. *Lactantius and Milton.* Cambridge: Harvard University Press, 1929.

Background on Hermes Trismegistus (*Idea*, 32–34); Phoenix passage at *Ep. Dam.*, 185–89 compared to ancient descriptions and held to be essentially based on Lactantius' *De ave phoenice* (pp. 115–21, 124–32).

81. Riley, Edgar H[eisler]. "Milton's Tribute to Virgil." *SP*, 26 (1929), 155–65.

M.'s attitude to Virgil in the Latin poems (pp. 157, 162–63).

82. Brodribb, C. W. "Milton and Buchanan."*N&Q*, 158 (Jan.–June 1930), 185.

Comparison of *El.* 5, *Q. Nov.*, and *Naturam* with Buchanan's poems; M. more original than Buchanan vis-à-vis the ancients.

83. Brodribb, C. W. "Milton and Persius." *N&Q*, 159 (July–Dec. 1930), 39.

Compilation of Persius references, quotations, and reminiscences in M.'s Latin works.

84. Brodribb, C. W. "Milton and Two Latin Poets." *N&Q*, 159 (July–Dec. 1930), 129.

    Reminiscences of Manilius in *Patrem* and *Naturam*.

85. Goode, James. "Milton and Sannazaro." *TLS*, 13 August 1931, p. 621.

    Compares *El.* 1, 21–22 and *El.* 5, 121–22 with passages in Sannazaro's *Elegies*.

86. Levinson, Ronald B. "Milton and Plato." *MLN*, 46 (1931), 85–91.

    Source of the Socrates reference at *El.* 4, 23–24 is Plutarch's *Alcibiades*, chs. 1 and 4; questions the generally accepted view of *Idea* as satire on the Aristotelian position (pp. 88–90).

87. MacKellar, Walter. "Milton and Pindar." *TLS*, 3 Dec. 1931, p. 982.

    El. 6, 23–26 "the only passage in the Latin poems that certainly shows an acquaintance with Pindar."

88. Bush, Douglas. *Mythology and the Renaissance Tradition in English Poetry.* Minneapolis: The University of Minnesota Press, 1932; rpt., New York: Pageant Book Company, 1957; rev. ed., New York: W. W. Norton, 1963.

    Brief sketch of M.'s adaptations of the classics in his Latin poetry (pp. 250–52; rev. ed., pp. 262–64, with substitution of Virgil for Horace as one of M.'s "teachers").

89. Brill, Mary Campbell. *Milton and Ovid.* Ph.D. diss., Cornell University, 1935.

    Ch. 2, "The Latin Poems" (pp. 23–61); separately paginated appendix, pt. 3, "Latin Poems" (pp. 11–111; collection of verbal and conceptual parallels). *Poemata* only.

90. Brodribb, C. W. "Milton and Valerius Flaccus." *N&Q*, 175 (July–Dec. 1938), 399.

    Parallels with *Mans.* and with the fall of Vulcan [*El.* 7, *Naturam*].

91. Fletcher, G. B. A. "Milton's Latin Poems." *MP*, 37 (1939–40), 343–50.

    Verbal parallels in ancient Latin writers and in Buchanan.

92. Koehler, [G.] Stanley. *Milton and the Roman Elegists: A Study of Milton's Latin Poems in Their Relation to the Latin Love Elegy.* Ph.D. diss., Princeton University, 1942.

    Ell. compared to Catullus, Propertius, the *corpus Tibullianum*, and the elegiac Ovid in respect of themes, vocabulary, versification, and rhyme and other special effects.

93. Samuel, Irene. "Milton's References to Plato and Socrates." *SP*, 41 (1944), 50–64. Revised as Ch. 1, "Milton as a Student of Plato," of her *Plato and Milton*, Cornell Studies in English, vol. 35 (Ithaca: Cornell University Press, 1947; rpt., 1965), pp. 3–25.

M.'s early references to Plato and Socrates (incl. *El.* 4, 23–24, and *Idea*) show no particular insight into, or commitment to, Platonic doctrine. *Postscr.*, though, shows Plato's influence on M.'s ethical theory (pp. 50–51, 55; *Plato and Milton*, pp. 6–7, 8–9). Additional comment in *Plato and Milton* (pp. 48–49) on *El.* 6, 77–78, and *Patrem*, 17–20; these recall accounts of poetic inspiration in the *Ion* and the *Phaedrus*.

94. Harding, Davis P. *Milton and the Renaissance Ovid.* University of Illinois Studies in Language and Literature, vol. 30, no. 4. Urbana: University of Illinois Press, 1946.

    Ch. III, "The Latin Poems" (pp. 42–57).

95. Starnes, D[e Witt] T. "Proper Names in Milton: New Annotations." In Arnold Williams, ed. *A Tribute to George Coffin Taylor.* Chapel Hill: The University of North Carolina Press, 1952. Pp. 38–61.

    Passages in M.'s poetry in light of entries in Renaissance reference books (includes *El.* 4, 14–16, *Eli.*, 20–22, *Q. Nov.*, 59–60 and 139–41; incorporated, with slight modification, in no. 96).

96. Starnes, De Witt T., and Ernest William Talbert. *Classical Myth and Legend in Renaissance Dictionaries: A Study of Renaissance Dictionaries in Their Relation to the Classical Learning of Contemporary English Writers.* Chapel Hill: The University of North Carolina Press, 1955.

    Passages from the Latin poems locatable through the index.

97. Turner, Amy Lee. *The Visual Arts in Milton's Poetry.* Ph.D. diss., The Rice Institute [now Rice University], 1955.

    Connects *vitreo rore* at *Carm. El.*, 12 with contemporary glass beadwork; description of the cups in *Ep. Dam.*, 181ff. could be based on locally available goldsmith's work as well as on passages in pastoral literature (pp. 61, 185).

98. Chaney, Virginia Miles. *The Elegies of George Buchanan in Relation to Those of the Roman Elegists and to the Latin Elegies of John Milton.* Ph.D. diss., Vanderbilt University, 1961.

    Ch. IV, "The Latin Elegies of John Milton" (pp. 153–207; descriptive survey with special attention to themes of classical Roman elegy and particular points of indebtedness); Ch. V, "Buchanan and Milton compared" (pp. 208–43; their general postures vis-à-vis the Roman elegists; specific comparison of Buchanan's *El.* 2 with M.'s *El.* 5).

99. Harding, Davis P. *The Club of Hercules: Studies in the Classical Background of Paradise Lost.* University of Illinois Studies in Language and Literature, vol. 50. Urbana: University of Illinois Press, 1962.

    General comment on M.'s use of verbal echo (p. 15); *El.* 5, 81–95 closely analyzed in light of M.'s "schoolboy techniques of imitation" (pp. 11–17).

100. Revard, Stella P. "Milton's Gunpowder Poems and Satan's Conspiracy." In *Milton Studies*, IV, ed. James D. Simmonds. Pittsburgh: University of Pittsburgh Press, 1972. Pp. 63–77. Reworked in her *The War in Heaven: Paradise Lost and the Tradition of Satan's Rebellion* (Ithaca: Cornell University Press, 1980), pp. 86–107.

   Gunpowder epigrams, *Q. Nov.*, and the conspiracy in *Paradise Lost* in light of the annual Gunpowder Plot sermons.

101. Kessner, Carole Schwartz. *George Herbert and John Milton's Use of the Hebrew Psalms*. Ph.D. diss., State University of New York at Stony Brook, 1975.

   M. may have retranslated *Ps. 114* in Greek because of "the beauty of the Hebrew original" (p. 218); scriptural backgrounds and classical/Judeo-Christian fusion in *Q. Nov.* and in the visions of heaven in *El. 3*, *Eli.*, *El. 6*, and *Patrem* (pp. 289–307, 343, 353–54).

3. General and Other

102. Accademia degli Svogliati, Florence. [Minutes of meetings]. Firenze, Biblioteca Nazionale, MS. Magliabecchiani cl. IX, cod. 60.

   Latin poems read by M. "noble" and "very erudite" (foll. 52–52v [1638–39]; reprinted in no. 5, I, pp. 389, 408–09, and in no. 140, I, ii, p. 499).

103. Milton, John. *The Reason of Church-governement Urg'd Against Prelaty*. London: Printed by E. G. for John Rothwell, 1641.

   Poems read before the Italian academies included memorized pieces from when M. was "under twenty or thereabout" and others patched up "in scarsity of books and conveniences"; M.'s reasons for abandoning Latin in favor of English (pp. 37–38; no. 32, III, pp. 235–37).

104. Milton, John. *Ep. Fam.* 10 [letter to Carlo Dati]. Dated 21 April 1647 in *Epistolarum Familiarium liber unus*. London: Brabazon Aylmer, 1674. Dated "Pascatis feriâ tertiâ" 1647 in the holograph copy in the New York Public Library.

   Contains references to *Ep. Dam.* (esp. lines 136–38 and the separate printing [no. 390]) and apologies for anti-papal matter in the *Poemata* (pp. 28–32; no. 32, XII, pp. 44–53 [385–86: collation with the holograph]).

105. Morhof, Daniel Georg. *Unterricht von der Teutschen Sprache und Poesie*. Kiel: Joachim Neumann, 1682. 2d ed., Frankfurt: Johann Wiedermeyer, 1700; rpt., Bad Homburg v. d. H.: Gehlen, 1969.

   M.'s Latin poetry shows his maturity even in his youth (p. 252; 2d ed., p. 231). Similar comment in Morhof's *Polyhistor*, Bk. 1, ch. 24 (1688 ed., pp. 304–05; 1732 ed., I, p. 302).

106. T[oland], J[ohn]. "The Life of John Milton." In *A Complete Collection of the Historical, Political, and Miscellaneous Works of John Milton*. Am-

sterdam [London]: n. p., 1698. 3 vols. I, pp. 5–47. Rpt. in Helen Darbishire, ed., *The Early Lives of Milton* (London: Constable, 1932; several
times reprinted), pp. 83–197.

Brief remarks on the earlier Latin poems (pp. 6–7) and on the later ones
(pp. 9–11).

107. Johnson, Samuel. "Cowley." In *The Works of the English Poets*. London:
H. Hughs for C. Bathurst, 1779–81. Vol. 57 (*Prefaces*, vol. 1). Rpt. in his
Lives of the English Poets, ed. George Birkbeck Hill (Oxford: Clarendon
Press, 1905; 3 vols.), I, pp. 1–69.

Comparison of M.'s Latin poems with those of May and Cowley, depre-
cating the former for lack of originality (Birkbeck Hill ed., I, p. 13).

108. Johnson, Samuel. "Milton." In *The Works of the English Poets*. London:
H. Hughs for C. Bathurst, 1779–81. Vol. 58 (*Prefaces*, vol. 2). Rpt. in his
Lives of the English Poets. ed. George Birkbeck Hill (Oxford: Clarendon
Press, 1905; 3 vols.), I, pp. 84–200 [page refs. to this edition].

M. a Latin poet of "classick elegance" (p. 87). *El.* 1, 11–16 a reference to
M.'s rustication (pp. 88–89). *Obiter dicta* on *Sals.*, *Mans.*, and *Ep. Dam.*
(pp. 95–97). General evaluation of the *Poemata* (pp. 161–62).

109. [Neve, Philip]. *Cursory Remarks on Some of the Ancient English Poets,
Particularly Milton*. London: n. p., 1789; rpt., New York: Garland Publishing, Inc., 1970.

General estimate of the Latin poems, emphasizing their relationship to Ovid
(pp. 116–17; the parallel between *El.* 5, 122 and Ovid, *A. A.*, 2.24 is new);
El. 3, 47–48 an example of the many "turns" in M.'s English and Latin
verse (p. 130).

110. Cowper, William. [Letters to Samuel Rose, Joseph Hill, and James Hur-
dis, 30 October, 14 November, and 10 December 1791]. In Thomas Wright,
ed. *The Correspondence of William Cowper*. London: Hodder & Stoughton, 1904. Vol. 4.

Versification of *Ell.* "equal to the best of Ovid" but their matter quite pu-
erile (p. 134); M.'s Latin poems as a whole "certainly good in themselves"
(p. 137); *pace* Johnson (no. 108), *Ep. Dam.* "equal to any of Virgil's *Bu-
colics*" (p. 142).

111. Hayley, William. "The Life of Milton, in Three Parts." In *The Poetical
Works of John Milton*. London: Printed by W. Bulmer and Co. for John
and Josiah Boydell and George Nicol, 1794–97. I, pp. [i]–cxxxiii. Rev. ed.,
London: Printed for T. Caddell, Junior and W. Davies, 1796. Rpts., Gaines-
ville, FL: Scholars' Facsimiles and Reprints, 1970, with an introd. by J[o-
seph] A[nthony] Wittreich, Jr.; New York: Garland Publishing, Inc., 1971;
German translation, no. 46; also reissued in Hayley, ed., *Cowper's Milton*
(Chichester: Printed by W. Mason for J. Johnson, 1810), vol. 1.

Latin poems discussed, pp. iv–v (1796: p. 4); vii–xvii (1796: 8–21; *Ell.* 4–7); xxii–xxvi (1796: 30–35; *Patrem*); xxviii–xxxvii (1796: 38–49; *Ep. Dam.*, poems of the Italian trip); xliv–xlvi (1796: 62–64; *Ep. Dam.*); lxxvii–viii (1796: 144; *Sylla*, with verse translation); cxx (1796: 210–11; *Naturam*). Translations other than that of *Sylla* are Cowper's (no. **45**) in an early version.

112. R., E. "Cantabrigiana." *The Monthly Magazine; or, British Register*, 16 (Aug.–Dec. 1803), 131–36.

Praise of the Latin poems; M.'s low opinion of Cambridge as reflected therein; verse translation of *Effig.* (pp. 133–34).

113. Symmons, Charles. *The Life of John Milton.* London: T. Bensley for J. Johnson, etc., 1806. [Vol. 7 of Symmons, ed., *The Prose Works of John Milton*]. 2d [rev.] ed., London: T. Bensley for Nichols and Son, 1810; 3d ed., London: G. and W. B. Whittaker, 1822 (rpt., New York: AMS Press, 1970).

General evaluation of the Latin poems of the Cambridge period (pp. 43–46; 2d ed., 83–86; 3d ed., 43–46). Discussions of individual poems and Symmons's verse translations of *El.* 1 (also prose translation of *El.* 1, 11–20), *Idea*, 3–5, *Sals.*, 23–41, *Leon.* 2, *Mans.*, *Ep. Dam.* (this tr. reprinted in no. **391**, pp. 126–33), *Salmas.* 1 and *Salmas.* 2 locatable through the index. Symmons's verse translation of *Patrem* in an appendix (pp. 536–40; 2d ed., 602–08; 3d ed., 454–57) plus parts thereof in three separate places in the main text. Verse translations by William Gifford, Charles Symmons, Jr., and Francis Wrangham entered elsewhere (nos. **396, 298, 309, 436**). Philological footnotes greatly expanded (with the help of Dr. Samuel Parr) in the 2d and 3d eds.; some of these abstracted in Symmons, C[harles], "Observations on Milton's Latin Poetry," *Classical Journal*, 9 (1814), 338–45. 2d ed. has relevant corrigenda on pp. 635–37.

114. [Montgomery, James. Review of Cowper's tr. (no. **45**), 1808 ed.] *Eclectic Review*, [o. s.] 4 (1808), 780–91.

M.'s descriptions of nature "more magnificent than just, more classical than correct"; objection to *exit* at *El.* 3, 32; *obiter dicta* on *Ell.* 3, 4, 5, *Patrem*, and *Mans.* (pp. 786–90). General comments slightly revised in no. **483**.

115. Anon. [Review of the same]. *The Monthly Review*, ser. 2, 58 (Jan.–April 1809), 285–302.

General appreciation of the Latin poems for their literary merits; specific comment on *Rous.* (pp. 290, 299).

116. Anon. [Review of the same]. *The British Critic*, 34 (July–Dec. 1809; printed 1810), 117–24.

Obiter dicta on *Ell.* 4 and 7, *Naturam*, *Patrem*, *Mans.*, and *Ep. Dam.*, plus high praise for the Latin poems as a whole.

117. Brydges, Sir Edgerton. "The Ruminator, Nos. XLIV–XLV: On the Latin Poems of Cowley." In his *Censura Literaria*. London: Longman, Hurst, Rees, and Orme, 1805–09). IX (1809; equals n. s., vol. 6), pp. 84–94. 2d ed., (London, 1815), VIII, pp. 291–301.

Leans towards Johnson's position (no. 107): *pace* Warton (no. 21) M.'s Latin poems have less originality than Cowley's (p. 90; 2d ed., p. 297).

118. Coleridge, Samuel Taylor. [*Notebooks* entry on paper watermarked "1820"]. Printed in Kathleen Coburn, ed. *Inquiring Spirit: A New Presentation of Coleridge from His Published and Unpublished Prose Writings*. New York: Pantheon Books, 1951; rev. ed., Toronto: University of Toronto Press, 1979. No. 123, pp. 156–59 (both eds.).

Critique of Johnson's position in no. 107; M.'s Latinity and his originality both on a par with those of the 15th-century Latin poets of Italy.

119. Landor, Savagius [i.e., Water Savage]. *De cultu atque usu Latini sermonis et Quamobrem poetae Latini recentiores minus legantur*. In his *Idyllia heroica decem*. Pisa: S. Nistri, 1820. Pp. 167–258. Rpt. with changes as *Quaestio quamobrem poetae Latini recentiores minus legantur* in his *Poemata et Inscriptiones* (London: Edward Moxon, 1847), pp. 264–352.

M.'s elegies written with an almost Ovidian *facilitas*; M. one of the chief modern Latin poets of the British Isles (1847 ed., pp. 272, 290).

120. [Hunt, Leigh]. "On the Latin Poems of Milton." *The Literary Examiner*, [1] (1823), 129–37, 145–49, 161–68. Rpt. in Lawrence H. and Carolyn W. Houtchens, eds., *Leigh Hunt's Literary Criticism* (New York: Columbia University Press, 1956), pp. 177–207.

Criticism of the *Poemata*, with verse translations of parts of *Ell.* 4 and 5 and *Naturam* and of *Idea* and *Leon.* 1 entire (translations reprinted in H. S. Milford, ed., *The Poetical Works of Leigh Hunt* [London: Oxford University Press, 1923], pp. 429–33; that of *Idea* also reprinted, with changes, in Hunt's *Poetical Works*, 1832 and subsequent eds.). In three sections, dealing with *Ell.*, the epigrams, and the *Sylvae*, respectively; stops with *Naturam* and *Idea* (a promised continuation apparently never written).

121. Coleridge, Samuel Taylor. [Marginalia in no. 21 (1791 ed.), copy now in the Houghton Library]. Rpts. in Drinkwater, John, "Notes of S. T. Coleridge in 'Milton's Poems,' by Thomas Warton," *The London Mercury*, 14 (1926), 491–505 (and as "Coleridge, Milton, and Warton," in his *A Book for Bookmen* [London: Dulau, 1926], pp. 63–91); in Thomas M. Raysor, ed., *Coleridge's Miscellaneous Criticism* (Cambridge: Harvard University Press, 1936), pp. 170–90; and in Roberta F. Brinkley, ed., *Coleridge on the Seventeenth Century* (Durham, NC: Duke University Press, 1955), pp. 559–72.

Written in late 1823. Comments on the prosody of *El.* 1, 70; conjectures *hanc* for *haec* at *Sals.*, 6 (Brinkley, p. 572).

122. Villemain, [Abel]. "Essai historique sur Milton." In his *Discours et mélanges littéraires*. Paris: Ladvocat, 1823. Pp. [310]–47.

    M.'s Latin poems show an elegance and sweetness quite unusual among Neolatin writers from northern countries (p. 311; the rev. ed. of V.'s *Discours*, etc. [Paris: Didier, 1847] lacks this essay).

123. [Macaulay, Thomas Babington. Review of Charles R. Sumner, tr., *Joannis Miltoni, Angli, De doctrina Christiana* (Cambridge, 1825)]. In *The Edinburgh Review*, 42 (Apr.–Aug. 1825), 304–46. Frequently reprinted, either as "Milton" (e.g., in his *Literary Essays Contributed to the Edinburgh Review* [London: Oxford University Press, 1913, etc.], pp. 1–50) or as "Essay on Milton" (e.g., in the annotated ed. by James Greenleaf Croswell [London: Longmans, Green, and Co., 1895]).

    Rebuttal of Johnson (no. 107) and praise of M.'s Latin verse, heightened by Macaulay's view of the general impossibility of writing Neolatin poetry of distinction (pp. 310–11).

124. Hall, John, tr. *Milton's Familiar Letters*. Philadelphia: E. Littell, 1829.

    El. 6, 48 an imitation of the phrase from Claudian quoted in *Ep. Fam.* 2 (p. 15, n. 1); prose tr. of *Barberini* (p. 45).

125. Mitford, John. "The Life of Milton." In no. 23 (1832; dedication dated "1831"); several times reprinted. Rev. and expanded ed. in Mitford, ed., *The Works of John Milton in Verse and Prose* (London: William Pickering, 1851), I (vol. 1 of 2-vol. "Poetical Works"), pp. [v]–clxxxviii.

    General praise of the Latin poems, with comments on their critical reception and with individual mention of *El.* 1, *Patrem*, and (esp.) *Idea* (1836 Boston ed., pp. lxxxiv–lxxxv; 1851 3-vol. *Poetical Works*, pp. lxxxvi–lxxxviii; 1851 *Works in Verse and Prose*, pp. cxxii–cxxiii). 1851 *Works in Verse and Prose* has new matter on *Coelum* and *Sylla* (pp. xxxvi, lxxxviii).

126. [Hunt, Leigh]. "Letters to Such Lovers of Knowledge as Have Not Received a Classical Education. Letter III: A Popular View of the Heathen Mythology." *Leigh Hunt's London Journal* (London: various publishers, 1834–35; rpt., New York: AMS Press, 1967), I, no. 9 (28 May 1834), pp. 65–66.

    M.'s Latin verses are Ovidian, but their "conscious and sonorous music" makes them his own (p. 66).

127. Coleridge, Samuel Taylor. *Specimens of the Table Talk of the Late Samuel Taylor Coleridge*. London: John Murray, 1835.

    M.'s Latin verses if thought to come from the age of Tiberius would be considered very beautiful (II, p. 270; also in Raysor and in Brinkley [see no. 121], pp. 431 and 552, respectively; conversation dated 23 October 1833).

128. Hallam, Henry. *Introduction to the Literature of Europe in the Fifteenth, Sixteenth, and Seventeenth Centuries*. Paris: Baudry's European Library, 1839. 4 vols.; frequently reprinted in various formats.

General appreciation of M.'s Latin poems; his hexameters more Virgilian than Ovidian (III, p. 303 [ch. V in eds. divided into Parts; ch. xxii in other eds.; always para. 75 of the chapter]).

129. [Landor, Walter Savage. Review of F. Doering, ed., *C. Valerii Catulli Veronensis Carmina* (Altona, 1834)]. *Foreign Quarterly Review*, 29 (1842), 184–203. Rpt. as "The Poems of Catullus" in his *The Last Fruit Off an Old Tree* (London: Edward Moxon, 1853), pp. 237–81; and in his *Complete Works*, ed. T. Earle Welby (London: Chapman and Hall, 1927–36), XI, pp. 177–225.

M. in his elegies "rather the fag than the playfellow of Ovid"; *Idea* his best Latin poem (p. 186; Welby, XI, p. 184).

130. Landor, Walter Savage. "Southey and Landor: Second Conversation." In his *Works*. London: Edward Moxon, 1846. Vol. 2. Rpt. in his *Complete Works*. ed. T. Earle Welby (see no. 129), V, pp. 281–334; and in his *Imaginary Conversations*, ed. Charles G. Crump (London: J. M. Dent, 1891), IV, pp. 246–302.

General discussion of the Latin poems, with a rebuttal of Johnson (no. 107) and with specific comments on virtually all of them (Welby, V, pp. 323–32; Crump, IV, pp. 291–300).

131. Hunter, Joseph. *Milton: A Sheaf of Gleanings After His Biographers and Annotators*. London: John Russell Smith, 1850.

Pace Todd (no. 22, 1809 ed., I, p. 17), *Patrem*, 67–76 hardly proves that M.'s father had destined him for the law (p. 21); *editio princeps* of *Coelum* (p. 23).

132. Edmonds, Cyrus R. *John Milton: A Biography*. London: Albert Cockshaw, 1851.

General comment (p. 10); comment on *Naturam* (p. 24); comment on poems of the Italian trip (pp. 32–33).

133. [Masson, David. Review of Mitford, ed., *The Works of John Milton in Verse and Prose* (see no. 125)], *North British Review*, 16 (1851–52), 295–335 [American ed., vol. 11, pp. 155–76]. Partial rpt. as "Milton's Youth" in his *Essays, Biographical and Critical: Chiefly on English Poets* (Cambridge: Macmillan, 1856), pp. 37–52.

Sketch of M.'s character, life, and works, stressing (pp. 296–302) a "solemn and even austere demeanor of mind" as the salient feature of his youth and early writings; M.'s earlier poems characterized (p. 326; not in "Milton's Youth").

134. Keightley, Thomas. *An Account of the Life, Opinions, and Writings of John Milton*. London: Chapman and Hall, 1855.

"Milton's Latin Writings," pp. 388–94: M.'s Latin poetry beautiful, but only that, as true literary achievement in modern Latin is impossible. *El.* 1 dated to after M. had been "two or three" years at Cambridge (p. 119).

135. Masson, David. *The Life of John Milton: Narrated in Connexion with the Political, Ecclesiastical, and Literary History of His Time.* Cambridge [later, London]: Macmillan, 1859–94. 6 vols. plus *Index.* Vol. 1, new and rev. ed., 1881; vol. 2, new and rev. ed., 1894; rpt., New York: Peter Smith, 1946.

   Poems discussed as follows: *El.* 1, with prose tr. (I, pp. 137–42; rev. ed., pp. 161–67, with verse tr.); *El.* 3, *Eli.* (I, pp. 142–43; 167–69); *Procan., El.* 2, *Q. Nov.,* and gunpowder epigrams (I, pp. 147–50; 172–80, with verse tr. of *Q. Nov.*); *El.* 4 (I, pp. 154–55; 184–85); *El.* 7, with prose tr. (I, pp. 158–61; 188–90); *Naturam* (I, pp. 170–72, 384; 199–203, with verse tr.; 329); *El.* 5., with prose tr. of opening lines (I, pp. 184–85; 218–19); *El.* 6, with prose tr. of most of the poem (I, pp. 192–94; 226–28, partly tr. in verse, partly in prose); *Idea,* with prose tr. (I, pp. 273–74; 305–06, with verse tr.); *Patrem,* with partial prose tr. (I, pp. 385–86; 333–37, with verse tr.; III, p. 643); *Leon.* 1–3, *Sals.,* with prose trs. (I, pp. 751–55; 803–07); *Mans.,* with prose tr. (I, pp. 765–68; 816–19, with verse tr.); verse tr. of *Barberini* (I, pp. 771; 823); *Coelum* (I, pp. 779; 833, with more comment); *Carm. El.* and *Asclep.* (I, rev. ed. only, pp. 303–05); *Ps. 114* (I, rev. ed. only, p. 624); *Ep. Dam.,* with verse tr. (II, pp. 84–94 [both eds.]; tr. reprinted in no. 353, pp. 134–41); *Poemata* of 1645 (III, pp. 452–59; verse tr. of *Effig.,* p. 459); *Rous.* (III, pp. 646–50); verse trs. of *Salmas.* 1 and 2 (IV, pp. 266 and 590); verse tr. of *Sylla* (V, p. 678); *Poemata* of 1673 (VI, p. 689, with comment on *Effig.*). Most of the verse translations reprinted in no. 25 (1890 ed.).

136. [Stebbing, William. Essay on the] "Works of Abraham Cowley." *The Christian Remembrancer,* n. s. 38 (1860), 457–88. Revised and enlarged as "Abraham Cowley" in his *Some Verdicts of History Reviewed* (London: John Murray, 1887), pp. 47–81.

   M.'s Latin verses sweeter and more delicate than Cowley's, but also less strong and showing both less freedom and less "power of thinking in the language" (p. 460; *Some Verdicts,* p. 51).

137. Dallas, E. S. *The Gay Science.* London: Chapman and Hall, 1866. 2 vols.

   Replies (II, pp. 199–206) to no. 133: M.'s early verse *not* an exception to the rule that poets in their youth show "a predominance of sensibility over principle."

138. [Héguin] de Guerle, Edmond. *Milton: sa vie et ses oeuvres.* Paris: Michel Lévy frères, 1868.

   Treats poems of the Italian trip, pp. 70–80 (prose summary of *Sals.,* 9–16; prose trs. of *Mans.,* 77–93 and *Coelum*).

139. Des Essarts, Emmanuel. *De veterum poetarum tum Graeciae, tum Romae apud Miltonem imitatione.* Paris: Ernest Thorin, 1871.

   Poems of the Cambridge period (incl. *Patrem*), pp. 7–10; poems of the Italian trip, pp. 28–32.

140. Stern, Alfred. *Milton und seine Zeit.* Leipzig: Duncker & Humblot, 1877–79. 4 vols. in 2.

Dates *El.* 4 to 1625 (I, p. 30, n. 1 [on p. 303]); treats poems of the Cambridge period (I, pp. 63–72, 85–86 [*El.* 6], pp. 116–17 [*Idea*]); *Ps. 114* (I, p. 239); poems of the Italian trip (I, pp. 284–91); *Ep. Dam.* (II, pp. 18–19); *Rous.* (II, pp. 342–43); *Sylla* (III, p. 231 [n. 2, on p. 284: rejects identification of Sylla with Monk]). Verse trs. of *Leon.* 1 and of *Mans.*, 78–84 (I, pp. 285, 290).

141. Brooke, Stopford A. *Milton.* London: Macmillan, 1879; rpt., New York, AMS Press, 1973.

Poems of the Cambridge period (pp. 6–10); poems of the Italian trip and *Ep. Dam.* (pp. 29–34).

142. Pattison, Mark. *Milton.* London: Macmillan, 1879; New York: Harper, 1880; frequently reprinted by both houses.

M.'s Latin verses differ from most Neolatin poems by being "a vehicle of real emotion"; specific comment on *Ep. Dam.* (London eds., p. 41; New York eds., pp. 38–39). *El.* 1 dated to 1627 (London eds., pp. 6–7; New York eds., p. 6).

143. Garnett, Richard. *Life of John Milton.* London: Walter Scott, 1890.

General comment on the Latin verse (pp. 42–43); *obiter dictum* on *Mans.* (p. 64); critical remarks on *Ep. Dam.* (p. 66).

144. Schlesinger, Alban. *Der Natursinn bei John Milton.* Leipzig-Reudnitz: Druck von Oswald Schmidt, 1892.

Treatments of *El.* 5 (pp. 2–4), *El.* 3, 39–50 (p. 18), *Eli.*, 65–67 (p. 48), *Sals.*, 41 (p. 102), and *Naturam* (pp. 112–13).

145. Schmidt, Immanuel. *Miltons Jugendjahre und Jugendwerke.* Hamburg: Verlagsanstalt und Druckerei A.-G., 1896.

M.'s Latin verse interesting but not really pleasing. Yet (esp. in *Eli.*) it does contain independent descriptions in which imaginative fancy breaks through the imitation and reminiscences (p. 13).

146. Serrell, Geo[rge]. "Milton as Seen in His Latin Poems." *Temple Bar*, 115 (1898), 547–63.

Brief biographical interpretation, with partial translations in verse (some Masson's, some Masson's adapted by Serrell, some Serrell's own) of the following poems: *Ell.* 1, 4, 5, 6, *Q. Nov., Mans., Ep. Dam.*

147. Mabley, Arthur Hull. "Milton's Latin Poems." *Western Reserve University Bulletin*, [n. s.] 2 (1899), 49–72.

Poemata treated both as biography and as literature. Prose trs. of small excerpts by Mabley, as well as verse tr. of *Patrem*, 1–5.

148. Trent, William P. *John Milton: A Short Study of His Life and Works.* New York: Macmillan, 1899.

Pt. II, ch. II, "The Latin Poems" (pp. 71–78; general appreciation and specific comment); Pt. II, ch. V, "The Elegiac Poems" (pp. 119–54; Latin funerary pieces discussed, pp. 149–53 [mostly *Ep. Dam.*]).

149. Scheifers, B[ernhard]. *On the "Sentiment for Nature" in Milton's Poetical Works.* Wissenschaftliche Beilage zum Jahresbericht der Realschule in Eisleben, Ostern 1901. Eisleben: Druck von Ernst Schneider, 1901.

Discussions of *Ep. Dam.* (answer to Stern [no. 140] on the poem's alleged lack of personal feeling) and of *Leon.* 1 (misidentified as *Leon* 2; lines 9–10 a pantheistic utterance), pp. 24 and 28.

150. Begley, Walter, tr. *Nova Solyma: The Ideal City; or Jerusalem Regained.* London: J. Murray; New York: Scribner's, 1902. 2 vols.

Translation of a Latin *prosimetrum* now generally ascribed to Samuel Gott but believed by Begley to be by Milton. Appendices II and III in vol. 2 have material on *Q. Nov.*, 139–54 ("Spenserian in style"), on onomatopoeia in the Latin poems, on M.'s use of *Belgia* (*El.* 3, 12), on false quantities in the Latin poems, and on the Phoenix passage in *Ep. Dam.* (apparently independent statement of Black's hypothesis [no. 402]).

151. Courthope, W. J. *A History of English Poetry.* London: Macmillan, 1895–1910. 6 vols.

Comments on M.'s earlier Latin verse, primarily in relation to his English writings but also on their structural principles (III [1903], pp. 381–83).

152. Mackail, J. W. "A Miltonian Romance." *Quarterly Review*, 197 (1903), 484–502.

Review of no. 150. Commends M.'s mastery of a variety of lyric metres in the *Sylvae*; damns *Q. Nov.* and *Sals.* (the only two poems specifically mentioned).

153. Wendell, Barrett. *The Temper of the Seventeenth Century in English Literature.* New York: Charles Scribner's Sons, 1904.

The Clark Lectures, 1902–03. Ch. 10, "Milton Before the Civil Wars" (pp. 267–301), has general comments on the Latin poems of M.'s "earlier years" (pp. 269–72), dismissal of the poems of the Italian trip (pp. 297–98), and comment on *Ep. Dam.* (pp. 299–301).

154. Anon. "Milton in His Latin Poems." *GM*, 300 (Jan.–June 1906), 497–512.

Poemata only; biographical and appreciative. Verse translations of *El.* 4, 83–96; *Patrem*, 101–08; *El.* 7, 47–80 and 87–102; *El.* 1, 63–64 and 71–72 (an adaptation); *Leon.* 2; *Ep. Dam.*, 18–25, 29–30 plus 36–49, 57–61, 93–111, 145–52, 198–211.

155. Allodoli, Ettore. *Giovanni Milton e l'Italia.* Prato: C. & G. Spighi, 1907.

Poems of the Italian trip (pp. 22–29); Bernardino Ochino's *Tragoedia* M.'s source for the infernal council in *Q. Nov.* (pp. 51–53).

156. Coleridge, Ernest Hartley. "A Note on Milton's Shorter Poems." In Percy W. Ames, ed. *Milton Memorial Lectures, 1908*. London: H. Frowde, 1909. Pp. 23–38.

Comments on the Latin poems (pp. 36–38).

157. Elton, Oliver. *Milton and Party*. English Association Leaflet no. 9. Oxford: Oxford University Press, 1909. Rpt. as "Milton and Parties" in his *A Sheaf of Papers* (Liverpool: University Press of Liverpool; London: Hodder & Stoughton, 1922), pp. 36–44.

Harmony in M.'s early English and Latin verse (through *Ep. Dam.*); *Ep. Dam.*, 201–03, 205–07 an early version of the farewell of Manoa to Samson in *Samson Agonistes* (*Sheaf*, pp. 43–44).

158. Thomas, Walter. "Le sentiment de la nature dans Milton." *Revue Germanique*, 7 (Jan. 1911), 29–49.

In regard to nature the Latin poems are imitative and artificial, revealing no observation of or feeling for natural phenomena except as these may serve as poetical symbols; specific treatment of *El.* 5 and *Naturam* (pp. 32–34).

159. Newbolt, Henry. "John Milton." *English Review*, 14 (Apr.–July 1913), 517–34.

Very brief survey with negative estimate of the Latin poems as poetry (pp. 520–22).

160. Sampson, Alden. "From *Lycidas* to *Paradise Lost*." In his *Studies on Milton and An Essay on Poetry*. London: John Murray; New York: Moffat, Yard & Co., 1913. Pp. 1–163.

M.'s Latin poetry ranks higher as poetry than as Latin (p. 18); verse tr. of *Leon.* 1 (p. 49); parallels between *El.* 7 and *Paradise Lost* (pp. 52–54).

161. Spaeth, Sigmund Gottfried. *Milton's Knowledge of Music: Its Sources and Its Significance in His Works*. Princeton: The University Library, 1913; rpt., Ann Arbor: University of Michigan Press, 1963.

M.'s terms for musical instruments in the Latin poetry (pp. 32–34); in the poems *carmen* invariably means "verse" or "poetry" (pp. 51–52); *El.* 6, 39–46, *Patrem*, 17–40, 50–66 quoted and annotated (pp. 100–101, 104–05); *Leon.* 2 glossed with a 17th-century description of a performance by Leonora, her sister, and her mother (pp. 130–31).

162. Ramsay, Robert L. "Morality Themes in Milton's Poetry." *SP*, 15 (1918), 123–58.

M.'s personifications of Death in the Latin poems; opposition in *Eli.* of the conceptions of Death as either a celestial or an infernal messenger repeats a theme from medieval morality plays (pp. 141–43).

163. Saurat, Denis. *La pensée de Milton*. Paris: Félix Alcan, 1920. Tr. as *Milton, Man and Thinker* (London: Jonathan Cape; New York: Dial Press,

1925; rpt., New York: Haskell House, 1970; rev. ed., London: Dent, 1944; rpt. 1946 and Hamden, CT: Archon Books, 1964.

Comments on *Ell.* 6 and 7 (primarily school exercises, full of rhetoric and cold, false mythological allusions, but also with some precise and lively touches) and on *El.* 5 (lines 67–78 show an exquisite feeling of the richness of nature), pp. 11–13 (Engl. tr., pp. 7–9 [rev. ed., pp. 5–8]).

164. Hanford, James Holly. "The Youth of Milton: An Interpretation of His Early Literary Development." In O. J. Campbell et al. *Studies in Shakespeare, Milton and Donne*. University of Michigan Publications, Language and Literature, vol. 1. New York: Macmillan, 1925; rpt., New York: Haskell House, 1964. Pp. 87–163. Rpt. in his *John Milton, Poet and Humanist* (Cleveland: The Press of Case Western Reserve University, 1966), pp. 1–74.

Pioneering study of M.'s early poetry through *Ep. Dam.* (excluding the poems of the Italian trip) as "a singularly coherent progression of experience"; considerable attention paid to the Latin poems.

165. Mutschmann, H[einrich]. *The Secret of John Milton*. Acta et Commentationes Universitatis Dorpatensis, B: Humaniora, vol. 8, no. 2. Dorpat: [the University], 1925.

Pp. 33–40 and 62 deal with *Ell.* 1, 3, 5, 6, 7, *Eli.*, and *Q. Nov.* in support of the author's theory that M. was an albino and contain occasionally useful observations on light, darkness, and color in these poems.

166. Nairn, J. A. "Milton's Latin Poetry." *Fortnightly Review*, n. s. 117 [o. s. 123] (1925), 500–13.

Appreciative survey; verse tr. of *Q. Nov.*, 90–101 (p. 507).

167. Hanford, James Holly. *A Milton Handbook*. New York: F. S. Crofts, 1926. Rev. ed., 1933; 3d ed., 1939; 4th ed. [publisher now Appleton–Century–Crofts], 1946; 5th ed., by Hanford and James G. Taaffe, 1970; all eds. but the last reprinted several times.

Ch. III, "The Minor Poems," has survey of the Latin poems with appreciative comment and matter on dating.

168. Vince, Charles Anthony. "Milton in Italy." *Central Literary Magazine*, 28 (1927–28), 195–200. Rpt. in his *Lectures and Diversions* (London: Elkin Mathews & Marrot, 1931), pp. 49–57.

M.'s Latin verse, though not the product of a "real" Latin poet, "at least as good as Dante's" (p. 199 [rpt., p. 55]).

169. Draper, John W. *The Funeral Elegy and the Rise of English Romanticism*. New York: The New York University Press, 1929.

Notes "mortuary touches" in *Ell.* 2 and 3 (p. 70).

170. Goode, James. *John Milton: The Making of An Epic Poet*. Ph.D. diss., University of Birmingham, 1929.

Poems of the Cambridge period (pp. 46–67; reply to Fletcher [no. 293] on the dating of *El.* 4, pp. 57–59); relations between these and M.'s English works (pp. 88–93); Latin and Greek as dead traditions (pp. 115–19); *Patrem* dated to 1637 (pp. 186–87); festive elements in *El.* 6 due to the influence of Diodati (p. 210); M. and Ovid (pp. 335–56); M. and Virgil (pp. 417–19, 426–27).

171. Siebert, Theodor. "Untersuchungen über Miltons Kunst vom psychologischen Standpunkt aus." *Anglia*, 54 (1930), 67–82.

M.'s Latin poems strikingly youthful, perhaps artificially so (p. 73).

172. Tillyard, E. M. W. *Milton*. London: Chatto and Windus; New York: Dial Press, 1930; frequently reprinted by Chatto. Rev. ed., 1966 (and New York: Barnes & Noble, 1967).

M.'s earliest Latin verse (pp. 10–11; rev. ed., 9–10); Cambridge poems (pp. 18–42; 16–38); *Patrem* (pp. 78–79; 68–69); poems of the Italian trip and *Ep. Dam.* (pp. 169–72; 144–47); *Rous.*, with prose tr. (pp. 170–71; 144–45); appendix on the date of *Patrem* (*ca.* Sept. 1637; pp. 384; 327).

173. Mabbott, Thomas Ollive. "Milton's Latin Poems." *TLS*, 27 Oct. 1932, p. 790.

Discovery of no. **390** suggests that other separate printings of M.'s Latin poems may be found; a list of candidates follows.

174. Raymond, Dora Neill. *Oliver's Secretary: John Milton in an Era of Revolt*. New York: Minton, Balch & Co., 1932.

Brief remarks on some of the Cambridge poems (pp. 12–16; also p. 5 for *El.* 4); comment on *Ep. Dam.* (pp. 46–47).

175. Tillyard, E. M. W. *Milton: 'L'Allegro' and 'Il Penseroso'*. English Association Pamphlet no. 82. London: Oxford University Press, 1932. Rpt. in his *The Miltonic Setting* (no. **186**), pp. 1–28.

Q. Nov., 139–50 may have been parodied by M. in *L'Allegro;* passage underlies parts of *Prolusion 1*. Invitation that led to *Lycidas* the result of M.'s reputation as a writer of elegies and other occasional verse while at Cambridge.

176. Baker, Charles E. *Milton's Italian Relations*. Ph.D. diss., Cornell University, 1933.

Cross-references betw. *Ep. Dam.* and *Ep. Fam.* 10 (pp. 37–38, 41, 46); sees references to *Naturam* in Dati's encomium and in Francini's ode prefixed to the *Poemata* (pp. 45, 59); *Leon.* 2's account of Tasso's madness "specific and realistic" (p. 70, n. 1).

177. Macaulay, Rose. *Milton*. London: Duckworth, 1934.

Treats Cambridge poems (pp. 13, 19–23), *Patrem* (pp. 32–33), *Leon.* 1–3 and *Mans.* (pp. 52–53), *Ep. Dam.* (pp. 56–58), *Rous.* (pp. 91–92).

178. Belloc, Hilaire. *Milton.* Philadelphia and London: Lippincott, 1935; London: Cassell, c1935; rpt., Westport, CT: Greenwood Press, 1970.

    M.'s Latin verses written "in profusion" (p. 80); *Q. Nov.* marked by a strong visual imagination (p. 87).

179. Parker, W[illiam] R[iley]. "Some Problems in the Chronology of Milton's Early Poems." *RES,* 11 (1935), 276–83.

    M.'s "*Anno aetatis* 17," etc. means "at the age of 17," etc.; the 1645 and 1673 *Poemata* show a deliberate attempt at chronological arrangement, with *El.* 7 a conscious exception and so signalled by the date (pp. 277, 279–80).

180. Card, William M. *Milton's Coming of Age.* Ph.D. diss., The University of Wisconsin, 1936.

    Study of M.'s personal and intellectual development through age 21. *El.* 4 (pp. 21, 50–51), *Ell.* 1 and 7 (pp. 77–83), erotic undertones in *Ell.* 2, 3, and 5 (pp. 90–93), *El.* 5. 15–20 related to *At a Vacation Exercise;* classical and Christian imagery in the earlier poems (pp. 136–39), suppression of erotic imaginings in the Latin poems (pp. 158–60), timidity and *El.* 7 (pp. 175–76), *El.* 6 (pp. 180–82).

181. Hanford, James Holly, ed. *The Poems of John Milton.* New York: The Ronald Press, 1936; 2d ed., 1953.

    Critical headnotes to trs. of *Ell.* 1, 5–7, *Patrem, Mans., Ep. Dam.*

182. Sills, Kenneth C. M. "Milton's Latin Poems." *Classical Journal,* 32 (1936–37), 417–23.

    An address to teachers of Latin and of Milton, calling attention to the general qualities of the Cambridge poems and *Ep. Dam.*

183. Ochi, Fumio. "Milton and Diodati." *SELit,* 18 (1938), 513–30. Japanese version in no. 362, pp. 1–24.

    M.'s attitudes to love and love- (and bacchanalian) poetry in *Ell.* 1, 6, and 7 (pp. 522–29).

184. Praz, Mario. "Milton and Poussin." In *Seventeenth Century Studies Presented to Sir Herbert Grierson.* Oxford: Clarendon Press, 1938; rpt., New York: Octagon Books, 1967. Pp. 192–210. Italian tr., "Milton e Poussin," in his *Gusto Neoclassico* (Firenze: Sansoni, 1940), pp. 9–34; French tr., 1967, see no. 55. Rev. version of "Milton e Poussin," in *Gusto Neoclassico,* 2d enl. ed. (Napoli: Edizioni Scientifiche Italiane, 1959 [Engl. tr., *On Neoclassicism* (London: Thames and Hudson, 1969)], pp. 1–38 [Engl. tr., pp. 11–39]).

    Comparative study, touching (pp. 199–201; pp. 22–26 in the Engl. tr. of the rev. version) on *El.* 1, 51–62, *El.* 5, 119–30, *Ep. Dam.,* 217–19, and *Procan.,* 41–44.

185. Tillyard, E. M. W. "Milton and the English Epic Tradition." In *Seventeenth Century Studies Presented to Sir Herbert Grierson* (see no. 184), pp. 211–34. Rpt. in his *The Miltonic Setting* (no. 186), pp. 168–204.

The "neophytic and ascetic tone" of *El.* 6 accords with M.'s self-dedication to heroic poetry; *Patrem*, 44–49 suggests both exemplary/heroic and Hesiodic/Bartasian epic; discussion of M.'s epic plans as evidenced in *Mans.* and *Ep. Dam.*

186. Tillyard, E. M. W. *The Miltonic Setting: Past and Present.* Cambridge: Cambridge University Press, 1938; several times reissued; rpt., New York: Barnes & Noble, 1966.

Has rpts. of nos. **175, 185.** New material includes "Milton and Keats" (pp. 29–42), with statement that *El.* 6 is testimony to M.'s self-dedication as a "writer of great poetry."

187. Wright, B. A., ed. *Shorter Poems of John Milton.* London: Macmillan, 1938; frequently reprinted.

Discussion of the Cambridge poems (pp. xiv–xvii).

188. Morand, Paul Phelps. *De Comus à Satan: l'oeuvre poétique de John Milton expliqué par sa vie.* Paris: Didier, 1939.

Cambridge poems (pp. 30–41); heaven in the Latin poems (pp. 45–46); *Patrem* (pp. 52–53); poems of the Italian trip and *Ep. Dam.* (pp. 68–73); *Postscr.* (p. 89). Includes partial prose trs. of *Ell.* 1, 3, 6, 7, *Eli., Q. Nov., Patrem*, and *Ep. Dam.*

189. Bradner, Leicester. *Musae Anglicanae: A History of Anglo-Latin Poetry 1500–1925.* The Modern Language Association of America, General Series, vol. 10. New York: Modern Language Association of America, 1940.

Rous. structurally a new form of ode (p. 107); general appreciation of the Latin poems and specific comment on *El.* 6, *Postscr., Patrem, Mans., Ep. Dam.*, and *Rous.*, plus speculation on the likelihood of M.'s having written more Latin poems than he chose to publish (pp. 111–18).

190. Parker, William R[iley. Review of no. 186]. *MLN*, 55 (1940), 215–17.

Carm. El. and *Asclep.* may have been "an abortive poetic exercise on the theme of the First Prolusion, abandoned in favor of *L'Allegro*"; *El.* 6 not personal self-dedication to heroic poetry but an academic exercise on the thesis that "song and feasting belong together."

191. Parker, William Riley. *Milton's Contemporary Reputation.* Columbus: The Ohio State University Press, 1940.

El. 3 and *Eli.* not parodies (reply to no. **174**; p. 8, n. 6); dates *Patrem* after *Comus* (p. 11, n. 12); *Phil. Reg.* perhaps written in 1644 and autobiographical in nature (pp. 19–20); 1645 *Poems* and *Poemata* advertised for sale well after publication (pp. 93, 94, 118).

192. Ochi, Fumio. "Milton's View of Rome," *SELit*, 21 (1941), 458–74.

    Coelum interpreted; it, *Q. Nov.*, *Prod. Bomb.* 1–4, *Ep. Dam.*, *Leon.* 3, and *Sals.* discussed from point of view indicated in the title.

193. Sparrow, John, comp. *Poems in Latin, Together With a Few Inscriptions.* London: Oxford University Press, 1941.

    M. excluded from this anthology of Anglo-Latin writing because "when he wrote in Latin [he] ceased to be a poet and became an imitator" (p. xii). This opinion slightly revised in no. 194.

194. Sparrow, John, comp. *Poems in Latin, Second Series.* N. p. [printed for the compiler at the Chiswick Press], 1942.

    Includes *Ep. Dam.*, 94–111, 113–23, and *Patrem*, 30–40 (pp. 11–13); these the only passages in M.'s Latin verse to move Sparrow "as a poem" (p. ix).

195. Ross, Malcolm Mackenzie. *Milton's Royalism: A Study of the Conflict of Symbol and Idea in the Poems.* Cornell Studies in English, vol. 34. Ithaca: Cornell University Press, 1943.

    Naturam, *Ell.* 1 and 6, and *Q. Nov.* the products of a mind unaffected by contemporary social frustrations and political differences (pp. 40–43, 47); *Q. Nov.* an experiment in writing national epic; comments on M.'s poetic use of James in *Q. Nov.* and the gunpowder epigrams (pp. 72–73).

196. Woodhouse, A. S. P. "Notes on Milton's Early Development." *UTQ*, 13 (1943–44), 66–101. Rpt. in no. 246, pp. 77–99.

    Survey of the Latin poetry through *Patrem* in its artistic relationships to M.'s experiences; *El.* 6 not as important as *Sonnet VII* in the history of M.'s decision to be a *sacer vates* (pp. 68–73).

197. Hirsch, Franz. *Die Rolle der klassischen Mythologie in der geistigen Entwicklung Miltons.* Ph.D. diss., Vienna, 1944.

    Antique modes of thought in *Ell.* 1, 5, and 7 (pp. 7–9); internalization of classical myth in poems of the Cambridge period, esp. *El.* 5 (pp. 20–26); Muses and invocations of them in *El.* 5, *Idea*, *Patrem*, *Sals.* (pp. 53–54).

198. Brooke, Tucker. "Milton's Latin Poems and Prose Works." In Albert C. Baugh, ed., *A Literary History of England.* New York: Appleton-Century-Crofts, 1948; 2d ed., 1967. Pp. 681–88.

    Survey, with *obiter dicta*, of the *Poemata* only (pp. 681–85).

199. Clark, Donald Lemen. *John Milton at St. Paul's School: A Study of Ancient Rhetoric in English Renaissance Education.* New York: Columbia University Press, 1948; rpt., Hamden, CT: Shoe String Press, 1964.

    Apol.; imitation of the ancients in the Latin and Greek poems (pp. 177, 206–08; *Phil. Reg.* a grammar-school piece, p. 206).

200. Hanford, James Holly. *John Milton, Englishman.* New York: Crown, 1949; rpt., London: Gollancz, 1950.

Cambridge poems (pp. 26–34), *Naturam* (p. 38), *Idea* (p. 42), *Patrem* (pp. 51–52), *Sals.* (pp. 72–73, 83), *Mans.* (pp. 86–87), *Ep. Dam.* (pp. 98–100).

201. Banks, Theodore Howard. *Milton's Imagery.* New York: Columbia University Press, 1950; rpt., 1954.

Survey of the topic in broad subject categories. *Patrem* (p. 73), *Q. Nov.* (pp. 162–64), *Ep. Dam., Q. Nov., El.* 2 (pp. 205–06), *El.* 1 (p. 210).

202. Bateson, F. W. *English Poetry: A Critical Introduction.* London: Longmans, 1950; 2d ed., 1966 (also New York: Barnes & Noble).

Ch. 7, "The Money-Lender's Son: 'L'Allegro' and 'Il Penseroso'" (pp. 149–64; 2d ed., pp. 105–15), have comments on *El.* 6, 89–90 (ref. is to the companion pieces [philological assistance from Eduard Fraenkel]; pp. 155–56; 2d ed., p. 109) and on *Postscr.* (*obiter dictum* and dating; p. 161; 2d ed., p. 113).

203. Dorian, Donald Clayton. *The English Diodatis: A History of Charles Diodati's Family and His Friendship With Milton.* New Brunswick: Rutgers University Press, 1950.

Suggests influence of Diodati's ode on the death of Camden upon *Procan.* (p. 109); Cambridge poems in light of M.'s familiarity with the Diodatis (pp. 113–18); *El.* 6 (pp. 127–30); *Ep. Dam.*, date and comment (pp. 176–81).

204. Gordon, George [S.] "The Youth of Milton." In his *The Lives of Authors.* London: Chatto & Windus, 1950. Pp. 44–86.

Comments on *Ell.* 1, 4, 6, 7, *Patrem,* Greek poems, poems of the Italian trip, *Ep. Dam.* Originally written for delivery in 1926.

205. Parker, William Riley. "Notes on the Chronology of Milton's Latin Poems." In Arnold Williams, ed. *A Tribute to George Coffin Taylor.* (See no. 95). Pp. 113–31.

El. 1 dated shortly before 19 April 1626; *El.* 3, Dec. 1626; *El.* 7, May 1630; *Procan.*, late Oct. or early Nov. 1626; *Q. Nov.*, late 1626; *Naturam* and *Idea*, 1630–32; *Patrem*, early autumn 1634; *Phil. Reg.*, Dec. 1634 or early 1635; *Sals.*, Nov. 1638; *Mans.*, Dec. 1638, plus or minus one month.

206. Le Comte, Edward S. *Yet Once More: Verbal and Psychological Pattern in Milton.* New York: Liberal Arts Press, 1953.

Repetition in the Latin poems and from them in the English poems (pp. 17–18, 103–08); reiterative figures in the Latin poetry (pp. 21–24).

207. Ochi, Fumio. [*Studies in Milton*]. Doshisha: Publishing Office of Doshisha University, 1953; 2d rev. ed., 1958.

In Japanese. Ch. 2, "The Organic Relation of Milton's English and Latin Poems" (pp. 14–18; page refs. to the 2d ed.); Ch. 4, "His Tour in Italy" (pp. 74–141); Ch. 5, "His Indebtedness to the Past Tradition" (pp. 142–200;

Homer, Virgil, etc.); Appendix, incl. "From 'Philomela' to 'Nightingale'" (pp. 285–99; *Carm. El.* [?]; *El.* 5). Ch. 3, "The Persons Surrounding Milton in His Younger Days" (pp. 19–73), a rpt. of no. **362**.

208. Allen, Don Cameron. *The Harmonious Vision: Studies in Milton's Poetry.* Baltimore: The Johns Hopkins Press, 1954; several times reissued. Enl. ed., 1970; rpt. New York: Octagon Books, 1979. Twelve lines in *Naturam* perhaps modeled on the end of Seneca's *Ad Marciam*; remarks on the Cambridge epicedia (pp. 50–52 [both eds.]).

209. Muir, Kenneth. *John Milton.* London: Longmans, 1955; frequently reissued.

Latin poems discussed (pp. 49–52, 57, 79) with verse trs. of the following: *El.* 5, 119–30 (also selections from no. **301**), *Mans.*, 80–84, *Ep. Dam.*, 162–68 and 171, 45–49 and 58–61 (pp. 50–52).

210. Woodhouse, A. S. P. *Milton the Poet.* Sedgewick Memorial Lecture. Vancouver: University of British Columbia, 1955.

Tradition, genre, and structure in the Latin poems (pp. 4–8; related to no. **196** and expanded in no. **246**, pp. 7–13); *Ep. Dam.* analyzed (pp. 9–10; related to no. **419**).

211. Fletcher, Harris Francis. *The Intellectual Development of John Milton.* Urbana: The University of Illinois Press, 1956–61. 2 vols.; no more published.

General comments (I, pp. 228–29); pre-Cambridge poems (*Apol.*; dates here "perhaps" *Ell.* 1, 4, 5, and one or two of the gunpowder epigrams [does *not* discuss *Carm. El.* and *Asclep.*]; I, pp. 237–40); the Greek poems (I, pp. 258–63); Milton as a Latinist (II, pp. 125–34; *El.* 4., pp. 128–30); Cambridge poems through 1632 (II, pp. 391–552).

212. Daiches, David. *Milton.* London: Hutchinson, 1957; 2d [rev.] ed., 1959; several times reprinted.

Brief, often critical remarks on the following: *Patrem* (pp. 11–12; page refs. the same in both eds.); *Naturam, El.* 1 (pp. 19–21); *Ell.* 2 and 3, *Eli., Procan., El.* 4 (pp. 25–28); *Ell.* 5 (extended treatment) and 7 (pp. 34–36); *El.* 6 (p. 38); *Mans.* and *Ep. Dam.* (pp. 97–98). Includes prose trs. of *Patrem,* 67–85; *Naturam,* 65–67; *El.* 1, 53–60; *Procan.,* 41–48; *El.* 4, 1–2 and 29–32; *El.* 5, 1–4, 5–6, 21–22, and 27–28; *El.* 6, 81–82; *El.* 5, 55–56; *Mans.,* 78–84; *Ep. Dam.,* 161, 162–72.

213. Maclean, Hugh N. "Milton's *Fair Infant.*" *ELH,* 24 (1957), 296–305. Rpt. in Arthur E. Barker, ed., *Milton: Modern Essays in Criticism* (New York: Oxford University Press, 1965), pp. 21–30.

Expands (pp. 296–98) on no. **208**: design of and classical and Christian elements in *El.* 3 and *Eli.*

214. Parker, William Riley. "Milton and the News of Charles Diodati's Death." *MLN,* 72 (1957), 486–88.

M. got the news at Naples in Dec. 1638 or Jan. 1639; *Mans.*, 78–100 a reflection of M.'s brooding over Diodati's demise. *Ep. Dam.*, in part a "thank-you" note to Italian friends, written probably autumn 1639.

215. Tuve, Rosemond. *Images & Themes in Five Poems by Milton.* Cambridge: Harvard University Press, 1957.

Classical and Christian fusion in *El.* 6 (pp. 41–42); M.'s use, as in *El.* 1 and *Mans.*, of *Phoebus* (p. 75).

216. Ochi, Fumio. ["Milton's Love Lyrics and His Epilogistic Palinode"]. *SELit*, 35 (1958–59), 51–74. Rpt. in no. 217, pp. 110–35.

In Japanese. Girl in *El.* 7 not the same as the one in the Italian sonnets, which it preceded by a few years; chronology of *Ell.*, including *Postscr.*

217. Ochi, Fumio. *Milton Ron-Kō [Researches into Milton].* Nan'undo, 1959.

In Japanese. Plants mentioned in M.'s English and Latin poems (pp. 220–40); rpt. of no 216 (pp. 110–35).

218. Saillens, Emile. *John Milton, poète combattant.* Paris: Gallimard, 1959. Tr. as *John Milton: Man, Poet, Polemist* (Oxford: Basil Blackwell, 1964).

Brief comments on *El.* 4 (pp. 29, 31; tr., pp. 13–14, 16); *El.* 7, *Postscr.*, *Naturam, El.* 5, *Idea, El.* 6 (pp. 38–44; 23–32); *Patrem* (pp. 55; 43); poems of the Italian trip (pp. 83–87 [prose tr. of *Barberini*, p. 87]; 73–75); *Ep. Dam.* (pp. 92–94; 84–86); *Rous.* (p. 141 [prose tr. of part of Strophe 2]; p. 138); *Sylla* (p. 220, with prose tr.; 230). Includes verse trs. of *El.* 7, 95–102; *Naturam*, 56–57, 60–69; *El.* 5, 11–14; *Idea*, 1–10, 19–24; *El.* 6, 49–51, 55–60, 67–71, and 77; *Patrem*, 101–104, 115–20; *Mans.*, 25–33, 80–84; *Ep. Dam.*, 112–23, 125–35, 155–60, 161–67; also bits from some of the poems in prose translation (verse trs. from the *Poemata* and the *Rous.* tr. represented in the Engl. tr. by equivalents from no. 51). Some of the trs. are adaptations.

218a. Broadbent, J. B. *Some Graver Subject: An Essay on Paradise Lost.* London: Chatto & Windus, 1960.

Brief comments on many of the Latin poems through *Ep. Dam.*, including arguments for late dating of *Postscr.* and against reading *El.* 6 as self-dedication to heroic poetry; prose trs., based on those in nos. 30 and 33, of *El.* 1, 47–62; *El.* 3, 45–48; *El.* 4, 118–22; *El.* 5, 15–21, 55–60, 95–96, 109–10, 127–30; *El.* 6, 49–66; *El.* 7, 1–4, 73–80, 85–88, 95–100; *Eli.*, 48–64; *Postscr.*; *Mans.*, 78–84; and *Ep. Dam.*, 155–68, 212–19 (pp. 25, 30–36).

219. Daiches, David. *A Critical History of English Literature.* London: Secker and Warburg; New York: Ronald Press, 1960. 2 vols.

Cambridge poems (I, pp. 393–96; prose tr. of *El.* 1, 49–60, p. 396); poems of the Italian trip and *Ep. Dam.* (I, pp. 415, 418–19).

220. Shawcross, John T. "Two Milton Notes: 'Clio' and Sonnet 11." *N&Q*, n. s. 8 (1961), 178–79.

Clio at *El.* 4, 31 and *Patrem*, 12 not the muse of historical writing (as at *Mans.*, 24) but the guardian of an individual's talents and of their outcome as represented in his or her life.

221. Semple, W. H. "The Latin Poems of John Milton." *Bulletin of the John Rylands Library*, 46 (1963–64), 217–35.

Survey of the *Poemata* with appreciative comment.

222. Shawcross, John T. "Milton's Decision to Become a Poet." *MLQ*, 24 (1963), 21–30.

Decision made in 1637; *Patrem* written in 1638 (see no. **365**) to explain it. *Ell.* 5 and 6 in their references to M.'s writing verse do not indicate more than occasional activity as a poet.

223. Shawcross, John T. "Of Chronology and the Dates of Milton's Translation from Horace and the *New Forcers of Conscience.*" *SEL*, 3 (1963), 77–84.

Arrangement (pp. 77–79) of the 1645 and 1673 *Poemata*; placing of *Effig.* and *Rous.*, though dictated by convenience, preserves the chronological order. Printer's copy for *Apol.* and *Rous.* may have been in M.'s own hand; this *Rous.* MS. may have been the exemplar of no. **435**.

224. Bush, Douglas. *John Milton: A Sketch of His Life and Writings.* New York: Macmillan; London: Collier-Macmillan, 1964; occasionally reprinted.

M.'s Latin poems may have echoed some of Alexander Gill's (p. 22); survey of the earlier poems through *Patrem*, with early versions of comments appearing in no. 6 (pp. 26–33); same for poems of the Italian trip (pp. 69–71).

225. Fallon, Robert Thomas. *Milton's Military Imagery: Its Growth and Function in His Art.* Ph.D. diss., Columbia University, 1964.

M.'s military images in his pre-Civil War poems (pp. 16–22; includes comment on *Eli.*, *Patrem*, and *Mans.*).

226. Fixler, Michael. *Milton and the Kingdoms of God.* [Evanston, IL]: Northwestern University Press, 1964.

El. 6, *Patrem*, *El.* 3, and *Eli.* treated (pp. 46–64) in the contexts of M.'s poetic vocation and of his developing expectation of an apocalyptic kingdom of God on earth.

227. Allen, Don Cameron. "Milton as a Latin Poet." In James E. Phillips and Don C. Allen, *Neo-Latin Poetry of the Sixteenth and Seventeenth Centuries.* Los Angeles: William Andrews Clark Memorial Library, 1965. Pp. 30–52. Rpt. as "John Milton: Elegy Five: 'In Adventum Veris'" in his *Image and Meaning: Metaphoric Traditions in Renaissance Poetry*, new enl. ed. (Baltimore: The Johns Hopkins Press, 1968), pp. 115–37; and under the original title in Earl Miner, ed., *Stuart and Georgian Movements* (Berkeley: University of California Press, 1973), pp. 23–45.

Ell. 5 (esp.) and 7 in light of their European tradition from classical and late antiquity through Neolatin literature; *El.* 5 analyzed as a poem about poetic inspiration. A Clark Library Seminar paper read in 1964.

228. Frye, Northrop. *The Return of Eden: Five Essays on Milton's Epics.* Toronto: University of Toronto Press, 1965. Rpt., with index, as *Five Essays on Milton's Epics* (London: Routledge & Kegan Paul, 1966).

Priestly discipline in *El.* 6 (p. 8; London ed., pp. 6–7); thematic connections between *Leon.* 1 and other poems of M. (p. 58; London ed., pp. 50–51); divine energy in *El.* 5 and in the conclusion of *Ep. Dam.* (pp. 49–50; London ed., p. 52); comparisons of Arthur in *Mans.* to Blake's Orc and of giant in *Idea* to figures in Blake, Shelley, Dylan Thomas, and M.'s *Of Reformation* (pp. 105–06; London ed., pp. 111–12).

229. Martz, Louis L. "The Rising Poet, 1645." In Joseph H. Summers, ed. *The Lyric and Dramatic Milton: Selected Papers from the English Institute.* New York: Columbia University Press, 1965. Pp. 3–33.

Arrangement of the 1645 volume, with comment on *Rous.*, *El.* 1 and *Ep. Dam.*, *Postscr.*, and *El.* 6 (the latter not taken as self-dedication to a life of divine poetry). Revised and expanded in no. **266.**

230. Daiches, David. "Some Aspects of Milton's Pastoral Imagery." In Ilva Cellini and Giorgio Melchiori, eds. *English Studies Today, Fourth Series: Lectures and Papers Read at the Sixth Conference of the International Association of University Professors of English, Held at Venice, August 1965.* Rome: Edizioni di Storia e Letteratura, 1966. Pp. 289–309. Rpt. in his *More Literary Essays* (Edinburgh: Oliver & Boyd; Chicago: The University of Chicago Press, 1968), pp. 96–114.

Ell., with specific comment on *Ell.* 4, 5, 7 and modifying remarks made in no. **212** (pp. 292–94; rpt., pp. 99–101); *Ep. Dam.* analyzed (pp. 294–96; 101–02).

231. Honigmann, E. A. J., ed. *Milton's Sonnets.* London: Macmillan; New York: St. Martin's Press, 1966.

Ordering of *Ell.* (pp. 61, 70, 72); *Ep. Dam.*, 133 a reference to M.'s Italian poetry (p. 79).

231a. Burden, Dennis H. *The Logical Epic: A Study of the Argument of Paradise Lost.* Cambridge: Harvard University Press, 1967.

Arthur references in *Mans.* and *Ep. Dam.* may be more poem-related than actual expressions of intent to write an Arthuriad (pp. 15–16).

232. Lawry, Jon S. *The Shadow of Heaven: Matter and Stance in Milton's Poetry.* Ithaca: Cornell University Press, 1968.

Survey of all the poems prior to *Comus* (incl. *Patrem* and *Phil. Reg.*), with comment on each (pp. 8–15).

233. Parker, William Riley. *Milton: A Biography.* Oxford: Clarendon Press, 1968. 2 vols., paged continuously.

Discusses virtually all of the Latin and Greek verse in chronological order. Excellent index makes location references here unnecessary.

234. Via, John Albert. *Studies in the Imagery of Milton's Poetry and Prose to 1642*. Ph.D. diss., The University of Illinois, 1968.

   Carm. El. and *Asclep.* (pp. 113–14); *Apol.* and *Phil. Reg.* (pp. 114–15); *Ell.* 1, 7, 5 (pp. 116–26); *Naturam, Idea, Q. Nov.*, and gunpowder epigrams (pp. 128–38); *Ell.* 2 and 3, *Eli., Procan.* (pp. 138–48); *El.* 4 (pp. 152–54); *El.* 6 (pp. 160–64); *Patrem* (pp. 275–81); *Sals., Mans.*, and *Ep. Dam.* (pp. 294–309). Related material in nos. 242, 250, and 355.

235. Friedman, Donald. "Harmony and the Poet's Voice in Some of Milton's Early Poems." *MLQ*, 30 (1969), 523–34.

   In *Procan.* and (to a lesser degree) in *El.* 3 and *Eli.* M.'s poetic persona largely subordinated to the decorum of the classical elegy (pp. 525–26).

236. Gros Louis, Kenneth R. R. "The Triumph and Death of Orpheus in the English Renaissance." *SEL*, 9 (1969), 63–80.

   M.'s allusions to Orpheus in *El.* 6 and *Patrem* align him in these poems with the Elizabethan concept of O. as "triumphant poet-civilizer" (p. 76).

237. Leishman, J. B. *Milton's Minor Poems*. London: Hutchinson, 1969; rpt., Pittsburgh: University of Pittsburgh Press, 1971.

   Ch. 3, "The Latin Poems" (pp. 40–44): *Ell.* treated as instances of a poetic requiring, in contradistinction to epic, "no special dedication"; *Ell.* 1, 5, 7 not spontaneous expressions of aspects of M.'s personality suppressed in the English poems (answer to no. 172); poems from *Patrem* through *Ep. Dam.* discussed in connection with M.'s conception of poetry and his plans for a poetic career.

238. Ricks, Christopher. "Milton. Part I: *Poems (1645)*." In Ricks, ed., *English Poetry and Prose, 1540–1674*. History of Literature in the English Language, vol. 2. London: Barrie & Jenkins, 1970. Pp. 249–81.

   M.'s Latin poems have "Poetic skill . . . , but not much poetic life"; imitation versus "originality" in Neolatin verse (pp. 253–54).

239. Wagenknecht, Edward. *The Personality of Milton*. Norman: University of Oklahoma Press, 1970.

   Biographical interpretation and specific comment on *Ell.* 1, 5, 7, and *Naturam* (pp. 5–7); *El.* 6 (pp. 10–11); *Patrem* (pp. 8, 79); *Ell.* 1, 5, 7, and *Leon.* 1 (pp. 101–03; interest in the opposite sex).

240. Weidhorn, Manfred. *Dreams in Seventeenth-Century English Literature*. Studies in English Literature, vol. 57. The Hague: Mouton, 1970.

   Inspirational dreams in *Patrem* and *El.* 5, visions in *El.* 3 and *Q. Nov.* (pp. 132–37).

241. Shawcross, John T. "*A Variorum Commentary on the Poems of John Milton*: Another View." *SCN*, 29 (1971), 1–4.

Criticism of vol. 1 of the *Variorum Commentary*, esp. of the section edited by Bush (no. **6**). Specific comment on *El.* 1, 57–58; *Sals.*, 4–5; *Prod. Bomb.* 3, 3–4; the *Rous.* MS.; *Patrem*, 35–37; *Ep. Dam.*, 9–13.

242. Via, John A[lbert]. "Milton's *The Passion:* A Successful Failure." *MQ*, 5 (1971), 35–37.

Brief comments on the topic of poetry as dealt with in *El.* 6, *Patrem*, and *Ep. Dam.* (p. 37).

243. West, Michael. "The *Consolatio* in Milton's Funeral Elegies." *HLQ*, 34 (1971), 233–49.

Study of M.'s developing ability to deal in these poems with problems presented by the description of heaven (*Ell.* 2 and 3, *Eli.*, *Procan.*, *Ep. Dam.*).

244. Wolfe, Don M. *Milton and His England.* Princeton: Princeton University Press, 1971.

Glosses the descriptions of London girls in *Ell.* 1 and 7 with two female portraits by Sir Peter Lely (plates 14, 16).

245. Cipolla, E[lizabeth] M. C. "Pastoral Elements in Milton's Latin Poems." *UniSA English Studies*, 10 (1972), 1–16.

El. 5, *Mans.*, and (esp.) *Ep. Dam.*

246. Woodhouse, A. S. P. *The Heavenly Muse: A Preface to Milton.* Toronto: University of Toronto Press, 1972.

Expands on no. **196**, pp. 66–77, and on no. **210**, pp. 4–8, including new material on *El.* 3 and *Postscr.* (pp. 15–37); rpt. of no. **196** (pp. 37–54); rpt., with minor changes, of no. **419** (pp. 83–98). Edited by Hugh MacCallum, who updates some footnotes and adds a substantial one of his own on dating (pp. 346–47). Revisions, expansions, etc. date from 1963–64.

247. Jenkins, R. B. *Milton and the Theme of Fame.* Studies in English Literature, vol. 77. The Hague: Mouton, 1973.

M.'s praise of rumor in *Q. Nov.* a break with classical tradition; despite the tone of *Rous.*, M. perhaps quite serious in wanting the good opinion of competent judges (pp. 16–17; 37).

248. Le Comte, Edward [S.] "Milton *versus* Time." In his *Milton's Unchanging Mind: Three Essays.* Port Washington, NY: Kennikat Press, 1973. Pp. 3–68.

Reasons for M.'s misdating of *Eli.* (p. 7); his "strange mixture of pride and humility" in the 1645 *Poemata* (title-page; age dates; *Patrem*, 115) and in *Rous.*, 3–6 (pp. 28–29); *Phoebicolis* (*El.* 1, 14) paralleled in Nicholas Felton's Latin poem on the death of Edward King (n. 25 on pp. 57–58).

249. Rivers, Isabel. "The Making of a 17th-Century Poet." In John Broadbent, ed. *John Milton: Introductions.* Cambridge: Cambridge University Press, 1973. Pp. 75–106.

Ovidian influence in the *Poemata;* characterization of *Ell.* 5 and 7 (pp. 100–101); *Mans.* written after M.'s return to England in 1639 (p. 104).

250. Via, John A[lbert]. "Milton's Antiprelatical Tracts: The Poet Speaks in Prose." In *Milton Studies,* V, ed. James D. Simmonds. Pittsburgh: University of Pittsburgh Press, 1973. Pp. 87–127.

Q. Nov. and treatments of the Anglican service in *Of Reformation* and in *Animadversions* (pp. 91–92, 122); wolf and reed imagery in *Ep. Dam.,* *Lycidas,* and the pamphlets; apotheosis theme from *El.* 3 and *Eli.* through *Ep. Dam.* to *Of Reformation* (pp. 102–05, 123); regeneracy as theme in *El.* 3, *Eli., El.* 4, *Mans., Ep. Dam.* (pp. 107–10); *Ell.* 1, 3, and 5 as "rarefied form" of M.'s early working in the modes of classical elegy (p. 119).

250a. Berkeley, David Shelley. *Inwrought With Figures Dim: A Reading of Milton's "Lycidas."* De Proprietatibus Litterarum, Series didactica, vol. 2. The Hague: Mouton, 1974.

Absence of beasts from Christian heaven in *El.* 3 and *Ep. Dam.* the result of M.'s horror of animal idolatry; comparison of Boccaccio's satyrs in Heaven (*Ecl.* 14) with the orgies at the end of *Ep. Dam.*; backgrounds for British worship of Apollo at *Mans.,* 35–38 (pp. 45–47).

251. Condee, R[alph] W[aterbury]. "The Latin Poetry of John Milton." In J. W. Binns, ed. *The Latin Poetry of English Poets.* London: Routledge and Kegan Paul, 1974. Pp. 58–92.

Chronological survey touching upon everything but the verse scraps; critical comment on most of the poems.

252. Condee, Ralph Waterbury. *Structure in Milton's Poetry: From the Foundation to the Pinnacles.* University Park, PA: The Pennsylvania State University Press, 1974.

Ch. 3, "The Early Latin Poems and 'Lycidas'" (pp. 21–41; *Ell.* 1–3, *Procan.;* draws on no. **284**); Ch. 4, "The Fair Infant, 'Elegia Quinta,' and the Nativity Ode" (*El.* 5, pp. 48–51); Ch. 5, "The Companion Pieces and 'Ad Patrem'" (*Patrem,* pp. 64–70); Ch. 7, "'Mansus' and the Panegyric Tradition" (pp. 85–103; reworking of no. **389**); Ch. 8, "'Epitaphium Damonis' as the Transcendence over the Pastoral" (pp. 105–22; reworking of no. **426**); Virgilian reminiscence at *Q. Nov.,* 92–93 (pp. 150–51).

253. Brodwin, Leonora Leet. "Milton and the Renaissance Circe." In *Milton Studies,* VI, ed. James D. Simmonds. Pittsburgh: University of Pittsburgh Press, 1975. Pp. 21–83.

Circe references in *Ell.* 1 and 6 in relation to aspects of the myth and to M.'s English writings (pp. 38–43); temptations in *Ell.* 1 and 7 antiintellectual as well as sexual (pp. 58–59).

254. Kerrigan, William. "The Heretical Milton: From Assumption to Mortalism." *ELR,* 5 (1975), 125–66.

Assumption in *Eli.* and the gunpowder epigrams; consolation in *Mans.* (pp. 130–31; 148).

255. Shawcross, John T. "Milton and Diodati: An Essay in Psychodynamic Meaning." In *Milton Studies*, VII, ed. Albert C. Labriola and Michael Lieb. Pittsburgh: University of Pittsburgh Press, 1975. Pp. 127–63.

Treatment of the relationship with interpretations of passages in *Ep. Dam.*, *Ell.* 1 and 6, and *Patrem*. Modifies no. 40 by dating *El.* 7 to "perhaps" 1630.

256. Viswanathan, S. "'In Sage and Solemn Tunes': Variants of Orphicism in Milton's Early Poetry." *Neuphilologische Mitteilungen*, 76 (1975), 457–72.

Stresses note of seriousness and personal involvement in *El.* 6, 55–70; influence of Orphic ideals in *El.* 6 and *Patrem* (pp. 460–62).

257. Camé, Jean François. *Les structures fondamentales de l'univers imaginaire Miltonien.* Etudes anglaises, vol. 59. Paris: Didier, 1976.

M.'s conceptions of the physical universe as shown in his writings (esp. the verse); organized under the rubrics of light and darkness, time, and space. No *index locorum;* of the *ca.* 75 references to the Latin poems the following, at least, are discussions rather than mere citations: *El.* 1, 21–22 (p. 403); *El.* 3, 23–26 (p. 63), 33–36 and 66–67 (p. 168); *El.* 5, 77 (p. 420), 79–82 (p. 358); *Q. Nov.*, 166–69 (p. 357); *Patrem*, 30–32 (p. 257); *Mans.*, 27–33 (p. 133); *Ep. Dam.*, 4–8 (p. 425).

258. Norford, Don Parry. "The Sacred Head: Milton's Solar Mysticism." In *Milton Studies*, IX, ed. James D. Simmonds. Pittsburgh: University of Pittsburgh Press, 1976. Pp. 37–75.

Solar figures (incl. Orpheus) and solar language in M.'s writings. Comment on *Patrem* and *El.* 5 (pp. 42–43; 45–46).

259. Harned, Jon William. *John Milton, 1632–1642: A Psycho-biographical Study.* Ph.D. diss., University of Virginia, 1977.

Tragedies and comedies in *El.* 1 (p. 139); moly and Haemonian herbs in *Ell.* 1 and 2 (pp. 145–46; "antidotes to castration"); *Ell.* 6 and 5 (pp. 10–15); *Patrem* (pp. 60–61, 69–71, 78–83, 85); poems of the Italian trip and *Ep. Dam.* (pp. 173–79); conclusion of *Ep. Dam.* "stunning" (p. 33).

260. Hill, Christopher. *Milton and the English Revolution.* London: Faber and Faber, 1977; rpt., New York: Viking Press, 1978.

Innuba in line 65 hints that M. may have seen himself as married to Diodati (p. 31); political stance in some of the subjects of the Cambridge poems (p. 35); erotic element in M.'s writings through *Ep. Dam.* (pp. 57–58); *Ps. 114* an instance of M.'s use of the Egyptian captivity as a contemporary political symbol (p. 206); *Postscr.* designed to differentiate M. from the libertines with whom he was associated by his opponents in the 1640s (pp. 451–52).

261. Schindler, Walter Leo. *Voice and Crisis: The Pattern of Invocation in Milton's Poetry.* Ph.D. diss., Yale University, 1977.

El. 6, 87–88 (pp. 29–30); *Patrem,* 1–7, 30–37, 50–55 (pp. 31–35).

262. Le Comte, Edward S. *Milton and Sex.* New York: Columbia University Press, 1978.

Ell. 1 and 7 in light of M.'s sexual stirrings (pp. 5–7); *El.* 3 and Ovid, *Amores,* 1. 5 (pp. 9–10, drawing upon no. **290**); Scientia in *Patrem* (p. 14); *Postscr.* itself a convention (p. 21); connections between *Leon.* 1–3 and *Comus* (p. 21); sexual imagery in *Mans.* and *Ep. Dam.* (p. 22).

263. Hill, John Spencer. *John Milton, Poet, Priest and Prophet: A Study of Divine Vocation in Milton's Poetry and Prose.* London: Macmillan; Totowa, NJ: Rowman and Littlefield, 1979.

Ch. 2, "Poetic Vocation," treats passages on poetry and the poet in the Latin poems, esp. *Ell.* 5 and 6 (the latter written *before* the Nativity ode was finished).

264. Tayler, Edward W. *Milton's Poetry: Its Development in Time.* Duquesne Studies: Language and Literature Series, vol. 2. Pittsburgh: Duquesne University Press, 1979.

El. 6, 81 states the main theme of the Nativity ode — peace (p. 37); sexuality of *Ell.* 1 and 5 (p. 136; specific comment on *El.* 1, 57).

265. Freeman, James A. *Milton and the Martial Muse: Paradise Lost and European Traditions of War.* Princeton: Princeton University Press, 1980.

El. 5, 39–40 and *Q. Nov.,* 139–56 related to M.'s unfashionably negative view of military force and fraud.

266. Martz, Louis L. *Poet of Exile: A Study of Milton's Poetry.* New Haven: Yale University Press, 1980.

Pt. 1, ch. 2, "The Rising Poet" (pp. 31–59), a revised and expanded version of no. **229**. Its Section II (pp. 39–43) is entirely new, dealing with *Postscr.* (perhaps composed for recitation before one of the Italian academies), the epigrams, and the *Sylvae* (arranged to show poetic development; Orphicism in *Leon.* 3 and *Sals.* as well as in *Patrem*). *Mans.,* 54–69, and Ovidian backgrounds (pp. 18–19).

267. Miller, Leo. "Dating Milton's 1626 Obituaries." *N&Q,* n. s. 27 (1980), 323–24.

Ridding died on 26 Sep. 1626; *El.* 2 therefore preceded *El.* 3, as the news of Andrewes's death in London (on 25 Sep.) reached Cambridge afterward. *Procan.* followed. *Eli.,* though revised for Gostlin's death, begun in 1625 as an exercise in emulation of Diodati's poem on the death of Camden (see no. **203**) and so dated by M.

268. Miller, Leo. "Milton's Clash With Chappell: A Suggested Reconstruction." *MQ,* 14 (1980), 77–87.

Associates M.'s rustication with heterodox views expressed in *Prolusions* 3 and 4; dates *El.* 1 and occasion of *El.* 7 to spring of 1627.

269. Pironon, J. "The Images of Woman in the Sonnets and in Some Minor Poems of John Milton." *Cahiers Elisabéthains,* no. 18 (Oct., 1980), 43–52.

Brief remarks on the images of woman in *Ell.* 1, 5, and 7.

270. Campbell, Gordon. "Francini's *Permesso.*" *MQ,* 15 (1981), 122–23.

Permessus reference in Francini's ode prefixed to the *Poemata* an acknowledgment of M.'s "accomplishment as an elegiac poet," F. having heard M. recite some of the *Ell.* in Florentine academy meetings; *Postscr.* applies to *Ell.* as a whole, as each has erotic content.

271. Lieb, Michael [J.] *Poetics of the Holy: A Reading of* Paradise Lost. Chapel Hill: The University of North Carolina Press, 1981.

Poet-priest in *Ell.* 5 and 6, *Patrem, Sals.,* and *Mans.* (pp. 43–45, 58, 63, 133); visions of the holy in *El.* 3, *Eli., Ep. Dam.* (pp. 64–65); sacred mount in *Ell.* 4 and 5, *Eli., Patrem, Mans.,* and *Ep. Dam.* (p. 146); animism in *Ps. 114* (p. 151); light in *Carm. El.* and *Ell.* 5 and 6 (pp. 187–88); M.'s approval of holy war seen in *Ps. 114* (pp. 269–70).

PART III: INDIVIDUAL POEMS (AND GROUPS THEREOF)

A. *Poemata*

1. *Elegiae* as a whole

272. Shawcross, John T. "Form and Content in Milton's Latin Elegies." *HLQ,* 33 (1969–70), 331–50.

Analyzes themes and structure of each poem. Most attention paid to *Ell.* 1, 4, 5, and 6, with a reading of *El.* 5 as characterized by ambivalence and as the maturing M.'s wistful glance back at the "golden age" of his early youth.

273. Whitehead, Louis Edward. *A Critical Study of Milton's Latin Elegies.* Ph.D. diss., Florida State University, 1976.

Close analysis of each poem in numerical order.

274. Fruchter, Barry George. *Studies in The English Elegy.* Ph.D. diss., State University of New York at Stony Brook, 1977.

Ch. 3, "Milton's Elegiac Persona" (pp. 42–92), begins and ends with *Lycidas* but is mostly devoted to an interpretation of the seven *Ell.* as "a series of valedictions to worldly values."

See also: nos. 66, 71, 92, 98, 216, 270.

2. *El.* 1

a. *Translations*

See: no. 219.

b. *Comment*

275. Peck, Francis. *New Memoirs of the Life and Poetical Works of Mr. John Milton.* London: n. p., 1740.

Lines 89–90 seem to deny any interpretation of lines 11–20 as a reference to M.'s expulsion or rustication (p. 35).

276. Warton, Thomas, ed. *The Life and Literary Remains of Ralph Bathurst, M.D.* London: Printed for R. and J. Dodsley, etc., 1761.

Discovery of information that M. was whipped helps explain lines 15–16, *caetera* referring to this punishment; *durus magister* is Thomas Bainbrigge, Master of Christ's College (p. 153, note ‡; rpts. in "New Anecdotes of English Writers," *GM*, 31 [1761], 221–22, and *London Magazine*, 3 [1761], 256–57).

277. [Blackburne, Francis]. *Remarks on Johnson's Life of Milton.* London: n. p., 1780; rpt., New York: Garland Publishing, Inc., 1974.

Rebuts nos. 108 and 276 on M.'s "flogging" and "exile" (pp. 27–36): *caetera* likely refers only to college exercises set as punishments, *vetiti laris* and *ex- ilium* need not signify either expulsion or rustication. M.'s absence from Cambridge probably the result of financial problems at home.

278. Bowle, John. "An Imaginary Blemish in *Milton's* Character Removed." *GM*, 52 (1782), 18–19.

Prints the "letter of a friend" arguing that M.'s *exilium* refers to vacation time only; asserts that an honest person would not have used line 18 to refer to a "publick indignity."

279. Monboddo, James Burnet, Lord. *Of the Origin and Progress of Language.* Edinburgh: Printed for J. Balfour and T. Caddell, 1773–92; rpt., New York: Garland Publishing, Inc., 1970. 6 vols.

Lines 9–10, 21–22 quoted as outstanding examples of elegiac verse and praised for their beauty, elegance, and sweetness (III, pp. 68–70, note).

280. [Marsden, John Howard]. *College Life in the Time of James the First, Illustrated by an Unpublished Diary of Sir Symonds D'Ewes.* London: John W. Parker and Son, 1851.

In line 90 *raucae murmur . . . Scholae* refers to disputations in the Public Schools (p. 65).

281. Hales, John W. "Milton and Gray's Inn Walks." *St. James Gazette*, 29 and 30 July 1891. Rpt. in his *Folia Litteraria* (London: Seeley; New York: Macmillan, 1893), pp. 220–30; and in Carmen J. Dello Buono, ed., *Rare Early Essays on Milton and Bunyan* (Darby, PA: Norwood Editions, 1981), pp. 126–36.

Lines 49–50 refer not to Horton but to Gray's Inn Gardens, a popular spot for promenading and "fairly rural" as late as 1780; quotes from Pepys's diary (30 June 1661, 4 May 1662) for the fashionable appearance of ladies strolling there.

282. Watson, Sara Ruth. "'Moly' in Drayton and Milton." *N&Q*, 176 (Jan.–June 1939), 244.

Drayton's references to the herb a possible source for M. [line 88].

283. Clark, Donald Lemen. "John Milton and William Chappell." *HLQ*, 18 (1954–55), 329–50.

    Pace Masson (tr. in no. 135), *durus* in line 15 means "rigorous" (p. 330).

284. Condee, Ralph Waterbury. "Ovid's Exile and Milton's Rustication." *PQ*, 37 (1958), 498–502. Slightly modified in no. 252, pp. 22–27.

    Poem's organizing principle the cross-comparison of the two exiles. Though M. arranges analogous material better in the companion pieces, *El.* 1 still "a subtle and often successful gibe" at his university.

285. Shawcross, John T. "Milton's *nectar:* Symbol of Immortality." *English Miscellany*, 16 (1965), 131–41.

    In lines 55–58 the nectar in the girls' necks and the Pelops reference indicate that M. is praising the divinely granted and immortal beauty of English womanhood (p. 139).

286. Patrick, J. Max. [Review of Vol. 1 of the *Variorum Commentary* (see no. 6)]. *SCN*, 29 (1971), 1.

    Line 3 suggests that M. knows the exact location of Diodati's residence in or near Chester; in lines 27–46 the dramas are deliberately invented by Milton.

3. *El.* 3

287. Mahood, M. M. *Poetry and Humanism*. London: Cape, 1950; rpt., New York: Norton, 1970.

    Baroque quality of lines 51–64 (p. 203).

288. Bush, Douglas. "An Allusion in Milton's *Elegia tertia*." *Harvard Library Bulletin*, 9 (1955), 392–96.

    Suggests James I and Maurice, Prince of Orange, as the figures alluded to in lines 9–10.

289. Stroup, Thomas B. *Religious Rite and Ceremony in Milton's Poetry*. Lexington: University of Kentucky Press, 1968.

    Lines 63–64, though based on Revelation, xiv, 13, may have been inspired by John Buckridge's funeral sermon for Andrewes (p. 13).

290. Le Comte, Edward [S.] "Sly Milton: The Meaning Lurking in the Context of His Quotations." *English Studies Collections*, 5 (1976), 1–15. Rev. version, *Greyfriar*, 19 (1978), 3–28.

    Opening of the article (expanded in the rev. version, pp. 1–7) outlines and examines parallels between Ovid, *Amores*, 1,5 and the second (and "better") half of *El.* 3.

4. *El.* 4

291. Dunster, Charles. *Considerations on Milton's Early Reading*. London: John Nichols, 1800.

Lines 29–32, *pace* Warton (no. 21), show M.'s gratitude not only for his first introduction to the classics but also for his initiation into "sacred poesy" (p. 231).

292. Stern, Alfred. [Review of no. 25, 1874 ed.]. *Göttingische Gelehrte Anzeigen,* [127] (1875), 833–45.

     Dates *El.* 4 to 1625 on the basis of *Ep. Fam.* 1 (pp. 842–44).

293. Fletcher, Harris [Francis]. "Milton and Thomas Young." *TLS,* 21 January 1926, p. 44.

     Interprets lines 33–38 as indicating that the poem was written before 26 March (1625, following Stern).

294. Grierson, H[erbert] J.C. "Milton and Thomas Young." *TLS,* 11 February 1926, p. 99.

     Response to no. 293. Prefers traditional dating to 1627 because of M.'s age date for the poem.

295. Barker, Arthur [E.] "Milton's Schoolmasters." *MLR,* 32 (1937), 517–36.

     Modifies view expressed in no. 291 by generalizing from "poesy" to "composition" (p. 517, n. 2).

296. Parker, William Riley. "Milton and Thomas Young, 1620–1628." *MLN,* 53 (1938), 399–407.

     Lines 29–38 mean that M. was either Y.'s first or his foremost student of classical literature (p. 403, n. 6; with the assistance of E. K. Rand); poem composed between 21 March and 28 April 1627 (p. 406).

297. Ochi, Fumio. ["Milton and Thomas Young—Viewed through Tutorship"]. In [*Essays and Studies in Honor of Professor Funahashi*]. Doshisha: The English Literary Society of Doshisha University, 1939. Pp. 49–68. Rpt. in no. 362, pp. 25–44.

     In Japanese.

5. *El.* 5

a. Translations

298. Symmons, Charles, Jr. Verse tr. of lines 1–30. In no. 113 (2d ed., pp. 540–43; 3d ed., pp. 404–05).

299. Boyd, H[enry]. "Part of the Fifth Elegy of Milton Imitated." *PRR,* [8] (1810–11; printed 1814), 181–83.

     Verse adaptations of lines 1–24, 25–30, 31–78.

300. Wassenberg, Franz. "*Frühlings Nahen.* Aus dem Lateinischen des John Milton." *Archiv für das Studium der neueren Sprachen und Literaturen,* 60 (1878), 122–25.

     Verse tr. of the entire poem.

301. Waddell, Helen. "The Coming of Spring." *The Listener,* 4 (1930), 1091.

Verse adaptations of lines 1–52, 55–66, 79–94. Revised version as two separate poems, "Spring Song" and "Spring Time," in her *More Latin Lyrics* (New York: Norton, 1977), pp. 357, 359–61.

See also: no. **306.**

b. Illustrations

302. Westall, Richard. "Elegia Quinta." In *The Poetical Works of John Milton.* London: Printed by W. Bulmer and Co. for John and Josiah Boydell and George Nicol, 1794–7. III, facing p. 247. Mediocre reproduction, entitled "Latin Elegia V: Pan and Syrinx [!]," in *The Complete Poems of John Milton* (New York: Crown [also in reduced format under Crown's Bonanza Books imprint], 1936; p. [648].

Sometimes referred to as "Sylvanus and the Violence in the Night." Faunus, in a grove and carrying his oread, stands over a drunken Sylvanus; two fleeing nymphs look back at the scene (lines 119–32). For comment, see the Birmingham [England] Public Library's catalogue, *Milton Illustrated: Visions of Paradise* (Birmingham: Birmingham Public Library, 1978), p. 31.

c. Comment

303. C[alton], J. [Article on readings in the text of *Gorboduc*]. *The History of the Works of the Learned,* 8 (July, 1740), pp. 1–12.

Explicates the mythological references in lines 49–54 (p. 4).

304. Sledd, James. "A Note on the Use of Renaissance Dictionaries." *MP,* 49 (1951–52), 10–15.

Supplements Harding (no. **94**) on *Lycaonius* in line 35 (pp. 11–12).

305. Lievsay, John Leon. "Milton among the Nightingales." *RenP,* 1958–60, pp. 36–45.

Read in 1959. Ovidian and non-Ovidian elements in lines 25–28; line 26 directly translated by M. at *Sonnet I,* line 2 (pp. 39–40).

306. Broadbent, J. B. "The Nativity Ode." In Frank Kermode, ed. *The Living Milton.* London: Routledge & Kegan Paul, 1960. Pp. 12–31.

Contrasts lines 55–60 with the Nativity ode, 32–44; prose tr. of the passage (p. 21).

307. Woodhouse, A. S. P. *The Poet and His Faith: Religion and Poetry in England from Spenser to Eliot and Auden.* Chicago: University of Chicago Press, 1965.

Poem suggests, "even in its imagery," Swinburne's "When the hounds of spring are on winter's traces" (p. 92).

308. Skulsky, Harold. "Milton's Enrichment of Latin Love Elegy." In J. IJsewijn and E. Kessler, eds. *Acta Conventus Neo-Latini Lovaniensis: Proceedings of the First International Congress of Neo-Latin Studies, Louvain 23–28 August 1971.* Louvain: Leuven University Press, 1973. Pp. 603–11.

Poem's underlying theme the association of the renewals of cosmic amorousness, of just order, and of prophetic vision; its treatment thereof a Miltonic solution to the Renaissance problem of adapting classical genres.

6. *El. 6*

a. Translations

309. Wrangham, Francis. Verse tr. of the entire poem. In No. 113 (1st ed., pp. 165–69; 2d ed., pp. 207–14; 3d ed., pp. 144–47). Rpt. in his *Sermons Practical and Occasional* (see no. 470), III, pp. 290–95.

b. Comment

310. Yoneyama, Hiroshi. ["Milton's Latin Poem: *Elegia sexta*"]. *Aries* (Kwansei Gakuin University), no. 3 (Nov. 1936), 74–82.

   In Japanese.

311. Fink, Z. S. "Wine, Poetry, and Milton's *Elegia Sexta.*" *English Studies*, 21 (1939), 164–65.

   M.'s references to wine as a source of poetic inspiration glossed with examples of Renaissance poetic doctrine.

312. Leishman, J. B. "*L'Allegro* and *Il Penseroso* in Their Relation to Seventeenth-Century Poetry." In English Association, *Essays and Studies*, n. s. 4 (1951), 1–36. Rpt. in Alan Rudrum, ed., *Milton: Modern Judgements* (London: Macmillan, 1968), pp. 58–93; and in no. 237, pp. 120–59.

   Refutes Bateson (no. 202) on the poem's referring to the companion pieces; translates parts of line 89 and refers it to the Nativity ode (p. 2, n. 1; no. 237, p. 121).

313. Carey, John. "The Date of Milton's Italian Poems." *RES*, n. s. 14 (1963), 383–86.

   Another answer to no. 202: the reference in lines 89–90 is to M.'s Italian verse.

314. Steadman, John M. "Chaste Muse and 'Casta Juventus': Milton, Minturno, and Scaliger on Inspiration and the Poet's Character." *Italica*, 40 (1963), 28–34.

   M.'s distinction between spiritual and secular types of poetic inspiration discussed in relation to the poem and to Renaissance poetical theory.

315. Koehler, G. Stanley. "Milton's Use of Color and Light." In *Milton Studies*, III, ed. James D. Simmonds. Pittsburgh: University of Pittsburgh Press, 1971. Pp. 55–81.

   sanguine nigro in line 75 an imitation of the Homeric practice of calling blood "black" (p. 68).

316. Bouchard, Donald F. *Milton: A Structural Reading.* Montreal: McGill-Queens University Press; London: Edward Arnold, 1974.

Treatment of death in lines 71–78 "merely a game" meant to enhance the power of the virtuous poet as exemplified by Homer (p. 33).

317. Hieatt, A. Kent. *Chaucer, Spenser, Milton: Mythopoeic Continuities and Transformations.* Montreal: McGill-Queens University Press, 1975.

The Odysseus matter in lines 71–76 perhaps meant by M., in the context of his epic plans, as "emblematic of the two sides of heroic life"; they and the heroic subjects of lines 55–58 suggest Spenserian influence on M.'s thoughts.

318. Roberts, Gareth. "Three Notes on Uses of Circe by Spenser, Marlowe, and Milton." *N&Q*, n. s. 25 (1978), 433–35.

Possible sources for Hecate's parentage as given in line 73 (p. 435).

319. Low, Anthony. "The Unity of Milton's *Elegia Sexta.*" *ELR*, 11 (1981), 213–23.

Poem unified by its festive spirit and by its structure.

320. Miller, Leo. "Milton's *patriis cicutis.*" *N&Q,*, n. s. 28 (1981), 41–42.

Similar wording in a Latin poem by May supports the view that the reference in lines 89–90 is to the Nativity ode.

7. *El.* 7 (including *Postscr.*)

321. Saunders, J. W. "Milton, Diomede and Amaryllis." *ELH*, 22 (1955), 254–86.

Biographical interpretation of *Postscr.* (pp. 258–60).

322. Potter, Lois. *A Preface to Milton.* London: Longman; New York: Scribner's, 1971.

Postscr. in relation to *El.* 7 and M.'s development; its tone "facetious" (p. 84).

323. Martyn, J. R. C. "Milton's Elegia Septima." In J. IJsewijn and E. Kessler, eds. *Acta Conventus Neo-Latini Lovaniensis.* (See no. 308). Pp. 381–87.

Analysis of the poem's structure, prosody, imagery, and tone (ironic); *Postscr.* not an apology.

8. Gunpowder epigrams

a. Translations

324. Brittain, Frederick, ed. and tr. *The Penguin Book of Latin Verse.* Harmondsworth: Penguin, 1962.

Prose tr. of *Prod. Bomb.* 1 on p. 325, preceded by text of the poem.

b. Comment

325. MacKellar, Walter. "Milton, James I, and Purgatory." *MLR*, 18 (1923), 472–73.

Prod. Bomb. 3, 1 a reference to James's dismissal of Purgatory in the 2d ed. of his *Apologie for the Oath of Allegiance.*

326. Gallagher, Philip J. "*Paradise Lost* and the Greek Theogony." *ELR*, 9 (1979), 121–48.

    Inv. Bomb. shows an unfavorable view of Prometheus (p. 147, n. 52).

327. Shawcross, John T. *With Mortal Voice: The Creation of* Paradise Lost. Lexington: The University Press of Kentucky, 1982.

    Inv. Bomb. shows the Son of God as superior to Prometheus (p. 187, n. 16).

9. *Leon.* 1–3.

a. *Translations*

328. Liebert, Gustav. *Milton: Studien zur Geschichte des englischen Geistes.* Hamburg: Otto Meissner, 1860.

    Verse tr. of *Leon.* 1 (p. 45).

See also: nos. **160, 331.**

b. *Comment*

329. Barker, E. H. "Error in Milton's Latinity Noticed, and Passages in Milton, Sophocles, and Aeschylus, Explained by the Doctrine of the Association of Ideas." *Classical Journal*, 7 (1813), 393–98.

    Questions use of *et* before *propter* in *Leon.* 2, 4; condemns use of *sibi* in *Leon.* 2, 12 (p. 394).

330. L[amb, Charles]. "Nugae Criticae, By the Author of Elia. No. I: Defence of the Sonnets of Sir Philip Sydney." *London Magazine*, 8 (July–Dec. 1823), no. 45, pp. 248–52. Rpt. as "Some Sonnets of Sir Philip Sydney" in his *The Last Essays of Elia* (London: Edward Moxon, 1833; standard modern ed. in E. V. Lucas, ed., *The Works of Charles and Mary Lamb* [London: Methuen, 1903–5], II, pp. 213–20); also in Roy Park, ed., *Lamb as Critic* (Lincoln: University of Nebraska Press, 1980), no. 17, pp. 170–03.

    Leon. 1 a near-blasphemous expression of the poet's love.

331. Ademollo, A[lessandro]. *La Leonora di Milton e di Clemente IX.* Milano: Ricordi, 1885.

    Although Leonora not likely to be the lady of the Italian verses, *Leon.* 1–3 show in their admiration M.'s love for their dedicatee; prose trs. of all three poems (pp. 8–10).

332. Pommrich, [Woldemar] Ewald. *Miltons Verhältnis zu Torquato Tasso.* Halle: Druck von Ehrhardt Karras, 1902.

    Nature of the Tasso reference in *Leon.* 2 makes it probable that *Leon.* 1–3 were composed in 1639 during M.'s second stay in Rome, i.e., after his conversations with Manso (pp. 9–10).

333. West, Robert H. *Milton and the Angels.* Athens: The University of Georgia Press, 1955.

    M.'s use of the Catholic idea of guardian angels at *Leon.* 1, 1–2 merely fanciful.

10. *Apol.*

334. Fletcher, Harris [Francis]. "Milton's *Apologus* and Its Mantuan [*sic*] Model." *JEGP*, 55 (1956), 230–33.

   Source is a fable from Mantuan's *Sylvae*.

11. *Q. Nov.*

a. *Translations*

See: no. 166.

b. *Comment*

335. Grosart, A. B., ed. *The Poems of Phineas Fletcher, B.D.* N. p., 1869. 4 vols.

   Pace Warton (no. 21), poem not influenced by Fletcher's *Locustae*, as the latter was published after *Q. Nov.* was written (I, pp. cccxviii–ix).

336. Gilbert, Allan H. "The Tower of Fame in Milton." *MLN*, 28 (1913), 30.

   Defends the reading *Mareotidas* at line 171.

337. Mutschmann, H[einrich]. *Milton's Projected Epic on the Rise and Future Greatness of the Britannic Nation.* Acta et Commentationes Universitatis Tartuensis (Dorpatensis), B: Humaniora, vol. 40, no. 1. Tartu: [the University], 1936.

   Poem inspired by one of the illustrations in printed accounts of the Gunpowder Plot; its "photophobic" character seen in the dark settings of its real action; correspondences with *Paradise Lost* (pp. 52–54).

338. Starnes, D[e Witt] T. "More About the Tower of Fame in Milton." *N&Q*, 196 (1951), 515–18. Expanded slightly in no. 96, pp. 253–56.

   Location of the tower described in lines 170–73; M.'s treatment of Fame perhaps indebted to Perotti's *Cornucopiae*, s.v. *Fama.*

339. Jeffrey, Lloyd N. "Virgil and Milton." *Classical Outlook*, 31 (1954), 69–70.

   Resemblance between lines 139–54 and Virgil, *Aen.* 6, 268–81.

340. Cheek, Macon. "Milton's 'In Quintum Novembris': An Epic Foreshadowing." *SP*, 54 (1957), 172–84.

   Virgilian elements in the poem (language, style, epic technique); aspects of Satan's characterization in relation to *Paradise Lost.*

341. Visiak, E. H. *The Portent of Milton: Some Aspects of His Genius.* London: Werner Laurie, 1958.

   Poem's attack on the Pope against a type, not an individual (p. 89).

342. Kastor, Frank S. *Milton and the Literary Satan.* Amsterdam: Rodopi, 1974.

   Satan's treatment in the poem discussed in terms of a role typology established earlier in the book: S. both "Prince of Hell" and "Tempter" (pp. 95–96).

343. Tung, Mason. "Milton's Adaptation in *In quintum Novembris* of Virgil's *Fama.*" *MQ*, 12 (1978), 90–95.

Compares lines 172–216 with Virgil, *Aen.* 4, 174–88.

344. Creaser, John. "Textual Cruces in Milton's Shorter Poems." *N&Q*, n. s. 29 (1982), 26–28.

Favors text of no. 17 at lines 147–50 (correction in no. 18 not authoritative).

12. *Naturam* and *Idea*

a. Translations

345. Boyd, H[enry]. "Nature Not Liable to Decay. From a College Exercise in Latin Verse by *Milton*." *PRR*, [5] (1805; printed 1810), 32–36.

Verse tr. of *Naturam*, entire.

346. Lewis, C. S. "From the Latin of Milton's *De Idea Platonica quemadmodum Aristoteles intellexit.*" *English*, 5 (1944–45), 195.

Verse tr. of *Idea*, 1–34, with appreciative comment.

b. Comment

347. Milton, John. *Ep. Fam.* 3 [letter to Alexander Gill, dated 2 July 1628]. In *Epistolarum Familiarium liber unus* (see no. 104), pp. 10–12; no. 32, XII, pp. 8–13.

Describes his verses written for the Cambridge great commencement of 1628 (generally taken, since Warton [no. 21], to be *Naturam*, though others consider *Idea* also a possibility).

348. Coleridge, Samuel Taylor. [Marginalium in vol. 5 of a set of Anderson's *British Poets* now in the Victoria and Albert Museum, p. 193]. Rpts. in Raysor and in Brinkley (see no. 121), pp. 190 and 552, respectively; and in Kathleen Coburn, ed., *The Collected Works of Samuel Taylor Coleridge* (Princeton: Princeton University Press, 1969–), XII (*Marginalia*, ed. George Whalley, vol. 1), p. 73, no. 30.

Idea a burlesque not of Plato but, instead, of the Aristotelian view of P.'s theory of ideas. Written *ca.* 1807.

349. Ferguson, A. S. "'Paradise Lost,' IV, 977–1015." *MLR*, 15 (1920), 168–70.

Naturam, 29–36 gives a cosmic setting to the image in Virgil, *Aen.* 12, 725–27 (p. 169).

350. Reiss, Edmund. "An Instance of Milton's Use of Time." *MLN*, 72 (1957), 410–12.

Naturam, 14–15 show M.'s view of time as a divine creation existing before the world.

351. Costello, William T. *The Scholastic Curriculum at Early Seventeenth-Century Cambridge.* Cambridge: Harvard University Press, 1958.

Naturam and *Idea* in the context of verses at disputations (pp. 17–19).

352. Zwicky, Laurie Bowman. *Milton's Use of Time: Image and Principle.* Ph.D. diss., The University of Oklahoma, 1959.

Rebuts no. **350**: M. using the Platonic identification of time and the motion of the heavenly bodies, in which sense "the heavens are the father of time" (pp. 59–62).

353. Hardison, O. B., Jr. "Milton's 'On Time' and Its Scholastic Background." *Texas Studies in Literature and Language*, 3 (1961–62), 107–22.

Naturam inconsistent in accepting the doctrine of the end of the world at the Last Judgment (pp. 121–22).

354. Shawcross, John T. "The Dating of Certain Poems, Letters, and Prolusions Written by Milton." *ELN*, 2 (1964–65), 261–66.

Dates *Naturam* and *Idea* to 1631 (pp. 263–64).

355. Via, John A[lbert]. "The Rhythm of Regenerate Experience: *L'Allegro* and *Il Penseroso*." *RenP*, 1969, pp. 47–55.

Opening movement of *Naturam* characterized by "ugliness" (p. 47).

356. Erlich, Victor. "Milton's Early Poetry: Its Christian Humanism." *American Imago*, 32 (1975), 77–112.

Naturam, 1–3 perhaps M.'s best description of the "eternal struggle to outgrow the oedipal victimization by one's parents" and a good introduction to all of M.'s early poetry (pp. 111–12).

13. *Patrem*

a. *Translations*

357. Burney, Charles. *A General History of Music, from the Earliest Ages to the Present Period*. London: Printed for the Author, 1776–89. 4 vols. Modern ed. by Frank Mercer (New York: Harcourt, Brace and Company, 1935). 2 vols.

Verse tr. of lines 55–66 (III, p. 135 [Mercer ed., II, p. 116], note z; rpt. in no. 361, p. 126, n. 11).

358. Cirillo, Albert R. Verse tr. of lines 17–23. In no. 7, IV, 40.

b. *Comment*

359. Thompson, Elbert N. S. *Essays on Milton*. New Haven: Yale University Press, 1914.

Poem "as much an apology for disregard of parental wishes as an elaborate compliment and expression of gratitude" (p. 39).

360. Fletcher, Harris [Francis]. "Grierson's Suggested Date for Milton's 'Ad Patrem.'" In Clarence D. Thorpe and Charles E. Whitmore, eds., *The Fred Newton Scott Anniversary Papers*. Chicago: The University of Chicago Press, 1929. Pp. 199–205.

Argues for 1640.

361. Brennecke, Ernest, Jr. *John Milton the Elder and His Music*. Columbia University Studies in Musicology, vol. 2. New York: Columbia University Press, 1938.

Poem discussed in light of the conflict from which it arose; appreciative comments (pp. 121–27).

362. Ochi, Fumio. [*Milton in His Younger Days — In Relation to His Friend, Teacher, and Father*]. Doshisha: Doshisha English Society, 1939; rpt. in no. 207, pp. 19–73.

["Milton and His Father"], pp. 45–60. In Japanese. Has tr. of no. 183 and rpt. of no. 297.

363. Little, Marguerite. "Milton's *Ad Patrem* and the Younger Gill's *In Natalem Mei Parentis.*" *JEGP*, 49 (1950), 345–51.

Gill's poem a possible inspirational source.

364. Barnett, H. A. "A Time of the Year for Milton's 'Ad Patrem.'" *MLN*, 73 (1958), 82–83.

Lines 38–40 indicate that the poem was written in early spring.

365. Shawcross, John T. "The Date of Milton's 'Ad Patrem.'" *N&Q*, n. s. 6 (1959), 358–59.

Reply to no. 205. Dates the poem to 1638.

366. Sirluck, Ernest. "Milton's Idle Right Hand." *JEGP*, 60 (1961), 749–85. Also in *Milton Studies in Honor of Harris Francis Fletcher* (Urbana: University of Illinois Press, 1961 [a rpt. of the Oct. 1961 issue of *JEGP*]), pp. 141–77.

Appendix, "Some Recent Suggested Changes in the Chronology of Milton's Poems," summarizes positions and dates the poem to 1637 or 1638 (pp. 784–85; rpt., pp. 176–77); supporting argument in main article (pp. 766–67; rpt., pp. 158–59).

367. Bush, Douglas. "The Date of Milton's *Ad Patrem*." *MP*, 61 (1963–64), 204–08.

Argues for 1631 or 1632.

368. Carey, John. "Milton's *Ad Patrem*, 35–37." *RES*, n. s. 15 (1964), 180–84.

Fiery spirit of these lines is M.'s disembodied soul; similarity to a passage in *Of Reformation* suggests a late date for the poem.

369. Kerrigan, William. *The Prophetic Milton*. Charlottesville: University Press of Virginia, 1974.

Lines 103–04 express a view that is not only elitist but also defensive (p. 123).

370. Hill, John Spencer. "Poet-Priest: Vocational Tension in Milton's Early Development." In *Milton Studies*, VIII, ed. James D. Simmonds. Pittsburgh: University of Pittsburgh Press, 1975. Pp. 41–69.

Poem most probably written in 1637 or 1638 (pp. 60–62).

371. Tobin, J. J. M. "'Metamorphoses' XI: An Influence on Milton's 'Ad Patrem.'" *N&Q*, n. s. 24 (1977), 206.

Imagery at line 107 partly derived from Ovid, *Met.* 11, 56–60, with the personification of Calumnia coming from Sandys's commentary in his 1632 *Ovid's Metamorphosis* (which would exclude a date earlier than June 1632).

372. Radzinowicz, Mary Ann. *Toward* Samson Agonistes: *The Growth of Milton's Mind.* Princeton: Princeton University Press, 1978.

Poem analyzed as a self-deprecatory debate on divine poetry and M.'s earliest attempts thereat (esp. his English trs. of Psalms 114 and 146); its date, stanzaic organization, purpose, and genre (pp. 190–93).

14. Greek pieces

a. Translations

373. Cowper, William. Verse trs. of *Phil. Reg.* and *Effig.* In British Library Add. MS. 30801, foll. 61–2. First printed in J. C. Bailey, ed., *The Poems of William Cowper* (London: Methuen, 1905), pp. 596–97, 726; rpt. in H. S. Milford, ed., *Cowper: Poetical Works,* 4th ed. with corrections and additions by Norma Russell (see no. 45), pp. 646–47.

Written in 1791–92. Two versions of *Effig.*, the later one ascribed by Bailey to William Hayley. Note by Cowper saying that *Ps. 114* needs no translation.

See also: nos. 4, 112, 377, 379, 380.

b. Comment

374. Milton, John. *Ep. Fam.* 5 [letter to Alexander Gill, dated 4 Dec. 1634]. In *Epistolarum Familiarium liber unus* (see no. 104), pp. 13–14; no. 32, XII, pp. 14–17.

Ps. 114, characterized as a recent, impulsive effort by one who is out of practice, is M.'s first and only composition in Greek since leaving St. Paul's.

375. Burney, Charles, [Jr.] *Remarks on the Greek Verses of Milton.* London: n. p., 1790. Rpts. in no. 21 [2d ed.], pp. 591–605; and in no. 22 [1st ed.], VI, pp. 275–91, [2d ed.], VII, pp. 277–99.

Critical evaluations of the poems; observations on grammatical and stylistic details.

376. Butcher, S. H. ["Remarks on Milton's Greek Verses"]. In no. 25 (1890 ed.), III, pp. 345–46.

General comments on each piece; criticism of diction, grammar, and metrics.

377. Mabbott, T[homas] O[llive]. "Milton's 'In Effigiei Ejus Sculptorem.'" *Explicator,* 8 (1949–50), item 58.

Poem intentionally ambiguous in that the portrait may be a bad picture by and of its engraver; verse tr. of the whole piece.

378. Goldman, Jack. *Milton's Knowledge of Hebrew and His Renditions of the Psalms.* Ph.D. diss., University of Detroit, 1973.

Has close comparison of *Ps. 114* with the Hebrew original.

379. Goldman, Jack. "Milton's Intrusion of Abraham and Isaac upon Psalm 114." *PQ*, 55 (1976), 117–26.

    M.'s view of the psalm as seen in his departures from the Hebrew original and in their likely sources in Judeo-Christian exegesis. Prose tr. of the poem (p. 118).

380. Hale, John K. "Milton's Greek Epigram." *MQ*, 16 (1982), 8–9.

    Pace nos. 376 and 377, Greek *men/de* does not require a contrast; *Effig.*'s second couplet intensifies the first and the epigram is thus successful in regard to form. Prose tr. of the piece.

15. *Mans.*

a. Editions

381. Laurens, Pierre, ed. and tr. *Musae Reduces: Anthologie de la Poésie Latine de l'Europe de la Renaissance.* Leiden: E. J. Brill, 1975. 2 vols.

    Mans. edited and translated in prose (II, pp. 455–63; notes to the poem, p. 523).

b. Translations

382. Sterling, Joseph. "Manso; from the Latin of Milton." In his *Poems.* Dublin: Printed by Joseph Hill, 1782. Pp. 84–88 (pp. 87–88 misnumbered 85–86). Rpt., with revisions, in his *Poems* (London: Printed for G. G. J. and J. Robinson, 1789), pp. 190–93.

    Verse tr. of the whole poem. Translator's name sometimes incorrectly given as "Stirling."

383. Cowper, William. "Stanzas on the Late Indecent Liberties Taken with the Remains of the Great Milton." In William Hayley, *The Life, and Posthumous Writings, of William Cowper.* Chichester: J. Seagrave for J. Johnson, London, 1803–06. II, pp. 296–97. Rpt. in H. S. Milford, ed., *Cowper: Poetical Works,* 4th ed. with corrections and additions by Norma Russell (see no. 45), pp. 398–99.

    Written in 1790. Lines 1–8 an expanded tr. of *Mans.,* 91–93.

See also: no. 381.

c. Comment

384. [Phillips, Edward]. "The Life of Mr. John Milton." In his tr. of M.'s *Letters of State.* London: n. p., 1694. Pp. i–[liv]. Standard modern ed. in Helen Darbishire, ed., *The Early Lives of Milton* (London: Constable, 1932; several times reissued), pp. 48–82.

    Calls poem an "Eclogue," perhaps viewing it as pastoral (p. xiv; Darbishire, p. 58).

385. Hunt, Leigh. "An Essay on the Cultivation, History, and Varieties of the

Species of Poem Called the Sonnet." In Hunt and S. Adams Lee, eds., *The Book of the Sonnet.* Boston: Roberts Brothers; London: S. Low, son and Marston, 1867. I, pp. 1–91.

Praise of Marino in lines 9–12 less than the preceding praise of Tasso; *prolixus* in line 11 ambiguous (pp. 42–43).

386. Tillyard, E. M. W. "The Christ of *Paradise Regained* and the Renaissance Heroic Tradition." *SP*, 36 (1939), 247–52. Rpt. in his *Studies in Milton* (London: Chatto & Windus, 1951; several times reissued), pp. 100–106.

Arthurian heroes of lines 80–84 examples of Christian Aristotelian magnanimity but hardly passive ones (p. 249; rpt., p. 102).

387. Fink, Z. S. "Milton and the Theory of Climatic Influence." *MLQ*, 2 (1941), 67–80.

Lines 24–43 in view of this theory, which M. clearly shared (pp. 71–72).

388. King, James Roy. "Psyche's Tasks—Milton's Sense of Self." In his *Studies in Six 17th Century Writers.* Athens: Ohio University Press, 1966. Pp. 193–218.

Lines 30–31 exemplify M.'s "constant celebration of the personality that comes to know itself and to value its own inner consistency" (p. 214).

389. Condee, Ralph W[aterbury]. "'Mansus' and the Panegyric Tradition." *Studies in the Renaissance*, 15 (1968), 174–92. Rpt. in no. 252, pp. 85–103.

Poem rearranges the topoi of the panegyric and reverses the traditional role of the *personae* to create a vision of a transcendent universe peopled by good men like Manso and united by the values of trust, respect, and affection.

16. *Ep. Dam.*

a. *Editions*

390. [Milton, John]. *Epitaphium Damonis.* [London: n. p., 1640?]. Reproduced in nos. 35 and 392.

The separate first printing. Only known surviving copy is in the British Library (pressmark: C.57.d.48).

391. Jerram, C. S., ed. *The Lycidas and Epitaphium Damonis of Milton.* London: Longmans, Green and Co., 1874; rev. ed., 1881.

Ep. Dam. treated in the introduction, pp. 31–36; text and notes, pp. 109–25. Verse trs. by Symmons and by Masson (see nos. 113, 135); pp. 126–33, 134–41. Page refs. the same in the rev. ed.; notes revised to take account of Masson's in no. 25 (1874, 3-volume ed.).

392. [Pollard, A. W.], ed. *John Milton's Epitaphium Damonis. Printed from the First Edition. With a New Translation by Walter W. Skeat.* Cambridge: Cambridge University Press, 1933.

Corrects five misprints and expands a contraction; otherwise a facsimile of the text of no. 390. Skeat's verse tr. revised in no. 50.

393. Harrison, Thomas Perrin, Jr., ed. *The Pastoral Elegy: An Anthology. English Translations by Harry Joshua Leon.* Austin: The University of Texas, 1939.

Text and Leon's prose tr., pp. 208–20; commentary and notes, pp. 293–97.

b. Translations

394. Langhorne, John. "The Pastoral Part of Milton's Epitaphium Damonis." In his *The Correspondence of Theodosius and Constantia, From Their First Acquaintance to the Departure of Theodosius.* London: Printed for T. Becket and P. A. Dehondt, 1765. Pp. 101–10 ("Letter XII"). Rpts. in Robert Anderson, ed., *The Works of the British Poets* (London: Printed for John & Arthur Arch, etc., 1795), XI, pp. 246–48; and in Alexander Chalmers, ed., *The Works of the English Poets* (London: Printed for J. Johnson, etc., 1810), XVI, pp. 462–63.

Verse tr. of lines 1–138.

395. Dermody, Thomas. "Milton's Epitaphium Damonis Translated." In his *The Harp of Erin.* London: Printed for Richard Phillips, 1807. I, pp. 266–87.

Written late 1785 or early 1786. Verse tr. of entire poem.

396. Gifford, William, verse tr. of lines 37–42, in no. 113, 2d ed. only, p. 188.

397. Auchmuty, Arthur Compton, tr. *Milton's* Epitaphium Damonis, *A.D. 1639.* Leominster: The Orphans' Printing Press, [1884].

Verse tr. of entire poem.

398. Waddell, Helen. Lament for Damon *Translated from the* Epitaphium Damonis *of John Milton.* N. p., 1943. Rpts. in *UTQ,* 16 (1946–47), 341–48, with a prefatory note by A. S. P. Woodhouse; in C. A. Patrides, ed., *Milton's* Lycidas: *The Tradition and the Poem* (New York: Holt, Rinehart, and Winston, 1961), pp. 19–26; and in her *More Latin Lyrics* (see no. 301), pp. 338–55.

Verse tr. of the entire poem, preceded by an introduction (lacking in the Woodhouse and Patrides rpts.) rebutting Johnson (no. 108) and commenting on M.'s use of pastoral convention and the Latin language to both mask and release his grief. Dame Felicitas Corrigan's introduction to *More Latin Lyrics* quotes W. as calling the poem "the one thing I know of Milton's that has real anguish in it" (p. 21). *Argumentum* not translated.

399. Blunden, Edmund. "Some Seventeenth-Century Latin Poems by English Writers." *UTQ,* 25 (1955–56), 10–22.

Verse tr. of entire poem, pp. 16–22, with prefatory remarks on the unsuitability of certain verse forms for this purpose. *Argumentum* not translated.

400. Kluncker, Karlhans. "Grabschrift für Damon: erste deutsche Übersetzung." *Castrum Peregrini,* 96 (1971), 66–89.

Verse tr. of entire poem, including eight pages of notes. Preceded (pp. 57–64) by a popularly written introduction, "Zu John Milton's 'Epitaphium Damonis.'"

401. Baldi, Sergio. "L' 'Epitaffio per Damone' di Giovanni Milton." *L'Albero*, 26 (1977), 11–27.

Verse tr. of entire poem. Introduction (pp. 11–21) offers interpretations of concealed bucolic references.

See also: nos. **392, 393.**

c. Comment

402. Black, John. *Life of Torquato Tasso.* Edinburgh: James Ballantyne for J. Murray, 1810. 2 vols.

Cups in lines 181ff. may be Manso's *Poesie nomiche* and *Erocallia* (II, p. 467, note).

403. Lloyd, Mary, ed. *Elegies: Ancient and Modern.* Trenton: Albert Brandt, 1903. "Volume 1" [all published].

Brief remarks on the poem and on some of its translations (pp. 92–93).

404. Hanford, James Holly. "The Pastoral Elegy and Milton's *Lycidas*." *PMLA*, 25 (1910), 403–47. Rpt. in his *John Milton, Poet and Humanist* (see no. 164), pp. 126–60; and, with editorial revisions including the loss of some footnotes, in C. A. Patrides, ed., *Milton's* Lycidas: *The Tradition and the Poem* (see no. 398), pp. 27–55.

M.'s relationship to the classical and Renaissance tradition of the pastoral lament. Poem discussed on pp. 408–09, 414–16, 430, 432, 446.

405. Kerlin, Robert Thomas. *Theocritus in English Literature.* Lynchburg, VA: J. P. Bell Company, 1910.

Theocritean elements in the poem; possible influence of Daniel Heinsius' 1604 ed. of that poet (pp. 40–41).

406. Myers, Weldon T. *The Relations of Latin and English as Living Languages in England During the Age of Milton.* [Dayton, VA: Ruebush-Elkins Co., printers, 1913].

M.'s use of English in *Lycidas* and Latin in this poem (p. 49).

407. Grierson, Herbert J. C. *Cross Currents in English Literature of the XVIIth Century.* London: Chatto & Windus, 1929; frequently reissued; rpt., Harmondsworth: Penguin, 1966.

Coldness and egotism in the poem (p. 243; Penguin rpt., pp. 229–30).

408. Bradner, Leicester. "Milton's 'Epitaphium Damonis.'" *TLS*, 18 August 1932, p. 581.

Announcement and description of the newly found copy of no. **390**, dating it to 1639 or 1640.

409. Anon. "Milton's *Epitaphium Damonis*." *British Museum Quarterly*, 7 (1932–33), 42.

Notice of Bradner's discovery; item purchased in 1857 as a work of Milton's but not so catalogued.

410. Gottfried, Rudolf. "Milton, Lactantius, Claudian, and Tasso." *SP*, 30 (1933), 497–503.

Tasso's description of the phoenix in his *Sette Giornate del Mondo Creato*, based on Lactantius and Claudian, may have influenced lines 185–89, which also draw directly on the same sources.

411. Harrison, Thomas Perrin, Jr. "The Latin Pastorals of Milton and Castiglione." *PMLA*, 50 (1935), 480–93.

Parallels between the poem and C.'s *Alcon*.

412. De Filippis, Michele. "Milton and Manso: Cups or Books?" *PMLA*, 51 (1936), 745–56.

Argues in favor of Black's hypothesis (no. **402**).

413. Dorian, Donald C[layton]. "Milton's *Epitaphium Damonis*, lines 181–197." *PMLA*, 54 (1939), 612–13.

Adduces Pindar, *Ol.* 7, 1–10, as additional evidence in support of De Filippis (no. **412**).

414. Whiting, George Wesley. *Milton's Literary Milieu*. Chapel Hill: The University of North Carolina Press, 1939.

Melancholy in the poem (pp. 143–45).

415. Egle, Artur. *Milton und Italien*. Freiburg im Breisgau: Druck von Rudolf Goldschagg, 1940.

Detailed survey (pp. 40–43) of the arguments on the matter of the cups in lines 181ff. "Cups or books" question probably unanswerable.

416. Montgomery, Walter A. "The *Epitaphium Damonis* in the Stream of Classical Lament." In Nathaniel M. Caffee and Thomas A. Kirby, eds. *Studies for William A. Read*. University, LA: Louisiana State University Press, 1940. Pp. 207–20.

Sets the poem against its classical background in a rather general way. *Ep. Dam.* an exception to M.'s usually pedestrian Latin verse.

417. Barker, Arthur E. *Milton and the Puritan Dilemma 1640–1661*. Toronto: University of Toronto Press, 1942; several times reissued.

Connects stress on Damon's virginity at the end of the poem with the antiprelatical tracts (p. 14).

418. Bush, Douglas. *English Literature in the Earlier Seventeenth Century 1600–1660*. The Oxford History of English Literature, vol. 5. Oxford: Clarendon Press, 1945; 2d ed., rev., 1962.

Unfavorable assessment of the poem (p. 368; 2d ed., pp. 387–88).

419. Woodhouse, A. S. P. "Milton's Pastoral Monodies." In Mary E. White, ed. *Studies in Honour of Gilbert Norwood.* Toronto: University of Toronto Press, 1952. Pp. 261–78. Rpt., with minor alterations, in no. 246, pp. 83–98.

     Analysis of the poem (pp. 263–72; rpt., pp. 84–92).

420. Shawcross, John T. "*Epitaphium Damonis*: Lines 9–13 and the Date of Composition." *MLN*, 71 (1956), 322–24.

     Crops referred to are Italian ones; hence poem written in autumn 1639, probably October or November. Answered by Baldi (no. 431).

421. Maddison, Carol. *Apollo and the Nine: A History of the Ode.* London: Routledge & Kegan Paul, 1960.

     Obiter dicta on the poem (pp. 330–31).

422. Brett, R. L. *Reason & Imagination: A Study of Form and Imagination in Four Poems.* London: Oxford University Press, 1960; rpt., 1968.

     Chastity and M.'s religious belief and poetic vocation as treated in the poem (pp. 48–49).

423. Fletcher, Harris [Francis]. "The Seventeenth-Century Separate Printing of Milton's *Epitaphium Damonis*." *JEGP*, 61 (1962), 788–96.

     Dates it after the *Poemata* of 1645 (perhaps "early in 1646"). Answered by Shawcross (no. 427).

424. Jones, William M. "Immortality in Two of Milton's Elegies." In Bernice Slote, ed. *Myth and Symbol: Critical Approaches and Applications.* Lincoln: University of Nebraska Press, 1963; rpt., 1967. Pp. 133–40.

     Poem's consolation chiefly that of earthly fame; M. serves as "God's fertilizing power" to produce an immortalizing work of literature.

425. Clavering, Rose, and John T. Shawcross. "Milton's European Itinerary and His Return Home." *SEL*, 5 (1965), 49–59.

     Rebuts Parker (no. 214): lines 9–13 taken with lines 129ff. show that M. did not hear of Diodati's death until after his second stay in Florence. In lines 14–15 *pecus relictum* more likely to refer to M.'s family than to the nation.

426. Condee, Ralph W[aterbury]. "The Structure of Milton's 'Epitaphium Damonis.'" *SP*, 62 (1965), 577–94.

     Structural significance of M.'s adherence to and breaks with the pastoral tradition; theme of "dynamic emergence" all-pervasive, aided by changes of meaning in the refrain. Reworked in no. 252.

427. Shawcross, John T. "The Date of the Separate Edition of Milton's 'Epitaphium Damonis.'" *Studies in Bibliography*, 18 (1965), 262–65.

     Reply to Fletcher (no. 423). Examination of the surviving copy suggests printer was that of *Comus*, not one of the printers of the prose pamphlets of the early 1640s. No. 390 probably printed in 1639 or 1640; its text probably the copy-text for that in the 1645 *Poemata*.

428. Nichols, Fred J. "'Lycidas', 'Epitaphium Damonis', the Empty Dream, and the Failed Song." In J. IJsewijn and E. Kessler, eds. *Acta Conventus Neo-Latini Lovaniensis.* (See no. **308**). Pp. 445–52.

M.'s use of the Neolatin tradition of pastoral lament at a crucial point in his poetic development.

429. Lambert, Ellen Zetzel. *Placing Sorrow: A Study of the Pastoral Elegy Convention from Theocritus to Milton.* University of North Carolina Studies in Comparative Literature, no. 60. Chapel Hill: The University of North Carolina Press, 1976.

Poem's audience; treatment of the poem in relation to *Lycidas* and, esp., to the Neolatin lament (pp. 83; 182–86).

430. Rowse, A. L. *Milton the Puritan: Portrait of a Mind.* London: Macmillan, 1977.

Obiter dictum on the poem; reason for using Latin (p. 37).

431. Baldi, Sergio. "The Date of Composition of 'Epitaphium Damonis.'" *N&Q,* n. s. 25 (1978), 508–09.

Rebuts Shawcross (no. **420**) on the number of harvests per annum in the Arno valley; date most likely autumn or winter 1640.

432. Mallette, Richard. *Spenser, Milton, and Renaissance Pastoral.* Lewisburg, PA: Bucknell University Press, 1981.

Theme and lack of true consolation in the poem, which is grouped with Castiglione's *Alcon* and Spenser's *Astrophel* as an example of an elegy whose pathos is heightened by "the bleakness of an empty future" (pp. 143–48).

433. Ryan, Lawrence V. "Milton's *Epitaphium Damonis* and B. Zanchi's Elegy on Baldassare Castiglione." *HL,* 30 (1981), 108–23.

Zanchi's poem (entitled *Damon* and edited here) a possible inspirational source; critique (pp. 112–13) of Harrison's argument for Castiglione's *Alcon* as source (no. **411**).

434. Hale, John K. "Sion's Bacchanalia: An Inquiry Into Milton's Latin in the *Epitaphium Damonis.*" In *Milton Studies,* XVI, ed. James D. Simmonds. Pittsburgh: University of Pittsburgh Press, 1982. Pp. 115–30.

Poem's diction and prosody and the use of Latin itself all support M.'s thought; comparison with *Lycidas* highlights M.'s transcendence of pastoral, especially in the poem's concluding movement.

17. *Rous.*

a. *Editions*

435. Oxford. Bodleian Library. MS. Lat. Misc. d. 77* (formerly, f. 15), attached to a copy of no. **17** cataloged 8° M168 Art (kept as Arch. G. f. 17); reproduced in no. **35**. Two leaves.

The *Rous.* MS., dated 23 January 1647. Holograph correction at line 71 (*Graiae*); otherwise not in M.'s hand.

b. Translations

436. Wrangham, Francis. Verse tr. In no. 113 (1st ed., pp. 231–4; 2d ed., pp. 277–80; partial tr.; 2d ed., pp. 610–13; 3d ed., pp. 198–200; full translation with some revision). Further revised version in his *Sermons Practical and Occasional* (see no. 470), III, pp. 296–301.

437. Landor, Walter Savage. [Untitled poem generally known as "Appendix to the *Hellenics*"]. In his *Hellenics*, new ed., enl. Edinburgh: James Nichol, 1859. Pp. 247–50. Standard modern text in Stephen Wheeler, ed., *The Poetical Works of Walter Savage Landor* (Oxford: Clarendon Press, 1937), III, pp. 472–74.

Lines 1–2 an adaptation of *Rous.*, 82 and 86.

See also: no. 172.

c. Comment

438. Shafer, Robert. *The English Ode to 1660: An Essay in Literary History.* Princeton: Princeton University Press, 1918; rpt., New York: Haskell House, 1966.

Structure of the poem based on choral ode of Greek drama and not on the Pindaric ode (p. 92, n. 57).

439. Finley, John H., Jr. "Milton and Horace: A Study of Milton's Sonnets." *Harvard Studies in Classical Philology*, 48 (1937), 29–73.

Lines 25–32 "eminently Horatian" in their treatment of serious themes in an ostensibly complimentary poem (p. 54, note).

440. Schuster, George N. *The English Ode from Milton to Keats.* New York: Columbia University Press, 1940; rpt., New York: Peter Smith, 1964.

Poem treated as an incorrectly formed Pindaric ode (pp. 72–73).

441. Parker, William R[iley]. "The Date of *Samson Agonistes.*" *PQ*, 28 (1949), 145–66.

Parallels between the poem's metrics and those of the choruses and monologues in *Samson* (p. 156).

442. Shawcross, John T. "Notes on Milton's Amanuenses." *JEGP*, 58 (1959), 29–38.

John Phillips may have been the scribe of no. 435 (pp. 36–37).

443. Shawcross, John T. "The Prosody of Milton's Translation of Horace's Fifth Ode." *Tennessee Studies in Literature*, 13 (1968), 81–89.

Scans lines 1–6 and comments on the metrics (p. 88).

444. Sage, Lorna. "Milton's Early Poems: A General Introduction." In John Broadbent, ed. *John Milton: Introductions.* (See no. **249**). Pp. 258–97.

Tone of the end of the poem; M.'s reasons for using Latin (pp. 259–60).

B. Uncollected pieces

1. *Carm. El.* and *Asclep.*

a. Editions

445. Netherby Hall, Longtown, Cumberland. MS. of unknown designation. One leaf. Autotype reproduction: Public Record Office, "Autotypes / Milton &c. / Fac. 6 / Library / Shelf 156a"; photographs thereof: British Library Add. MS. 41063I, ff. 84–85.

M.'s holograph of the "Early Prolusion" and of *Carm. El.* and *Asclep.* (on verso). Reported by Mabbott et al. (no. **453**) to be "in excellent condition."

446. Horwood, Alfred J., ed. *A Common-place Book of John Milton, and a Latin Essay and Latin Verses Presumed to Be by Milton.* Camden Society, London, [Publications], n. s. 16. Westminster: Printed by Nichols and Sons for the Camden Society, 1876; rev. ed., 1877.

MS. discussed in the introduction (pp. xvi–xix; dated to either M.'s years at St. Paul's or early in the Cambridge period). Text of the two poems, printed as though they were one (pp. 62–63); rev. ed. has new punctuation and some revised readings.

b. Comment

447. Brodribb, C. W. "Milton's 'Asclepiadean' Verses." *N&Q*, 162 (Jan.–June 1932), 188.

Corrects MacKellar's punctuation (in no. **30**) at end of *Asclep.*, 3; suggests *strato* instead of Mabbott's suppletion *toro* (no. **32**, I, pp. 328 and 598) in *Asclep.*, 4.

448. Mabbott, Thomas Ollive. "Milton's 'Asclepiadean' Verses." *N&Q*, 162 (Jan.–June 1932), 263–64.

Reply to Brodribb (no. **447**), defending *strato* as more in keeping with characters legible in the British Library photograph.

449. Mabbott, Thomas Ollive. "Milton's 'Asclepiadean' Verses." *N&Q*, 163 (July–Dec. 1932), 170.

Supplement to no. **448**. A reexamination of the photograph shows *toro* to be at least as possible as *strato*.

450. Gaselee, S. "Milton's Asclepiadean Verses." *N&Q*, 163 (July–Dec. 1932), 249.

In *Asclep.*, 4 *stratus* at the beginning of the line makes *strato* at the end "inconceivable"; "errors" in M.'s Latinity defended.

451. R[endall], V[ernon]. "Milton's Asclepiadean Verses." *N&Q*, 163 (July–Dec. 1932), 371.

Reply to Gaselee (no. 450). M. meant *stratus . . . toro* but instead wrote *stratus . . . strato.*

452. Candy, Hugh C. H. "Milton's *Prolusio* Script." *The Library*, 4th series, 15 (1934–35), 330–39.

Handwriting of no. 445, with a reproduction of part of the "Early Prolusion."

453. Mabbott, Thomas Ollive, J. Milton French, [and] Maurice Kelley. "The Columbia Milton; Fourth Supplement." *N&Q*, 195 (1950), 244–46.

Corrects no. 32 (I, p. 597; XII, p. 390) in regard to no. 445 (p. 245).

454. Kelliher, W. Hilton. "Erasmus' *Adagia* and Milton's *Mane citus lectum fuge.*" *MQ*, 5 (1972), 73–74.

The *Adagia*, which quote Homer, *Il.* 2, 23–24 (as does M.) to illustrate the commonplace, *non decet principem solidam dormire noctem*, probably a source for the "Early Prolusion" [and hence, because of its subject matter, for *Asclep.*].

2. Justinian

455. Ariosto, Lodovico. *Orlando Furioso in English Heroical Verse, [tr.] by John Harington.* London: Imprinted by Richard Field, 1591. Copy in private ownership.

Justinian inscribed on sig. ¶ 2 verso.

3. Barberini

a. Editions

456. Vatican City. Biblioteca Apostolica Vaticana. MS. Barb. lat. 2181.

Miscellaneous collection of letters, mostly to Lukas Holste. Foll. 57–58 (reproduced in no. 458) the original of *Ep. Fam.* 9, containing *Barberini*. Dated 29 March 1639.

457. Milton, John. *Epistolarum Familiarium liber unus.* London: Brabazon Aylmer, 1674.

Ep. Fam. 9 in its first printing, dated 30 March 1639 (pp. 25–28; *Barberini* on p. 28).

458. Bottkol, Joseph McG. "The Holograph of Milton's Letter to Holstenius." *PMLA*, 68 (1953), 617–27.

Ep. Fam. 9 transcribed from no. 456 (photographs also provided) and collated with the text in no. 457. Tense change in *Barberini* noted (p. 622).

b. Translations

459. Tillyard, Phyllis B., tr. *John Milton: Private Correspondence and Academic Exercises.* Cambridge: Cambridge University Press, 1932.

Prose tr. of *Barberini* (p. 21).

See also: no. 124.

4. *Coelum*

460. Harvard University. Houghton Library. MS. Sumner 84.

The album of Camillo Cerdogni (Cardouin, Cardoyn). *Coelum* on p. 110; reproduced in no. 35 and, *inter alia*, in nos. 244 (plate 40b) and 462 (plate XIV; description on pp. 73, 106).

5. Euripides marginalia

a. Editions

461. Oxford. Bodleian Library. Printed Books. Don. d. 27 and 28. (Euripides, *Tragoediae quae extant* [(Geneva:) Paulus Stephanus, 1602]. 2 vols.).

M.'s Euripides, with his marginalia in both volumes.

462. Sotheby, Samuel Leigh. *Ramblings in the Elucidation of the Autograph of Milton.* London: Printed for the Author by Thomas Richards, 1861.

Selections from the marginalia, including the tr. of *Rhesus*, 1–5, reproduced in plate XV (facing p. 108).

b. Comment

463. Kelley, Maurice, and Samuel D. Atkins. "Milton's Annotations of Euripides." *JEGP*, 60 (1961), 680–87.

Reduces considerably the number of marginalia that can safely be ascribed to M. Translations not discussed but validated as his work.

6. Pieces from the *Defensiones*

a. Editions

464. Milton, John. *Joannis Miltoni Angli Pro Populo Anglicano Defensio Contra Claudii Anonymi, aliàs Salmasii, Defensionem Regiam.* London: Du Gard, 1651.

First ed. of the *Defensio prima* (with *Salmas.* 1 in *cap.* 8 [page nos. vary in eds. of this year]; reprod. in no. 35).

465. Milton, John. *Joannis Miltoni Angli Pro Populo Anglicano Defensio Secunda.* London: Thomas Newcomb, 1654.

First ed. of the *Defensio secunda* (with *Salmas.* 2 [pp. 38–39] and *De virtute* [p. 64]; *Salmas.* 2 reproduced in no. 35).

b. Translations

466. Anon., tr. *Joannis Miltons Engelsmans Verdedigingh des gemeene Volcks van Engelandt, tegens Claudius sonder Naem, alias Salmasius Koninck-lijcke Verdedigingh.* N. p., "1651."

Verse tr. of *Salmas.* 1 (pp. 240–41).

467. [Washington, Joseph], tr. *A Defence of the People of England, by John Milton: In Answer to Salmasius's Defence of the King.* N. p., 1692.

Verse tr. of *Salmas.* 1 (pp. 187–88; rpt. in no. 469 [I, p. 203]).

468. Cowper, William. Verse tr. of *Salmas.* 2. In British Library Add. MS. 30801.

Written 1791 or 1792. Reported by Bailey (see no. 373), p. 722.

469. Burnett, George, ed. and tr. *The Prose Works of John Milton.* London: Printed for John Miller, 1809. 2 vols.

Verse trs. of *Salmas.* 2 and *De virtute* (II, pp. 353–54, 372; reprinted in no. 32 [vol. 8]).

470. Wrangham, Francis, tr. *Milton's "Second Defence of the People of England."* London: C. Baldwin, 1816. Also in his *Sermons Practical and Occasional* (London: Baldwin, Cradock, and Joy, 1816), vol. 3.

Verse trs. of *Salmas.* 1 and 2 and *De virtute* (pp. 50, 51, 80; page refs. identical in both eds.). Tr. of *Salmas.* 1 a revision of that by Symmons in no. 113; tr. of *De virtute* an adaptation of William Gifford's tr. of the Juvenalian original.

471. Bernhardi, Wilhelm, tr. *John Miltons Politische Hauptschriften.* Berlin [later, Leipzig]: Erich Koschny, 1874–79. 3 vols.

Verse trs. of *Salmas.* 1 and 2 and *De virtute* (I, p. 285; II, pp. 190, 204).

472. Blackford, Paul Weldon, tr. *The Defence of the English People by John Milton Englishman in Answer to the Defence of the King by Claudius Anonymous alias Salmasius.* Ph.D. diss., Northwestern University, 1950.

Prose tr. of *Salmas.* 1 (p. 222).

c. Comment

473. Wood, Anthony à. *Athenae Oxonienses.* London: Printed for Thomas Bennet, 1691–92. 2 vols. New ed., with additions and a continuation by Philip Bliss (London: Printed for F. C. and J. Rivington, 1813–20). 4 vols.

M. a liar in accusing Saumaise [as in *Salmas.* 2] of receiving money from Charles for the *Defensio regia* (II, p. 770; new ed., IV, c. 152).

474. Oldfather, W. A. "Pro Ioanne Miltono poeta populum Anglicanum iterum defendente." *PQ,* 19 (1940), 88–89.

Metrics of *Salmas.* 2 and emendations therein. Answered in no. **475.**

475. Hendrickson, G. L. "Milton, Salmasius, – and Synizesis." *PQ*, 20 (1941), 597–600.

    Reply to no. 474. Emendations unnecessary. In lines 9–10 the reference is to the *libraries* of the fishmongers.

476. French, J. Milton. "Some Notes on Milton." *N&Q*, 188 (Jan.–June 1945), 52–55.

    Section III, "Salmasius's Reward for Writing his Defensio" (pp. 53–54), adduces from no. 60 S.'s denials that he was paid the hundred jacobuses [as alleged in *Salmas.* 2].

477. McNeill, W. "Milton and Salmasius, 1649." *English Historical Review*, 80 (1965), 107–08.

    Prints Sir William Boswell's letter to S. inviting him to write the *Defensio regia*; notes that it provides no support for the idea [as alleged in *Salmas.* 2] that S. was hired for pay.

7. *Sylla*

a. *Editions*

478. Milton, John. *The Readie and Easie Way to Establish a Free Commonwealth*. London: n. p., 1660.

    The 2d ed.; *Sylla* on title page.

b. *Translations*

479. Hughes, Merritt Y., ed. *John Milton: Prose Selections*. New York: The Odyssey Press, 1947; often reissued.

    Prose tr. by Hughes (p. 356, n. 1).

480. Lewalski, Barbara Kiefer, ed. "The Political and Religious Tracts of 1659–1660." In J. Max Patrick, ed. *The Prose of John Milton*. New York: New York University Press, 1968. Pp. 437–557.

    Prose tr. by Lewalski (p. 550, n. 1).

See also: nos. 111, 481.

c. *Comment*

481. Godwin, William. *Lives of Edward and John Philips, Nephews and Pupils of Milton*. London: Longman, Hurst, Rees, Orme, and Brown, 1815.

    Sylla part Juvenal, part Milton; reference is to the advice given to Cromwell in the *Defensio secunda*. Verse tr. of the piece (p. 31).

PART IV: REPUTATION AND INFLUENCE

482. Coleridge, S[amuel] T[aylor]. *Biographia Literaria*. London: Rest Fenner, 1817; rpt. ed. J. Shawcross. Oxford: Clarendon Press, 1907; frequently reissued. 2 vols.

Johnson's comparison of M. and Cowley (in no. 107) a "caprice"; *Mans.*
and *Patrem* read with enthusiasm by an Italian poet "last summer" (II,
p. 209, note).

483. Montgomery, James. "Memoir of Milton, With Strictures on His Genius
and Writings." In the 1843 Tilt and Bogue *Poetical Works.* (See no. 58).
I, pp. i–lii. Several times reprinted.

Revision of general comments in no. 114 preceded by assertion that M.'s
Latin poems "command little attention, except as curiosities of literature"
(pp. xviii–xix).

484. Good, John Walter. *Studies in the Milton Tradition.* University of Illinois
Studies in Language and Literature, vol. 1, nos. 3–4. Urbana: The University of Illinois, 1915; rpt., New York: Johnson Reprint Corp., 1967.

Late 18th-century reception of the Latin poems (pp. 40–41, 213).

485. Sherburn, George. "The Early Popularity of Milton's Minor Poems." *MP,*
17 (1919–20), 259–78, 515–40.

Reception of the minor poems before 1740. Annotated *testimonia,* some
bearing on the *Poemata* (pp. 262–77).

486. de Selincourt, Ernest, ed. William Wordsworth, *The Prelude.* Oxford:
Clarendon Press, 1926. 2d ed., revised by Helen Darbishire, 1959.

Prelude I, 179–80 [168–69] may be in part a reference to M.'s epic plans
in *Ep. Dam.* (p. 503; 2d ed., p. 513).

487. Plunkett, Frank Willis. *The Milton Tradition in One of Its Phases: The
Criticism of Milton as Found in the Leading British Magazines of the Pre-
Romantic and Romantic Periods (1779–1832).* Ph.D. diss., Indiana Uni-
versity, 1931.

Remarkable lack of interest in the Latin poems (p. 172); these thought in
general to show "great learning, but little genius" (p. 230). Views of *El.* 1
in relation to M.'s "flogging" (p. 74). Bibliography of magazine items (pp.
347–58).

488. French, J. Milton. "Moseley's Advertisements of Milton's Poems, 1650–
1660." *HLQ,* 25 (1961–62), 337–45.

No. 17 repeatedly advertised by the publisher before his death in 1661.

489. Riffe, Nancy Lee. *A Study of Milton's Eighteenth Century Reputation in
British Periodicals.* Ph.D. diss., University of Kentucky, 1963.

Treats the period 1711–78. Very little attention paid to the Latin poems
(pp. 96–97). Appendix K (pp. 307–15) an 18th-century Milton bibliography,
not restricted to periodicals; other appendices are topical bibliographies.

490. Maxwell, J. C. "Pope's Spring and Milton's In Adventum Veris." *N&Q,*
n. s. 13 (1966), 212.

El. 5, 129–30 may have influenced lines 57–58 of Pope's poem.

491. Wittreich, Joseph Anthony, Jr., ed. *The Romantics on Milton: Formal Essays and Critical Asides.* Cleveland: The Press of Case Western Reserve University, 1970.

    Compilation of English-language criticism; matter on the Latin poems locatable through the index.

492. Kreuder, Hans-Dieter. *Milton in Deutschland: Seine Rezeption im latein- und deutschsprachigen Schrifttum zwischen 1651 und 1732.* Quellen und Forschungen zur Sprach- und Kulturgeschichte der germanischen Völker, n. F., 43. Berlin: de Gruyter, 1971.

    Poemata discussed, pp. 119–21, 123–24, 154, 161, 180, 203.

See also: nos. 13, 14, 125, 175, 191.

INDEX NOMINUM

Listed below, and keyed to entry numbers, are the names of persons cited either as authors or editors of reference works dealing with the Latin and Greek verse or as editors, translators, illustrators, or commentators of or on these pieces. Entries for lifetime editions and manuscript material written or overseen by Milton are included under his name. Anonymous entries are omitted.